THE HORIZON BOOK OF

ANCIENT ROME

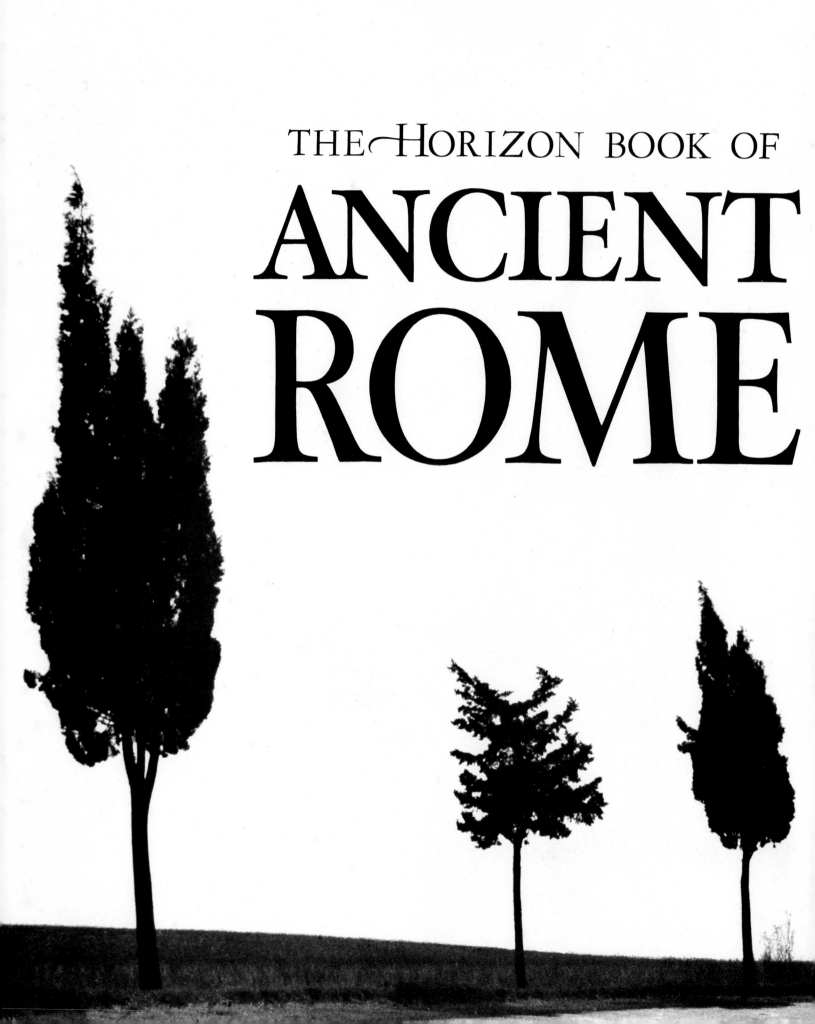

THE HORIZON BOOK OF
ANCIENT
ROME

BY THE EDITORS OF HORIZON MAGAZINE

EDITOR IN CHARGE WILLIAM HARLAN HALE

AUTHOR ROBERT PAYNE

INTRODUCTION BY GILBERT HIGHET

PUBLISHED BY AMERICAN HERITAGE PUBLISHING CO., INC., New York

BOOK TRADE DISTRIBUTION BY DOUBLEDAY & COMPANY, INC.

AMERICAN HERITAGE
PUBLISHING CO., INC.

PRESIDENT
James Parton

EDITOR-IN-CHIEF
Joseph J. Thorndike

EDITORIAL DIRECTOR, HORIZON
Oliver Jensen

EDITORIAL DIRECTOR, BOOK DIVISION
Richard M. Ketchum

ART DIRECTOR
Irwin Glusker

———

Staff for this Book

EDITOR
William Harlan Hale

ART DIRECTOR
Emma Landau

ASSOCIATE EDITOR
William B. Cummings

ASSISTANT EDITOR
Jane Hoover Polley

PICTURE EDITORS
Ellen Bates
Martha Fine, *Assistant*

COPY EDITORS
Kaari I. Ward
Jill Felsen, *Assistant*

EDITORIAL ASSISTANT
J. Muriel Vrotsos

EUROPEAN BUREAU
Gertrudis Feliu, *Chief*

———

Horizon Magazine is published quarterly
by American Heritage Publishing Co.,
Inc., 551 Fifth Avenue, N.Y. 17, N.Y.

Printed in the United States of America
Library of Congress Catalog Card
Number: 66–18667

———

At right is a Pompeiian wall painting
representing Venus lolling on her seashell.
POMPEII; SONJA BULLATY

HALF-TITLE PAGE: The head of Jupiter-
Ammon is symbolic of Rome's receptive-
ness to ideas from other cultures and of its
ability to spread them farther; the bronze,
representing a god who was half Roman
and half Egyptian, was found in France.
TOWN HALL, SAINT-LAURENT-DU-CROS, FRANCE;
MADAME GUILEY-LAGACHE

TITLE PAGE: All roads once led to Rome.
Many have perished, but the routes of
others survive. Italian roads like this recall
the Romans' sovereign engineering skills.
SONJA BULLATY

INTRODUCTION: A relief shows a chariot
being led to the starting line at a race
course. The hardheaded Romans always
found time for the exuberance, gambling,
and danger that accompanied the games.
MUSEO NAZIONALE, NAPLES; ANDERSON

CONTENTS

SWORD AND SPIRIT

Rome. It has a resonance like a deep bronze bell. It clangs like a heavy shield struck by a heavy sword. It is the keynote of a noble theme in which other names are overtones: Caesar, triumph, legion, forum, senate, emperor, pope. The majestic word has rung through twenty-seven centuries. It is one of the greatest utterances of mankind: it is heard all round the world and will not soon be silenced.

It means, first of all, Power. The appellation *Rome* was a mystery to the Romans themselves: they did not know what meanings were concealed within it; perhaps originally it was no more than the name of a noble Etruscan family. But in Greek there was a noun *rōmē*, meaning "strength," "vigor," "might." As the Greeks watched the little Italian city making itself into the head of a league of neighboring cities, and then dominating other Italian peoples, and fighting off foreign invaders of Italy, and conquering the whole peninsula, and extending its strength and its laws and its roads and its tax system and its language and its morality farther and farther outward from the Capitol, they came to believe that the name expressed the nature of the city and its people. Power.

And that was the center of the Roman achievement. Starting from almost nothing, a city of a few thousand citizens built up the greatest structure of political power that the western world has yet seen. It was greatest in extent, for at its widest it covered most

of the known world, from Scotland to Arabia and from the Straits of Gibraltar to the Black Sea. It was greatest in durability, for it survived, in the area commanded by Constantinople and still designated the Roman empire, until the fifteenth century of our era, to fall only a generation or so before Columbus discovered the new continent. Or, looked at in another way, the Roman empire, which started from Romulus and fell before the barbarians in the fifth century of the Christian dispensation, did not die, but continued to exist for another thousand years in the Holy Roman Empire, and still exists, transformed and spiritualized, in the Holy Roman Catholic Church, whose language is Latin and whose central seat is Rome.

Roman power was more constructive than destruc-

tive. All power systems destroy those who resist them and strive to eliminate those who compete with them; so did Rome. But it rebuilt. It did not glory in building pyramids of heads as did the Assyrians or leaving mighty cities in ruins as did the Mongols. Where it conquered, it made roads and bridges and aqueducts, market places and meeting halls. In many, now desolate, regions of Turkey and North Africa and Spain and Yugoslavia, one still finds those ruined fragments of its civilizing structures that the peasants used to point to and say: "Giants made these."

Rome's power sprang from some spiritual source. What that source was, the Romans themselves did not surely know. Nor do we. Their greatest poet, Vergil, gave a simple, lofty explanation of it. The dominion of Rome, he said, was willed by almighty God in order to bring peace to the warring world. Christian interpreters have often thought that, although born a pagan, Vergil was a "naturally Christian soul," and foresaw something of God's purpose in making Rome the capital of the Prince of Peace. There were others, in Vergil's day and earlier, who had a harsher explanation. These men were cultured Greeks, who saw their little city-states losing identity in the vast power system of Rome, who watched helplessly as massive wars between Romans and foreign foes or Romans and Romans devastated whole countrysides and swept through their fields and streets in a bloody avalanche, and who saw their intellectuals demoralized and their art treasures removed by rich and tasteless Roman collectors. They said that the power of Rome had no rational cause whatever and sprang from no comprehensible source. It was merely a disaster for civilization—as we ourselves should think if a race of giant apes were to emerge with irresistible weapons and dominate mankind. It proved, they held, that the world was ruled not by God but by Chance, not by Fate but by Fortune: capricious, silly, and cruel. For such men the triumph of Rome made life a "tale told by an idiot, full of sound and fury, signifying nothing." Such a conclusion was a shallow and spiteful answer to the problem. Vergil wrote his *Aeneid* largely in order to propose a nobler explanation that would harmonize with the willing acceptance of Roman majesty and might by many half-barbarous peoples and with the selflessness of many great Romans.

Other thoughtful men, both Roman and Greek, believed that the explanation must be that the Romans had painfully acquired, through centuries of historical struggle, a particularly strong and sensitive talent for communal effort. In the second century B.C. a well-educated and intelligent Greek called Polybius was deported to Rome as a political prisoner. He met the cultivated Roman statesmen and generals such as Scipio, the final conqueror of Carthage; traveled with them on their expeditions; watched them in their staff conferences and political meetings; and concluded that the Romans possessed a real genius for administration and for corporate achievement, which they transmitted by advice and example from one generation to the next; this was the source of their strength.

One of the principles thus transmitted was the subordination, not the sanctity, of the individual. They were keen, greedy, energetic, ambitious people, and so they devised a check on themselves. A man was unimportant in comparison with his family: it was his duty to make the family great or to maintain its greatness. A citizen was unimportant in comparison with the whole body of the citizens: he could live only through them, and if he must die for them, his death was good. A magistrate was important only during his term of office and within the limits of his authority: he had power, and majesty, and honor only because he was the embodiment of the whole community past and present.

For five hundred years the Romans governed themselves through elected magistrates. This was their main period of growth. The chief authority lay in the hands, not of one man, but of two; and not for life, but for one year, during which time the consuls were watched for any sign of personal ambition. On lower levels the other magistrates served as checks and balances on one another's power; a dictator, when an emergency compelled the state to appoint one, held his authority only for the duration of the crisis and was then forced to surrender it; and the highest power of all was not single but dual—the Senate and the Roman people.

Eventually this magnificent system was corrupted from inside by the destructive disease that it was created in order to control: personal ambition and the selfish competition of families and factions. There had been a number of dictators in the five hundred years of the republic, and many men had held absolute power for a time; but when Julius Caesar became perpetual dictator, and later when his adoptive son Augustus founded a dynasty so that power should no longer be held and transmitted by the Senate and the Roman people, but by one individual and his immediate family and kinsmen, then a noble historical enterprise came to an end. The republic fell. The empire was created on its ruins. The republic had been debilitated by personal ambitions, class enmities, and civil wars. Julius Caesar gave it the deathblow. His barely disguised monarchy lasted for four years until he was struck down by lovers of the republic in 44 B.C. Then, after enormous effort and a war that exhausted the Mediterranean world, his monarchy was re-established under tactful concealment by the brave, kindly, far-sighted, generous, surely almost godlike Gaius Julius Caesar Octavianus, who became Augustus. Less than seventy years later, his descendant Gaius Julius Caesar Germanicus, the emperor Caligula, was challenging almighty Jupiter to wrestle, and insisting that his statue be put in the Temple at Jerusalem. Not long after him came Nero.

How did Rome survive, first the early struggles against foreign enemies, and then the tyranny of crazy individualist rulers? Through another of the principles in which its growth was rooted—adaptability. The Romans never claimed to be original. They borrowed nearly everything from others and amalgamated their borrowings into their system. Yet at the same time they were scrupulously conservative. So, when Julius and then Augustus made themselves monarchs in fact, they did not abolish the Senate. They and their successors, even the lunatics and criminals, often sat in it and often held the rank of consul. Thus, the Senate survived for many centuries more and was a counterweight, however light and mobile, to the power concentrated in a single emperor.

Adaptability was not only the secret of survival for Rome. It was the secret of its civilizing mission. From the Greeks it learned poetry, philosophy, the fine arts:

it resisted them for some time, but then assimilated them, producing poetry, philosophy, and art of its own, based on Greek form and imagination but changed by Roman strength and Italian fancy into something new, equally viable, often equally noble. From the Greeks it borrowed gods who could embody the impersonal numinous presences of its own religion: it made them into its own pantheon with its own names for them. So the faceless divinity named Grace acquired the heavenly smile and bewitching body of the Hellenic Aphrodite, and is now, as lady Venus, better known to the world than her Greek model. When a new conception of deity was born in Judaea its representatives came to Rome. They were resisted by some, welcomed by others; they struggled, and suffered, and proved themselves, and in due course they made their way into the Senate and the emperor's palace, and their message was at last accepted; and now, across the Tiber, rises the mighty Roman dome of St. Peter's crowned by the cross.

One of the most difficult things for a modern western man is to understand the three roots of our civilization: Greece, and Rome, and Judaea. Each of the three cultures is so complex that it is a lifetime's work to appreciate it fully. And it is hard to do justice to one without downgrading the others. Anyone intoxicated by the clarity of Greek art and Greek philosophy, anyone dominated by the overpowering Jewish-Christian vision of man as a grain of dust in the Creator's hand, is tempted to dismiss Rome as the supreme assertion of materialism. Marching armies as efficient and cruel as the ancient Assyrians or the modern Germans, massive buildings as graceless and senseless as the Egyptian pyramids or the American skyscrapers, the world plundered to enrich a single city when the city's favorite amusement was to watch men hunting animals or men in pairs killing each other—surely it can scarcely be called a civilization except in the external sense, wealth and vulgar pleasure, a titanic body without a heart. That would be true indeed, except for the fact that the body as it grew acquired a heart and a soul. We can hear the beating of the heart and share in the soul's strivings when we read the *Dream of Scipio*, which is Cicero's loftiest work, his assertion of the pettiness of this world and the grandeur of the cosmos and the law of duty linking the two; when we study Vergil's epic poem, hearing behind every line an echo of Homer or of Greek tragedy, seeing in the entire structure an adaptation of a Greek symphonic plan, and yet realizing as the whole wealth of its music and meaning sweep through us that there is something here which is Greek but different from Greece, which is Roman but higher than Rome itself. For noble thoughts, these men and others molded, out of a crude and narrow dialect, a masterful and subtle language in which great thoughts could be expressed. And later, when the classical speech was hardening into polite rigidity, such men as Tertullian and Saint Augustine took it over and stretched it and strained it and simplified it and strengthened it once again to carry the new message of Christianity. At first little more than the power of the sword carried Rome forward; but as it grew, it acquired the power of thought, the power of the law, and the power of religious and poetic vision. These are the spiritual powers which it bequeathed to its heirs, the modern nations of the western world.

GILBERT HIGHET

OCEANUS GERMANICUS
(North Sea)

GERMANIA

HIBERNIA

BRITANNIA

Eboracum *(York)*

Camulodunum
(Colchester)

Isca Silurum

Londinium
(London)

GERMANIA
INFERIOR

Colonia Agrippinensis *(Cologne)*

Rhenus (Rhine)

Maguntiacum *(Mainz)*

Albis (Elbe)

Augusta
Treverorum
(Trier)

BELGICA

OCEANUS ATLANTICUS

Lutetia *(Paris)*

Sequana (Seine)

LUGDUNENSIS

GERMANIA
SUPERIOR

RHAETIA

NORICUM

PANNONIA

Aquincum
(Budapest)

Vindobona
(Vienna)

Carnuntum

Danubius

ILLYRICUM

Siscia

Liger (Loire)

GALLIA

Alesia

Augustodunum

Lugdunum
(Lyons)

AQUITANIA

Vienna
(Vienne)

Rhodanus (Rhone)

Glanum
(St.-Rémy)

GALLIA
CISALPINA

Aquileia

Verona

Mantua

Ravenna

Padus (Po)

DALMATIA

Salonae

Spalatum
(Split)

MARE ADRIATICUM

Burdigala
(Bordeaux)

Nemausus
(Nîmes)

Arelate
(Arles)

Genua

Pisae

Arretium
(Arezzo)

Tiberis

ITALIA

Dyrrha
(Dura

Tolosa
(Toulouse)

NARBONENSIS

Massilia
(Marseilles)

Roma

Tibur
(Tivoli)

Ap

Narbo Martius
(Narbonne)

Ostia

Capua

Cannae

Brundisium
(Brindisi)

CORSICA

Puteoli

Tarentum
(Taranto)

Bracara Augusta

TARRACONENSIS

Iberus (Ebro)

Barcino
(Barcelona)

Pompeii

Heraclea

Salmantica

Segovia

Caesar Augusta
(Saragossa)

Tarraco

SARDINIA

MARE TYRRHENUM

HISPANIA

Saguntum

BALEARES

Messana
(Messina)

LUSITANIA

Toletum
(Toledo)

Valentia

Lilybaeum
(Marsala)

SICILIA

Syracusae

Emerita Augusta
(Mérida)

Olisipo
(Lisbon)

Carthago Nova
(Cartagena)

Agrigentum

BAETICA

Cordoba

Utica

Carthago

Munda

Caesarea

Cirta

Zama

Thapsus

MARE INTER

Gades
(Cadiz)

NUMIDIA

Tingis
(Tangiers)

Thamugadi
(Timgad)

AFRICA

MAURETANIA

Sabrata

Leptis Magna
(Lebda)

GROWTH OF AN EMPIRE

Some five hundred years elapsed from the date of Rome's presumed founding to the time, in the third century B.C., when it won control of Italy. Yet within another century or two it was fated (in the words that Shakespeare applied to Julius Caesar) to "bestride the world like a colossus." This map shows four stages in the building of the empire, tracing its growth from the time of Rome's victory in its desperate war for survival against Hannibal of Carthage, to the time, little more than three hundred years later, when one of its greatest emperors, Trajan, extended Roman power to its outermost geographical limits.

SARMATIA

MARE CASPIUM

ALBANIA

IBERIA

COLCHIS

CHERSONESUS
TAURICA

(Plovdiv)

PONTUS EUXINUS
(Black Sea)

• Artaxata

ARMENIA

PARTHIA

Sinope •

PONTUS

ASSYRIA

Tigris

Odessus •
(Varna)

MOESIA

Heraclea • • Zela

BITHYNIA

CAPPADOCIA

MESOPOTAMIA

Ister (lower Danube)

Carrhae •

• Ctesiphon

THRACIA

Philippopolis
(Plovdiv) •

Byzantium •

Nicomedia
(Izmit)

Euphrates

Nicaea •

GALATIA

CILICIA

Philippi •

ASIA

LYCAONIA

Tarsus •

ARABIA

DONIA

• Pergamum
(Bergama)

PAMPHYLIA

• Antiochia
SYRIA

essalonica
Saloniki)

Smyrna •

Sardes •
Ephesus •

CYPRUS

Heliopolis •
(Baalbek)

• Palmyra

ydna

Pharsalus •

LYCIA

Halicarnassus
(Bodrum)

• Damascus

	Rome after the Second Punic War (201 B.C.)
	Rome in the time of Marius (100 B.C.)
	Rome at the death of Augustus (A.D. 14)
	Rome at the death of Trajan (A.D. 117)

RUS

Nicopolis •

• Corinthus

MARE AEGAEUM

• Tyrus
(Tyre)

• Bostra

Athenae •

JUDAEA

ACHAIA

RHODUS

Hierosolyma •
(Jerusalem)

Sparta •

CRETA

• Petra

ARABIA
PETRAEA

Alexandria •

M

n)

Memphis •

Cyrene •

AEGYPTUS

SINUS
ARABICUS

CYRENAICA

Nilus

• Coptus

(Red Sea)

THE REPUBLIC

Period	Leaders	Political and Military Affairs	Culture and Technology
EARLY PERIOD Conquest of Italy c.500–c.275 B.C.		753 B.C. Legendary date of Rome's founding	6th century B.C. Etruscan building program in Rome; forum area drained by Cloaca Maxima; first temple to Jupiter on the Capitoline; Circus Maximus; first temple of Vesta; temple of Janus; Regia; Servian Wall
		c.616–c.509 Etruscan period; Tarquin kings rule Rome	
		c.509–c.500 Tarquins deposed; Roman republic established	
		c.500–c.350 Intermittent warfare against Etruscans, Latins, Umbrians, and other neighboring peoples; Latins defeated at Lake Regillus (c.496)	
		c.494 Tribunate established	
		c.451 Twelve Tables, first written code of Roman law	
		c.450 Romans begin to found colonies in Italy	c.400–c.200 Latin gradually wins ascendancy over other Italic languages
	c.440–c.365 Camillus	443 Office of censor created	
	c.350–c.280 Appius Claudius Caecus	390 Rome sacked and burned by Gauls	c.367 Temple of Concord
		343–290 Samnite wars; Rome wins ascendancy in central Italy	
		312 Censorship of Appius Claudius Caecus	312 Appian Way, first of great Roman paved roads, is begun; Aqua Appia, first major aqueduct built in Rome
		280–275 War with Pyrrhus of Epirus; power of Greeks in south is broken	
ERA OF SENATE SUPREMACY Beginning of Overseas Expansion c.275–c.110 B.C.		264–241 First Punic War; Carthage cedes Sicily, Corsica, and Sardinia (241)	c.250–184 Plautus, *dramatist*
	c.265–217 Gaius Flaminius	225 Gallic invasion repulsed at Telamon, in northern Italy	239–169 Ennius, *poet*
		218–201 Second Punic War; Hannibal invades Italy (218); Romans defeated at Lake Trasimene (217) and Cannae (216), victorious at Metaurus (207) and Zama (202); Carthage cedes Spain and other overseas colonies (201)	c.220 Flaminian Way
	237–183 Scipio Africanus Major		
	234–149 Cato the Elder	214–148 Four Macedonian wars; phalanx defeated by Roman legions at Cynoscephalae (197) and Pydna (168); Macedonia becomes Roman province (148)	c.205–c.125 Polybius, *historian*
	185–129 Scipio Africanus Minor	c.190 Defeat of Syrian king Antiochus III at Magnesia; Rome gains Asian foothold	c.195–159 Terence, *dramatist; Adelphi* staged (160)
			184 Basilica Porcia, first basilica in Rome
	163–133 Tiberius Gracchus	156–155 Dalmatia is Romanized	180–102 Lucilius, *satirist*
	153–121 Gaius Gracchus	150–146 Third Punic War; Carthage destroyed; province of Africa created (146)	144 Aqua Marcia, six-mile-long high aqueduct
		133 Pergamum (*later province of Asia*) bequeathed to Rome	116–27 Varro, *scholar*
		133–121 Social reforms attempted by the Gracchi	
		112–106 Jugurthine wars; Numidia conquered	
LATE PERIOD The Civil Wars c.110–27 B.C.	c.155–86 Marius	107–100 Consulships of Marius; army reorganized	106–43 Cicero, *philosopher and statesman; Orations against Catiline* (63); begins *The Republic* (54); *On Duty* (44); *Philippics* (44-43)
	138–78 Sulla	102 Cimbri and Teutones repulsed in north	
		91–88 Social War in Italy	c.98–55 Lucretius, *poet; On the Nature of Things* (c.60)
		86 Sulla takes Athens	
		82–79 Dictatorship of Sulla	c.86–c.34 Sallust, *historian; Histories* (c.37)
	c.115–53 Crassus	73–71 Slave revolt led by Spartacus	c.84–54 Catullus, *poet*
	106–48 Pompey	67–62 Pompey subjugates Pontus, Syria, and Cilicia	70–19 Vergil, *poet; Eclogues* (37); *Georgics* (29)
	100–44 Julius Caesar	60 First Triumvirate formed (*Pompey, Caesar, Crassus*)	65–8 Horace, *poet; Satires* (c.33); *Epodes* (29)
		58–51 Caesar conquers Gaul	59–A.D.17 Livy, *historian*
		53 Parthians defeat seven legions at Carrhae; Crassus killed	55 Theatre of Pompey
		49 Caesar crosses Rubicon, occupies Rome, is made dictator	51 Caesar's commentaries on *The Gallic War*
		48 Pompey defeated by Caesar near Pharsalus	c.50–c.15 Propertius, *poet; Elegies* (c.30-15)
		48–45 Caesar campaigns in Egypt, Asia Minor, Africa, Spain	
	c.82–30 Mark Antony	44 Caesar assassinated	c.48 Caesar initiates building program in Rome; forum of Julius Caesar begun
	63–A.D.14 Octavian (*Augustus*)	43 Second Triumvirate formed (*Antony, Octavian, Lepidus*)	45 Julian calendar introduced
		42 Battle of Philippi; Brutus dies	43–A.D.17 Ovid, *poet*
		31 Naval battle at Actium; Antony and Cleopatra defeated	36 Regia rebuilt
		27 Octavian founds principate, takes name Augustus	

THE EMPIRE

Periods:
- EARLY PERIOD — The Roman Peace, 27 B.C.–A.D. 180
- AGE OF MILITARY EMPERORS — Beginnings of Barbarian Migrations, A.D. 180–284
- LATE PERIOD — Imperial Divisions and Fall of Western Empire, A.D. 284–476

EMPERORS (reigns)

The Julio-Claudians
- 27 B.C.–A.D. 14 Augustus
- A.D. 14–37 Tiberius
- 37–41 Caligula
- 41–54 Claudius
- 54–68 Nero

The Flavians
- 69–79 Vespasian
- 79–81 Titus
- 81–96 Domitian
- 96–98 Nerva
- 98–117 Trajan
- 117–138 Hadrian

The Antonines
- 138–161 Antoninus Pius
- 161–180 Marcus Aurelius
- 180–192 Commodus
- 193–211 Septimius Severus
- 211–217 Caracalla
- 218–222 Elagabalus
- 222–235 Alexander Severus
- 235–270 Maximinus, Gordian III, Philip, Decius, Gallus, Valerian, Gallienus, Claudius II
- 270–275 Aurelian
- 276–282 Probus
- 284–305 Diocletian
- 286–305 Maximian
- 306–337 Constantine
- 337–350 Constans
- 337–361 Constantius II
- 361–363 Julian
- 363–364 Jovian
- 364–375 Valentinian
- 364–378 Valens
- 375–383 Gratian
- 375–392 Valentinian II
- 379–395 Theodosius

(in West)
- 395–423 Honorius
- 425–455 Valentinian III
- 455–476 Puppet emperors

POLITICAL AND MILITARY AFFAIRS

- 24 B.C. Augustus assumes tribunician powers
- 15 B.C.–A.D. 6 Empire extended to Danube line
- 12 B.C. Death of Agrippa
- c.4 B.C. Birth of Jesus Christ
- A.D. 9 Three Roman legions defeated in Germany
- c.29 Crucifixion of Christ
- 43 Conquest of Britain
- 64 Fire in Rome
- 70 Siege and capture of Jersusalem by Titus
- 79 Destruction of Pompeii
- c.78–c.85 Agricola governs in Britain
- 101–106 Trajan's Dacian campaigns; Dacia becomes province (106)
- 113–117 Trajan conquers Armenia and Parthia, pushes imperial boundaries to Persian Gulf and Caspian Sea; empire at its largest (117)
- 117–118 Hadrian abandons Trajan's conquests east of Euphrates River
- 131 Edictum salmanum, codification of the laws
- 131–135 Revolt and war in Judaea
- 162–166 Parthian invasion repulsed in East
- 165 Plague depopulates Rome
- 166–179 Marcomannic wars; barbarian invasions of Dacia, Pannonia, Noricum, Rhaetia, and northern Italy repulsed; beginning of defensive wars
- 197 Parthian wars renewed
- 212 Citizenship granted to free inhabitants of empire
- 228 Beginning of wars against Sassanid Persia
- c.250–c.265 Plague rages through empire
- c.250–305 General persecution of Christians
- 258 Invading Alamanni checked at Mediolanum (Milan)
- 260 Shapur I of Persia captures Emperor Valerian
- 262 Goths defeated at Naissus
- 270–275 Aurelian pacifies Gaul and Palmyra; Queen Zenobia captured
- 286 Diocletian divides empire, makes Maximian ruler in the West
- 293 Diocletian establishes tetrarchy (two augusti supported by two caesars)
- 312 Constantine defeats Maxentius at battle of Mulvian Bridge
- 313 Edict of Milan proclaims toleration of Christianity
- 324 Constantine becomes sole ruler of reunited empire
- 325 Council of Nicaea
- 330 Founding of New Rome (Constantinople)
- 378 Visigoths kill Valens at Battle of Adrianople
- 395 Empire redivided at death of Theodosius
- 407–409 Franks invade Gaul; Vandals move into Spain
- 410 Sack of Rome by Visigoths under Alaric
- 429 Vandals overrun Africa
- 452 Attila's Huns turn away from Rome after intercession by Pope Leo I
- 455 Vandals sack Rome
- 476 Romulus Augustulus, last of emperors in the West, is deposed

CULTURE AND TECHNOLOGY

- c.27 B.C.–c.A.D.14 Augustan or golden age in the arts; Vergil's *Aeneid: Odes of Horace; Livy's History of Rome.* Forum and mausoleum of Augustus; Ara Pacis; baths of Agrippa; theatre of Marcellus; Basilica Julia
- c.4 B.C.–A.D. 65 Seneca, *philosopher and dramatist*
- c.A.D.20–66 Petronius, *satirist*
- 62–69 Baths of Nero; Nero's Domus Aurea
- c.40–c.104 Martial, *epigrammatist*
- 46–c.120 Plutarch, *biographer*
- c.55–c.118 Tacitus, *historian; Annals* (116)
- c.60–c.140 Juvenal, *satirist; Satires* (c.116–130)
- c.75–82 Colosseum; temple of Vespasian; baths and arch of Titus
- c.62–c.113 Pliny the Younger, *writer and administrator*
- 113–c.115 Forum, column, and baths of Trajan
- c.120–127 Pantheon rebuilt; villa of Hadrian at Tivoli; wall of Hadrian in Britain
- c.135 Temple of Venus and Roma; mausoleum of Hadrian begun
- 140–142 Wall of Antoninus in Britain
- c.174 *Meditations of Marcus Aurelius*
- c.193 Column of Marcus Aurelius completed
- c.203 Arch of Septimius Severus
- c.160–c.230 Tertullian, *Christian apologist*
- 215 Baths of Caracalla
- 260–c.340 Eusebius of Caesarea, *Christian historian*
- c.271 Wall of Aurelian begun
- 306 Baths of Diocletian
- 310–c.320 Basilica of Constantine
- 315 Arch of Constantine
- 340–397 Ambrose, *Christian bishop and theologian*
- c.340–420 Jerome, *Christian historian and theologian*
- 354–430 Augustine, *Christian philosopher; The City of God* (c.426)

I

THE ETRUSCAN MYSTERY

The sum of things is ever being replenished, and mortals live one and all by give and take. Some races wax and others wane, and in a short space the tribes of the living are changed, and like runners hand on the torch of life.

Lucretius, On the Nature of Things

Italy is a stern and rugged land that makes hard demands upon its people. There are not very many places where the earth is fertile; only the Po Valley, the lowlands of Latium around Rome, and the volcanic regions of the Campania to the south produce a natural abundance. The mountains ride the land hard; there are few rivers, few harbors, few plains. The Apennines form a spiny ridge down the whole length of the country, dividing it in two, making it difficult in ancient times to form a united people. The land was always an enemy to be conquered, and it bred tough, resourceful men. Even today it offers them backbreaking labor and few rewards.

We think of Italy as a boot poised delicately over the Mediterranean, but to the Italians themselves it resembles a muscular and thickly veined arm plunging out of Europe into a dangerous sea. We remember the calm sunlight and the ripening fruits, but the Italian peasant is more inclined to remember the bitterness of winter. The gaunt mountains, the remote valleys, and the lack of communications fostered the growth of isolated communities of farmers, shepherds, and woodsmen living out primitive lives in secluded hamlets, maintaining themselves with difficulty, and living in fear of the next hamlet over the hill. Yet this narrow arm of Europe, forbidding in many respects, was inviting in others. It offered temperate climate, good pasturage, ample timber, and a strategic position with eventual promise of raid or trade.

When we see Italy first in the interval between the darkness of prehistory and the dawn of the first, large, settled communities, the original inhabitants are being pushed deeper and deeper into their remote fastnesses by invaders who have come down from central Europe over the Alpine passes or from the Balkans by way of the bend of the Adriatic. The invaders came in wave upon wave, and just as the aboriginal inhabitants were pushed back into more desolate regions, so they in turn were dispossessed and forced to occupy less desirable lands. It was the time of the great folk wanderings that marked the end of the Bronze Age and that set the whole Mediterranean area astir with new blood. Men known as Dorians were moving down into Greece, superseding the ancient cultures of Mycenae and Crete. In Italy nameless tribes moved like shadows over the land, leaving scarcely any trace of themselves. At the beginning of the last millennium before Christ we cannot yet speak of a civilized presence there. Most of the peninsula, however, had been occupied by Indo-European tribes speaking related dialects. They raised horses, sheep, and cattle, lived in round huts made of mud-daubed wattle, and farmed their lands with the same primitive instruments they had employed before they entered Italy. They were not a nation, but formed independent tribal communities. One last wave of these Indo-European tribesmen, known as the Latins, entered Italy in the ninth or eighth century B.C. and established itself among the dark crater lakes and high cone-shaped mountains of the Alban hills: these were to become the Romans.

The boundaries of the tribes were unstable and continually changing. We know that the Veneti occupied the territory at the head of the Adriatic, the Piceni occupied the central Adriatic coast, the Samnites were in the hill country east of Campania; the Sabines, Aequi, and Volscians were in the regions northeast, east, and south of the Latins. There were also countless subtribes, each with its local loyalties and local gods. Here and there small pockets of the original neolithic inhabitants remained, but they too were falling under the sway of the invaders.

About this time there began to appear on the western coast of Italy a new tribe that challenged the settled habits of the invaders and radically changed the fortunes of Italy. They were a hard, warlike people determined to carve out new settlements. These were the Etruscans, whose origins remain cloaked in mystery, but who were to stride forth as the first civilized folk in Italy, immensely gifted and original in art and governance. They were to contribute to the making of Rome a vast store of skill, from the use of the arch and the organization of a town to the ceremonials of majesty, the first structure of civil polity, and the rituals of augury and respect for the gods. As they expanded from their coastal settlements, near the Tyrrhenian Sea, they became Italy's first city builders and men of money, at a time when the Latin tribes to the south of them were still little more than unlettered peasants bent on local feud and harvest. Any chronicle of Rome must begin with these extraordinary settlers of Etruria, who both awakened and for a time ruled the future capital. Their influence upon the Romans was to remain profound over the centuries, matched in later years by that of Greece, to which the Etruscans themselves had also become beholden. The composite civilization we know as Roman owed immense debts to both.

There are so many mysteries about the origin of the Etruscans that scholars despair of a solution. In the fifth century B.C. the Greek historian Herodotus declared that they came from Lydia in Anatolian Asia Minor. He tells how the Lydians, suffering from famine, quietly reconciled themselves to their fate and for eighteen years amused themselves by playing dice, knucklebones, and ball. However, when conditions did not change King Atys decided that half the population should be sent away to colonize a more fruitful land. At Smyrna (the present Izmir) they built a fleet,

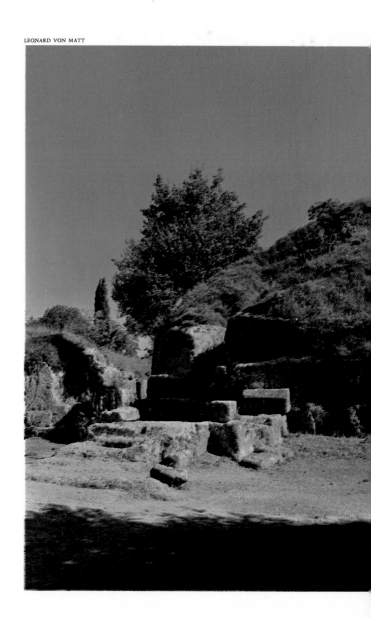

Tombs such as the one above dot the countryside of Tuscany. Filled with wall paintings, art objects, and utensils, they are the primary source of information about the mysterious Etruscans, whose civilization preceded—and influenced—that of Rome.

Tuscany was rich in ore deposits, which the Etruscans capitalized on from early in their history, trading crude metal and wrought goods. The iron kitchen utensils above (similar to those in use today) are probably typical of their exports. A water bottle is depicted at left, and at top right there is a colander; in the center from left to right are a grater, a spoon, and a hand, shaped from metal, for picking up ashes; at bottom is a collection of ladles.

put their household objects on board, and set sail under the command of Tyrrhenus, the king's son. It was evidently a long voyage, for we are told that they skirted many lands. When they settled in Italy they no longer called themselves Lydians, but adopted the name of Tyrrhenoi after their princely leader. (It should perhaps be noted here that the hellenized term *Tyrrhenoi,* meaning the "Etruscans," has also been thought by modern scholars to derive from the word *Tyrra,* which was the name of a locality in Lydia.)

According to Herodotus, the Lydians were a charming and resourceful people who enjoyed pleasure and the wealth that flowed down to them in the gold-bearing streams of Mount Tmolus. Herodotus believed that they were the first people to engage in retail trade and the first to mint gold and silver coins. He describes, too, how the Lydians built a tomb in Sardes to honor the father of King Croesus with five columns bearing inscriptions showing who had contributed to the work, and notes that the prostitutes had contributed more than the merchants and the artisans. Herodotus, who saw the tomb, described it as one of the wonders of the world, comparable to the pyramids and the works of the Babylonians.

Herodotus is not, of course, an infallible guide, but since he is often surprisingly accurate when he seems to be telling old wives' tales, he deserves to be read sympathetically. He is quite certain that the Lydians settled in Etruria, and he was not alone in this belief. Among the Roman historians it was generally believed that the Etruscans originally came from Lydia, and Vergil, Horace, and Ovid often call the Etruscans Lydians in their poems.

Four centuries after Herodotus, the Greek historian Dionysius of Halicarnassus rejected the theory of an oriental origin for the Etruscans. He said they were an indigenous people who had inhabited Italy from time immemorial, and he pointed out that they neither spoke the Lydian language nor worshiped the Lydian gods. He wrote that "they cannot be said to preserve any trait which may be considered to derive from their supposed homeland" and dismissed all those chroniclers who thought otherwise as pure fantasists.

Living in the age of Augustus, Dionysius of Halicarnassus had advantages over modern scholars. He was living at a time when the Etruscan language was still being spoken and their sacred books and traditional histories were still in existence. As late as Cicero's time we hear of Roman aristocrats sending their sons to Tarquinii, the old Etruscan capital, to learn the language and to study the sacred lore, and in the first century A.D. we find the emperor Claudius writing a history of the Etruscans in twenty volumes, which are now lost. A vast amount of written information about them was available. Still, Dionysius was not wholly dependable, if only because he was composing a history designed to prove that Rome's founders were in reality Greeks.

Today scholars are still divided: there are those who hold that Etruscans were indigenous to Italy and those who follow Herodotus and accept an Asiatic origin. In any event, there are resemblances between the arts of the Etruscans and those of the Lydians. Vaulted tombs with painted frescoes found in Lydia are remarkably similar to the painted tombs of the Etruscans. Etruscan names like Tarchon, Tarquinii, and Tages are common in Asia Minor, where Tarkhuni was the name of a storm god. Though we know comparatively little about the language of the Etruscans, we know that they employed the genitive case ending -al, which is also found in Asia Minor. In 1885 there was discovered on the island of Lemnos, in the Aegean, a seventh-century B.C. funerary stele bearing the portrait of a warrior grasping a spear with two inscriptions in Greek characters, though the language was not Greek. Scholars pointed to an apparent similarity between these words and others found in Etruria. A similar stele, with a design of a warrior grasping a two-bladed axe, was subsequently discovered in Vetulonia, in Etruria. For the first time a link between the ancient cultures of Lydia and Etruria seemed to have been established. Yet, though Etruscan art suggests Asiatic influences, it was also rooted in the earthy vigor of the Italian soil.

Wherever these mysterious people came from, they were a people with a highly developed civilization far superior to that of the earlier Indo-European invaders. They were not only farmers and fishermen, but merchants and adventurers, with a taste for grandeur and ostentatious luxury, proud of their artistic skills. Determined colonizers, they were soon spread out from Tuscany to Umbria and Latium, building their fortified cities on hilltops. Their fleets sailed out into the Tyrrhenian and Ionian seas. They appear to have established colonies in Corsica and to have traded with Sardinia (then under Carthaginian influence) and with the Balearic Islands, possibly setting up posts there as well. During the seventh and sixth centuries B.C. they were carving out a small empire of their own, reaching up the Po Valley in the north and toward the Greek settlements clustered in southern Italy and Sicily. They were a people on the march.

The presence of Greeks on the peninsula was also a result of great stir and movement throughout the Mediterranean area. Dorian and Ionian invaders had descended upon mainland Greece before the start of the millennium. Then they had spread over the

As early as the eighth century the Etruscans went to sea in boats that were even less sturdy than the one depicted in the seventh-century B.C. ivory above. The development of navigation was one of the most important factors in the evolution of Etruscan civilization; it enabled the country to raise its standard of living through the profits of trade and brought Etruscans into contact with other peoples such as the Greeks, who had a profound influence on them.
MUSEO ARCHEOLOGICO, FLORENCE; FOTO SOPRINTENDENZA ANTICHITA

THE GOLDEN AGE OF ETRURIA *Italy in the sixth century* B.C. *was virtually an Etruscan peninsula. Vigorous colonies of seafaring Greeks and Carthaginians lined the coasts of southern Italy and Sicily, but the disunited Italic peoples who occupied most of the central and southern mainland were completely overshadowed by the city-building Etruscans, then at the peak of their power. Rome was, at this time, little more than an Etruscan satellite.*

Aegean islands and the Asia Minor coast, founding local colonies or city-states as they advanced. The next step, beginning in the eighth century B.C., saw these individual settlements engaging in colonization efforts of their own as they grew and as the eyes of many of their citizens turned westward in search for ampler space. A highly imaginative technique was worked out by Greeks and specifically by those of Euboea and Corinth and Ephesus: it was that of encouraging citizen groups to sail forth and found daughter-cities that would be bound to the parent city by ties of blood, interest, and worship of common local gods, but that would be politically almost autonomous. Thus, colonists from Euboea (the long island that flanks and hugs the seaward site of Attica) in about 750 B.C. established a western offshoot at Cumae, on the Campanian shore of Italy, from which the city of Naples was to emerge. Further south, Megara and Croton (the latter to become the seat of the philosopher Pythagoras) also came into being. Sicily saw the founding of the Greek outposts of Syracuse and Acragas, well selected by colonizers and sailors for their harbors and commanding coastal positions. The thrust of the Greeks led them to found colonies or trading stations as far west as Marseilles and along the Spanish coast.

The western Greeks, as historians have called them, were adventurous men, profoundly tied by ancestry and culture to the emerging life of the Greek mainland. From at least the seventh century B.C. on, they were a major civilizing influence in the central and western Mediterranean. They carried over into western Europe the skills and fine craftsmanship they had learned in the East. They came as colonizers, not conquerors.

While the western Greeks were diffusing their culture in the central Mediterranean, the Carthaginians were exerting formidable naval power from their bases along the North African coast. The trade routes and spheres of influence of the three contending peoples—Greeks, Etruscans, and Carthaginians—were continually crossing, and conflicts were inevitable. In the West the advantages lay with Carthage and Etruria, which set about forming an uneasy alliance against the Greeks.

In this struggle for domination the Etruscans possessed one great advantage denied to their adversaries: the rich and extensive iron deposits on the island of Elba. In addition they made good use of the deposits of lead, copper, and iron at Volaterrae, Vetulonia, and Populonia, on the mainland. Iron gave them armor, battle-axes, grappling hooks, the sharp prows of their ships. The Greeks credited them with the invention of the iron anchor (though scholars since have disputed this). Iron, indeed, appears to have been the basis of their economy and their power.

One would scarcely guess how great a part iron played in their culture by looking at their ruined towns and surviving works of art. Iron rusts and crumbles away, and few of their pots and pans, sometimes shown in charming relief on the walls of their funeral chambers, have survived. A good deal of their wealth may have come from the export of everyday kitchen hardware. That they were indeed wealthy is shown by the gold ornaments—bracelets, necklaces, and pectorals of exquisite delicacy—found in their tombs.

Unlike most of the Indo-European invaders of Italy, the Etruscans possessed a body of laws, believed to have been transmitted to earth by the gods. Cicero in the first century B.C. tells the legend of a plowman at Tarquinii who was once working his field when his plow turned up from a furrow the god Tages, who had the appearance of a child and the wisdom of an old man. The plowman cried out in surprise and wonder, and soon a crowd assembled to see the prodigy who had risen from the earth. Tages then revealed to the assembled Etruscans the laws for interpreting omens. According to another story, a nymph named Vegoia appeared to them and revealed the divine laws governing ritual and even the principles of measurement. Codes were established, governing the study of thunder and lightning and the entrails of beasts for purposes of divination. The Etruscans became adept in the arts of augury.

These arts were well known in ancient Babylon, where examination of entrails and the study of storms were practiced assiduously. The Babylonians, like the Etruscans, interpreted the meaning of a peal of thunder according to the particular day or month. The Etruscan augurs, facing southward, divided the sky into sixteen segments—eight on their left, eight on their right—and sought to foretell the future by observing the direction from which a bolt of lightning fell, and by the brilliance and color of its light. Lightning on the left promised good fortune; on the right, evil tidings. The lightning of the supreme god Tinia was always blood red, whereas the other gods wrote across the sky in other colors. In this way the gods spoke to the people, sometimes promising abundance of crops, sometimes foretelling a coming drought or a future victory. The Etruscans also examined the entrails of the animals they sacrificed, and they were especially concerned to examine the liver, which they thought of as representing the seat of life.

The entire doctrine of divination was later taken over by the Romans, who translated the original texts. Plutarch wrote in the first century A.D. that when Romulus founded Rome he called upon Etruscan priests to superintend the foundation rites. They

The golden tablet above is one of three found in 1964 near Rome; the inscribed sheets constitute the most important discovery yet made relating to the almost undeciphered Etruscan language. This tablet, like the second, is in Etruscan, but the third bears the same information in Punic, a language already known.

The bronze handle (above) representing a panther gorging on a human head was fashioned about 500 B.C. The artist was undoubtedly inspired by a favorite Etruscan pastime, the gladiatorial contest, which arose from their primitive funeral rites. The practice of pitting one man against another man or some ferocious beast was adopted by the Romans early in the third century.

consulted their laws, ordered a circular trench to be dug, and filled it with offerings and first fruits. The trench was called *mundus,* a word which the Etruscans used both for the circle of a city and for the circle of the heavens. In time the Romans used the word to mean the "world." And many other strange customs of the early Romans were probably inherited from the Etruscans.

Yet it would be a mistake to suggest that the Etruscans were a solemn people burdened with mysteries. Magic and divination were the commonplaces of the ancient world, and the Greeks in the age of Socrates often practiced strange rites of divination, summoning up the dead and holding converse with the moon. Such practices were an essential part of ordinary living. The men of Etruria, who dug tunnels through hills, drained lakes, diverted rivers, built furnaces, and sailed into the Atlantic, combined their dependence on omens with bold adventure.

They were a people who lived in the open and enjoyed dancing, horse racing, and gladiatorial contests. They especially relished the theatre, and Livy credited them with the invention of satirical drama. Their women possessed remarkable sexual freedom. The Greek historian Theopompus, writing in the middle of the fourth century B.C., tells how Etruscan women were shared "in common"; Herodotus describes them as exercising in the nude with men and mentions that they attended banquets not with their husbands but in the company of the men who pleased them. Herodotus may have been exaggerating, but the Roman comic poet Plautus, writing a century later, reproached the Etruscan girls for being inveterate wantons. Few children, it was said, knew their fathers. Sexual relations were conducted openly, without shame. Men enjoyed the same liberty as women, and Theopompus observes that "though the men approached the women with great pleasure, they derived as much pleasure from the company of adolescents and boys." Aristotle noted that Etruscan men and women dined together on the same couch with a common mantle over them.

Both the Romans and the Greeks somewhat wistfully regarded the Etruscans as devotees of sexual freedom, lovers of luxurious living, gaily indifferent to the moral codes. The early Romans were especially shocked by the freedom given to the women of Etruria, since they themselves kept their wives subordinate and permitted them no voice in government or civil affairs. Unlike early Roman women, Etruscan women spoke their mind in public and regarded themselves as men's equals. Theopompus tells us that their women were unusually beautiful, and the paintings in funeral chambers and terra-cotta images confirm this. The charge of profligacy may not be generally applicable, for there are countless paintings and funerary statues showing husband and wife reclining on the same couch, embracing with exquisite tenderness.

But if the private lives of the Etruscans were free, their public lives were severely disciplined by their aristocratic rulers, one for each of the twelve city-states that formed the Etruscan confederacy. The people worked hard, there were continual wars, and there can have been few prolonged periods of rest. They were building ships, mining iron, spreading across northern Italy, and reaching toward the Adriatic, where they founded the naval port of Spina, now silted over, but once a place of great power and wealth. The bronze statues of their warriors show lean, hard-muscled men armed with spears or short stabbing swords; they have the look of conquerors.

Power belonged to the local prince, the *lucumon*, who appears to have combined the roles of magistrate and high priest. His person was surrounded with brilliant panoply, and it was deliberately intended that he should live in a world so remote from the common people that he would have the appearance of a god. He presided over audiences once a week, but it would appear that only the nobility attended. One of the *lucumones* was chosen to act as king of the confederacy, but in practice the powers of the local prince were probably autonomous. The confederacy consisted of a loose linking of independent states, all of which had a common culture and a common purpose.

The emblems and privileges of the *lucumones* were worked out with special care. When the *lucumon* appeared in public everything about him glittered. He wore a gold diadem, a toga patterned with palms, or with the images of the gods. He sat on an ivory folding stool decorated with plaques of ivory and carried an ivory scepter and took part in processional triumphs in a gilded, four-horse chariot with gold horse trappings. In front of him marched the lictors bearing the emblem of sovereignty, a bundle of elm rods tied with a scarlet strap and enclosing an axe, the head of which jutted above the rods. These emblematic weapons, known as fasces, symbolized the prince's absolute authority over life and limb. The historian Diodorus Siculus wrote that the Etruscans were "the authors of that dignity which surrounds rulers." The Romans, vividly aware of the impression created by the dazzling appearance of an Etruscan prince, wore the entire panoply, and their consuls and magistrates unashamedly borrowed the same clothing and carried the same insignia as the *lucumones*. The military standard topped with a bronze eagle was originally Etruscan; so, too, was the scarlet military cloak worn by a Roman general in

A detail (above) of a tomb painting shows a rider astride a spirited steed; the Etruscans were excellent horse breeders. Through the centuries they had learned to use the animals for war and leisure as well as for transporting goods; they developed the war chariot, then transformed it into a racing vehicle. The sport became one of their (and the Romans') passionate interests.

the field and the purple-bordered toga of the nobility.

The Etruscans handed down to the Romans a multitude of forms, traditions, and observances, which were assimilated into the body of Roman customs. And while panoply and divination were among the greatest gifts transmitted to the Romans, there were also smaller gifts. Etruscan words entered the Roman vocabulary, and some of them have survived into our own language. *Antenna, histrio, persona, magister, atrium, sacer, caerimonia* were all originally Etruscan words. *Antenna* was originally a yard-arm, *histrio* comes from *hister*, the Etruscan word for an actor, *persona* appears to be derived from the Etruscan word *phersu*, denoting a mask. Scholars are still attempting to find out how many other Etruscan words are concealed in Latin vocabularies, and what effect Etruscan grammar may have had on Latin grammar in its formative stages. Though philologists have worked for decades, they are still far from solving these problems, because the Etruscan language has proved curiously difficult to translate. Some ten thousand inscriptions, usually very brief, have survived, but only about one hundred root words can be translated with accuracy. A few are surprisingly close to modern English. The Etruscan *cupe* means "cup," *nefis* means "nephew" or "grandson," and the Etruscan *mi* means "me."

But it was in the realm of religion that Etruscan influence on Rome went deepest. "In the West, in antiquity, there was no people more given to rites of all sorts than the Etruscans," writes the modern authority Raymond Bloch, adding that "this constant attitude of anxiety vis-a-vis the divine powers who regulate the life of man is undoubtedly one of the characteristic traits of this extraordinary nation." Ancient writers, as Bloch observes, also noticed this. Thus the Roman historian Livy remarked that they were a people all the more devoted to religious rites because they excelled in the art of performing them. The body of revelation gathered in the sacred books known as the *disciplina Etrusca*, set forth complex codes of ritual and behavior—so complex that only the Etruscan college of priests could interpret them. The priests presented themselves as the sole interpreters of the divine will; and the *lucumon*, moving in a divine radiance and acting as the supreme pontiff, would interpret the will of the gods with regard to important matters of state.

The Etruscan gods who ruled the earth from their abodes in the high heavens are generally depicted with a quiet and kindly gravity. Tinia, the lord of the skies, was the most powerful, for he was granted three thunderbolts, whereas the other gods were granted one. He was not the absolute master of heaven, but the chairman

The sarcophagus showing an affectionate married couple reclining on a couch (below) was fashioned in the sixth century B.C. The Etruscans believed that if the soul was properly supplied with the necessities of life as well as some of its luxuries, it would stay in the houselike tomb that had been prepared for it. The relatives of the deceased had dual motives for taking good care of the dead; naturally they wanted the soul to live happily ever after, but they also believed that if the spirit became discontent it would leave its abode to return to haunt the living.

of the board who looked for advice to the other gods. He was permitted to hurl one thunderbolt at his pleasure; he could hurl the second only after he received the approval of the rest; and the terrible third bolt could only be hurled when all the gods in concert demanded it. Tinia was usually flanked by his wife Uni and his virgin daughter Menerva. There was a god of fire called Sethlans, who was especially worshiped in the iron-smelting centers, and a goddess of female beauty and enchantment called Turan (Venus), which may mean the "lady" or simply the "goddess." Maris was the god of war and Turms was the god of trade. As contacts with the Greeks increased we find the Greek gods entering the Etruscan pantheon. Under the names of Apulu and Artumes we find the familiar figures of Apollo and Artemis. The Etruscan Hercle is of course Heracles. These gods were taken over bodily and no attempt was made to disguise their origin; and with the gods came their legends.

While the Etruscans entertained a deep affection for the Greek gods, they did not follow the Greeks in their form of worship, nor did they copy the shape of the Greek temple. They had their own way of venerating the gods, with a direct and concentrated approach to divinity. Whereas the Greek temple was designed to be beautiful on all four sides and to radiate its presence in all directions, the Etruscan temple was designed to be beautiful only from the front. There were usually two entrances to the Greek temple, on the east and west; there was only one entrance to the Etruscan temple, which backed against the wall of the sacred enclosure. The temple was approached by a high stairway reaching to a platform with a colonnaded portico opening on three chambers, the larger chamber being occupied by a powerful god while the side chambers were occupied by his divine attendants. All over ancient Etruria we find traces of such temples. When they built the great temple to Jupiter on the Capitoline hill, the Romans imitated the Etruscans by building a high stairway, a portico, and three chambers—one for Jupiter, one for Juno, and one for Minerva. They probably employed Etruscan architects, and it is known from historical records that they employed an Etruscan sculptor to make the terra-cotta images of the gods.

Among the Romans there was a tradition that during the first one hundred seventy years following the foundation of Rome there were no statues of deities at all. The gods were mysterious presences, having neither form nor features; they were felt rather than seen. Sometimes the gods took up their abodes in trees or stones, and sometimes altars were raised to them; here they were placated with offerings and sacrifices. From the beginning the

21

The Etruscans not only believed that the deceased would have a better life in the tomb if he were pictured doing happy things, but they also went to pains to preserve the ashes, for they felt that the soul stayed with the remains. The fifth-century B.C. statue of a mother and child above is in fact a cinerary urn.

Etruscans made their gods in the images of men. Like the Greeks, they rejoiced in their gods in human form and saw no reason to worship the invisible presences.

They fashioned their gods nobly, and many statues of them have survived. In the Museum of the Villa Giulia, in Rome, there stands the Apollo with a hole in his back and one leg half destroyed, found in 1916 among the ruins of Veii; but the springing energy in the warm life-sized terra-cotta figure remains undiminished by time. The Apollo (see illustration on page 23) dates from the end of the sixth century B.C., a time when, according to Livy, the influence of Etruria extended over the whole of Italy, from the Alps to the Straits of Messina. It is Apollo in all his majesty, superbly in command. He leans slightly forward, the curve of his body forming a benediction, an archaic smile hovering on his lips. Although he betrays his Greek origin, he is fashioned with purely Etruscan feeling. This warmth of feeling, combined with a suggestion of Hellenic influences, is also present in the terra-cotta figure of an enthroned woman with child, which has been thought by some to represent the Mother Goddess. Her strong hands hold the child in its swaddling clothes with an exquisite tenderness; and there is about that statue, now lost in one of the dark corners of the museum, a quiet and brooding monumentality. In looking at a photograph of it (left) you would hardly guess that it is only three feet high.

But it is in the painted tomb chambers and funerary sculptures that we come closest to the religious and human feeling of the Etruscans. Terra-cotta statues (such as the one illustrated on pages 20–21) show husband and wife reclining together in death on a couch, the sculptor suggesting their continuing affection for one another, their silent enjoyment of each other's presence. These are people who gaze on death calmly, looking out on the world as though they had just awakened from a refreshing sleep. In the painted tomb chambers in the hills above Tarquinii there is a sense of spaciousness and airy lightness, as though another sun were shining in the underworld. The colors are apple green, sky blue, red, orange, yellow, the colors of spring; in one painting we see musicians and dancers, wrestlers and jugglers, youths on their high-stepping horses, lovers caught in an eternal embrace. There are chariot races and bullfights. Always there is the sense of movement, of life's pleasures continuing after death. Only rarely are there moments of solemnity as in the Tomb of Augurs, where among hovering birds we see professional mourners standing before blood-red gates that symbolize the barrier between the living and the kingdom of death. Sometimes, too, we encounter the demons of hell with their bright blue faces and serpentine hair; yet their presence is rare. Far more frequent are scenes of banqueting. For the function of these paintings was more than a decorative one; it had a magical intent, designed to re-create for the dead man in his tomb the surroundings of his earthly life and to prolong by means of pictures his relationship with the living.

Etruscan art suggests a people charged with energy, vividly alive, sinewy and alert, delighting in color and the joys of the flesh, but capable of enduring the hardships of war. They were not, one would have thought, a people who would vanish from the earth, and in fact they did not vanish entirely. The Romans destroyed the confederacy of the twelve city-states, but the Etruscans remained in Umbria, Tuscany, and Latium, giving their features and their gifts to their descendants. As a people they survived until 82 B.C. when Sulla ordered a general massacre. Then, at last, they lost the remnants of their independence. By the second century A.D. there was scarcely anyone alive who could speak Etruscan or read the sacred books. Yet as late as the fifth century A.D. a few Etruscan priests could be found among the entourage of the emperor Julian.

The mystery is how so great a culture could have perished. A strange silence surrounds them. We have the paintings, the sculptures, the jewelry, a host of stone inscriptions, but the living voice is absent. If all the books written by the Greeks had perished, and we knew them only by their works in the world's museums, we would conclude that they had reached marvelous heights in artistic expression, but we would know little about their thoughts. We do not know just what was said in the long-lost sacred books of Etruscan ritual and divination, and we might not comprehend them even if we found them. Most of what we know about the Etruscans comes down through Roman legends. We would know more about the Etruscans, and perhaps more about their language, if the history of the Etruscans written by the emperor Claudius had survived. No Etruscan grammar or dictionary by Roman scholars has been found. A recent discovery at San Severo, near the site of the ancient seaport of Caere, of three thin gold plates inscribed in Punic and Etruscan to record the dedication of a temple to the Carthaginian goddess Astarte, may have provided a clue in the form of a parallel text, and scholars of Punic may be able to solve a problem which has baffled scholars of Etruscan for centuries. Meanwhile the Etruscan enigma remains. All we know is that there arose in early Italy a brilliant and charming people whose influence fed into the mainstream of Italian culture and helped to shape the destinies of Rome.

One of the most famous Etruscan works of art, the Apollo of Veii, *was created at the end of the sixth century* B.C. *Apollo was one of many gods adopted by the Etruscans directly from the Greeks. Apparently even his functions as god of order and reason and artistic inspiration were not changed by the move.*
MUSEO DI VILLA GIULIA, ROME

23

ROME'S ETRUSCAN TUTORS

While their origin remains a mystery, there is no doubt as to the Etruscans' immense influence upon emerging Rome. Inventions, ideas of government, and many aspects of religion, social custom, and taste were to pass from them to their successors. In the eighth century B.C. the civilized Etruscans made their appearance among the semibarbaric tribes of the Italian peninsula. They occupied the central area of Italy (modern Tuscany), where there were extensive ore deposits, from which they were quick to profit. Enriched by their trade in iron, the Etruscans built an army unmatched among the tribes, and by the time they reached their zenith in the sixth century B.C., they controlled Italy from the Po Valley to the Campania.

They came into contact with Rome early in the city's history and occupied it because of its strategic position on the Tiber: an Etruscan dynasty probably ruled Rome for almost a century. But by the fourth century B.C. the Romans had become organized and powerful enough to defeat the bickering cities of their former masters; by the beginning of the Christian era they were to completely engulf Etruria, the state that had prepared the way for the Roman empire by spreading cultural unity over Italy and leading the way to an urban civilization. The Etruscans left brilliant, if silent, testimony to their life in the form of art, as in the wall painting (left) of an Etruscan couple.

TOMB OF SHIELDS, TARQUINIA; LEONARD VON MATT

ETRUSCANS AS BORROWERS

The Etruscan civilization, which so greatly influenced Rome, was itself a product of crosscurrents of influences. It was deeply affected by constant contact with Greece and Phoenicia. In addition Etruria came into contact with many other cultures, for its natural resources and navy made it a strong trading nation; its merchants saw other societies first-hand, and goods from many areas of Europe and the east that flowed through its ports were sold throughout the country. When its ideas and works of art took shape, therefore, they were at once unmistakably Etruscan and distinctly cosmopolitan.

The Etruscans' propensity for absorbing from other cultures is most visibly demonstrated in their artifacts. The figures with wide staring eyes on the seventh-century B.C. *cinerary urn from Chiusi (far left) are Sumerian in character; the bronze censer (left), though Etruscan work, is of Phoenician design. Etruria most frequently borrowed from Greece; the vase above is Greek in shape, design, and motif. The costume as well as the elegant design of the figure at right came from Crete.*

OVERLEAF: *A tomb painting probably depicts the offering of a libation. The Etruscans, an almost fanatically religious people with a primitive theology, spent a great deal of time at divination and the performance of rituals. The Romans inherited something of their attitude and many of their gods.*

TEACHERS OF WARRIORS

In the fifth century B.C., 306 members of a powerful Roman clan set out for Veii seeking vengeance for the murder of one of their kin. Warned of the attack, the Veientines cleverly deployed their men, lured the Romans into ambush, and destroyed them. The military situation was to change drastically, however. In 396 B.C., after a ten-year siege, the Romans captured Veii, hastening Etruria's decline from power. Ironically Rome was to defeat the Etruscan cities by using Tuscan techniques. Roman leaders learned that victory came more easily when they arrayed their infantry in three tight ranks. They adopted the idea of a cavalry and even used Etruscan studs for breeding. They probably also borrowed Etruscan weapon and armor designs; when they added these things to their own talent for organization they replaced their teachers as the strongest fighting force in Italy.

Etruria's expansion in Italy during the seventh and sixth centuries B.C. took place because its armies were made up of trained and disciplined soldiers like the haughty warrior at right. Due to their skill at working with metals, Etruscans had weapons far superior to their opponents'. Opposite, a panel from a chariot shows two combatants heavily armed and armored in the Etruscan style; even the seventh-century bowman above was a terror in his time.

PURSUIT OF PLEASURE

Etruscan women were considered equal to their men; although Roman ladies did not enjoy all the same privileges, many aspects of the aristocratic Roman way of life were determined by luxurious tastes and habits inherited from their Etruscan predecessors. Noble Etruscans had found countless ways—which Roman sybarites later adopted—to sate their appetites for sumptuous living. At banquets guests reclined on couches covered with costly materials, watching dancers and other entertainers as slaves served them course after course of exquisite food and poured fine wine into their silver goblets. Dancing, athletic contests, and stage shows were also favorite pastimes. As Rome passed from republic to empire it drew more heavily on this heritage—possibly to its detriment, for many historians feel it was partly responsible for Rome's downfall.

Because no Etruscan literature has been found, we are entirely dependent on art and artifacts for our knowledge of daily life in Etruria; fortunately these are abundant. A detail (opposite) of a fourth-century B.C. tomb painting depicts an elegant noblewoman. Her hair has been meticulously dressed (probably by a slave), and she wears rich clothes set off with gold jewelry. Her taste for grandeur was the product of many generations; three centuries earlier her forebears had worn pins such as the delicately wrought fibula at top. At left is a bronze canister incised with mythological scenes; the handle represents two Amazons bearing a fallen comrade. Etruscan women used these beautiful coffers as containers for cosmetics and jewelry. A relief (above) from a sixth-century cinerary urn shows two women sharing the pleasures of the banquet with their husbands. They feast to the music of a flute player as a slave brings them more wine.

33

THE UNDERWORLD

For a people with such a great capacity for enjoying life's pleasures the Etruscans spent a surprising amount of time preparing for death. They believed that if properly provided for, a man's spirit would live on. Consequently tombs were equipped with everything from weapons to crockery, and scenes of earthly revelry were painted on the walls. To ensure the comfort of the deceased several rites were performed. Customarily the body was the guest of honor at a lavish banquet in its new home, and sacrifices and funeral games were presented to supply the soul with sustenance. When the Etruscans came into contact with the Greeks they adopted the concept of an underworld, but they apparently felt no need to reconcile the two theologies, for their funerary practices remained essentially unchanged.

Whole cities of the dead have been found in Tuscany, each tomb being built like an elaborate home. At right is the Tomb of Reliefs in which all the utensils and weaponry the dead might need have been provided by reliefs on the wall. Cinerary urns like that below were common in early Etruria; it was believed that the spirit would stay in a humanoid form.

A CULT OF CRUELTY

The Etruscans loved luxury and gaiety, but sometime after the start of the fifth century B.C., a dark, cruel side of their character appeared. Apparently because Etruscans believed that the dead needed blood to survive in the other world, funeral games developed which involved the death of the contestant who lost, and human sacrifice at a tomb was common practice. Such observances can be partially explained by the fact that religion was a very important element in Etruscan life, but the zeal and imagination with which they depicted maiming and killing, or set man against man or beast are hard to rationalize. This Etruscan preoccupation became their least healthy legacy to the Roman people, whose lust for blood never had religion for an excuse. Rome staged its first Etruscan-style gladiatorial contest in 264 B.C., and these shows, next to chariot races, were to remain Rome's most popular spectacles.

*Many tomb paintings dwell on
murder as does the bloody detail
(left) depicting a slaughter, from
a Vulci burial site. Yet coun-
terbalancing these gory creations
are others, whimsical and hu-
morous. Some artisan, tired of
conventional shapes, formed the
drinking horn at top left.
Etruscan ladies must have liked
a jest, for one of them used the
ceramic head (top right) as a
vessel for her perfume, and another the wheeled bronze above.
Tuscan artists loved to represent
animals like the lion at right.*

II

THE SEVEN HILLS

According to a pleasant Roman fiction Rome was founded by a chieftain named Romulus on April 21, 753 B.C., at about eight o'clock in the morning.

This story appears in Plutarch. Archaeologists and historians, however, have long looked upon the tale as unsubstantiated and outside the realm of record. They are inclined to doubt whether the city's foundation took place as early as the eighth century. They are not sure that anyone called Romulus ruled over the Romans. So many layers of legend have accumulated over the figure of Romulus that if there ever was such a man, he has all but vanished beneath their weight. At various times before the dawn of history many chieftains and many tribes must have contended for those hills that rose strategically out of the marshes to dominate the Tiber. But Rome's actual origins remain dark. There is a sense in which the small, precarious settlement was less the result of the work of men's hands than of the marriage of the river and the hills.

When we first become aware of these hills in early time, they are occupied by various tribes fighting for the control of river crossings that offered passage between the south and what was to become Etruria, and perhaps also to the salt flats near the river's mouth. There were many tribes and each had its own totems, its own gods, its own customs. Though most of them shared a common Indo-European heritage, they showed no particular love for one another, each tribe being jealous of its own power and its own divinities. The tribesmen were shepherds, hunters, farmers, cattle thieves, occasional merchants and lived in small huts crowding the wooded heights. The hut poles were planted firmly in the soft volcanic tufa; there was a hearth or earthenware furnace in the center of the hut and a roof hole to draw off smoke. Such primitive dwellings, often round in shape, are found even today in the Campania, south of Rome, and their design has scarcely changed over the centuries.

No names can be attached to the first settlers. They represent various Iron Age cultures. We know that some buried their dead in hollowed-out oak trees; others cremated them and stored the ashes in votive jars. These remains have been unearthed in the Roman Forum, about five acres of land between the Palatine and Capitoline hills that were to become the center of a vast empire. In early days the Forum was nothing more than a marsh, fed by springs, with here and there a few dry knolls rising above it. In the rainy season it became a lake. Yet this marshland had a special importance, for the pathways from the south and the east met there, whereas beyond the river were those to the north. The word *forum* means "the place outside the door." It was the area outside the little hill settlements of the early tribesmen, where they could meet and exchange goods without trespassing on one another's land. Even as Rome grew, *forum* always kept its dual meaning—"meeting place" and "market."

Gradually, as time passes, we are able to recognize some of the tribes on the hills. The Sabines, congregating from the mountain valleys in central Italy, which their Indo-European ancestors had settled, were entrenched on the Quirinal, worshiping the sun and moon and the god Quirinus, whose name was thought to mean the "lance bearer." Generally they were a rather phlegmatic people, but they were ferocious in battle and famous for their long shields. Some Greek influence had touched them, and there was a vague tradition that they came originally from Sparta.

On the Palatine there lived a Latin tribe formed of refugees from Alba Longa, a settlement on the shores of the Alban Lake, about a dozen miles southwest of Rome. The Latins' presence was explained by early chroniclers in the tale of Romulus and Remus. According to the myth, Romulus and Remus were the twin sons of Rhea Silvia of the royal house of Alba Longa. She was a vestal virgin, who had made a vow of perpetual chastity. When she produced children her uncle, who had usurped the throne, imprisoned her and ordered the babies to be drowned, even though she claimed she had been raped by the god Mars. The men who were ordered to drown the babies, instead, left them on the banks of the flooded Tiber, where they were suckled by a wolf and fed by a woodpecker, which made its home in the shelter of a sacred fig tree. The wolf, the woodpecker, and the fig tree were probably tribal totems arranged to lend a kind of sanctity to the children of Rhea Silvia. A shepherd, Faustulus, found them at last and carried them home to be brought up by his wife. The brothers grew up to be robbers who shared their spoils with Faustulus. One day Remus was caught and taken before the king of Alba Longa. Romulus came to help his brother, and together they killed the monarch. After they had restored the rightful king to the throne, they left their native town, but they took with them a small band of landless and masterless men.

Romulus took possession of the Palatine hill and founded a new principality, marking out its limits by plowing the boundaries of a special area on the hill and sanctifying them by sacrifice. He was a man of daemonic energy and a forceful diplomat. Romulus and Remus soon became rivals, however, for Remus declared that he in turn would build his own settlement on the Aventine hill nearby. As the city walls of Romulus were rising, the rivalry grew

Rome, which was to become the jealous guardian of an empire, had as its emblem a bronze likeness of a she-wolf, the animal that suckled Romulus and Remus in the legend of the city's founding. The ancient Etruscan statue was discovered on the Capitoline; the twins were added during the Renaissance.

intense. Remus jumped over his brother's wall in a symbolic gesture that was part jest, part challenge, and Romulus killed him. It was a senseless crime that could never be expunged. At intervals throughout their history, the Romans felt the spell of this original bloodguilt and acted out the myth with monotonous frequency in their fratricidal civil wars and palace murders.

Romulus does not appear to have confined his realm to the Palatine alone. He is said to have swelled the ranks of his followers by appealing to the heterogeneous and fugitive elements—the young, the landless, the murderers. He offered them land, booty, and a lawless life, and prepared for them a retreat on the Capitoline hill which was called the *asylum inter duos lucos* (that is, a place of refuge between the two wooded heights of the Capitoline). Dimly discernible behind the legend is the familiar image of the bandit chieftain, the resourceful man of war and stratagems, towering above his band of followers because he possesses an indomitable spirit of violence.

The attentive reader of legends soon learns to look for chains of logic concealed among the fairy tales, and sometimes the most improbable legends contain their own logic. Even in fable Romulus seems to be acting out a consistent role. The stories told about him have a ring of truth; those of his origins are such as a bandit might deliberately invent in order to impress his followers. It is said that when he died he was carried up to heaven in a thundercloud, and this too is the kind of legend that might be invented about a war chief venerated by his followers. A loftier tale, immortalized by Vergil, set forth the idea that the primordial father of Rome was Aeneas, the Trojan chieftain who survived his city's fall at the hand of the Greeks and brought his followers to a promised land, where he sired the breed that produced Romulus (see summary of and excerpts from the *Aeneid* on pages 210–16). The Aeneas legend was surely splendid poetic invention; yet the Romulus of the myths has the appearance of being the memory of an actual man.

The famous story of the rape of the Sabine women is plausible, given the character that legend assigns to the followers of Romulus. A lack of wives to share the beds of the outcasts and fugitives and to produce offspring may have provoked this first Roman assault upon neighbors. The Roman stratagem was a simple one. Romulus announced that somewhere in his territory an altar to the god Consus had been found buried in the earth. Then, as now, buried objects possessed magical significance in the Mediterranean world, and people would travel a great distance to see them. According to legend, the neighboring tribesmen (most of whom

ROME BEFORE 500 B.C.
1. Circus Maximus
2. Temple of Diana (probable site)
3. Cloaca Maxima
4. Temple of Jupiter, Juno, and Minerva
5. Curia (first meeting place of the Senate)
6. Temple of Janus
7. Temple of Vesta
8. Regia (palace of the early kings; under the republic the residence of the *pontifex maximus*)

On the map:
VINCIAN

SERVIAN WALL

QUIRINAL

VIMINAL

WALL OF AURELIAN *(built c. A.D. 271-75)*

S E P T I M O N T I U M *(7th century B.C.)*

TOLINE

FORUM

ESQUILINE

VELIA

PALATINE

CAELIAN

AVENTINE

APPIAN WAY *(paved in 312 B.C.)*

N

CITADEL ON THE TIBER *Archaeological finds have made it possible to trace the growth of Rome during its earliest days. The village on the Palatine became, not more than a century after its founding, part of a federation of settlements called the Septimontium. (The name indicates that the area may have included seven hilltop villages, although it embraced only three of the seven great hills later enclosed by the Servian Wall.) By the middle of the sixth century Rome was a full-fledged city on the Etruscan model. Among the imposing new structures was a city wall that fully exploited the defensive advantage offered by many natural escarpments. Attributed to Servius Tullius and rebuilt sometime after 390 B.C., the Servian Wall was later to intimidate such formidable invaders as Pyrrhus and Hannibal. It was the last wall to be built around Rome until the reign of the emperor Aurelian.*

were of Sabine stock) were invited to attend the ceremonies in honor of the newly discovered altar and to bring their womenfolk. They came willingly and they were unarmed. Romulus and his followers, who were armed, had no difficulty in capturing the women and speeding off with them. According to the Mauretanian king Juba II, who became one of the most learned antiquarians of the Augustan age, 683 women were captured. Another tradition states that only 30 women were seized. Whatever the number, Romulus had acquired a useful addition to the population and had shown that he was perfectly capable of defying the gods by breaking the sacred truce. Though few in number, his followers had administered a psychological shock to the Sabines, who were unlikely to recover without winning a full-scale war against Rome.

Yet curiously we hear of no war, only of a series of retaliatory campaigns that met with little success. The long truce that appears to have followed had enduring consequences, for it laid the foundations for the dual government which was to be characteristic of Rome in later years. Since neither side had won, an agreement was made that the seven hills should be governed jointly by Romulus and by Titus Tatius, the chieftain who ruled over the Sabines. This system of joint rule was to be revived at intervals throughout Roman history. When Rome was ruled by consuls, they were generally appointed in pairs; nearly all the important officers of state also worked in pairs, each checking the activities of the other. The Romans were proud of this safeguard against tyrannical rule, and in later years it pleased them to remember that they had brought reason and intelligence into the art of government.

Far from being the conqueror of all the hills of Rome, Romulus appears to have been merely the chieftain who finally accepted a life of amity with the neighboring Sabines. Following his death they are said to have taken possession of the Palatine, and the small principality founded by Romulus was joined to the far larger community of the Sabines.

In time more and more legends accumulated around the memory of Romulus, "the son of the she-wolf." He was credited with the capture of Alba Longa, the original seat of his royal house, and with a great but unlikely victory over Veii, an almost impregnable Etruscan citadel some twelve miles north of Rome. He was remembered as the founder-father, the shaper of destinies, the stern lawgiver, and the great harasser of the countryside; and his memory was kept alive by his followers. Primitive ceremonies arose about him, many to survive for a thousand years. At the festival of Lupercalia, youths sacrificed goats in the cave where the wolf had suckled Romulus and Remus, below the western slope of the Palatine, and then ran around the hill wearing loincloths; they carried strips of goatskin with which they struck women to promote fertility. The Sabines paid tribute to Romulus in their own way by calling him Quirinus after their own god of war, with the result that the Romans eventually adopted Quirinus as a second war god, to rule with Mars. It was as though the dual system of government extended even to the deities.

The legendary Romulus remains a mysterious figure. He left no dynasty, no body of doctrine, no tables of law. Yet some emanation of dynamic purpose was believed to flow from him after his death. In Romulus, the Romans found the symbol of an all-powerful king. In the Forum there survives a part of a four-sided column, which may represent the cenotaph of Romulus, bearing in archaic lettering an inscription intended perhaps as a proclamation of divine vengeance against those who would pollute a place that was sacred to a king. We can read only a few words: *sakros, recei, kalatorem, iouxmenta*—"sacred," "for the king," "attendant," "beasts of burden." This broken stone—the city's oldest surviving document—suggests the awe surrounding the kingship.

The immediate successor of Romulus was the Sabine king Numa Pompilius, whose long reign was devoted, if we can trust the chroniclers, to the pursuit of peace. Tradition ascribed to him the kingly virtue of benevolence. He inaugurated many rites that were to endure with little change until the advent of Christianity, and he was especially remembered as the king who installed the pontiffs in their office. The word *pontiff* comes from the Latin *pons*, a "bridge," and has been a problem for generations of commentators, who have wondered why a priest should have anything to do with bridges. One explanation may be that the bridges across the Tiber were regarded as having special sanctity, since the command of the river crossings gave Rome its power and prestige in the ancient world; but it is just as possible that the word was used in an abstract sense. Among the Jains of India the greatest saints bear the title *tirthankara*, meaning "the maker of the river crossings." So we may imagine the pontiffs building their sky bridges to the gods.

The college of pontiffs, presided over by the *pontifex maximus*, the chief bridgebuilder, preserved the sacred books, superintended all public religious ceremonies, and drew up the calendar of festivities. We hear of other priestly colleges instituted by Numa, so many that he seems to be the inventor of all the rituals that the Romans practiced assiduously, long after their original meaning had been forgotten. They thought of him almost as the

The shape of the earliest type of Roman dwelling is known from traces of post holes on the Palatine hill and from models in the form of small funerary urns such as that above, dating from the eighth century B.C. *The Roman village and others of that period consisted of a cluster of frame huts of daub and wattle, each barely large enough to shelter a single family. The weight of the thatched roof was supported by a central post.*
SOPRINTENDENZA FORO ROMANO E PALATINO

42

personification of ritual, strangely detached from affairs of everyday life: the story was told that when a messenger came running to him to say that the enemy was approaching, Numa replied, "Hush, I am worshiping." Above all, Numa stands against Romulus in the Roman saga as the peacekeeper and the embodiment of a lost golden age when no wolves attacked the flocks and no armies breached the walls. Romans were told, too, that he had built the small temple to the god Janus, ordering the doors to be closed in peace and kept open in war. After his benevolent reign they were rarely closed.

Under his successor, Tullus Hostilius, whose very name sounds warlike, the doors flew wide open. The new king appears to have been a throwback to Romulus, fiery and energetic. After long and difficult campaigns, he destroyed the city of Alba Longa, which, according to legend, had been founded by the son of Aeneas and had been the birthplace of Romulus and Remus. (Castel Gandolfo, the summer residence of the pope, stands on the site of the ancient city.) This ruthless act helped to give Rome the primacy among the Latin tribes and cities.

Next in the legendary line of kings came Ancus Marcius, who was credited with re-establishing the traditional Sabine reign of peace, with founding a colony at the Tiber's mouth, and with encouraging agriculture and trade. It may well have been that he built a bridge across the Tiber, thereby promoting commerce between Etruscan merchants, who were then pushing southward across the Latin plain, and Greek settlements in the south.

The next king, however, was neither Sabine nor Roman. He was half Etruscan and half Greek, and with him—or at least in his time—the configuration of Rome changed profoundly. Like Romulus and Numa, Tarquinius Priscus left his enduring imprint on the Roman mind. According to tradition, he was the son of a rich Corinthian immigrant named Demaratus, who had settled in Etruscan Tarquinii. Being considered a half-breed he moved to Rome and established himself there, becoming the adviser to Ancus Marcius. Upon the latter's death, Tarquinius led a bloodless revolution which bore him to the throne. Presumably this took place just before the end of the seventh century B.C., and Tarquinius became the master of the primitive hill town, seeking to convert it into an Etruscan metropolis.

Roman historians were inclined to view Tarquinius Priscus in the same magical light in which they viewed Romulus and Numa. It was said that when he first drove up to the gates of Rome in an open cart with his Etruscan wife Tanaquil, an eagle swooped out of the sky, lifted Tarquinius' cap, and then set it down on

While sophisticated Etruria was influencing the development of Rome, another advanced culture, that of the Greeks, was shaping the civilization of southeastern Italy. A tomb painting of the fourth or third century B.C., *discovered in the city of Cumae, in Campania, combines Greek and Italic elements. It shows an upper-class Samnite matron in Greek dress, attended by a maid, preening herself for a ritual wedding in the realm of the dead.*
MUSEO NAZIONALE, NAPLES; REV. RAYMOND V. SCHODER, S.J.

The small temple of Janus, its closed gate signifying that Rome is at peace, is depicted on a coin at top. The original temple, whose foundations have been uncovered, was supposedly dedicated by Numa, an early king of Rome. Also recalling the city's beginnings is a rendering of the legendary rape of the Sabine women in the time of Romulus.

his head. Tarquinius was heaven-sent and therefore above reproach. The chroniclers omit all reference to the southward march of Etruscan power. They regard him as a Roman king, Greek by accident of birth, wed to an Etruscan woman. In fact he—or someone like him at that time—began the process of Rome's advancement by introducing the half-barbarous people to the cultivated habits of Etruria. The several lakes in the Forum were drained and channeled to the Tiber through the Cloaca Maxima, a sewer which survives to this day as a testimony to the engineering skill of the Etruscans. Hills were fortified with stone walls, and foundations were laid on the Capitoline for the great temple to the Etruscan deities Tinia, Uni, and Menerva. In time Tinia became identified with the god Jupiter, and the goddesses Uni and Menerva, their names only slightly changed to Juno and Minerva, were retained in the Roman pantheon. Tarquinius is thought to have either built or greatly enlarged the Circus Maximus, the race course below the steep cliff of the Palatine where games and contests were held. Etruscan words, ideas, techniques, and customs poured into Rome. As the Romulus of story gave the Romans a taste for conquest, and Numa gave them a deep-seated affection for ritual, Tarquinius gave them a delight in luxury, in vast buildings, and in civilized comforts. The Romans were presented with the evidence of the Etruscan splendor and succumbed avidly to the temptations offered by their conqueror.

In a hundred different ways Etruscan influence penetrated the minds and hearts of the Romans. It was felt particularly in the arts, in ceremony, and in divination, and perhaps most of all in a sense of spaciousness, as the Romans absorbed the characteristics of the Etruscans and moved on to conquests of their own. The colorful emblems of Etruscan rule were taken over, and Roman historians preserved for posterity a record of the insignia and titles of the royal Tarquins.

With the Etruscans came aristocratic rule, formality, a taste for elegance, a superb sense of style, and though the Romans later condemned aristocratic elegance, they were rarely to free themselves from it. The Etruscan influence took deep root, and in their private lives the rich retained the imprint of Etruscan ways long after Etruria had vanished into the limbo of the past. Etruscan influence, however, also had its dangers, for by introducing a method of government that was tyrannical and hierarchic, its kings brought about an inevitable conflict between classes, and particularly between themselves and men of landed property. And on that rock the power of the Etruscans was eventually broken.

Greek influence, too, was being felt in Rome. It was the age of luxury-loving Pisistratus, ruler of Athens. The expanding Greek colonies in Sicily and southern Italy were increasing in wealth and splendor. Direct traffic between Rome and such Greek settlements as Syracuse and Acragas, however, was still in its infancy, so that Greek influence filtered into Rome chiefly through Etruria. We hear of Greek artisans working near the ancient Etruscan city of Caere. Greek pottery was used and adapted in Tarquinian Rome.

Under the Tarquinian rule Rome made war on its Latin neighbors, starting with the conquest of the city of Apiolae; and the returning soldiers brought so much booty that the Romans were able to indulge their new taste for luxury. Tarquinius offered elaborate games with race horses and boxers imported from Etruria. Dancers and musicians were also brought in, and the Etruscan ceremonial dances and modes of music were imitated by the Romans. Rome was becoming a large and prosperous city adorned with monumental architecture. By 500 B.C. it may have had a population of twenty or twenty-five thousand spread over the seven hills. Moreover, by seizing neighboring villages in the Latin plain and by extending its domain from the Tiber's mouth into the Alban hills and beyond, it was growing into a nation that may then have numbered a few hundred thousand. One modern authority holds that even before the year 500 Rome had won control of some three hundred fifty square miles in just one advance.

The rule of the Tarquins lasted, according to tradition, from 616 B.C. to 509 B.C. Modern scholars, while prepared to accept these dates and to regard Tarquinius as an Etruscan conqueror, are puzzled by his successor Servius Tullius, whose origins are as obscure as the events of his reign. Romans said he was the good king who built the first stone wall around Rome—portions of the Servian Wall (see map on pages 40–41) still exist—and who signed a treaty with the Latin League, a confederacy of villages and tribesmen dedicated to joint worship of Jupiter on the Alban Mount. He is said to have built a temple to the goddess Diana on the Aventine as a sanctuary for the Latin people, thus showing his sympathy for the Latin communities, who regarded Diana with special veneration. Roman records make the claim that he was a Roman or a Latin and describe him as a man of peace. Yet the antiquarian Emperor Claudius, who made a prolonged study of Etruscan history, identified Servius Tullius with Mastarna, an Etruscan soldier of fortune.

The tyrannical majesty of the first Tarquinius was equaled only by Tarquinius Superbus, who was perhaps the son of the man reputed to have brought Etruscan civilization to Rome. The name

ANDERSON

FOTOTECA UNIONE

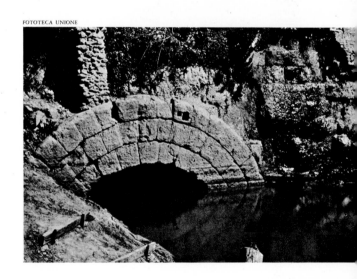

The earliest known Roman inscription (top) marks a grave which some ancient Romans believed to be that of Romulus. At bottom is the Tiber outlet of the Cloaca Maxima, greatest of the sewers and canals built to drain Rome's marshlands by the sixth-century Tarquins. The surviving arch replaced an earlier one some time after 200 B.C.

Superbus seems to have been given him by an admiring people; it could mean "the proud," but is more likely to have meant "the magnificent." He is said to have completed the works begun by Tarquinius Priscus, employing the artist Vulca from Veii to adorn the temple of Jupiter, Juno, and Minerva on the Capitoline, and he seems to have made war chiefly to acquire slaves to build the great monuments intended to immortalize his fame. Livy says that he led his army into the territory of the Hernici and the Volsci, despoiled their lands, and established armed camps among them. He abolished the civic rights bestowed on the people by Servius Tullius and brought Rome to a position of dominance as the head of the Latin League. He was more powerful than any king of Rome before him, and he reveled in his power.

The temple he built to the trio of gods on the Capitoline was to be his most lasting memorial and the first major monument in Rome. The historian Dionysius of Halicarnassus tells us that "it stood on a high base and was 800 feet in circuit, each side measuring close to 200 feet." (The Periclean Parthenon at Athens, built nearly half a century later, is only 228 feet in length and 101 feet in width.) The temple appears to have been a structure in the Etruscan style, its figures of gods no larger than life-sized. Later, under the republic, it was to be peopled with towering statues reaching to its lofty roof. Gilt shields were to ornament its pediment, trophies to adorn its interior; stucco facings and floor mosaics were also to appear. In 83 B.C. it burned down, to be replaced by a second temple of the same size but of greater magnificence. Pillared with marble and roofed with gilded bronze, this was to be the shrine which the poet Horace called *Capitolium fulgens*, the shining Capitol. There was a tradition that when the foundations of the first temple were being laid, a human head (*caput*) was found buried in the earth. Soothsayers interpreted this as meaning that Rome was to become the head of all Italy, and indeed the words *capital* and *capitol* both mean "the head place." The Romans always regarded this sanctuary as the most sacred of all: it was the true habitation of Jupiter, the most powerful of the gods, and the place where the supreme offerings were made. Within the walled enclosure that surrounded it, stood the altar at which sacrifices were offered at the start of each year and in celebration of triumphs. Today only its foundations and some fragments of its marble columns survive.

The temple was still unfinished in 509 B.C. when (again, according to tradition) a palace revolt, led by the king's nephew Lucius Junius Brutus, brought about the fall and expulsion of Tarquinius Superbus. The historical basis of such an uprising

The head of Hermes was part of a group of terra-cotta figures that, from about 500 B.C., adorned the roof of the temple of Apollo in the Etruscan city of Veii, some twelve miles northwest of Rome. It became a spoil of war for the Romans in 396 B.C., when Veii fell to a besieging army led by the general Camillus.

remains obscure; and though Brutus himself may be legendary, there is no doubt that at about this time the Romans threw off Etruscan overlordship as well as the institution of kingship as a whole, replacing it by a republic. It is known that under the kings a strong class of nobles had arisen to challenge their power. These men were patricians, landholders who claimed descent from the leading families of Rome's earliest times. A council of elders, or a *senatus*, had come into existence, composed of persons selected by the king from among the patricians. It held only advisory powers, but upon the death of the king it had the very important function of choosing one or more viceroys, or *interreges*, who in turn would nominate the next king for the Senate's approval. A tribal assembly of all citizens, known as the Comitia Curiata, had also come into being to witness and vote on certain acts—another early step toward representative government. Even though the plebeians, or folk without patrician lineage or property, were regarded as citizens, they appear to have had little political power as against the clans of the nobles. The time of the plebs lay ahead; what occurred at the end of the sixth century was undoubtedly an uprising of the "best" families.

In Roman history Lucius Junius Brutus was depicted as a popular leader, the personification of liberty, the stern lawgiver who gave direction and purpose to the republic he supposedly founded. But this was a legend invented to give substance to the claim that the expulsion of the kings came about as the result of a popular movement. Some chronicles also have it that Brutus, the revolutionary aristocrat, soon proclaimed himself dictator, thereby merely exchanging one form of tyranny for another. Plutarch described him as "a man like steel of too hard a temper, who never had his character softened by thought or study." His portrait, or what is believed to be his portrait, shows him as a person with deep-set eyes and powerful features half hidden by a thick and unruly beard. In the imagination of the Romans he was a man so loyal to the state and so remote from pity that he could watch unmoved when his two sons, arrested as traitors, were executed before his eyes. To Brutus was given the credit of founding the republic and shaping it in accordance with his own vigorous and puritanical character.

There seems to be no doubt that someone like Brutus lived and played an important role in the expulsion of the Tarquins. What is in doubt is whether he actually founded the republic. We learn that his dictatorship was short-lived, and that he was soon compelled to accept as co-ruler a certain Lucius Tarquinius Collatinus, evidently another member of the royal family. Then

A powerful bronze bust dating from the third century B.C. *exhibits lingering traces of the Etruscan style, but contains more than a promise of what was to be one of Rome's greatest contributions to world art—its mastery of uncompromising portraiture. The head may be that of Lucius Junius Brutus, who expelled the Tarquins.*
PALAZZO DEI CONSERVATORI, ROME; HERSCHEL LEVIT

The evolution of Rome's republican institutions was far enough advanced by the early fifth century B.C. to allow considerable stability of government even under the divided rule of two consuls. Many years were to pass, however, before private citizens could cast private ballots. A coin minted in 137 B.C. gives evidence of such an innovation; it shows a Roman dropping a stone tablet into a voting urn.

both were overthrown and the last vestiges of Etruscan rule were extinguished. When the Etruscans departed, Rome came under the personal rule of Publius Valerius, a man descended from an ancient family reputed to have taken part in the promotion of peace between the Sabines and the Romans.

With Publius Valerius we may emerge from legend into fact—though his historicity has been doubted. Kindly in peace, generous to his enemies in war, ruthless in his determination to win for Rome its place in the sun, he gives the impression of a man with a carefully-thought-out political philosophy. His first test came, according to Livy, when the Etruscans massed their forces, demanding the subjugation of the city that had dared to expel them. Under Lars Porsenna of Clusium, wave upon wave of Etruscan cavalry was thrown against Rome; but a Roman soldier, Horatius, heroically defended the Tiber's bridge. For a time the invaders held the Janiculum hill; they also occupied large areas of the city. Publius Valerius was compelled to come to terms with the common people, exasperated by more than a century of aristocratic rule and in no mood to fight for its prolongation.

According to classical sources it was at this time that Valerius issued a series of extraordinary enactments giving to the people powers which they had never previously enjoyed. He set about creating a popular army. He introduced the death penalty for anyone who attempted to make himself a tyrant against the will of the people. The same penalty was reserved for anyone who attempted to usurp a public office. He gave the right of appeal to citizens sentenced to death. He ordered the treasury to be removed from the keeping of the chief magistrates known as consuls, and it was entrusted to civil servants called quaestors, who became the chief financial agents of the republic with offices of their own in the temple of Saturn. He inaugurated the custom whereby a consul on entering the assembly must part the axes and the rods of his ceremonial fasces and lower them before the people. The story is told by Plutarch that when Publius Valerius heard the people murmuring against the splendor of his mansion on the Velia, he simply ordered the house and everything in it to be destroyed and then went about asking for lodgings in a friend's house. A grateful populace gave him the name Poplicola, meaning "the friend of the people." Probably it was he who was the father of the republic that was to endure for nearly five hundred years.

Meanwhile there were wars to be fought, not only against the Etruscans but also against those Latin tribes which saw advantages in destroying Rome and allying themselves with the powerful princes of Etruria. These savage wars at times reduced Rome to the size of a small provincial town cut off from foreign trade, impoverished, with pestilence running through the streets. But it was characteristic of Rome to be most resolute when it was weakest. It fought back. Thirteen years after the expulsion of the Tarquins, Rome won a resounding victory over the Latins at Lake Regillus. Then at last there was peace with the Latins and no longer any real fear of the Etruscans. Rome had shown its mettle.

The text of the treaty of peace with the Latin tribes has survived. It says: "There shall be peace between the Romans and all the communities of Latins as long as heaven and earth endure. They shall not wage war with each other, nor summon enemies into the land, nor grant passage to enemies; and when any community is attacked, they shall render help in concert, and whatever is won in joint warfare shall be equally distributed." The treaty was signed in 493 B.C. In the previous year a popular revolt led to the creation of a new government office which was to have even more enduring consequences, for in that year the first tribune of the people was elected.

By granting new powers to the people, by which he meant the middle classes, Publius Valerius Poplicola had set in motion a process that could be stopped only with the greatest difficulty. Liberty once given inevitably attracts more liberties to itself. The poor—the peasants, the farm workers, the artisans, the small landholders—demanded their own liberties, and when these were refused they marched out of Rome in a body, encamped on the Sacred Mount on the river Anio, three miles from the city, and refused to return until their demands were met. What they wanted above all was freedom from arbitrary punishment and from the abuses of power; they would return only if the Senate—the governing body made up largely of rich landowners, aristocrats, and leaders of the army—agreed to protect their rights by giving full powers to their representatives. A class war had begun.

Because all the ordinary work and life of the city as well as of the farms had come to a halt, the Senate was compelled to accept the demands of the plebs. It was agreed that a magistrate or tribune representing the plebs should enjoy full powers of veto against the decisions of the senators. His person was to be inviolate, and the entire body of the Roman citizenry was to be under his protective care. From time to time the number of tribunes changed: there were never less than two, sometimes there were as many as ten. In the slow and laborious history of the development of the democratic process the tribunes of the people occupy a special place. Even Athens, fount of the idea of popular government, had not gone so far as this.

Statesmanship and oratory were interdependent arts in classical times, and the Romans excelled in both, communicating some of their proficiency to the people they conquered. This life-sized bronze, probably dating from the time of the Punic wars, was found near Lake Trasimene. The inscription reveals it to be the likeness of a local magistrate, possibly an Etruscan. The pose is that of a Roman orator.
MUSEO ARCHAEOLOGICO, FLORENCE

49

With the establishment of the tribunate came a proliferation of Roman law, for although the tribunes were in theory armed only with the power of veto, in fact they sometimes became the lawmakers, and the decisions of the plebeian assembly, expressed through the tribunes, were regarded as binding once the Senate confirmed them. In effect the plebeian assembly which came into existence in 471 B.C. and comprised the greater part of the population, had become a powerful political force determined, if possible, to wrest power from the patrician rulers or at least to hold them in check. There was now a system of government by different representative groups and a growing body of enactments, rules, customs, and covenants which eventually was to produce the magnificent Roman legal structure, with its many safeguards and checks and balances.

The machine, so carefully contrived to put an end to acts of tyranny, was far from perfect. It often creaked badly and sometimes came to a standstill. The inviolate tribunes were sometimes murdered, or they were bribed, or they themselves became tyrannical. In times of crisis dictators emerged and made a mockery of the laws. But the tribunate survived until the last days of the republic, and even when the republic was finally overthrown the emperors took the proud title of *tribunus plebis*. Then, at last, the title lost all meaning.

In the fifth and fourth centuries B.C., however, the wars in central Italy went on like brush fires that could not be put out. Every year there was a new campaign or a drawn-out war against the neighboring towns; the Latin League split up and the various fragments fought against one another. From these wars Rome emerged as an increasingly strong power, driving itself dangerously close to exhaustion and suffering periodically from famine and plagues which the chroniclers record with the air of men recording events as inevitable as sunrise and sunset.

There was nothing yet to suggest that Roman power would soon extend over large areas of Italy. Rome dominated little more than the plains on both sides of the Tiber, and the endless border wars were little more than skirmishes. There had been no prodigious gains of territory, and indeed there was very little to show for the wars. Yet the period between the expulsion of the Tarquins and the great upheaval at the hand of the Gauls which was to reduce the Romans temporarily to impotence—those decades which saw the rise of the plebeians to a position of importance in government—showed that an intellectual expansion was taking place. It was not only that new forms of government were being hammered into shape, new offices were being created, and new

The lid of a fourth-century B.C. bronze container from Praeneste, in Latium, has a handle that represents two warriors carrying a slain comrade. These figures may be either Romans or Latins, but there is no doubt that in their weapons, clothing, and armor they closely resemble the soldiers of Rome who tried unsuccessfully to stem the Gallic invasion in 390 B.C.

aspects of rule were being explored, but the Romans were demonstrating a passionate concern for a just society, a more mature way of living. Those years left an enduring heritage, and in later days when the republic was destroyed by the revival of autocratic government, the Romans would look back on that period with a sense of longing. They recognized that during that embattled century they had laid the foundations of their greatness.

These tough-minded hill people had come far. They had built a workable civilization, absorbed the arts of the Etruscans, shown themselves to be possessed of a ferocious spirit of independence, and could look forward to increasing their influence. Then quite suddenly in a single day they lost the gains of centuries.

Unknown to the Romans, a power much greater than the combined ones of all the Latin states and principalities was massing in the north. The Gauls were on the march. They were herdsmen who had drifted westward from the plains of central Europe, and for a century they had been pouring along the valley of the Danube River into France and Spain. They were tall, large-limbed, and fair-haired; they fought from chariots with long swords and spears. They struck at Etruria, which never completely recovered from their assaults. In 390 B.C. they met the Roman army on the banks of the river Allia, eleven miles north of Rome. The battle was soon over, as the Romans fled in the direction of Veii, recently conquered by Marcus Furius Camillus, the most resourceful of Rome's generals. Three days later the Gauls marched into Rome to find only the temple on the Capitoline defended; they plundered the city at their leisure and left most of it a smoking ruin. There is a legend that they found the senators sitting tranquilly on ivory thrones in their homes near the Forum, and massacred them. For seven months the Gauls are said to have ruled over the city, abandoning it only when they were offered a ransom to withdraw. According to Plutarch, the amount was to be a "thousand weight" of gold; but the Gauls were discovered cheating in the weighing of it, upon which their chieftain Brennus contemptuously threw his own sword and belt upon the scales, crying, "*Vae victis* (Woe to the defeated)!" Whatever the truth of the stories, the Romans never forgot they had been beaten to their knees.

Rome all but perished, only to rise again. Within a hundred years it grew into a power that threatened the entire Mediterranean world. Then the Romans, not the Gauls, carried the message "*Vae victis!*" Coming from them, it had a more ominous import. Although it could still mean death or slavery to a defeated warrior, it could also doom his nation to centuries of Roman rule or even to annihilation.

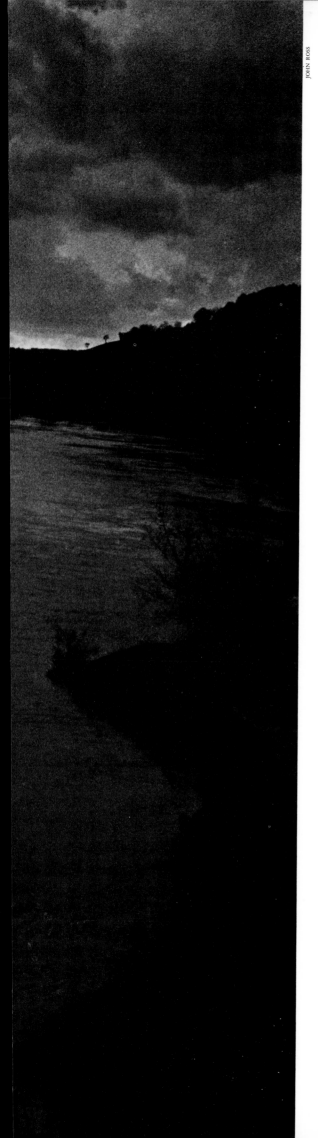

LAND OF
THE ROMANS

Italy was in ancient times, as it is now, a land of vivid contrasts and contradictions, one that could both challenge and reward a hardy people. The long, volcano-studded peninsula, which the Romans were to make their own through centuries of determined effort and almost ceaseless fighting, offered mineral wealth and fertile soil in some areas, windswept wastes and pestiferous marshes in others. But it was a peninsula well-situated to serve as a base for conquest, and it was a land bountiful enough to support a remarkable growth in population—not the least of Rome's advantages in its long march toward empire.

The early Roman world was confined to the rolling fields of northern Latium. A familiar feature of that world was the shallow, muddy Tiber, shown at left meandering sluggishly toward the city of Romulus. The river afforded access to the sea and served as a line of defense; a bridge built across it at Rome funneled through the Roman countryside much of the overland traffic between prosperous Etruria and the civilized Greek cities of the south. The Romans had good reason to colonize the land that bordered the Tiber, but a less ambitious people might never have come to know the rugged, hostile mountains from which the river issued, or the rocky shoreline of Campania, or the parched fields of Calabria. When at last the whole of the Mediterranean world was theirs, the Romans had come to cherish all of Italy as their homeland.

Neither ground haze nor a delicate screen of leafless birch trees can disguise
the massiveness of a peak in the northern Apennines (above). The Apennine
chain extends the length of Italy. It influences the Italian climate, conceals
valuable ores, and in antiquity it bred peoples who were among the fiercest
enemies of Rome. At right, clinging to gentler slopes on the island of Capri,
gnarled olive trees flourish as they did in the ancient days of Tiberius.

The Italian coastline, like the land itself, is at once inviting and forbidding. The Romans were to become very familiar with the headlands of Campania (above), which shelter some of the Mediterranean's finest harbors.

ROLOFF BENY

OVERLEAF: *Latin writers did not lack sources of inspiration in nature. This spring-fed, poplar-shaded pool, sixty miles north of Rome, was described by Pliny the Younger in the second century* A.D.; *it has changed little.*

ENTE NAZIONALE INDUSTRIE TURISTICHE

Until Roman times, the sandstone foothills of the Apennines, such as those at left, served for little but pasturage. As Italy's population grew, furrows began to spread from the valleys to the hillsides. The poor man planted cereals, whereas the landowner who could afford to wait a few years to harvest the first crop often cultivated grapes or olives. Above is a vineyard in Tuscany.

OVERLEAF: *Rome's success in agriculture led a confident Cicero to ask, in the first century* B.C., *"Why, what soil is there so thin and miserable that it cannot be broken up by a plow?" Yet even in his day overcultivation, erosion, and sudden droughts were producing, in some regions, land as stubbornly resistant to life as this arid, sun-baked field of southern Italy.*

III

FAITH AND THE STATE

The first herdsmen and farmers who settled in Rome brought with them the beliefs they had nourished for generations in the countryside. They were men with a brooding love of the earth and its fruits, and they saw no reason to change their beliefs when they became town dwellers. The gods of the woodland and the harvest, of storm and clear skies, of budding leaf and warming flame accompanied them from their hamlets into Rome, and even after the Romans had conquered most of the known world seven or more centuries later, these gods were still being worshiped. Some of the early deities grew old and died and were replaced by others with names borrowed from different tribes encountered during the long wars, but always at the heart of the Roman religion there were the gods and spirits of the hearth and countryside.

When the Romans were still an unlettered, agricultural folk, their first or chief god appears to have been Janus, at various times thought of as the sun god, the sky, the thunderer, and the governor of all beginnings and entrances. He was also associated with the door, or *ianua*, of a house. Doorways were invested with magical or numinous significance; Janus, present in every household, exerted great power over the household's undertakings. In some way he was connected with the goddess Diana, who evolved from a wood spirit with some governance over the cycles of the moon and of women into the goddess of fertility, of the woodland and protectress of huntsmen. Diana was to retain her power over the Roman imagination through the ages; but at some very early period in Roman history all-powerful Janus was superseded by other gods, led by Jupiter. The reasons for this remain obscure, though the explanation has been set forth that the Romans, becoming more mature and literate, felt a need for godheads more advanced than Janus. Yet the Romans never completely forgot his former eminence, and the god was invoked before any other god, even before Jupiter, at the beginning of any important undertaking. The memory of his ancient, warlike powers was preserved in his small temple located in the Forum and dedicated to military prowess; the temple gates being thrown open in times of war and closed in times of peace.

When we first see Jupiter, who was eventually to preside over the entire pantheon, he is the god of the oak forest, the thunder and the rain, and the maintainer of peace who presides over tribal loyalties and the making of oaths. His shrine is a grove of oaks; and his presence is revealed in the trembling of leaves that announce a storm. Originally he was perhaps simply the power of the sky, manifesting itself in various ways: as Jupiter Lapis, his image was a meteorite or a stone; as Jupiter Pluvius, he gave rain to the land; as Jupiter Fulminator, he was the hurler of lightning; as Jupiter Tonans, he was the thunderer.

From those earliest days, only Diana and Vesta survived unchanged. Vesta was the goddess of the hearth-flame, which was kept burning continually. The flame symbolized communal life, the continuity of the family and its welfare; it cooked the meats, kept the wild beasts at bay, and dispelled the horrors of the night. To this ever-burning flame the Romans paid tribute by instituting ritual offerings in each household, while each tribe had its own public hearth-fire, tended only by maidens known as vestal virgins, who offered special prayers in its honor. When Rome became master of a great and powerful empire the vestal virgins, living in the Forum in a round temple evidently shaped to resemble the ancient wattle huts, continued to tend the flame with quiet decorum. Their persons were sacrosanct, and according to Plutarch, if they passed a condemned criminal, the criminal was freed. Some mysterious power was believed to reside in the maidens as long as they remained virgin. The worship of the flame was one of the most ancient and most enduring of all surviving Roman rituals, for the flame continued to burn long after Rome was ruled by a Christian emperor, being extinguished only in A.D. 382 during the reign of Emperor Gratian.

Roman household worship took forms different from the emerging state religion, though both relied on consultation of omens and auspices, and on propitiatory rituals. The state cult, too, was to adopt many festivals from home observances. The high priest of the household was the paterfamilias—father of the family, breadwinner, preceptor, and judge—and he was to be regarded with awe and reverence. He possessed powers of life and death, his word was law, and through him the gods and the spirits influenced the household. He was the guardian of the family; a long-lived patriarch might rule despotically over the lives of his grandsons and great-grandsons. His daughters, however, once they were married, could pass out of the orbit of his command. Originally *pitir* or *pater* seems to have meant "power" or "authority" rather than a man who had begotten children.

As high priest of the family the paterfamilias superintended the household rites. He made offerings to the lares and penates, guardian spirits of the home. The lares were originally the spirits who presided over the land outside the house, and the penates protected the food in the store cupboards and the grain in the bins. They were familiar, friendly spirits, grateful for small offerings. They were depicted on household altars, and offerings were placed before them—myrtle wreaths, honeycakes, cups of wine. They

Rome's growing state religion eventually led to the building, throughout the empire, of imposing temples or elegant ones like that above in Nîmes, France. Colleges of priests served in the gods' buildings, performing rituals designed more to obtain practical benefits for Rome than to assert spiritual values.

fostered gaiety and good living, and were especially remembered when the family sat at table. For the Romans there was always something holy about sitting together at a meal, under the presiding eyes of the lares and penates. These spirits, too, survived the pagan empire, and the Christian emperor Theodosius was compelled to issue an edict against those who offered burnt sacrifices to the lares and perfumes to the penates. Even today some traces of the worship of the household gods are to be found in villages in Italy.

Beyond the realm of the paterfamilias lay the world of nature, where he had little or no authority. In this world the gods of harvest, rain, and lightning wielded their powers, and the entire community would take part in prayer and offerings. They were the gods of the fields and the woods, and the nymphs who hovered over springs and lakes. There were hundreds of these minor gods, some of them scarcely more than sprites. There was sweet-tempered Faunus, a god of the woodlands; Pomona, the goddess of orchards, who was especially fond of apple trees; Silvanus, who presided over timber lots and saw that the boundary stones were kept in place; Pales, who guarded shepherds from danger. Not all the little gods were kindly: Robigus was a malevolent deity who would place a blight on the crops unless he was properly propitiated with offerings of wine and the sacrifice of dogs. The lemures and larvae were even more intractable deities; they were ghosts of the dead, mysterious specters who hovered invisibly in the air, to be propitiated by the head of the household, who would fill his mouth with beans and then spit them out saying, "I throw away these beans, and with them I redeem myself and mine."

We do not have any complete account of the ancient rituals practiced by the Romans. We hear of magic spells and incantations that were derived from the distant past and were still being used in republican times. The Romans, aware that many of the gods were nameless, sometimes addressed their prayers to an unknown deity, *sive deo sive deae* ("whether god or goddess"). Beyond the known gods was an infinite number of unknown ones, who also had to be placated and given offerings. Sometimes the ritual took the form of a re-enactment of an ancient legend, illustrated by the fact that the claimant for the priesthood of the goddess Diana at Nemi obtained his office only by killing his predecessor; often it took the form of a sacred dance performed to the accompaniment of music. An early surviving fragment of a hymn that was addressed to Mars in the days when he was still a god of fecundity and husbandry reads:

Official worship evolved from more simple rites in the home; the paterfamilias made sacrifices and poured out libations on little household altars like the one at right, located in a courtyard in Rome. The altar was dedicated to gods who watched over the family and the home. Below, a bronze sculpture represents one of the family gods, a lar, whose specific care was the house. The college of vestal virgins (shown in the relief below right) was perhaps the first of many large groups of state-supported priests who supervised public worship over the centuries.

Enos Lases iuvate.
Neve lue rue Marmar sins incurrere in pleores.
Satur fu, fere Mars: limen sali, sta berber.
Semunis alternei advocapit conctos.
Enos Marmor iuvato.
Triumpe, triumpe, triumpe, triumpe, triumpe!

Come, help us, O lares.
Let neither blight nor ruin hasten upon the people.
Be satiated, fierce Mars: leap the threshold, stay the scourge.
Summon in turn the gods of the harvest.
Come, help us, O Mars.
Triumph, triumph, triumph, triumph, triumph!

In this way, with a fierce flourish of excitement and with the clang of resounding drums, the Roman peasants leaped to imitate the growing grain and called to the earth to feed them. There was a directness in their approach to the gods in the primitive times, the village community gathering together to give commands to the gods during high holidays. In later times an intricate priesthood would come between the public worshipers and the gods; but in the villages the ancient hymns with their direct summons to the gods survived, and they were still being sung long after the advent of Christianity.

Then there were the great gods, who held the destiny of the country in their hands; they were massive and spectacular, accumulating power by virtue of some extraordinary process of accretion, restlessly seeking to spread their dominion wider. These were the gods of the state cult, remote from the lives of the peasants. Their origins were often lowly: Mars, the god of the ripening grain, became god of war; and Jupiter, who once dwelt in the oak trees, presided over the heavens and the earth. Many of the great gods were simply borrowed and reshaped to serve Roman needs. In pre-Roman times Jupiter appears to have been worshiped particularly in Alba Longa as a sky god of magical powers. When his cult was brought to Rome it lost its strength and became relatively stable only when he took on some of the characteristics of Tinia, the sky god of the Etruscans, and of Zeus, worshiped by the Greek settlers in southern Italy with whom the Romans came into early contact. Under the Etruscan kings he was conceived of as the protector of the city and the people, the supreme legislator of their destinies, at the same time retaining his empire over the heavens and the works of nature. As the divine king with all the radiance of majesty he became Jupiter Optimus Maximus—the best and greatest of all gods —honored by a temple on the steep rock of the Capitoline overlooking the Forum. The Etruscan sculptor Vulca of Veii may

As was true of other ancient religions, in Roman belief superstition was intertwined with more purely religious thought. The people employed any number of charms, incantations, and magical rites and words to ward off evil spirits, which they felt lurked everywhere around them. In a mosaic from a Roman colony, eleven different talismans, including a raven, a scorpion, and a serpent, attack an evil eye.

PALAZZO DEI CONSERVATORI, ROME; ALINARI

have been the first to fashion his image; in 385 B.C. a terra-cotta statue of the god was placed in the temple. Jupiter came to Rome in the company of Uni and Menerva. Uni became Juno and Menerva became Minerva, retaining the name even when she was linked with the Greek goddess Athena.

Jupiter was derived from several gods. Not only Tinia and Zeus went into his making, but he took over many of the powers of the fallen Janus. He became the guardian of the Roman state, the loftiest representative of Roman power; but he was divided into many shapes and functions, and bore many titles. He was a complex, restless figure, though outwardly he appeared to have an unnerving calm and to possess a simple, single-minded purpose. He presided over the seasons, but so did Anna Perenna. He decided battles, but so did Mars and Quirinus. He helped the grapes to ripen, but so did Bacchus and Liber. He was worshiped at the beginning of the harvest, but so was Janus. He was the light bringer, but so was Apollo. Though called the best and the greatest, he was never, like Zeus, the supreme arbiter of the universe and the governor of the world. Zeus reigned from the heights of Mount Olympus, Jupiter from a low and easily accessible hill. Zeus belonged to the shining space of the air, while Jupiter, as represented by the Romans, belonged as much to the earth as to the sky. Zeus was free, Jupiter was rigid. When we compare the two gods, we find we are comparing the imagination of the Greeks to the imagination of the Romans; they had almost nothing in common.

Under the empire Jupiter was represented in the form of Olympian Zeus, heavily bearded and curly-haired, with a look of wisdom and calm maturity. All that was known of his legendary life was borrowed from the Greeks. It was difficult to imagine him smiling (though he does so on two occasions in the *Aeneid*) or plunged into deep gloom. Duty, dignity, inflexibility, oath, power —these are the words that seemed to come from his impersonal lips. Though earthbound, he was remote; and though physically present, he was curiously inaccessible. He was concerned above all with law and morality; he watched over justice and truth. Though he blessed the vineyards, brought down the rain when it was required, permitted the sacrifice of white cattle in his honor, and sometimes indulged in prophecies, revealing the future and showing his approval or disapproval of contemplated undertakings by the Roman state, these were all minor activities which he could perform using only a small part of his available power. Where he excelled in the eyes of the Romans was in the divine personification of authority. He represented the archetypal image of the paterfamilias, ruling gravely over his enormous family of Romans.

It is necessary to understand the stern, austere Jupiter, because in a sense he is the *only* god of the Romans. As Jupiter Optimus Maximus, he was the god from whom most was expected, the one whose favor was most desired and whose blessings were most efficacious. The other great gods—Saturn, Ceres, Venus, Neptune, Mercury, and the rest—served as decorations for his throne, deriving their powers from him. Jupiter was almost an abstraction, but one with hard outlines. In his temple on the Capitoline was kept a flint stone or meteorite, and when men swore oaths in his name, they sometimes spoke of him as Jupiter Lapis—Jupiter the Stone. Stonelike he loomed over Rome.

For those who wielded power over the Romans and their rapidly expanding empire, the state cult of Jupiter served a useful function. The ceremonies and rituals in his temple were unexampled in magnificence, and his temple was the largest and most imposing of all. His high priest, the *flamen Dialis*, was traditionally granted extraordinary powers and hedged with equally extraordinary taboos. He was never allowed to perform any physical labor or to see others at work; a herald preceded him to warn the people to stop working in his presence. He must wear nothing binding, not even a ring, nor touch anything that was binding, like the tendrils of a vine hanging from a trellis. He must never mount a horse or see a dead man or come in sight of a funeral. He must not touch iron. Insofar as it was possible, he must live in perfect freedom and detachment as did the god he served. He wore the purple-edged toga of the magistrate and sat on a curule chair. The *flamen Dialis* was the earthly representative of Jupiter; and to maintain the cult he was assisted by a flock of priests whose powers and taboos were equally strange, derived from customs so old that no one could remember their origins. In the name of Jupiter the Romans went to war, and when the conquering general returned to receive a triumph, the procession followed the Sacred Way and then mounted the Capitoline hill to reach the temple of Jupiter. There the general made a sacrifice to the god and laid his laurel wreath on the god's lap.

The temple on the Capitoline, then, was the focus of the state religion, the place from which divine power was believed to radiate. There the pontiffs, who supervised all sacred observances under the *pontifex maximus*, and the augurs, who examined the entrails of sacrificial victims or the play of lightning to foretell the will of the gods, had their priestly colleges and pronounced their verdicts. Originally there were three pontiffs and three augurs, all elected from the patrician families, but their num-

To assure divine approval of state undertakings the entire Roman calendar was set up on a religious basis. Not only did it indicate the days on which business could be conducted, but there were almost fifty official festival days honoring the gods. The eight mosaics are part of a pictorial agricultural calendar. In the left column, from top to bottom, are a sacrifice to Ceres, a sowing scene, fruit being picked, and a bull representing spring; in the right column, ground is broken, a man places loaves in an oven, men press grapes, and two men pour a libation.

LOUVRE; GIRAUDON

69

bers were continually changing: there were sixteen pontiffs and sixteen augurs in the time of Julius Caesar. The first college was entrusted with guardianship of the divine law, or *ius divinum*, and the calendar; the second with the power to read omens, or *auspicia*; the result was an extraordinary exercise of priestly power within the state. While Greeks turned to the Delphic oracle on the distant heights, Romans turned to well-connected interpreters within the walls. Here, too, the texts of the sacred books were kept, to be consulted at times of grave emergency, and there they remained until the time of Augustus, who, in his special reverence for Apollo, removed the books to a vault in the new temple to the god he had had erected on the Palatine.

Apollo was only one of many Greek gods who successfully invaded the Roman pantheon. Mercury was the Greek god Hermes, Venus was Aphrodite, Neptune was Poseidon, Ceres was Demeter. They came to Rome wearing the Greek dress and were given high positions among the gods. But sometimes the mythologies of Roman gods were incorporated with those of the Greek gods; the result was that some gods were encrusted with layer upon layer of mythology. On the other hand Ceres, an ancient Roman goddess of agriculture, took on all the legends connected with Demeter and shed her Roman past almost completely. In Rome the service of the goddess was performed in Greek by women of Greek extraction in a temple built on the Greek model. Such tributes to Greek origins were rare.

Venus, originally perhaps a goddess of the flowers, became a love goddess when Aphrodite was grafted onto her. From a love goddess she was changed into the queen of fecundity, rivaling Ceres, but this was only the beginning of her transformations. She became the generative force of the universe and the goddess who presided over the destinies of Rome. The philosopher-poet Lucretius, living in the first half of the first century B.C., described her as the fountain of all blessings and the divine mistress of Rome, greater than Jupiter because she governed all created things:

> *O guardian Mother of Rome, joy of gods and mortals,*
> *Venus, who beneath the march of the swimming stars*
> *Dost make the many-voyaged ocean teem with fish*
> *And the earth with fruit, through thee alone*
> *All living things owe their conception,*
> *And through thee alone they rise toward the Sun.*

Even as Lucretius was writing, the goddess was in the process of transformation. Under Julius Caesar, who claimed descent from her, she was to become the goddess who guided the destinies of his imperial family. When he became the unquestioned ruler of

The Romans borrowed many of their gods and most of their mythology from the Greeks, either indirectly through the Etruscans or by direct contact. One such acquisition was Sol, depicted above moving across the sky in his chariot; the Roman god of the sun differed from the Greek god Helios only in name.

Rome, he built in the Forum a shrine in her honor, which was also a temple to his own glory.

Venus continued to rule in Rome, growing in power and influence long after Julius Caesar was dead. She became almost indistinguishable from the civic goddess Roma, and under the emperor Hadrian, a strange, new, double temple was built where Venus and Roma sat back to back. It was as though Hadrian had come to the conclusion that the equation Venus equals Rome could be solved satisfactorily only by placing them under a single roof. In the imperial age Venus became the symbol of the beauty of conquest, the serene embodiment of the Roman world empire. That the humble goddess of flowers should have grown in power and acquired so many virtues only demonstrates the changing nature of Roman mythology, which became amazingly intricate and almost unmanageable.

Since the beginning of their history the Romans had been accustomed to borrowing the gods of other tribes and nations. The result was that they accumulated more gods than they needed and more festivals and games than any single person could attend. Nearly every day there was a local feast honoring some god, with prayers and sacrifices and gifts to be given to the priests. The Roman religious calendar, perhaps established in the days of Numa Pompilius, was overflowing with names of gods and holy days. Some were so ancient that no one any longer remembered their precise significance or understood the meaning of the prayers spoken in an archaic language by priests who themselves had forgotten what the prayers meant.

What purpose was served by the multiplicity of gods? The Romans would have answered that they could see no harm in numbers. No god must be left without the proper sacrifices and prayers for fear that he might take umbrage, punish those who had rejected him, and perhaps even visit punishment on rival gods who were receiving too much worship. Above all, it was necessary to maintain peaceful relations with the gods by scrupulously observing the proper amenities and by addressing them in the way that was most pleasing to them. When the Romans spoke of *pax deorum* ("the peace of the gods") they were speaking of a state of affairs that resembled peaceful relations between neighboring states. To preserve the peace and to draw favor from the gods was the duty of every Roman. It was one of his many obligations, like fighting for his country, paying taxes, and raising a family, and perhaps it was neither more nor less important than any of these.

The sense of duty, or *pietas*, was inculcated in the Roman from his youngest years. The stern, grave expression that appears on

The relief above depicts the objects used in religious sacrifice. Clockwise from top left are a libation dish, a knife, a sacrificer killing a bull, a ram and cock—common sacrificial animals—and a sacred vessel next to an altar. In the relief below, the donor pours a libation on the altar as the animal is killed, and a piper plays so that no impure sound will render the gift unacceptable. To the Romans a sacrifice was more than an expression of piety; they were offering sustenance to a god who was then obligated to help them.

71

Roman portraits reflects their sense of *gravitas*—the conscious acceptance of burdens or the disposition to take things seriously. They saw themselves as a people dedicated to the gods, and the religious ceremonies were far more formal and ritualistic than those of the Greeks, who were often lighthearted in their devotions. The Greeks told amusing stories about their gods and were on familiar terms with them; they laughed and sorrowed with them, and they liked to imagine the gods' lives as being very similar to their own. They approached their gods openly, without knocking on the doors, and they would never have thought to veil themselves in the presence of the deities as the Romans did, drawing their togas over their heads.

The word *religion* comes from *religare*, "to bind." Basically Roman religion was a contract between men and divinities, who offered service in exchange for gifts given. It provided favors and accommodation, but little in the way of what we would call a moral code. It filled the people's lives more with holidays than with meaning, and in time it was doubted or rejected by intelligent men. The very oaths uttered to the gods were composed in legalistic language. *Do ut des* ("I give so that you may give") was one of the principles of worship, though it was not the only one. Especially in the countryside, worship provided an excuse for communal gaiety, and the contractual obligations to the gods were forgotten in merrymaking, in which the gods themselves were assumed to take part. The Romans enjoyed the great processions and games held in the honor of the gods, and some were also dedicated to the little, familiar gods of the household, the fields, and the orchards.

The gods provided so many holidays that these seriously interfered with the normal conduct of affairs. The Roman year opened in March with the ceremonial rededication of the vestal flame and the lively clanging of the sacred shields removed from the temple of Mars. The twelve Salii, or dancers and leapers who clanged the shields, wore armor and conical caps, which may have represented the thrusting of seeds. For many days the Salii danced in procession through the streets, halting at all the temples and shrines, feasting every night, then continuing their wild processional dance the next morning to the accompaniment of piercing trumpet blasts. March was a noisy month, for there was also the festival of the Liberalia in honor of the ancient god Liber, who demanded unrestrained merriment. April was crowded with festivals. There were festivals for Tellus, mother of the earth; for Ceres, bringer of fruitfulness; and for Jupiter, in whose honor the wine of the previous year had been broached. At the end of the month came

The details of two sculptured reliefs depict different kinds of religious ceremonies. Processions, whether they were for returning heroes or for the funeral of an important personage, were a favorite Roman entertainment. At top is a sacrificial procession led (background) by lictors carrying fasces; they are followed by trumpeters, a priest, and the beasts on their way to be slaughtered for the gods. The bottom relief depicts a moment in a funeral when the mourners all cry out, a ritual meant to call back the soul.

the Floralia in honor of the goddess Flora, when men decked themselves and their animals in flowers, and women set aside the staid costumes they had worn during the winter and put on colorful dresses. With May came solemn ceremonies, as though to atone for the gaiety and license of April. Despite the Roman spring, it was a time of danger, doubt, and foreboding, of offerings to the dead and fearful pleas to the gods to permit the crops to grow. Then in June came the great celebrations connected with the ripening of the harvest.

So it was throughout the year, the rhythm of the festivals following the rhythm of the seasons, and sometimes there were strange alterations of mood as the people withdrew into themselves and gave in to their fears, only to burst out joyfully again a few weeks later. December and January were months of wild festivity, February was a month of gloom.

The Romans found a deep satisfaction in these festivals. Worship was entertainment as well as duty, release from toil as well as the fulfillment of an obligation. Significantly there were no important underworld divinities, and the Romans themselves felt no great dread of death. Although their religion was not a very exalted one, it permitted them to live fully and colorfully, without a gnawing sense of inadequacy and with the certainty that the gods, however malevolent and unruly on occasion, would fight for them to the end. It was a religion that had grown almost casually over the centuries, with no obvious plan, no body of doctrine, no contours. We speak sometimes of the Roman religion as though it possessed a firm basis, but in fact it was constantly changing, the gods melting away and being replaced by others. Although such continual flux was at times disconcerting—nothing comparable to this had existed among the ancient Greeks—it must be interpreted as a sign of health.

Ultimately the religion failed to satisfy all the needs of the Romans. The divine machinery often creaked, and if the restless borrowing of gods was sometimes a sign of imagination and strength, it was also a sign of weakness. Too many questions were left unanswered. The religion said little about death and afterlife; it was sternly masculine and therefore had comparatively little to say to women; it derived its sanctions from ancient legends and therefore it had little to say about the present. By the end of the republic, educated men regarded state religion as a survival from an archaic past. They preserved an antiquarian interest in the gods, discussing them endlessly, but they were beginning to wonder whether their worship served any useful purpose. Although Cicero proclaimed his belief in the supreme gods and professed to regard

The painting from Herculaneum depicts priests of the Egyptian goddess Isis, an underworld goddess of procreation and birth, performing rites in her honor. Even before the first century A.D. many Romans had become disenchanted with the spiritually unrewarding state religion and turned to personal foreign deities.

divination as the proper vehicle by which the gods communicated with men, it is clear that he shared the skepticism of the Stoics and Epicureans, who regarded the gods as uncertain and scarcely probable denizens of an uncertain and scarcely probable heaven. Pythagoras of Samos had spoken of the one god who ruled the universe without the aid of any divine servants. Varro, the great encyclopedist of the late republic, wrote of a time when all the minor gods would be swept away, leaving Jupiter in sole command. He would abolish the worship of the images, pointing out that in the early days the Romans had neither altars nor temples nor statues, and the gods were numinous presences. What was the purpose in dressing them in the shapes of men? He would permit the country festivals to continue because the countryfolk delighted in them, but he would put an end to the offering of sacrifices. Did Jupiter really derive pleasure from the sight of slaughtered bulls and sheep at his altar? But Varro admitted that Roman religion, with all its faults and inconsistencies, had served a great purpose. It had trained men to be pious and obedient to the demands made by the state.

Cicero, too, felt that the state cult was necessary for the survival of the empire. He had only a distant and troubled affection for the gods and was not quite sure whether they existed, but he was certain that the people needed them. "We must persuade our citizens that the gods are the lords and rulers of all things and what is done, is done by their will and authority; and they are great benefactors of men, and know who everyone is, and what he does, and what sins he commits, and what he intends to do, and with what piety he fulfills his religious duties." But this was a counsel of despair, for he was simply restoring the gods to their high places because they were useful to government; he was offering no justification for their existence. Lucretius, however, went further. Though he opened his great poem *De rerum natura* (*On the Nature of Things*) with an invocation to Venus as the supreme goddess of all blessings, his purpose was to remove from men the fear of the gods and to show them how little justification there was for the existence of the deities, even for the ones who were officially encouraged by the state. If Lucretius and Cicero could come to directly contrary opinions regarding the gods, clearly the status of the gods was in jeopardy.

In the first century B.C. strange, exotic cults were emerging in Rome itself to satisfy a people thirsting not only for novelty but more importantly for spiritual fulfillment. Isis, Mithra, and a host of minor deities from Egypt and Asia Minor were being worshiped in Rome by sects that had abandoned the formal state religion for far more colorful religions that grew up on the eastern shores of the Mediterranean. These religions spoke of the promise of immortality, provided complex and exciting rituals, and were directed at the most intimate hopes and fears of the worshipers; they celebrated the individual, not the state. The white-robed Egyptian priests waving their softly tinkling sistrums were poles removed from the harsh-voiced priests of Mithra, who bathed their converts in the blood of freshly killed bulls; but both promised a continuing life after death and painted its glories. Mithraism, which derived from Persia, became the favored cult of the Roman army, and Mithraic temples have been found in all the regions of the Roman empire. (Recently, the remains of a Mithraic temple were discovered in the heart of London.) Neither Isis nor Mithra succeeded in entering the Roman pantheon. Unlike the Greek gods they could not be assimilated into the state cult, and therefore they were kept a little apart in a kind of annex reserved for strange gods whose powers were still unexplored and whose presence was disturbing. Efforts were made to ban them; laws were passed against them; Varro prayed for the day when foreign cults would perish from the earth; but they remained. The more the devotees were punished, the more they flourished.

Isis and Mithra opened the way for Christianity, with its demand for a revolutionary reversal of values. Instead of *gravitas* there was to be a quiet joy; instead of brute strength there were to be meekness and gentleness; instead of a pious veneration of the state there was to be indifference to the state. Ten years after the Crucifixion there were Christians in Rome, rejoicing in something so foreign to Roman beliefs—the imminent Second Coming of Jesus of Nazareth and the end of the world—that it is understandable that the Romans found them incomprehensible. Like Mithra and Isis, Jesus was excluded from the Roman pantheon, and although a pagan emperor might worship a statue of Jesus in private, Christianity remained obstinately remote from the state cult. Christ and Jupiter belonged to different worlds, and there could be no peace between them.

The triumph of Christianity in Rome was to have prodigious consequences—not the least of these was that Christianity itself was colored by Roman religious practices. The robes of Christian priests, the shape of Christian churches, the order of services, the offerings at the altars, the title of the supreme pontiff, and the very language of Christian ceremonial were derived from the Romans. For a thousand years a hard, stubborn, earthy people had built a pragmatic edifice of belief, and though it was to be superseded by a far loftier one, many of its foundation stones survived.

In a crypt below a Christian basilica in Rome, an altar of the Persian god Mithra still stands. Although the Mithraic cult was brought to Rome by pirates and soldiers, it had a sophisticated moral code. Followers were adjured to be pure and love the truth; if they did their souls would live forever in heaven.
LEONARD VON MATT

DEITIES
HIGH AND LOW

In very early times when Rome was less a city than a collection of villages, its religion was a rather undefined belief in a vast number of spirits who watched over house and fields. Later, religious ceremonies that had been performed in the home came to be enacted for whole clans or tribes, and during the sixth century B.C. the government began organizing public rites for the most-worshiped gods.

Eventually a great hierarchy of state priests developed whose function was to perform public rituals, interpret omens, offer sacrifices, and generally bargain with the gods. In fact the practicality in the Romans' character was reflected in their relations with the gods, to whom they offered rewards in return for services given.

The state religion was not a very elevated one: it had no doctrine and little mythology that had not been borrowed; it offered neither a moral code nor promise of an afterlife. But as long as the state prospered, common men accepted official religion and usually allowed themselves to be controlled by its pronouncements and promises of circuses and holidays. Although they respected the austere, cold, government gods, the masses turned to new cults and to old, familiar, household gods for spiritual warmth and personal help. (Some of the most important state gods appear at left. Depicted from left to right are Hercules, Minerva, Bacchus, Jupiter, Ceres, Juno, Mercury.)

ROME'S FAVORITE COUPLE

Venus and Mars, like almost all of the earliest state gods, were elevated to national importance from a lowly place in the fields. As Rome became more and more urbanized, these gods had to accept new responsibilities or be washed into obscurity by the flood of new deities from other countries. Thus, as the Roman lust for conquest grew, Mars, who appears to have been originally a god of vegetation and fertility, became increasingly important as a god of war. Eventually he took on most of the myths and symbols of the Greek Ares—but while Ares was detested as a posturing, foolish presence by Greeks, Mars was one of the most popular gods in Italy. Venus, often linked with Mars, was suddenly transformed from an obscure and modest garden goddess into a thorough-going seductress when she acquired the attributes of the Greek deity Aphrodite.

The number of representations of Venus found in Pompeii indicates that she was a favorite goddess in that licentious city. The wall painting of the marriage of Venus and Mars from Pompeii shows her at far left being fondled by her husband-to-be as the wedding party, including a doleful Cupid (in the center), looks on.

79

BORROWED PRESENCES

The early Roman gods were not rational gods, although they had certain powers that controlled qualities like fertility in people or animals or earth. They sometimes had names, but they rarely had myths attached to them and were almost never anthropomorphic. Three of the most important gods of the state cult—Jupiter, Juno, and Minerva—had begun as vague and formless Italian deities. Jupiter had been a sky god somehow responsible for light and weather; Juno watched over women, and Minerva, handicrafts. Then Greek and Etruscan gods lent them personal characteristics and the trio, raised to the eminence of state cult objects, were given a temple together, and each had individual rites and holidays. Even though an immense number of complicated functions accrued to Jupiter, he never became quite convincing as father of the gods; so too with many other Roman deities who did not always wear comfortably their borrowed mantles of myth and personality.

These illustrations show Jupiter and Minerva in their most humanistic aspect. At left is a detail of a Roman bust of Jupiter carved in the Greek style. The sculpture of helmeted Minerva in her role as goddess of victory (at right) was once the capital of a column.

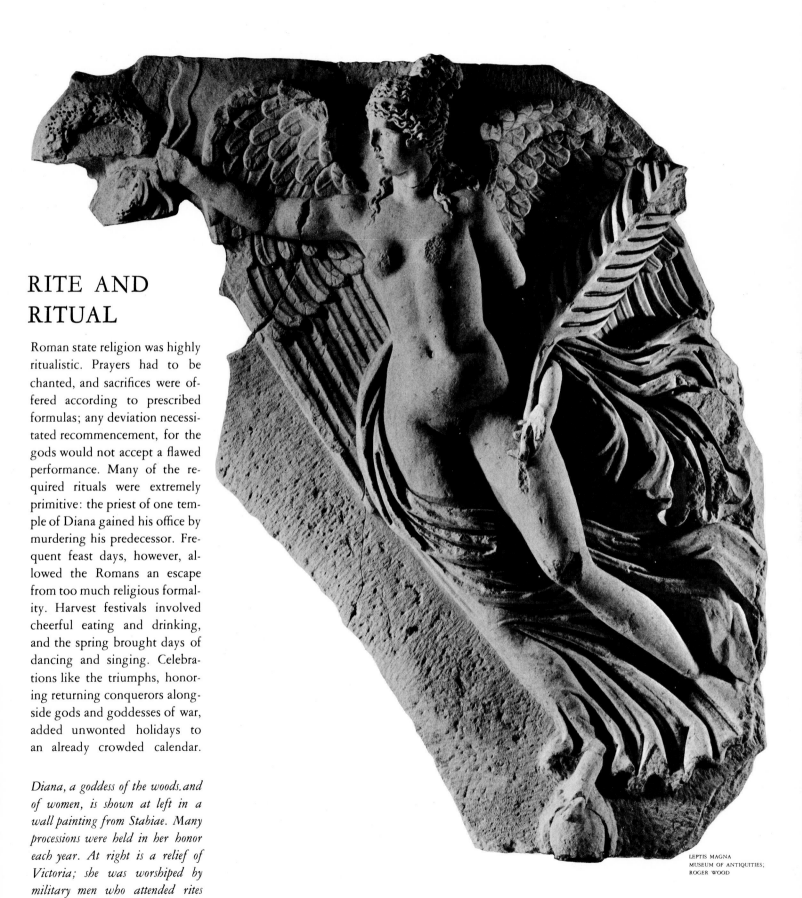

RITE AND RITUAL

Roman state religion was highly ritualistic. Prayers had to be chanted, and sacrifices were offered according to prescribed formulas; any deviation necessitated recommencement, for the gods would not accept a flawed performance. Many of the required rituals were extremely primitive: the priest of one temple of Diana gained his office by murdering his predecessor. Frequent feast days, however, allowed the Romans an escape from too much religious formality. Harvest festivals involved cheerful eating and drinking, and the spring brought days of dancing and singing. Celebrations like the triumphs, honoring returning conquerors alongside gods and goddesses of war, added unwonted holidays to an already crowded calendar.

Diana, a goddess of the woods and of women, is shown at left in a wall painting from Stabiae. Many processions were held in her honor each year. At right is a relief of Victoria; she was worshiped by military men who attended rites in her temple atop the Palatine.

CEREMONIAL
RELEASE

By about 180 B.C. government misuses of religion were so flagrant that even the masses had become skeptical about the state gods. (For example, state priests reversed a public election by announcing that the gods did not favor the outcome.) Their disillusionment led many to accept the Bacchanalian religions that veterans of eastern campaigns were bringing back with them. Participants gained deep satisfaction from the drunken and orgiastic rites; the individual was able for an ecstatic moment to blend the self with the totality of being. The state outlawed the sects as seditious; however, finally realizing that the people would not give up the new religions, it imposed severe limitations on the cults and reinstated them.

The Romans adopted Bacchic cults from the east and spread them to Europe and Africa. At left, a satyr shoulders a wineskin that will soon be empty. The Tunisian mosaic above depicts the drunken god Silenus riding an ass. The Roman-crafted silver dish opposite was found in England. The outer rim depicts a Bacchanalia; Bacchus, god of wine, surrounded by his followers, the frenzied maenads and satyrs, stands with his foot on a lion.

OVERLEAF: *Another Tunisian mosaic depicts Neptune, originally a god of fresh water, driving a sea chariot.*

IV

THE THRUST OF POWER

Moribus antiquis res stat Romana virisque.
"It is through the ways of old and through the heroes of old that Rome stands fast."
                                                    Ennius

In the year 390 B.C. the Romans were at the lowest ebb of their fortunes, their city sacked and looted by the Gauls, their power reaching no farther than to a few neighboring villages. But before the close of the century Rome, risen from the ashes, was beginning to be a major Mediterranean power. By the end of the third century B.C., it had broken the power of Carthage and was well on the way to becoming the mistress of all the lands bordering the sea. In this phenomenal revival and masterly assertion of strength, all its resources of character and energy were made manifest.

When the Romans returned to their city after the withdrawal of the Gauls, they found no gods to console them for their defeats —all the religious statues and sacred objects had either been buried by the priests or removed to Caere for safekeeping—and only a few houses were left standing. Here and there they came upon a palatial residence formerly occupied by a Gallic chieftain or some storerooms that the Gauls had not troubled to fire, but among the deserts of rubble they had difficulty in making out the shapes of the streets or even the sites of the temples. February had come; the cold winds blew over the Tiber; there was no shelter among the ruins. So little of Rome had survived that many Romans thought it would be best simply to uproot themselves and abandon the city; they would march to the former Etruscan citadel of Veii and settle there, leaving Rome to its ghosts.

This is as Plutarch and Livy tell the story. Modern scholars have come to doubt whether the destruction was as general as ancient chroniclers claim, writing as they did with dramatic and heroic intent. The episode of the proposed migration to Veii may be fictional. But the figure who now moves to center stage—the veteran general Marcus Furius Camillus—appears to be historical, though his exploits may have been greatly embellished by writers anxious to enlarge the saga. They said he had been in exile at the time of the battle against the Gauls on the river Allia; thus, he was one of the few surviving generals who bore no responsibility for the defeat. He was a stern taskmaster, a brilliant organizer, a fearless general, who won so many battles that legend credits him with driving the Gauls from Rome. But the Gauls were not driven from the city; they abandoned it in their own good time after removing everything of value and making it uninhabitable; and Camillus was confronted with the task of building a new city on the rubble.

He went about this with extraordinary intelligence and cunning. First, he ordered a ritual purification of the city. He sent the priests probing among the ashes and the broken walls in search of foundation stones and sacred relics, and drew a map indicating the sites of temples. He needed their protection, but he also needed the protection of Romulus, and so it came about that the priests in charge of recovering the sacred sites found the lituus, or augural staff, of Romulus hidden deep below the ashes in the burnt-out temple of Mars. A lituus was an object of special potency because it was used by diviners to quarter the heavens; and Romulus, according to a long-established tradition, had made use of the staff on the day of the foundation of Rome. When Camillus heard that people were discussing abandoning the city, he argued with them. There was a long silence after he had finished speaking; in the silence was heard the loud voice of a centurion who accompanied a standard-bearer: "Halt! Fix the standard! Here is the place to stay!" Stay they did; and almost singlehandedly Camillus assumed the responsibility for rebuilding the city. An awed and grateful people was to call him the second founder of the city.

Camillus belongs to a type that recurs frequently in Roman legend and history. He appears at a time when Rome is given over to anarchy and the edifice is crumbling; he restores order by his commanding presence and the energy of his personality; in alliance with the aristocracy and the military leaders, he presents himself as the savior of his country; and having stamped Rome with his own image, he spends his last days in a melancholy quarrel with the people. The theme of the dictator as savior was to be repeated not only under the republic but during the empire and through the Middle Ages and the Renaissance into our own day.

Whatever his precise nature, Camillus is the first Roman general with a credible history and a recognizable program of action who can be seen in three dimensions. As he grew older, he grew increasingly stern and authoritarian. Conservative to the core, he was impatient with the popular demand for a greater voice in government and a better share of economic reward. In bringing forth the institution of the people's tribunes in the fifth century B.C., the republic had seen a marked advance in plebeian power; the tribunes held the right to veto any enactment by the aristocratic Senate that ran against the interests of the organized plebs or any individual member of it. But this much power only whetted the appetite for more. Since the Gallic invasion the economic situation of the plebs—urban artisans, traders, free peasants, and immigrants—had deteriorated seriously. Their chief grievances concerned the gathering of land into great estates and the harsh laws against those who failed to pay their debts. Roman seizures and colonization had indeed brought in considerable tracts of public land, which were widely assigned to private holders, thereby easing the land hunger of a fast-growing populace. While large holdings generally were profitable, small ones were uneconomical. More-

Begun about 312 B.C., the Appian Way was the first strand in what was to become a great web of paved highways extending from Rome to the outermost boundaries of the Mediterranean world. Such a road network had no precedent in ancient times. Without it, Rome could not long have administered the tremendous empire carved out by its armies.

over, the small holder in need of cash could not raise a mortgage on his property, he had to do so on his own person, which made him a bondsman of his creditor. Failure to work off his debt, often made at usurious rates, could lead to his imprisonment, sometimes for life, or sale into slavery.

In about 367 B.C. the plebs, struggling under the poverty of postinvasion years, made three demands that were to usher in a crisis of classes in Rome. They called for drastic reform of the debt laws and for remission of interest; for restrictions on the amount of land held by any one owner (many plebeians had sold their holdings to wealthy creditors in lieu of debt service); and thirdly, for re-establishment of the consulship (suspended under Camillus' dictatorship), with the provision that one of the two consuls be chosen from the plebs.

When Camillus heard that these revolutionary demands were being seriously presented, he was outraged. He immediately ordered that the Forum, which had become the place of public debate and the seat of the government, be cleared by the lictors, and he characteristically threatened to administer the oath of service to all men of military age and to lead them out of the city. His aim was to stifle all opposition; the aim of the tribunes was to silence him. They had power to impose fines and decided on the sum of fifty thousand drachmas if he continued to obstruct the popular will. Camillus was in his seventies. He had no stomach for further quarrels with the Romans and soon retired, pleading ill-health—though he was recalled to repel another incursion of the Gauls. He had served his country well and had no desire to see himself banished from Rome nor to have his legend destroyed, his wealth confiscated, his power shattered. Meanwhile, under the tribunes Sextius and Licinius, a new law was promulgated requiring that one of the consuls be chosen from the plebs. It was a notable victory for the majority. Camillus had vowed to build a temple to Concord if ever there was an end to the struggle between the orders, and in about 367 B.C. the temple was built, or at least begun, at the northwestern corner of the Forum, as a perpetual reminder of the new relationship existing between the aristocracy and the people. We are told that the temple was originally constructed of wood and ornamented with terra-cotta plaques in the Etruscan manner, so deeply was Etruscan influence felt long after the expulsion of the kings.

The temple to Concord, though often rebuilt, survived through the centuries. Camillus, we are told, presided over its dedication. It was his last official act; he died of the plague two years later. In time the Etruscan ornaments vanished, and the wooden columns were replaced by marble ones. Today little remains except the concrete base and the marble threshold beside the winding road leading to the Capitoline; but in the history of democracy this temple has a special place, for it was built to celebrate the day the plebs gained equal rights with the aristocracy to elect from among their number the highest magistrates of the republic.

The break-through by the plebs was to lead to a whole series of laws limiting the privileges of the aristocracy. The promised agrarian reforms were carried out, some debts were remitted, and new measures were passed making it an offense to hold a debtor in slavery; his goods could be placed under bond, but not his person. By the beginning of the third century B.C. the plebs, economically strengthened, were entering the priestly colleges and exercising the functions previously reserved for the aristocracy—with the result that a new class of rich plebeians emerged to ally themselves with their former enemies. The struggle for democracy therefore had to be renewed, and with the Lex Hortensia, passed in 287 B.C., a further victory was won through its provision that resolutions of the plebeian assembly should be binding upon all Romans—patrician no less than commoner. The growing machinery of public administration had already involved the creation of many new offices, many of them held by plebeians: there were praetors (or magistrates) and aediles (roughly equivalent to mayors), who together with the censors (tax and census officials and drafters of senatorial lists) divided many powers previously held by the consuls. Therefore the essential elements of a working democracy were in existence when the Romans set out to create an empire in about the middle of the first century B.C.

Into the creation of the empire went a singular belief of the Romans in the benefits they brought to the people they conquered. Not the least of these was the system of government, which they had hammered out in the fourth century B.C., with its scheme of two consular magistrates, a senate, and a popular assembly. Roman imperialism was the product of Roman democracy, but it was also to a far greater extent the product of a particular kind of mind that takes grave comfort from disaster and pleasure from risk. The Romans were a people who were always drawing strength from their wounds. They were hard and unyielding, thrifty, cautious, and simple in their tastes in spite of the overlay of Etruscan splendor. In every family absolute and unquestioning obedience was owed to the paterfamilias, who had power of life and death over his wife and children. In much the same way as conquerors, they imposed themselves on their subjects, laying a heavy hand on them, yet at the same time admitting

Traditionally a nation of farmers and footsoldiers, Rome scored its first naval success in 260 B.C. It defeated a Carthaginian fleet by using vessels that grappled enemy ships and made possible their capture by boarding-parties of legionaries. A first-century A.D. mural, depicting ships whose decks bristle with spears, shows the persistence of the Roman conception of the warship as a floating infantry unit.
HOUSE OF VETTII, POMPEII; SCALA

them step by step to the rewards of membership in the Roman family. The subjects were regarded by the Romans somewhat in the manner of children over whom the state should cast its protection, raising them in due time—if they behaved—to full citizenship. So Vergil placed in the mouth of Anchises, father of Aeneas, legendary ancestor of Rome, a prophecy of world empire and a warning to administer the empire according to law:

> Remember, Roman, to guide the nations with authority.
> Let these be your arts: impose the laws of peace,
> And spare the humbled and lay low the proud.

Long before Vergil the Romans were aware of their heritage.

They had scarcely recovered from the destruction of their city by the Gauls when they embarked on the long, arduous, and dangerous adventure that was to lead to world empire. The Latin tribes, with whom the Romans had blood ties and with whom they had long ago struck up alliances against the Etruscans, had taken the occasion of Rome's disaster to break away from the city's leadership of the Latin League and to enlarge themselves before Rome did. Calls for independence were made; a fear of Roman hegemony was in the air—a justified fear, it turned out, for the Romans in their treaty with Carthage in 348 B.C. asserted the right to speak for the towns of the Latin coast. Revolts, border wars, raids, and counterraids marked several decades, resulting in 338 in Rome's subjection of almost all the Latin tribes around it, and of the troublesome Volscians of the Latin hills in particular. Town after town surrendered and gave up its independence and its property in exchange for a promissory note of leniency and participation in the rising Roman state. The Latin League was dissolved, to be succeeded by a federation of Latin colonies owing loyalty to the Romans. Each colony had a Roman garrison, which kept the peace and watched over municipal officers and saw to it that people obeyed Rome's laws. However, with each conquest, Rome made a particular settlement, leaving some people with a modicum of independence and incorporating others into the Roman system. The result of this carefully graduated scheme of submission, occasional freedom, and participation in rewards overcame further rebellion and attached great numbers of people to Rome. The success of this policy became manifest when Rome, in the collision with Carthage across the sea, far from finding another revolt by Latins on its hands, found them to be friendly or at least quiescent.

The Latins enjoyed many rights of citizenship; in theory they remained free, in practice they were subordinate to the whims of the local garrison commander. If they intermarried with the Romans, their children acquired Roman citizenship. In Roman eyes this was a supreme privilege granted to them only because they were regarded as natural allies of the same stock. Two towns, Tibur (Tivoli) and Praeneste (Palestrina), were permitted independence because they possessed ancient historical ties with Rome; but they were the exceptions that proved the rule that Rome permitted no independent authority anywhere in its domains. Tibur and Praeneste were both near Rome and could still be watched closely.

Already in the fourth century B.C. the Romans were working out their laws of conquest. Like the Israelites, they saw themselves as divinely inspired missionaries serving a divine purpose and regarded war as a religious vocation not to be undertaken without suitable rituals, prayers, and sacrifices. Strange magical rites were practiced in order to induce the gods of a besieged city to abandon it and defect to Rome. The enemy city would be consecrated to the infernal gods, and the general in command would sometimes offer himself as a willing sacrifice. Such a *devotio* was pronounced by the consul Publius Decius Mus during one of the wars with the Latins. The Roman army was about to be overwhelmed when Decius covered his head with his toga and communed with the gods, urging them to visit the enemy with fear, shuddering, and death. It was not enough that they should die; they must learn in fear and trembling that the gods fought on the side of the Romans. The Latins must die in agony, suffering the punishment inflicted on them by the gods. Then having addressed all the known and unknown gods, Decius leaped onto his horse and hurled himself into the thick of the fighting. He did not live to see the end of the battle, for he was killed at its turning point. "It was as though," wrote the historian Livy, "he had been sent from heaven to expiate all the wrath of the gods and to deflect destruction from his own people onto his enemies."

The institution of the *devotio* was a peculiar one, for it involved vast and awesome claims. The consul, leading his army on the field of battle, was far more than a general. He saw himself as a religious leader in communion with the gods, possessing powers not given to ordinary mortals, capable of calling down the lightning on his adversaries; the heavens and the earth beneath were engaged in the struggle. The general became a shaman; the enemy could be cursed into defeat on condition that the general or someone chosen by him was prepared to sacrifice his life. If the man who pronounced the *devotio* died in battle, there were no further ceremonies; he was remembered gratefully in the hearts of the people he had saved. If he survived, his image was buried seven

Latin soldiers are represented on a pair of ivory plaques (opposite and above). The cities of Latium, which were Rome's closest neighbors and earliest enemies, proved to be among its most steadfast allies in the critical wars of the third century B.C. Thereafter, Roman armies frequently included Latin units commanded by Latin officers.
MUSEO DI VILLA GIULIA, ROME; ALINARI

93

feet deep in the earth, and a guilt offering was sacrificed over the so-called tomb that contained the image of a living man. The guilt offering was made because he had not died; the gods had demanded his death, but a miracle or the word of an unknown god had saved him. In this strange war, guilt and sacrifice came together in a rite that was at once mysterious and terrible in its consequences. Never again was the man who had devoted his life permitted to take part in religious ceremonies either on his own or on behalf of the state. He had become a man without an existence, for he was neither dead nor alive, and the place where his image lay was sacred.

The wars changed and the methods of fighting changed, for the Romans continually learned from their adversaries. The organization of warfare, down to its last-minute particulars, was their constant study. Originally they had fought in the formation known to Greeks as the phalanx: the heavy infantry drawn up in an unbroken line many ranks deep, the massed shields acting as armor, the long spears serving as their weapons of offense. Their tactic was to crush the enemy by the weight of those spears. After the Gallic invasion they learned the need for greater maneuverability. While fighting the Latins they seem to have experimented with combinations of a modified phalanx, using detached units capable of inflicting damage and then retiring under cover of the phalanx.

By about 326 B.C. the Romans were fighting the Samnites, sturdy mountaineers from the southern uplands of the Apennines, who fought in detachments of no more than twenty or thirty men, armed with javelins and short stabbing swords. About that time the Romans abandoned the phalanx and introduced the maniple, consisting of about one hundred twenty men, as the principal unit of organization in their armies. The small, round shield of the Roman soldier was replaced by a larger, oblong one; the long spear, which had earlier proved ineffective against the huge Gallic long swords, gave way to the javelin; and the cutting sword was altered into a stabbing weapon. The heavy javelins, nearly seven feet long, could be hurled at the enemy from a distance of several yards before the Romans closed for an encounter with swords. (The same principle was followed in modern wars when machine-gun fire opened the way for a bayonet charge.) Instead of the great shock of the phalanx there was now a series of shocks in rapid succession. Over the years the weapons were continually changing: new weapons were developed; old weapons were adapted, but the basic elements were retained. The Spanish sword replaced the old Roman one; the sling made of sinews became the sling staff, four feet long with leather thongs; the heavy artillery, which the Romans

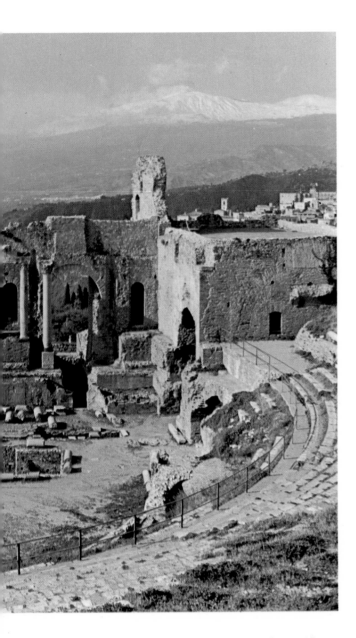

Overlooking the sea at Taormina, in eastern Sicily, are the remains of a theatre originally built by the Greeks, who founded many cities along the Sicilian coast. The Romans came to know those cities during the First Punic War (264–241 B.C.) when they engaged in seemingly endless campaigns to drive the Carthaginians from western Sicilian bases. For the Roman soldier exposure to the sophisticated culture of the Greeks was one of the few rewards of a long and thankless war on alien soil.

HERSCHEL LEVIT

designated with the word *tormenta*, came into being. But it was the highly maneuverable maniples that conquered the world.

The wars against the Samnites in the Campania were long and costly, fought with a vigor and a savagery that threatened to bleed both armies white. Though many historical questions remain as to the origin and extent of this fighting, there is no doubt that over a period of many decades Rome grew vastly by subjugating these settlers allied to the Greek colonists in the south. Given the presumptive dates 343–341 B.C. for the first war, 328–304 for the second, and 298–290 for the third, the Romans remembered thirty-one processional triumphs in which they led their Samnite captives across the Forum, displaying the heaped booty to the cheering crowds; but they suffered nearly as many defeats. In 321 B.C. at the Caudine Forks, between Capua and Beneventum, the Samnites trapped a Roman army in a defile by closing it at both ends. The Romans tried to fight their way out and then realized that if they continued fighting there would be no survivors. They sought for terms, but the Samnite general was all for massacring them to the last man. Finally he was prevailed upon to save the lives of the Romans on condition that they admit defeat and not make war. The Romans were compelled to surrender their arms, their equipment, and all their clothes except their undergarments, and they were forced to bend their necks under a yoke of spears. They solemnly signed a treaty of peace, which they later disavowed, claiming that it had been obtained under duress. War soon broke out again and continued for decades, the Romans mounting one punitive expedition after another. Then, at last, in 290 B.C. they captured the Samnite general whose magnanimity had saved them at the Caudine Forks, bound him in chains, led him in triumph through Rome, and beheaded him. The gods disapproved, for they sent a pestilence.

With the subjection of the Samnites the Romans opened the way for the conquest of all southern Italy. They had already secured their northern frontier by striking deep into the heart of Etruria. They were building military roads to the north, the south, and the west. Treasure was pouring in from the conquered territories and the ancient taste for opulence was revived. Stern republicans might offer warnings against Samnite gold, but the warnings went unheeded. The many-colored robes of the Samnite warriors, their silver scabbards, gold sword belts, and gold-embroidered saddlecloths passed into the hands of the Romans, who marveled at so much finery and learned after centuries to don it again.

Saturated with Samnite opulence, Rome began to mint silver coins, having only recently learned to mint bronze. The Forum was beginning to be crowded with the gilded statues of victorious generals. On the roof of the great temple on the Capitoline, as a visible sign of Roman dominance, there was now a statue of Jupiter riding in a four-horse chariot. Within the temple itself a new statue of Jupiter was fashioned from the breastplates, greaves, and helmets of the Samnites.

The Greek colonies in the boot of Italy held the promise of even greater loot. They were a temptation too great to resist; they were also a threat to the growth of Rome. Tarentum (Taranto) was a city of wealth, built around a great harbor, with a powerful navy composed of men proud of their Spartan descent. In 282 B.C. a Roman squadron of ten ships appeared offshore, and the Tarentines, remembering a treaty with Rome that forbade the passage of ships through their waters, decided to attack in force. All the available ships of Tarentum put to sea. Four Roman ships were sunk, one was captured, the rest fled. The Roman commander was killed in the fighting, and the captives were either executed or sold into slavery. Then, elated by the easy victory, the Tarentines turned their attention to the neighboring Greek city of Thurii, which had placed itself under the protection of the Romans, with a Roman garrison to keep the people in order. They attacked the city, forced the Roman garrison to withdraw, and returned in triumph to celebrate their victory.

These were not the acts of an excited, irresponsible mob, rather they were the result of a carefully-thought-out policy. Rome clearly intended to conquer the Greek world to the south. It could be stopped only by a superior force determined to prevent its expansion. The Tarentines, counting on the exhaustion of the Roman army after the long Samnite wars, may have decided that the time had come to assert the independence of the Greek colonists in Italy; and when a Roman envoy came to Tarentum to demand safeguards against future attacks, he was refused a hearing. We are told by Roman historians that the mob laughed at his bad Greek and pelted him with filth, and that he said, holding up his stained robe so that all could see it: "Laugh now, but this robe shall remain uncleansed until it is washed in your best blood." Rome was offering peace in exchange for domination. The Tarentines nevertheless prepared for war.

The future of the Greek colonies in southern Italy and Sicily was at stake. The Tarentines summoned help from Greece. Pyrrhus, king of Epirus, an ambitious and tempestuous prince, a kinsman of Alexander the Great, crossed into Italy with a force of 20,000 infantry, 3,000 cavalry, and 20 elephants. He, like Alexander, was tempted with visions of world empire. All southern

Pyrrhus, king of Epirus, was the first great Hellenic general to face the Romans. In 280 B.C., at the request of the Greeks of Tarentum, he invaded Italy with a skilled mercenary force. His phalanx twice defeated Roman legionary armies, but decisive victory eluded him. His departure in 275 left Rome in undisputed control of the central and southern portions of Italy.
MUSEO NAZIONALE, NAPLES; ALINARI

Italy, he thought, would fall to him, then Sicily and Spain and Africa. He held Tarentum in an iron grip, ordered the theatres closed, drilled the citizens, prepared to destroy any Roman army that dared to take the field. At Heraclea in 280 B.C. a Greek army encountered a Roman army for the first time. The Greek phalanx was confronted by massed maniples; Pyrrhus' force was tight and solid with its thick forest of bristling spears, man touching man in ranks sixteen deep. The Romans stood in open order at arm's length from one another, with their javelins and stabbing swords. Pyrrhus kept his best weapons in reserve: his Thessalian cavalry and armored elephants, which were thrown into battle when the Romans were giving ground. Pyrrhus, author of a celebrated treatise on the art of war, was a good general, and he had calculated his precise moment of attack to perfection. The Romans had never before seen elephants, and they fled in panic, leaving 7,000 dead on the field. Yet Pyrrhus had lost 4,000 of his Epirote veterans. According to Plutarch, when he returned to Tarentum to offer the spoils to the temple of Zeus, he remarked to one who congratulated him that another such victory would utterly undo him.

Later Pyrrhus marched on Rome, but when he was sixteen miles from the city he decided that it would be hopeless to lay siege to those impregnable walls and looked for another opportunity to destroy the Roman armies on the field. The opportunity came the following spring when the battle of Heraclea was fought all over again at Asculum, in Apulia. Once more the elephants were thrown into battle and the Romans retired in panic. But the losses on both sides were great, and Pyrrhus returned to Tarentum. There he learned that the Romans were allied with the Carthaginians, and the Gauls were overrunning Greece. No more reinforcements could be expected from Epirus, Macedonia, and Thessaly.

Carthage dominated the western Mediterranean. The power of its empire extended from the borders of Cyrenaica, in northern Africa, to the legendary Pillars of Hercules, at the western end of the Mediterranean Sea, and beyond. The descendants of Phoenician settlers, from Syria and Lebanon, had built a fortress-city on the Gulf of Tunis and ringed it with a triple line of walls. Homer describes the Phoenicians as "greedy men, famous for their ships," by which he meant perhaps nothing more than that they were fine sailors and cautious merchants. Unlike the Romans, they were content with their possessions and had little liking for war; instead of raising a citizen army, they employed mercenaries who were led by Carthaginian officers. These mercenaries were tribesmen from the African interior, Numidian light-horsemen, Libyan archers, Balearic slingers, and there was a leavening of

The invading army of Pyrrhus included twenty elephants. They frightened the Romans, who had never before encountered them in battle. The elephants, on the other hand, had never encountered pigs and, on one occasion, became panicky and unmanageable at the sight of these animals in a Roman camp. The Romans were to commemorate the rout of the elephants on copper bars (above) which they used as currency.
BOTH: BRITISH MUSEUM

By the third century B.C. *the Roman legion combined the esprit de corps* that made the Macedonian phalanx formidable with flexibility, which the phalanx lacked. The legion was divided into thirty maniples, each consisting of two centuries made up of thirty to sixty men. It went into battle with its youngest soldiers leading the attack, secure in the knowledge that two lines of seasoned veterans stood ready to relieve them. The maniples of the third line, including the steadiest legionaries, could wheel to repel an attack against the rear. Light infantry and cavalry auxiliaries were relegated to minor roles.

Gauls, Spaniards, and Greeks. Their trading centers in Spain, Sardinia, and Sicily prospered; gradually southern Spain, most of Sardinia, and all of western Sicily fell into their grasp. But they did not want land as much as a command of the seas, and both the Romans and the Greeks knew there were sea routes forbidden to them by the Carthaginians.

When the Greek cities appealed to Pyrrhus for help, he turned his attention to the Carthaginians. He chose to fight them on land, where they were most vulnerable. He swept across Sicily, reducing their fortresses one by one. He laid siege to Lilybaeum (Marsala), the strongest and westernmost Carthaginian citadel. The city held out so long that he was compelled to raise the siege. Once again he returned to Tarentum and built up an army capable of fighting the Romans. But an indecisive battle at Beneventum in 275 B.C., in which his troops were mauled during a night attack, was the signal for the abrupt termination of his campaigns, and he sailed for home, his dream of becoming a new Alexander shattered.

On leaving Sicily after his failure at Lilybaeum, Pyrrhus is said to have remarked, "What a battlefield I have left for the Romans and the Carthaginians!" With Pyrrhus gone, the Greek settlements in southern Italy and Sicily were left in a power vacuum, and before long a confrontation was bound to take place between the force expanding from the north and the strength radiating from the African shore. The battlefield of this great collision between former friends was to be not Sicily alone but the entire western Mediterranean. The first and second struggles of the Punic wars (264–241 B.C. and 218–201) were waged with increasing ferocity. The contestants were evenly matched: Carthage was larger and wealthier than Rome and could more readily face the costs of a large navy; Rome, however, was superior to Carthage in manpower and in the enthusiasm of its citizen soldiery. No quarter was given. Savagery became a way of life and massacre a commonplace. When the long struggle was over, Carthage lay in ruins and the fields of Italy were a desert.

After Pyrrhus' departure, Rome and its supporting cities had found it an easy task to put down remaining opposition in the south of the peninsula, thereby crushing not only Greek resistance but that of the Samnites, Oscans, and Lucanians as well. In 264 B.C. the Romans stood at the Strait of Messina—but a Carthaginian garrison stood opposite. After much debate in the Senate, Rome responded to an appeal by the autonomous city of Messina, on the Sicilian side, to form an alliance and protect it against the Carthaginian attack. Once landed, Roman forces were soon driving against a number of Punic settlements on the island, and the war to the death had begun. In an astonishingly short space of time the Romans built a fleet to challenge Carthage's mastery of the sea. A Carthaginian quinquereme, cast ashore on Bruttium (Calabria), provided the model to which the Romans added an ingenious device they referred to as the *corvus*, or "raven." This was a thirty-foot gangway, with a heavy curved spike at one end serving as a grappling-iron, which could be lowered from the ship's mast by pulleys. With the aid of the corvus the Romans proposed to transform naval war into a kind of land war, the aim being not to sink the enemy ships but to board them and fight the enemy on the deck. These tactics were more successful than they had dared to hope. Early in 260 B.C. the consul Gaius Duilius encountered a Carthaginian fleet off Mylae (Milazzo), on the northern coast of Sicily, and engaged it in battle. When the two sides pulled clear, the Romans had captured thirty-one of the Carthaginian ships and sunk fourteen. The Romans had won their first naval victory with their first fleet. Gaius Duilius was awarded the honors of triumphator; the strange, savagely decorated beaks of Carthaginian ships adorned the column in the Forum where the proud admiral walked, attended by flute player and torchbearer.

Emboldened by this victory, and believing that it had acquired command of the seas in a single stroke, Rome decided to invade Carthage. Four years later an enormous fleet of about three hundred thirty ships sailed for Carthage. The Carthaginians, too, had been building a new fleet. The two fleets met off the southern coast of Sicily in the greatest naval battle yet fought, and once more the corvus settled the issue. The Carthaginians were routed; the Romans sailed on to Carthage, confident that in a few weeks they would conquer the enemy. However, when Rome demanded in harsh terms that Carthage surrender, the Carthaginians were fired to a desperate resistance. Under the command of a Spartan general they hurled themselves at the Roman lines, and the Romans fled. The first landing on Africa was a disaster; only a small remnant of the invading army was able to make its way back to Rome.

Such catastrophes occurred at intervals during the long-drawn-out war. Whole armies, whole fleets vanished. Weeks, months, years would pass while the opponents painfully reassembled their forces, and then once again they would engage in a sudden, murderous conflict, from which they retired in disorder, bruised and broken, only to resume the fighting when they recovered their strength. At last, in 241 B.C., after twenty-three years of struggle, another Roman naval victory brought about a treaty of peace. The Carthaginians were ordered to pay an indemnity, to refrain from sailing their warships in Roman waters, and to abandon all claim to

At a time when Roman power was still confined to Italy and barely able to cope with a Greek invader, Carthage was a great trading nation with colonies scattered throughout the western Mediterranean area. The influence of Carthaginian culture in Spain is reflected in fourth- and third-century Spanish art objects such as the terra-cotta female figurine above.

MUSEO ARQUEOLOGICO, IVIZA

99

CANNAE—Stage 1

CANNAE—Stage 2

CANNAE—Stage 3

Hannibal of Carthage was to teach Rome much about military strategy. By far the costliest lesson was that administered in 216 B.C. to eight Roman legions and their allies near Cannae, in southern Italy. The Roman consul Varro, hoping to take advantage of his greater numbers, massed his heavy infantry in unusually close formation. Hannibal, by allowing the center of his own line to fall back under Roman pressure, lured the Romans into a pocket that further compressed their ranks and reduced their mobility. Then, in a vise-like double envelopment, the Romans were attacked on the flanks by African heavy infantry and in the rear by the cavalry of Hannibal's brother Hasdrubal. In the ensuing slaughter at least 50,000 died.

Sicily. The Romans declared they had won a crowning victory, but it was nothing more than a truce—a truce that was to last no longer than the war that preceded it.

The period between the first and second Punic wars was an important one for Rome. Sardinia and Corsica became Roman outposts, the raids of Illyrian pirates in the Adriatic were halted, and by the conquering of Corcyra (Corfu), off western Greece, the Romans obtained a foothold on Greek soil. These goals were obtained with little effort. More difficult was the conquest of northern Italy, or Cisalpine Gaul, which extended Rome's frontiers to the Alps and made it considerably more secure against the constant threat of invasion by northern Gauls. These were the years of the great break-through. Now Roman command posts stood in an unbroken chain from the Alps to Sicily. Nor were the Carthaginians resting on their laurels; they were pushing northward through Spain, bringing all the tribes under their sovereignty, securing the wealth of silver and other mines to restore their finances and the strength of manpower for their armies.

Hamilcar Barca, a soldier who had proved himself in Sicily, became governor of Carthaginian Spain. In eight years of brilliant activity, he built up a state, a treasury, and an army, placing great new resources into Punic service. Some years after his death, his son Hannibal was raised to the governorship. He was only a youth; at the age of nine he had vowed to dedicate his life to the destruction of Rome, and he very nearly accomplished it.

A strange impersonality attends Hannibal, for the records of Carthaginian historians are lost and the Romans never described his person, except to say that he was lean, hard-muscled, and possessed piercing eyes. They saw him as power incarnate, and no one else ever terrified them so much or wounded them so deeply.

Hannibal's plan was simple, effective, and deadly. He proposed to lead African and Spanish levies across the Pyrenees and across the Alps into Italy, and to strike at Rome from the north. He counted on the Cisalpine Gauls to flock to his standards, and after the Gauls, all the conquered tribes of Italy. The great expedition, supported by many war elephants, took place in 218 B.C. At first all went well. On the river Trebia and by the shores of Lake Trasimene, Hannibal tore to pieces the Roman armies sent to block his progress. At Cannae, with superb strategy, he induced the Romans to fight on his terms, surrounded them, then slaughtered possibly 50,000 of them at a cost of only 6,000 of his own men, the greater part of whom were Gauls. It was told that many of the Roman dead were found with their faces buried in the earth. They were the wounded who preferred to choke themselves to death rather than to be killed in a manner determined by their conquerors.

The army of Hannibal was intact; three huge Roman armies had been destroyed. "In five days' time," said the Carthaginian officers, "we shall dine in the Capitol." But without siege trains, and without a general uprising by the Italian tribes against Rome, Hannibal knew that he was powerless to occupy and hold the city and thus bring the Romans to their knees.

He appealed to the Italians and Greeks to join his forces, but his appeal failed; central Italy remained loyal to Rome. He learned that victory in the field is a faulty substitute for the capture of the enemy's citadel. His brother Hasdrubal crossed the Alps with Spanish reinforcements only to be defeated on the Metaurus. By 206 B.C., Roman armies had almost completely wrested Spain from the grip of Carthage. For nearly four more years Hannibal camped in the wild and mountainous regions of Bruttium, his veterans around him, hoping against hope that help would come from Carthage, from Philip of Macedonia, from the Italians; but none came.

Then once more, the Romans decided that their most promising course would be to carry the war to the enemy's homeland. In 204 B.C. the young and popular general Publius Cornelius Scipio sailed for Africa with an army, landed at Utica, and attempted to raise the tribes of Africa against Carthage. He was more successful than Hannibal in efforts at subversion; the Numidian king Masinissa had already gone over to the Romans on the promise of receiving an enlarged kingdom. Hannibal, undermined, abandoned Italy, sailed for Carthage with his veterans, and fought a combined Numidian Roman army at Zama, some eighty miles southwest of Carthage. His veterans fought superbly, but when he threw his elephants into the battle, the Romans, no longer frightened by those beasts, simply opened their lines and let them pass. The half-trained Carthaginian citizen-soldiers broke; the Numidian cavalry hammered at the wavering line; long before nightfall it was over. Hannibal escaped from the battlefield unharmed, having lost in a day's fighting all the advantages he had gained in a lifetime of victories.

When peace was concluded in 201 B.C., Carthage was prostrate. Though the city was permitted to retain its African possessions, it was compelled to surrender Spain and all its remaining foreign trading posts. The war elephants became the property of the Romans, and the great fleet, with the exception of ten triremes, was towed into the harbor and solemnly burned. As the ships burned low to the waterline, the Carthaginians standing on shore saw that their command of the sea, and therefore their power, was gone forever. The Mediterranean was already a Roman lake.

A profile of Hannibal on a Punic shekel is one of few known likenesses of the great commander who campaigned in Italy for more than a decade and brought Rome to the brink of destruction. In the long run, Carthage proved less durable than Rome, whose Italian allies refused to desert it. Hannibal's first defeat by a Roman army, at Zama in North Africa in 202 B.C., ended the Second Punic War.
BRITISH MUSEUM

THE ROMAN WAY OF WAR

From the early days of the republic, Rome's military might derived principally from the high quality of its heavy infantry—the celebrated legion. Organized in small, mobile companies and made up of four to six thousand men, the legion was flexible enough to meet a great variety of military challenges. It also proved adaptable to the changing political needs of the state. At first it was essentially an expeditionary force recruited among the wealthy classes. By 100 B.C. military service no longer appealed to the well-to-do, and reforms instituted by the consul Marius—particularly the extension of the terms of service of recruits—began to produce the professional standing army that Rome needed to police an empire. The imperial age saw the emergence of an arrogant, new, military elite, the Praetorians (pictured at left). Created as the emperor's home guard, the well-paid Praetorian cohorts spent much of their time in or near the city of Rome. The legions, on the other hand, were usually stationed on distant frontiers. The imperial legionary, unlike his earlier counterpart, might spend a lifetime in the service of Rome without setting foot in Italy. He fought less for the glory of the state than for the honor of his legion and the sanctity of his pension, but this shift in allegiance did not reduce his effectiveness as a soldier. The columnar reliefs, illustrated on the following pages, indicate that his military exploits did not go unremembered in the imperial capital.

THE LEGION IN ACTION

The Marian reforms of the late republican period
may have profoundly affected the nature of military
life, but they did not greatly alter the way in which a
Roman army fought. Though the legion of thirty
maniples (see table on page 98) gave way to the
legion of ten cohorts, its smallest constituent unit
was the century—a company of less than fifty to
more than a hundred men commanded by a centurion. Under the eye of this key officer (often a gifted
soldier who had risen from the ranks), legionaries
trained in various specialized tasks and drilled to
fight in close formation. Although new tactics were
continually being devised, a standard method of de-
ploying troops for battle may be discerned. As illustrated in the diagram below, the centuries were
ranged in a modified checkerboard formation, often
in three lines, each of which was normally several
men deep. Brief gaps in the lines divided the companies until sometime after A.D. 100 when the phalanx formation with its unbroken front was reintro-
duced. Light-armed auxiliaries often went into
action first, discharging a volley of spears at the
enemy and subsequently retiring to the rear. Cavalry
units were usually placed on one or both wings.

ROMAN ORDER OF BATTLE

ENEMY ARMY

Light Infantry

Cavalry

First Line

Second Line

Third Line

THE LEGION

*A relief (right) from Trajan's column shows Roman
legionaries attacking a Dacian camp beyond the Danube
early in the second century* A.D. *By linking their shields
overhead, the soldiers have formed the so-called tortoise,
a makeshift but effective shelter that served to protect them
against missiles thrown from the walls by the defenders.*

COLUMN OF TRAJAN; GERMAN ARCHAEOLOGICAL INSTITUTE

A detail (upper left) of a relief portraying cavalry in action includes horsemen who have dismounted to fight on foot in the time-honored Roman tradition. On the march a legionary carried most of his own equipment and armor; mule-drawn carts, one of which is pictured at left, were used only to transport the heavier supplies. At right is a Roman war galley with a deckload of infantry. Roman warships were usually rowed by slaves; this left the soldiers fresh for the task of boarding enemy vessels and subduing crews of tired oarsmen.

106

SUPPORTING SERVICES

The success of their legions made the Romans reluctant to think of war as anything other than a series of infantry actions. They failed to develop an effective cavalry, and from the second century B.C., recruited cavalrymen only among their non-Italian allies. The Roman navy was born during the First Punic War as a fleet of troop carriers, becoming almost at once an efficient extension of the Roman legion. It was later used by Pompey against pirates. In imperial times, for want of enemies, it atrophied into little more than a marine police force.

THE LONG AFTERNOON OF THE LEGIONARY

The legionaries, who sometimes jokingly referred to themselves as Marius' mules, could complain with some justice that their work was never done. When in the field, they were as much builders as fighters. From earliest times, they seldom ventured into battle or retired for the night without first preparing a fortified camp, a practice unknown among their enemies. Thus, after a day's march during which the soldier may have carried over eighty pounds of equipment—including weapons and armor, cooking utensils, an axe, a spade, a saw, a basket, tent stakes, and two-weeks' rations of meal—he was frequently called upon to fell trees and construct defenses.

The large relief at left shows soldiers assembling timber fortifications. Above is a reconstruction of a fortified camp of the kind built for overnight use by legionaries on the march; the arrangement of the tents seldom varied, each company being assigned to a specific area. The camp was surrounded by a defensive ditch and an earth wall surmounted by a palisade, shown in cross section at left. Along frontiers that were regarded as more or less fixed, soldiers erected more substantial quarters of timber, stone, or brick, as pictured in the small panel at upper left.

ENGINES OF WAR

The Roman's practical turn of mind contributed greatly to the effectiveness of his armies. Just as a variety of military tactics was developed to deal with specific problems in the field, many ingenious weapons were invented (or adapted from foreign models) to meet special military needs. When attacking an enemy fortress or fortified city, the legionary could count not only on his own training in the assembling of rams, siege towers, and various sheltering devices but also on the support of ready-made artillery pieces such as catapults that threw stones weighing several hundred pounds and gigantic crossbows that propelled twelve-foot spears. The catapult illustrated below—a Roman precursor of the modern mortar—hurled its heavy missile in a high trajectory.

A pair of reliefs from Trajan's column (opposite and above) illustrates the advantages that the Romans enjoyed over less sophisticated enemies in battles that involved the storming of major fortifications. In the background of the smaller panel mechanical slings are moved into place to assist Roman legionaries on the attack. By contrast, above, barbarians armed with nothing more formidable than bows and arrows and a simple ram would seem to stand little chance of breaching the massive walls of a Roman fort protecting the northeastern frontier.

THE BRIDGE BUILDERS

As they added territory to their empire, the Romans lost little time establishing roads between their new strongholds and their old bases of supply. This work was often begun by Roman soldiers during the course of military campaigns. The legionary became especially adept in the construction of bridges, the simplest type consisting of connected wooden frames covered with planking and supported by pontoons. Where the current was rapid, a more stable kind of bridge, secured by pilings driven into the river bed, might be erected. The most famous of such spans, illustrated in the drawings below, was the one built across the Rhine by Caesar in 55 B.C. Soldiers of a later era succeeded in constructing a half-mile-long bridge over the lower Danube.

A pontoon bridge wide enough to accommodate two-way traffic is depicted in the relief at upper left. The drawings above represent vertical and horizontal projections of a section of Caesar's Rhine bridge and are based on the detailed description of that structure by Caesar himself in his Gallic War *(the passage appears in translation on page 144). Included in these sketches is one of the ingenious V-shaped guards erected on the upstream side of the bridge to protect the piers from damage by objects borne by the powerful Rhine current. The relief at left shows a simple bridge of logs supported on pilings. At right, an elaborate pontoon bridge bears the weight of many officers and standard-bearers.*

OVERLEAF: *A panel from the column of Marcus Aurelius, dating from the late second century* A.D., *shows the decapitation of German prisoners on the northern frontier. The enforcers of the Roman peace were not noted for charity toward a beaten enemy. The usual lot of captives was either death or slavery.*

V

A REPUBLIC DIVIDED

When a commonwealth, after warding off many great dangers, has arrived at a high pitch of prosperity and undisputed power, it is evident that, by the lengthened continuance of great wealth within it, the manner of life of its citizens will become more extravagant; and that the rivalry for office, and in other spheres of activity, will become fiercer than it ought to be.

Polybius, Histories

Though the Romans had triumphed over Carthage, there must have been many who wondered whether victory had not been bought at too high a price. In sixteen years of fighting Rome had lost nearly a quarter of her population, four hundred towns had been destroyed, and half the farms of Italy had been devastated. Profound social changes had been set in motion. Slaves won by conquest flooded the labor market, and any Roman who could afford to feed them could have as many as he pleased; the number captured in the first half of the second century B.C. may have reached two hundred fifty thousand. The result was a growth of great estates worked by slaves and the displacement from the land of large numbers of independent farmers. They flocked to the towns, only to discover that they were unwelcome there, and soon became part of the restless Roman mob. A rising class of shrewd business promoters, the equites, mounted large-scale commercial ventures, taking advantage of the fact that the senators—august representatives of the old, landholding aristocracy—were prohibited by law from engaging in overseas trade. New wealth pouring in from the granaries of Sicily, the fields of North Africa, and the mines of Spain made the rich richer, but left the poor poorer.

In the past the Romans had been peasants and woodsmen, men of the countryside who brought into the towns the discipline of the seasons. They owed their strength to hard work, to the frugality of their lives, to their respect for household and public gods, and to their effort to embody such qualities as *gravitas*, *virtus*, and *diligentia*. But the conquest of Carthage had brought not only wealth and upheaval but subtle changes in the Roman character as well. The hard and grasping qualities that the Romans had possessed from the beginning assumed more dangerous forms. Never remarkable for their pity, they now became remarkable for their pitilessness, and victory, far from leaving them sated, only whetted their appetite for more.

Physically Rome burgeoned immensely in the period following the Punic holocaust. Despite all losses, by the middle of the second century B.C. the population of the city may have numbered half a million. In the same period national wealth is thought to have doubled or trebled. Industries, such as the manufacture of pottery, tools, cordage, and ships for the military or carrying trade, rose and thrived. According to the modern scholar H. H. Scullard, the great slag heaps discovered at Populonia, opposite the island of Elba, suggest that "an average of ten million tons of iron ore were treated each year during the last centuries of the republic." Finished goods went out across the entire Mediterranean; and in turn raw materials poured into Italy—along with some manufactured ware, and spoils and art treasures from Sicily and Greece.

To sustain a fast-growing populace and to aid the spread of Roman power, programs of public works were undertaken by official and private enterprise. Drainage canals were dug and aqueducts were built to control water supply, irrigation, and urban sanitation. Rome's paved road system, begun in the fourth century B.C. with the building of the Appian Way, grew and eventually linked all the major communities of the peninsula in an unprecedented network. In addition to wooden bridges, the Romans built great bridges of stone—a particular feat of early Roman engineering. The Mulvian Bridge, across the Tiber, was constructed in about 109 B.C. Provisions were set up whereby the equites, who may have numbered ten thousand in the later days of the republic, could engage in competitive bidding for public contracts and set up companies in which any Roman citizen could buy a share.

In theory Rome was still a republic. In fact it was an oligarchy ruled by the three hundred aristocratic senators, who had been elected for life and who replaced the annually appointed consuls, the tribunes, and the popular assembly as the fount of authority. The change had come about gradually as the Punic war effort demanded an increasing concentration of power. The popular assembly and the Comitia Centuriata continued to meet, and the tribunes still possessed a theoretical power of veto, but all the important decisions were made by the senators, who had control of military appointments, of the treasury and the judiciary, of regulating all revenues and expenditure, and of determining foreign policy, receiving ambassadors, and ratifying treaties. Although the senators supposedly acted as an advisory body, they acquired supreme judicial authority by appointing committees empowered to act on all matters concerning the safety of the state. Though excluded from trade, they nevertheless granted public contracts, and in this way assisted the growing mercantile class. The consuls were simply the agents of the senatorial majority. The Senate was a self-perpetuating body; it was not in direct contact with the plebeian assembly, and it was jealous of the privileges enjoyed by the assembly. Edicts announced in the name of the Senate and the Roman people—*senatus populusque Romanus*—merely represented the will of the senators.

Such a vast accumulation of power by a few privileged aristocrats could lead only to revolution, and almost inevitably it would be headed by a small and determined group within the senatorial party. The revolution, when it came, was broken because its leaders were murdered, and the remaining years of the republic only served to show that oligarchies and dictatorships were adept at employ-

The old man with the staff in the detail above personifies the Roman Senate; the youth symbolizes the people. Together they administered the growing realm, at least in theory. In fact, during the late republic senators and plebeians, soldiers and intellectuals fell into bitter strife that spawned civil war.

ing republican forms as a means to achieving their purposes.

All the advantages were on the side of the Senate, for the plebs were without resources. Virtually unlimited power was at the disposal of the Senate; it was not burdened with a sense of responsibility to the people. It fed and entertained them with bread and circuses. To keep the people in a good temper it increased the number of public holidays and provided games, dramatic performances, and gladiatorial shows. And more games were offered by candidates for high office. The gift of bread and circuses resembled a loan secured on the good behavior of the plebs.

Entrenched in their privileges, possessing vast estates tilled by slaves, having little or no respect for the laws, the senators dominated Rome as though it were a conquered city obedient to their whims. Of the three hundred senators, perhaps twenty formed the inner cabinet. Family ties bound them together; they rejoiced in their exclusiveness and their secrecy, so that we rarely know who was responsible for the great decisions nor do we know much about the debates that took place in the inner councils. The inner cabinet ruled, and those who defied it suffered the consequences.

Publius Cornelius Scipio, known as Scipio Africanus after his victory at Zama, both reached the peak of power in the Senate and incurred its displeasure. He was one of those rare men who combines so many virtues that the man himself seems to vanish and becomes a copy-book maxim. All the gifts were showered on him. Wealthy, wellborn, violently courageous, at times calmly meditative, scholarly, and deeply religious, believing himself close to the gods, he went through life as though he were in a dream. In his youth he had shown a girlish beauty, but no one thought he was effeminate. He wore his hair long in the Greek fashion, preferred Greek robes, and was admired for his graceful gestures, but there was a diamondlike hardness at the core. Scipio fought through the three disastrous battles of Ticino, Lake Trasimene, and Cannae and distinguished himself still further when the handful of dispirited survivors of the battle of Cannae threatened to leave Italy and take service in Greece. He held his sword over the head of the leader of the malcontents and threatened to kill him unless he went on fighting Hannibal. Scipio was then nineteen years old and already a veteran and an officer.

For generations members of his family had held high office. Within the family shrine there were said to be thirty death masks of ancestors who had held consular rank. His boundless self-confidence came perhaps from the knowledge of his aristocratic heritage, but there was a vein of mysticism in his nature which set him apart from other men and from his own family. The greatest mili-

The vast changes that took place in the economy and society of Rome during the first century B.C. were largely a result of the wealth that poured in from new provinces. The relief above depicts grain from African colonies being unloaded. The detail (left) of an Iberian relief shows miners entering a pit. As well as supplying Rome with silver, lead, tin, and iron, Spain provided many of the slaves brought into Rome in the late republic. Rome's conquests enriched her in intellectual ways too; below, a Greek slave appears to be tutoring his master and mistress.

tary commander of his time, fired with visions of Rome's destiny, he was also an intellectual drawn to Greek thought and presence. Though a member of a class rooted in tradition, his personal impulses were directed toward sweeping and civilizing change.

During Scipio's lifetime Greek cultural influence was beginning to be widely felt in Rome. The conquest of southern Italy and Sicily (then filled with beautiful Greek cities) had opened the invaders' eyes to Greek art. In 212 B.C. the general Marcellus had returned from Syracuse in triumph, with statues of that cultivated city as trophies. When Roman forces in the Second Punic War crossed into Greece itself, closer contact with Hellenic ways resulted, along with more booty. Adaptations of Greek plays had appeared on Roman stages in the third century B.C., and by the middle of the second century B.C. Rome produced its first playwrights of note in the comic writers Plautus and Terence, both of whom derived their plots from Greek New Comedy. The poet Quintus Ennius, a profound student of Greek literature, chronicled in dactylic hexameters the history of Rome from its beginnings to the age of Scipio. In 167 B.C. the consul Lucius Aemilius Paullus, another philhellene, was to bring from conquered Macedonia the library of King Perseus and form the first large collection of books in Rome. Greek traders, artists, teachers, and slave-tutors converged on the city and brought to it the testimonies of a superior culture and a new landscape of the mind. Greek philosophy and Hellenistic grace entered Rome; rich Roman youths went to Athens to study and returned with a reverence for Attic thought. With the looting of Greece's art treasures and with the importing of Greek ideas, a more mature Rome came into being—one in which worldliness and self-indulgence mixed with individuality and enlightenment.

In this cultural expansion, for it was nothing less, Scipio played a leading role. He was the innovator who threw the gates wide open, and in time he came to be regarded as being more Greek than Roman. Made censor and *princeps senatus* in 199 B.C., he seemed to occupy a position of unassailable authority. His family and his friends continued his Hellenizing effort.

But such men invite enemies. Scipio's most dangerous and rancorous enemy was Marcus Porcius, who bore the nickname Cato, which means "shrewd one." He came from a humble background in the Sabine farm country and owed his advancement to his friendship with powerful members of the aristocracy and to the courage he had displayed as a soldier in the ranks in the Second Punic War. At the age of thirty he became quaestor to Scipio in Sicily; six years later, in 198 B.C., he served as praetor in Sardinia,

A bust from Herculaneum conveys the energy and distinction of the greatest member of the aristocratic Scipio clan, Scipio Africanus. Leading soldier and statesman, innovator not only of war tactics but of ideas, he was dedicated to Greek culture and brought its liberalizing influence to bear on old Roman ways. This won him the deadly enmity in the Senate of conservatives like Cato (opposite).

where he expelled usurers and made himself widely known as an apostle of strict morality and traditional Roman virtues. In another three years he achieved the consulship, and in 184 B.C. he became a censor—an office that Scipio had held. Thus he had immense influence over public morals and the disposition of offices and funds. He enlarged his functions, making himself in effect the puritanical policeman of Rome, bent on suppressing the Hellenizing and liberalizing influences of Scipio and his clan.

Farmer, soldier, lawyer, writer, political chieftain, Cato was an extraordinary presence. Robust and somewhat rustic, he had a gift for blunt speech raised to the power of genius. He had a fiery red face, steely eyes, large teeth, and a harsh, bellowing voice—vibrant and unforgettable, it commanded attention as he proclaimed his adherence to the ancient republican virtues and damned the fashionable Hellenism of Scipio and all newfangled things. As an orator Cato was among the greatest that Rome ever saw. He maintained that an orator's task was to "hold fast to the matter, the words will follow." Yet Cicero, the most polished speaker of his time, admired Cato's diatribes as showing "all the qualities of great oratory." His hatreds, which were many, belong to a recognizable type: women must be kept in their place; slaves must feel the whip; nothing good ever comes from philosophy. He liked to say that he wore homespun clothes, allowed no plaster or whitewash on the walls of his house, and drove the plow with his own hands. In his view too many people gathered in the Forum to gossip, and he wished that the Forum were paved with sharp-edged shells.

Cato was almost a caricature of the archreactionary, the uncompromising upholder of an ancient patriarchal age which never existed except in his sturdy imagination. He was a man without sentiment who could write in his *De agricultura* that everything that was old and sick and worn-out on the farm should be sold, including "old and sick slaves, and whatever else is superfluous." Profit should be the main motive of the good husbandman—profit, and nothing else. A farm hand should receive a smock, a blanket, and a pair of wooden clogs every other year, and the farmer should keep the threadbare cloaks to make caps from.

The grave and brilliant Scipio, at home in Greek poetry and philosophy, was confronted by the rough and spirited Cato, who regarded Greek poetry and philosophy as luxuries that would assuredly destroy the fabric of the Roman state. He was even more uncompromising: he turned from reproving spiritual luxuries to attacking extravagances in dress and jewelry. As censor he sent his inspectors to examine the wardrobes of the rich and taxed the contents far above their value; in this way he earned the favor of the poor. He also saw to it that riots were put down mercilessly—even grumbling was punished—and in this way he earned the favor of the rich, who wanted above all an orderly and obedient people.

By brilliantly exploiting the conflicting interests of rich and poor, Cato became the most powerful figure in Rome. From a soldier in the ranks and farmer he rose to become the acknowledged lawgiver and judge, giving his name to one of the buildings in the Forum containing law courts. Senators feared him because as preserver of public morality he possessed sweeping powers and could call for their personal records and arrest them if he found any documents that displeased him; and everyone else feared him too, because his inspectors were everywhere. He was highhanded, vindictive, and always cautious, keeping to the letter of the law.

Scipio's influence, however, remained strong. When war broke out against Philip V of Macedonia in 200 B.C., Scipio's influence was such that the Senate gave orders to the Roman general Titus Quinctius Flamininus to proclaim to the Greeks that he had come, not as their enemy, but as their liberator from Macedonian tyranny. In 197 B.C. Flamininus defeated Philip at Cynoscephalae in a strange battle fought in the mist. The next year Flamininus attended the Isthmian games. A herald marched into the arena and spoke words meant to stir the Greeks to the depths of their souls: "The Roman Senate and the proconsular general Titus Quinctius have conquered King Philip and the Macedonians, and they now declare the Corinthians, the Phocians, Locrians, Euboeans, Achaeans, Magnesians, Thessalians, and Perrhaebians to be free, without garrison or tribute, subject to their own ancestral laws."

The Greeks had not expected the grant of freedom from the conquering Romans and became delirious with joy. Valerius Maximus says the birds in the air were stunned by the thunder of applause, and Livy says the Isthmian games came to an abrupt end because the Greeks were too happy to watch them. There was a vast outpouring of affection for the thirty-three-year-old imperator. Flamininus became the idol of the Greeks, and hymns were sung in his honor: "Hail, Paean Apollo, hail, Titus our Savior." As the months went by, it seemed as though Greeks and Romans were bound by ties of enduring friendship, and the two civilizations would fuse and there would be no more war. The philhellenes in Rome were overjoyed; the world they desired was taking shape.

Six years later, in 190 B.C., Antiochus III of Syria, known as Antiochus the Great, an eager voluptuary who had conquered the Greek cities of Asia Minor, fought a Roman army at Magnesia, near Smyrna. Scipio Africanus accompanied the army to the east,

Crusty, unpolished, of peasant birth, yet immensely impressive in person and speech, Marcus Porcius Cato (shown in a bust carved long after his death) was the leader of the traditionalist faction that opposed Scipio's Hellenizing influence. Though renowned, Scipio was unable to break the demagogic spell Cato had cast over the Senate, and a Cato-led faction successfully plotted to bring Scipio low.

VATICAN; ARCHIVO FOTOGRAFICO

serving under the command of his brother Lucius Cornelius Scipio. Although the army of Antiochus outnumbered the Roman army two to one, the Syrian phalanx was cut to pieces by the Roman cavalry, and heavily armored troops were not even engaged in the battle. Antiochus returned to Syria and abandoned half his kingdom, saying that he was grateful to the Romans for saving him the trouble of ruling so large an empire. The triumph of Lucius Scipio was the most dazzling ever seen in Rome. In the procession that wound across the Forum there were 224 military standards, 1,231 ivory tusks, 37,420 pounds of silver, and an immense quantity of gold. Lucius Cornelius Scipio was awarded the title of Asiaticus.

The two Scipios had won the two most significant battles of their age. They were the darlings of Rome, at once conquerors and leaders of an intellectual elite. Cato, however, was biding his time. Three years passed before he decided to attack them. Although he directed the attack against Lucius by demanding an account of the spoils of victory, he was actually aiming at the far more famous brother. Such a demand had never before been made, for generals were accustomed by tradition to distribute rewards to their officers and soldiers as they saw fit, and most of the treasure automatically made its way to the state treasury. Africanus was incensed, and instead of defending himself or his brother, brought his records to the Senate and tore them into shreds in full view of all the senators. Because the official records of the spoils had disappeared, Cato could no longer press his attack.

The law, however, was on Cato's side. He knew all its intricate workings, he had his spies in the Scipionic circle, and he knew his whole future depended upon destroying the influence of his two greatest enemies, who were too proud or felt too secure to attack him. Again he waited three years, and then quite suddenly, when everyone thought the matter had been forgotten, he ordered Lucius Scipio to appear before the plebeian assembly to render his account. The great Africanus stood beside his brother. Nevertheless a heavy fine was imposed on Lucius, whose refusal to pay brought him a sentence of imprisonment. The power of the Scipios was broken; the family that had risen to such great heights was now disgraced. They were the cultivated men who had hoped to marry Rome to Greek culture; but instead of peace and friendship, the Greeks were to be offered interminable wars, which were little more than butcheries. Scipio Africanus vanished from the scene, moving to his country estate at Liternum, on the coast of the Campania, far from Rome. He never returned. Broken in health and spirit, bewildered by the ingratitude of the Romans, he died in

Rome's first important victory in the east was won by Flamininus, who defeated Philip V of Macedonia in 197 B.C.; the victor's image appears above. Though offered extremely liberal peace terms, Macedonia was not satisfied and renewed threats against Rome, causing the Senate to make a decision that forever affected Rome's foreign policy: defeated countries were all to become Roman provinces. By about 145 B.C. most of the Hellenistic world had been made into provinces. They proved to be prosperous ones, taking part in cultural exchange (exemplified at right in the Syrian votive offering to a deity with traits of Jupiter and a sun god) as well as trade (demonstrated by the heavily laden wagons in the relief below from Asia Minor).

184 B.C. at age fifty-two. Cato outlived him by thirty-five years.

For Cato the only good foreigners were dead foreigners or slaves. His conception of the Roman empire was one of unlimited despotism, the subject nations to be ruled by an iron hand. He sowed the seeds of tyranny, scattering them in handfuls, and more than anyone he shaped a century that was to become tragic.

In 150 B.C. or shortly before, Cato, who was then in his late eighties, sailed for Carthage at the head of a commission to arbitrate a dispute between Carthage and Numidia—still being ruled by Masinissa, who was also nearing ninety. The two old men had much in common, and they shared an intense hatred and horror of the Carthaginians, who had survived defeat to become once more a great trading power. Masinissa's Numidians, loyal allies of the Romans, were in a privileged position. Since Carthage was forbidden by terms of peace with Rome to wage war on them, they could and did threaten it with impunity. They had absorbed one Punic province and were preparing to absorb another. Cato had been sent to mediate the dispute; instead he encouraged Masinissa in his designs and returned to Rome to plead the cause of the Numidians. At the end of every speech, whatever the subject, he would add the words: "And furthermore I move that Carthage must be destroyed!"

He meant exactly what he said—the city must be wiped off the map, with no building left standing, no people permitted to live within the ruined walls. His demand was obeyed three years after his death: the Senate gave the task of destroying Carthage to Publius Cornelius Scipio, known as Scipio Aemilianus Africanus Minor, the adopted grandson of the great Africanus. Carthage fell. For six days the Romans fought within its walls before the citadel surrendered. The thirty-nine-year-old commander watched the destruction impassively, but there came a moment when he turned to his close friend and secretary, the Greek Polybius, and said: "It is all so beautiful, and yet I have a foreboding that the same fate may fall on my own country." In the manner of a well-bred Roman he recited lines of Homer and wept a little.

For seventeen days the fires blazed over Carthage, then the buildings and walls were razed—a lengthy task, for some of the walls were nearly fifty feet high and over thirty feet broad—and then a plow was driven over the rubble and salt was sown into the furrows. Finally a solemn curse was spoken over the whole city; it forbade any crops to grow or any people to live there under pain of disastrous punishment by the gods. With the destruction of a city that had endured for about seven centuries, the long history of the Punic wars finally came to a close.

Long before the time of Julius Caesar, republican Rome had extended its sway west of the Alps to provide land routes along the Mediterranean coast to its faraway outposts in Spain. A key stronghold along the route was the city of Narbo Martius; the view from a nearby hillside fortress is shown above.

The Romans showed no interest in preserving even the vestiges of Punic culture. The libraries found during the sack of the city were scattered among the tribal princes of the interior; not a single book has survived. Little remains of their temples, their palaces, their bronzes, or their marble statues. Archaeologists must work with potsherds and a few inscriptions and with such reference to Carthaginian customs as survived in Greek histories.

Scipio Aemilianus was a cultured man of great personal distinction who could excuse his part in the destruction of Carthage by saying that he had merely obeyed the orders of the all-powerful Senate. To the end he remained a philhellene, encouraging Polybius to write his long and superbly intelligent history of republican Rome. The tragedy was that Scipio Aemilianus had had to perform the terrible acts that Cato had demanded.

It was a time of tragedies; never had the Romans shown themselves to be so bloodthirsty nor so destructive. The Greeks came out in rebellion, protesting that the promises of Flamininus were not being kept. "You pretend to be friends, but you behave like tyrants," declared the Greek philosopher Critolaus. The rebellion was put down by Lucius Mummius, who won the title of Achaicus by transforming Greece into the Roman province of Achaia. Corinth fought more furiously for her promised freedom than the rest and received the same punishment as Carthage. The walls were razed, the people were massacred or sold into slavery, and whatever was valuable was removed to Rome. For four centuries Corinth had been renowned for her arts; now all the bronze and marble statues were transported to Rome to decorate the temples, the Forum, and the private houses of the senators. To the ships' captains taking the treasure to Rome, Mummius gave the formidable instruction: "If any statue is damaged, it must be replaced by another of equal value."

But the lost statues could never be replaced, and there was little left of Roman *virtus*, by which was meant decency, sobriety, and courage. The dream of an empire founded on trust and fair dealing was going down in the blood of conquest. The march took Roman armies westward around the great bend of the Ligurian coast, past what are now Genoa and Nice, to fight off raiders threatening Rome's long-standing Greek allies established at Massilia (Marseilles) and then in 124 B.C. to strike up the Rhone valley and build outposts against the Gauls. Next they set up a key stronghold at Narbo Martius (Narbonne) to control the coastal route to Spain. To safeguard western sea routes, revolts were put down in Sardinia and colonies were established on Majorca, which had known the Phoenicians and Carthaginians in turn.

In 133 B.C. most of the kingdom of Pergamum, in Asia Minor, was annexed as a new Roman province. In the fastnesses of eastern Europe, battles were fought against the Cimbri and Teutones in 113 B.C. near what is now Ljubljana, in Yugoslavia. Booty and prisoners were paraded through the streets of Rome, and the conquerors were decked out in the robes of Jupiter. Europe and Asia bled. Those who were not killed were treated like cattle.

The Romans too suffered from the wars. A grandson of Scipio Africanus, Tiberius Sempronius Gracchus, pointed to the vast estates of the rich and then to the soldiers who had fought the Roman wars, with no property they could call their own, abandoned by the state to wander aimlessly through the countryside, unemployed, starving, and discontented. "The savage beasts have their particular dens in Italy . . . ," he declared, "but the men who bear arms, and expose their lives for the safety of their country, enjoy in the meantime nothing more in it but the air and light; and having no houses or settlements of their own, are constrained to wander from place to place with their wives and children." Though the Roman soldiers were called the masters of the world, he went on to say, they did not possess one foot of ground which they could claim as their own.

Tiberius Gracchus was known for his bravery in battle and his quiet earnestness of speech. Becoming tribune in 133 B.C., he proposed to revive an old law limiting the size of the great estates, and vastly to reduce the amounts of public land that had fallen into a few private hands and distribute it to the poor. He made no effort to warn the Senate prior to making his speech before the plebeian assembly. As tribune he had, or thought he had, the right to offer bills to the lower house, conveniently forgetting that the Senate had long ago usurped this right, employing its own docile instruments for this purpose. A docile instrument was found. Another tribune appeared in the assembly to veto the bill, but was thrown out. At that moment the social war began that was to sound the knell of republican Rome.

In defiance of the Senate, Tiberius Gracchus appointed a board of three to supervise the breakup of the great estates. The board consisted of Gracchus, his brother, and his father-in-law. The selection was unwise; in the eyes of the senators the board had been constituted illegally and represented only Tiberius Gracchus. No funds were granted to the board, and almost no capital was granted to the new farmers. In the following year Tiberius Gracchus presented himself as a candidate for the tribunate for the second time. When the returns showed that he was winning, the Senate decided to act. The young revolutionary and some three

---

REPUBLICAN GOVERNMENT
(c. 250–81 B.C.)

The long evolution of Rome's republican forms represented a continuing effort to achieve a system of checks and balances not only between lawmakers and officeholders but also between the classes of citizens—the hereditary aristocracy of patricians, the rising mercantile order called the equites, and the mass of plebeians. The result was a complex structure with its chief powers vested in the SENATE: *Membership:* three hundred; *term of office:* life; almost always chosen by censors from among the ex-officeholders, usually of patrician rank; supposedly an advisory body, actually the seat of policymaking, overseeing foreign affairs and military matters, finance, disposition of public lands, appointments, state religion.

POPULAR ASSEMBLIES
COMITIA TRIBUTA: Representative, legislative assembly of all citizens who voted by tribes; elected tribunes and quaestors; enacted laws, conducted minor trials. COMITIA CENTURIATA: Assembly of men of military age from all over Italy; primarily elected consuls, censors, praetors; had final power to declare war and ratify peace.

HIGH PUBLIC OFFICES
CONSULS: *Number:* two; *term of office:* one year; joint supreme magistrates and heads of executive branch; presided over Senate; commanders-in-chief in wartime. CENSORS: Two; eighteen months; usually elected from among former consuls; oversaw census taking; set taxes; assigned citizens to proper class; named senators; supervised public morals. PRAETORS: Six; two years; high judges; empowered in consul's absence to convoke and preside over Senate or assembly. TRIBUNES: Ten; one year; elected by Comitia Tributa to be guardians of rights of plebeians; broad veto power over senators and other officeholders. AEDILES: Four; one year; in effect, mayors of city. QUAESTORS: Eight; annually elected administrative officers; custodians of state treasury. PROCONSULS: Sent to govern provinces after serving term as consul.

hundred of his followers were attacked by hired bravos outside the temple on the Capitoline. All were killed. Tiberius Gracchus was beaten to death with a chair leg.

Eleven years after the death of Tiberius, his younger brother Gaius Sempronius Gracchus was elected tribune, and put forward further measures of land reform. He was a more vehement orator than his brother, and was even more popular. The Senate prepared for the inevitable moment when Gaius Gracchus would have to step down after a year in office. Once more the bravos were thrown at the revolutionaries. Three thousand of Gracchus' followers made a last stand on the Aventine hill. Gaius Gracchus either was killed or committed suicide; his followers were cut down or made prisoners, to be strangled in their cells. The Senate acted toward the reformers as it had acted toward Carthage; it annihilated them. A special law was passed forbidding the wives and children of the dead to put on mourning.

The Senate was supreme, but it was no longer respected amid the growing division of the state. Corrupt, ingrown, and murderous, it pursued its own purposes with no regard for the people. The African king Jugurtha, out to win sole control of Rome's allied state of Numidia, bribed many a senator in order to win support for his aim. Summoned to Rome to reveal their names, he remarked, "Rome is a city for sale, and doomed to perish if it can find a purchaser." Finally there was open war with Numidia; and this struggle, begun in 112 B.C., brought into prominence the two men who were to lead Rome on a new path to dictatorship. One was the hard and rugged Gaius Marius, the son of a farmer from the Volscian mountains, a *novus homo*, or "new man" who rose by his own merits without the patronage of the Senate which he despised. The other was Lucius Cornelius Sulla, a patrician, determined to uphold the senatorial privileges at all costs. A man of moods, dangerously impulsive, he would order a blood bath as calmly as he would read a Greek poem.

Marius and Sulla had been comrades, working closely together during the Jugurthine War. Marius received the credit for bringing it to a victorious end; but Sulla, the capable diplomat, was the one who trapped Jugurtha by inviting him to a conference, guaranteeing his safety, and then placing him under arrest. Jugurtha, chained, graced the triumph of Marius against whom Sulla now plotted revenge.

Both were great generals who served the republic well in war but helped to destroy it in time of peace. Marius fought and destroyed the hordes of barbarian Cimbri and Teutones as they descended from the north; Sulla overcame the armies of Mith-

The social structure of ancient Rome changed profoundly in the fifty years after the Second Punic War ended in 202 B.C. Those who had property became extremely rich: the nobles through provincial land acquisition, and the equites, who formed a middle class, through trade. The wall painting at left is from one of the many luxurious villas built near Pompeii during that period. The relief below depicts landowners collecting rent from peasants; the peasant class was rapidly being displaced by a vast slave population made up of peoples defeated by the Romans. The peasants gathered in the capital where there was free food and entertainment, and formed a poverty-stricken mass which was new to Rome.

TRIER MUSEUM; PHOTO MARBURG

ridates in Greece. The two conflicting parties were bringing on a tragedy in Rome: the one intent on breaking the power of the Senate, the other on maintaining senatorial privilege. Marius, whose military reforms turned the citizens' legions of Rome into professional standing armies, was consul seven times during the last twenty-one years of his life. In 87 B.C., he and his supporters slaughtered the leaders of the Senate and thousands of members of the aristocratic class. Sulla, in turn, after winning battles against partisans of Marius after the latter's death in 86 B.C., resorted to even greater butchery, setting up lists of outlawry that gave his followers the right to kill his and their own enemies at will and take over their properties. Countless numbers perished.

Once in command, Sulla had himself elected to the ancient emergency office of dictator. He held extraordinary powers and dominated Rome in near-regal state. The people, watching him parade through the streets surrounded by his bodyguard, observed that he was preceded by twenty-four lictors—a number perhaps even greater than that which had preceded the ancient kings. His announced scheme was to write new laws that would reorganize the republic. Believing in firm government by established leaders of the upper classes, he strengthened the powers of the Senate and reduced those of the tribunes and the popular assembly; moreover, a man could now become consul only after having served in the Senate for eight years. In this way he would prevent rule by plebeian chieftains (such as Marius) or future autocrats (such as himself). But the Senate was so ineffective, and the best men of Rome in both parties were so decimated, that uncertainty lay ahead. The Senate was in fact only the instrument of the dictator's will. His chief agents, the men who carried out his laws, were ten thousand young and sturdy slaves recruited from the households of the men he had killed, owing allegiance to him and murdering at his pleasure. This brotherhood of assassins acquired the family name of the dictator: they were known as the Cornelii. The forms of republican rule continued, but under a reign of terror.

Sulla himself seemed to revel in it. He ordered the severed heads of many of his enemies to be heaped before him in the Forum and gazed on them with quiet satisfaction. One of his most brilliant lieutenants, Catiline, was sent to murder a nephew of the late Marius; the killing was performed with all the refinements of slow torture. Sulla called himself Felix, meaning that he was the happiest of men and blessed by the gods. Yet the Roman people were not equally blessed. In the wake of Marius and Sulla, other rival military chieftains—Crassus, Pompey, and Caesar—were to arise to put an end to the republic.

127

THE VOICES OF REPUBLICAN ROME

The language of the Romans was, at first, only one of many related tongues spoken by the peoples of Italy. A minor branch of the Indo-European family of languages, it was confined to a small part of the Latin coastal plain. In about 400 B.C. Latin began to spread across the Italian peninsula on the tide of Roman power, gradually drowning out neighboring Italic tongues and slowly evolving from a stiff, archaic dialect into the superbly precise and expressive instrument wielded by Vergil. In southern Italy, in the fourth and third centuries B.C., it encountered Greek —a language that had already produced its major literary masterpieces. The birth of Latin literature postdates this encounter; Roman writing, despite its authentic accomplishments, was never to be wholly free of a debt to Greek models and Greek thought.

The republican or pre-Augustan era was the first of three distinct periods of Roman literary splendor. It opened late in the third century on a frivolous note with the farces of Plautus —a popular playwright who adapted the plots of Greek New Comedy to frame his satirical thrusts at the hypocrisies of his fellow Romans. The era reached its climax and conclusion in the first century B.C. with the work of some of Rome's greatest writers, including a pair of very dissimilar poets, Lucretius and Catullus, and a gifted philosopher-statesman, Marcus Tullius Cicero, the articulate defender of the republican ideal in its dying days. Julius Caesar and his contemporary Cicero belong in that lonely company of men (Marcus Aurelius, Jefferson, Churchill, and a few others) who bridge the gap between political accomplishment and literary excellence. The inspired pragmatism of Caesar, reflected in his commentaries, prevailed in the political sphere and helped to bring down the republic; but ironically the age in which he lived is often remembered as the Ciceronian.

. . . nothing seems to me a nobler ambition than to be able to hold by your eloquence the minds of men, to captivate their wills, to move them to and fro in whatever direction you please.
Cicero, On the Orator

An ancient bust portrays Cicero as a mature, distinguished senator in about 50 B.C.

THE LAUGHTER OF PLAUTUS

Of the surviving voices of Latin literature, the earliest are those of the quarreling fools and hysterical women created by the Umbrian-born comic dramatist Plautus, whose lines were shouted by actors performing outdoors on makeshift wooden stages before noisy audiences. Plautus (c. 250–184 B.C.) seems to have had something in common with Shakespeare, for he borrowed old plots, possibly acted in his own plays, and while satisfying unrefined tastes, displayed enough invention to influence succeeding ages of dramatists. In his Amphitryon, he relies heavily on mistaken identity for his broader comic effects; but in the final act, reproduced here in a modern translation, he achieves a more subtle kind of humor as he comments on the capacity of man to adapt himself to loss of honor when profit appears to be in the offing.

AMPHITRYON, Act V
(*translated by Lionel Casson*)

(*Amphitryon is unconscious, sprawled full length on the ground in front of his house. The thunder and lightning continue for a few moments and then gradually cease. Suddenly the door flies open, and Bromia, Alcmena's maid, her hair disheveled and her clothes in disarray, bursts out. Without noticing Amphitryon, she rushes downstage and addresses the audience.*)

BROMIA (*hysterically*)

My mind has given up the thought that I've any chance to
survive,
My heart's abandoned every hope—I'll never stay alive!
It seems to me that everything—the earth, the air, the sky—
Have all conspired against my life, have willed to see me die.
The strangest things went on in the house! God knows what I
should do!

(*Gasping for breath*)

Oh, god! I'm sick! Some water, please! My end is near, I'm
through!
My head aches so, my hearing's gone, my vision's not what it
should be.
No other woman's this miserable, no other ever *could* be!

(*Stops, gets hold of herself, and resumes much more calmly.*)

It's what Alcmena had happen to her. Once in labor, she prayed
to god.

Then, bang and crash! Thunder and lightning! So sudden, so
near, so hard!
The sound knocked over all of us; we fell in our tracks, struck
dumb.
And then a mighty voice called out, "Alcmena, help has come!
Don't fear! a god from heaven's on hand to shed his favor on
thee."

"And rise, all you," it said to us, "who fell through fear of me."
I rose, since I had fallen too. The lightning gleamed so, I
Was sure our house had caught on fire. Then I heard Alcmena's
cry.

For a moment, horror held me fast—but fear for her won out.
I ran to see what she'd called me for. Amazed, I look about:

She'd given birth to twins, two boys. It was all a mystery,
A birth none saw or had foreseen.

(*Suddenly noticing Amphitryon*)

My god, what's this I see?
Who is the gentleman stretched out here, before our very door!
Some victim of Jove's thunderbolt? By Jove, he looks it, for
He's laid out there as if he's dead. I think I'd better run
And check. Perhaps I know the man.

(*Rushing up to Amphitryon and taking a look; startled*)

My master, Amphitryon!

(*Shouting in his ear*)

Amphitryon!

AMPHITRYON (*groaning*)

I'm dead.

BROMIA

Get up!

AMPHITRYON (*as before*)

A corpse.

BROMIA (*reaching out and taking his hand*)

Here, let me have your hand.

AMPHITRYON (*feebly*)

Who's holding me?

BROMIA

Your Bromia.

(*She hauls mightily and succeeds in pulling him to his feet.*)

AMPHITRYON (*holding his head, his eyes closed; dazedly*)

But *I* don't understand—
That crack from Jove has me numb with fear. I feel as if I died
And have just come back from the underworld.

(*Finally pulling out of his stupor and looking at her curiously*)

But what brings *you* outside?

BROMIA (*nervously*)

The same fear and dread gripped all of us.

(*Pointing to the door; dramatically*)

In there, the house where you dwell,
I saw such a wonder I'm still unnerved.

(*Covering her face, hysterically*)

Amphitryon, it's hell!

AMPHITRYON (*pulling her hands from her face and forcing her to look at him*)

Now answer this: am I your master? Am I Amphitryon?

BROMIA
Of course you are.

AMPHITRYON
No, look again.

BROMIA (*as before*)
Of course you're Amphitryon.

AMPHITRYON (*to the world at large, bitterly*)
The only one of my household here who's preserved her sanity.

BROMIA (*reproachfully*)
No sir, we're all completely sane.

AMPHITRYON (*as before*)
There's one exception—me.
The shameful conduct of my wife has driven *me* insane.

BROMIA (*passionately*)
But you, yourself, will admit you're wrong as soon as I explain! (*Stops for a moment to make sure he is willing to listen, then continues gently*) Yes, you'll realize that your wife is a decent and honorable woman. It will take me only a moment to tell you some things that will prove it beyond any doubt. (*She pauses, then begins again, observing him keenly to note the effect of her words.*) To begin with, Alcmena has just given birth to twins, two boys.

AMPHITRYON (*blankly*) Twins, you say?

BROMIA Twins.

AMPHITRYON (*hopelessly*) God help me!

BROMIA (*impatiently*) Please let me go on—I want to show you that god *is* helping both you and your wife.

AMPHITRYON Go on.

BROMIA (*excitedly*) When her time came, and she went into labor, your wife, as women in childbirth always do, washed her hands, covered her head, and prayed to god to help her. The next second, there was a mighty clap of thunder. At first we all thought your house would come crashing down; the lightning gleamed so, the whole place looked as though it were made of gold.

AMPHITRYON (*savagely*) Will you kindly let me go as soon as you're through having fun with me? (*Shrugs as Bromia gestures helplessly and falls silent*) All right, what happened next?

BROMIA (*resuming excitedly*) During all this, not one of us heard your wife utter a groan or a cry. It was a completely painless delivery.

AMPHITRYON (*grudgingly*) Well, I'm glad to hear that—in spite of all she's done to me.

BROMIA (*impatiently*) Forget all that and just listen to what I'm going to tell you. (*Resuming her excited narrative tone*) When it was all over, she told us to wash the babies down. We started right in. Well, I can't tell you how big and strong the baby was that I was bathing! There wasn't one of us who could pin the diapers and clothes around him.

AMPHITRYON (*scratching his head*) This is an incredible story.

If it's true, my wife certainly received a lot of help from heaven.

BROMIA (*eagerly*) Believe me, what comes next you'll say is even more incredible. (*Resuming her narrative tone*) I had just put him in his cradle when there slithered down through the skylight two serpents with crests, both of them simply enormous. The next minute, there they were, the two of them, with heads raised looking about.

AMPHITRYON (*shuddering*) Oh, my god!

BROMIA (*reassuringly*) Nothing to be afraid about. (*Resuming her narrative tone*) The serpents eyed everyone there. As soon as they spotted the children, they made a rush for them. I pulled the cradles back and steered them away; I was frightened for myself but even more afraid for the babies. The snakes followed after, fiercer than ever. Then that child, the one I had bathed, saw them. He jumped right out of his cradle, went straight for them, and, in a flash, had one gripped in each hand.

AMPHITRYON Incredible! This is a very dangerous deed you've described! Just hearing about it gives me the shudders! What then? Go on?

BROMIA The baby strangled both those serpents. And, while he was doing it, a mighty voice was heard calling to Alcmena—

AMPHITRYON (*interrupting angrily*) Who was the man?

BROMIA Man? It was the lord of men and of gods, almighty Jove! He announced that he had had intercourse with Alcmena in secret and that the child that had killed the snakes was his. (*As an afterthought*) The other, he said was yours.

(*For a full moment Amphitryon stands buried in thought.*)

AMPHITRYON (*suddenly his old vibrant self*) Well, I certainly have no cause for complaint when I'm given the chance to share my goods with Jove. Go inside and have the ritual utensils made ready for me right away. I want to pray hard and long, and beg almighty Jove for peace. And I'll call in Tiresias, the prophet, and ask what he thinks I should do. At the same time I'll tell him how this whole business happened. (*A tremendous clap of thunder is heard.*) What's that? Thunder—but so loud! (*Falling to his knees*) Oh god, help me, please!

VOICE FROM OFF STAGE (*slowly and impressively*) Take heart, Amphitryon. I am here to help you and your family. There is nothing to be afraid of. Prophets, fortune tellers—don't bother with any of them. I will tell you both the future and the past much better than they, for I am Jove.

To begin with, I borrowed your Alcmena's body, slept with her, and conceived a son by her. You too conceived a son, when you left to go to the front. She has brought forth both together, in one birth. The one sprung from my seed will do deeds that will make your name great forever. Go back now to Alcmena and live with her in the harmony you two have always known. She deserves no reproaches; *I* forced her to do what she did. And now I must return to the heavens.

AMPHITRYON I'll do as you command—but I beg you: don't forget your promises. I'll go inside now to my wife, and I won't bother with Tiresias. (*He rises from his knees, walks downstage and addresses the audience.*) And now, ladies and gentlemen, for Jove's sake, a good loud round of applause!

THE ATOMIC WORLD OF LUCRETIUS

One of the greatest masterpieces of Roman writing is the long, apparently unfinished didactic poem entitled De rerum natura (On the Nature of Things). *It is the single surviving work of Lucretius, a philosopher-poet of the early first century* B.C. *about whom very little is known. The six-part poem, composed in hexameters, expounds the doctrine of Epicurus and seeks, not with dry argument but with a vivid description of a material and sensuous world, to banish all fear of death and the supernatural from the heart of man. In Book II, passages of which are rendered here in prose translation, Lucretius elaborates Epicurean "atomic theory" into a remarkably modern view of an infinitely varied, infinitely complex universe composed of constantly moving submicroscopic particles, which he calls "the first-beginnings of things."*

from ON THE NATURE OF THINGS
(translated by Cyril Bailey)

Sweet it is, when on the great sea the winds are buffeting the waters, to gaze from the land on another's great struggles; not because it is pleasure or joy that any one should be distressed, but because it is sweet to perceive from what misfortune you yourself are free. Sweet is it too, to behold great contests of war in full array over the plains, when you have no part in the danger. But nothing is more gladdening than to dwell in the calm high places, firmly embattled on the heights by the teaching of the wise, whence you can look down on others, and see them wandering hither and thither, going astray as they seek the way of life, in strife matching their wits or rival claims of birth, struggling night and day by surpassing effort to rise up to the height of power and gain possession of the world. Ah! miserable minds of men, blind hearts! in what darkness of life, in what great dangers ye spend this little span of years! to think that ye should not see that nature cries aloud for nothing else but that pain may be kept far sundered from the body, and that, withdrawn from care and fear, she may enjoy in mind the sense of pleasure! And so we see that for the body's nature but few things at all are needful, even such as can take away pain. Yea, though pleasantly enough from time to time they can prepare for us in many ways a lap of luxury, yet nature herself feels no loss, if there are not golden images of youths about the halls, grasping fiery torches in their right hands, that light may be supplied to banquets at night, if the house does not glow with silver or gleam with gold, nor do fretted and gilded ceilings re-echo to the lute. And yet, for all this, men lie in friendly groups on the soft grass near some stream of water under the branches of a tall tree, and at no great cost delightfully refresh their bodies, above all when the weather smiles on them, and the season of the year bestrews the green grass with flowers. Nor do fiery fevers more quickly quit the body, if you toss on broidered pictures and blushing purple, than if you must lie on the poor man's plaid. Wherefore since in our body riches are of no profit, nor high birth nor the glories of kingship, for the rest, we must believe that they avail nothing for the mind as well; unless perchance, when you see your legions swarming over the spaces of the Campus, and provoking a mimic war, strengthened with hosts in reserve and forces of cavalry, when you draw them up equipped with arms, all alike eager for the fray, when you see the army wandering far and wide in busy haste, then alarmed by all this the scruples of religion fly in panic from your mind, or that the dread of death leaves your heart empty and free from care. But if we see that these thoughts are mere mirth and mockery, and in very truth the fears of men and the cares that dog them fear not the clash of arms nor the weapons of war, but pass boldly among kings and lords of the world, nor dread the glitter that comes from gold nor the bright sheen of the purple robe, can you doubt that all such power belongs to reason alone, above all when the whole of life is but a struggle in darkness? For even as children tremble and fear everything in blinding darkness, so we sometimes dread in the light things that are no whit more to be feared than what children shudder at in the dark, and imagine will come to pass. This terror then, this darkness of the mind, must needs be scattered not by the rays of the sun and the gleaming shafts of day, but by the outer view and the inner law of nature.

Come now, I will unfold by what movement the creative bodies of matter beget diverse things, and break up those that are begotten, by what force they are constrained to do this, and what velocity is appointed them for moving through the mighty void: do you remember to give your mind to my words. For in very truth matter does not cleave close-packed to itself, since we see each thing grow less, and we perceive all things flow away, as it were, in the long lapse of time, as age withdraws them from our sight: and yet the universe is seen to remain undiminished, inasmuch as all bodies that depart from anything, lessen that from which they pass away, and bless with increase that to which they have come; they constrain the former to grow old and the latter again to flourish, and yet they abide not with it. Thus the sum of things is ever being replenished, and mortals live one and all by give and take. Some races wax and others wane, and in a short space the tribes of living things are changed, and like runners hand on the torch of life.

If you think that the first-beginnings of things can stay still, and by staying still beget new movements in things, you stray very far away from true reasoning. For since they wander through the void, it must needs be that all the first-beginnings of things move on either by their own weight or sometimes by the blow of another. For when quickly, again and again, they have met and clashed together, it comes to pass that they leap asunder at once this way and that; for indeed it is not strange, since they are most hard with solid heavy bodies, and nothing bars them from behind. And the more you perceive all the bodies of matter tossing about, bring it to mind that there is no lowest point in the whole universe, nor have the first-bodies any place where they may come to rest, since I have shown in many words, and it has been proved by true reasoning, that space spreads out without bound or limit, immeasurable towards every quarter everywhere. And since that is certain, no rest, we may be sure, is allowed to the first-bodies moving through the deep void, but rather plied with unceasing, diverse motion, some when they have dashed together leap back at great space apart, others too are thrust but a short way from the blow. And all those which are driven together in more close-packed union and leap back but a little space apart, entangled by their own close-locking shapes, these make the strong roots of rock and the brute bulk of iron and all other things of their kind. Of the rest which wander through the great void, a few leap far apart, and recoil afar with great spaces between; these supply for us thin air and the bright light of the sun. Many, moreover, wander on through the great void, which have been cast back from the unions of things, nor have they anywhere else availed to be taken into them and link their movements. And of this truth, as I am telling it, a likeness and image is ever passing presently before our eyes. For look closely, whenever rays are let in and pour the sun's light through the dark places in houses: for you will see many tiny bodies mingle in many ways all through the empty space right in the light of the rays, and as though in some everlasting strife wage war and battle, struggling troop against troop, nor ever crying a halt, harried with constant meetings and partings; so that you may guess from this what it means that the first-beginnings of things are for ever tossing in the great void. So far as may be, a little thing can give a picture of great things and afford traces of a concept. And for this reason it is the more right for you to give heed to these bodies, which you see jostling in the sun's rays, because such jostlings hint that there are movements of matter too beneath them, secret and unseen. For you will see many particles there stirred by unseen blows change their course and turn back, driven backwards on their path, now this way, now that, in every direction everywhere. You may know that this shifting movement comes to them all from the first-beginnings. For first the first-beginnings of things move of themselves; then those bodies which are formed of a tiny union, and are, as it were,

nearest to the powers of the first-beginnings, are smitten and stirred by their unseen blows, and they in their turn, rouse up bodies a little larger. And so the movement passes upwards from the first-beginnings, and little by little comes forth to our senses, so that those bodies move too, which we can descry in the sun's light; yet it is not clearly seen by what blows they do it.

Herein we need not wonder why it is that, when all the first-beginnings of things are in motion, yet the whole seems to stand wholly at rest, except when anything starts moving with its entire body. For all the nature of the first-bodies lies far away from our senses, below their purview; wherefore, since you cannot reach to look upon them, they must needs steal away their motions from you too; above all, since such things as we can look upon, yet often hide their motions, when withdrawn from us on some distant spot. For often the fleecy flocks cropping the glad pasture on a hill creep on whither each is called and tempted by the grass bejewelled with fresh dew, and the lambs fed full gambol and butt playfully; yet all this seems blurred to us from afar, and to lie like a white mass on a green hill. Moreover, when mighty legions fill the spaces of the plains with their chargings, awaking a mimic warfare, a sheen rises there to heaven and all the earth around gleams with bronze, and beneath a noise is roused by the mighty mass of men as they march, and the hills smitten by their shouts turn back the cries to the stars of the firmament, and the cavalry wheel round and suddenly shake the middle of the plains with their forceful onset, as they scour across them. And yet there is a certain spot on the high hills, whence all seems to be at rest and to lie like a glimmering mass upon the plains.

Now come, next in order learn of what kind are the beginnings of all things and how far differing in form, and how they are made diverse with many kinds of shapes; not that but a few are endowed with a like form, but that they are not all alike the same one with another. Nor need we wonder; for since there is so great a store of them, that neither have they any limit, as I have shown, nor any sum, it must needs be, we may be sure, that they are not all of equal bulk nor possessed of the same shape. Moreover, the race of men, and the dumb shoals of scaly creatures which swim the seas, and the glad herds and wild beasts, and the diverse birds, which throng the gladdening watering-places all around the riverbanks and springs and pools, and those which flit about and people the distant forests; of these go and take any single one you will from among its kind, yet you will find that they are different in shape one from another. Nor in any other way could the offspring know its mother, or the mother her offspring; yet we see that they can, and that they are clearly not less known to one another than men. For often before the sculptured shrines of the gods a calf has fallen, slaughtered hard by the altars smoking with incense, breathing out from its breast the hot tide of blood. But the mother bereft wanders over the green glades and seeks on the ground for the footprints marked by those cloven hoofs, scanning every spot with her eyes, if only she might anywhere catch sight of her lost young, and stopping fills the leafy grove with her lament: again and again she comes back to the stall, stabbed to the heart with yearning for her lost calf, nor can the tender willows and the grass refreshed with dew and the loved streams, gliding level with their banks, bring gladness to her mind and turn aside the sudden pang of care, nor yet can the shapes of other calves among the glad pastures turn her mind to new thoughts or ease it of its care: so eagerly does she seek in vain for something she knows as her own. Moreover, the tender kids with their trembling cries know their horned dams and the butting lambs the flocks of bleating sheep: so surely, as their nature needs, do they run back always each to its own udder of milk. Lastly, take any kind of corn, you will not find that every grain is like its fellows, each in its several kind, but that there runs through all some difference between their forms. And in like manner we see the race of shells painting the lap of earth, where with its gentle waves the sea beats on the thirsty sand of the winding shore. Wherefore again and again in the same way it must needs be, since the first-beginnings of things are made by nature and not fashioned by hand to the fixed form of one pattern, that some of them fly about with shapes unlike one another.

It is very easy by reasoning of the mind for us to read the riddle why the fire of lightning is far more piercing than is our fire rising from pine-torches on earth. For you might say that the heavenly fire of lightning is made more subtle and of smaller shapes, and so passes through holes which our fire rising from logs and born of the pine-torch cannot pass. Again light passes through horn-lanterns, but the rain is spewed back. Why? unless it be that those bodies of light are smaller than those of which the quickening liquid of water is made.

And so, we are all sprung from heavenly seed; there is the one father of us all, from whom when live-giving earth, the mother, has taken within her the watery drops of moisture, teeming she brings forth the goodly crops and the glad trees and the race of men; she brings forth too all the tribes of the wild beasts, when she furnishes the food, on which all feed their bodies and pass a pleasant life and propagate their offspring; wherefore rightly has she won the name of mother. Even so, what once sprung from earth, sinks back into the earth, and what was sent down from the coasts of the sky, returns again, and the regions of heaven receive it. Nor does death so destroy things as to put an end to the bodies of matter, but only scatters their union. Then she joins anew one with others, and brings it to pass that all things thus alter their forms, and change their colours, and receive sensations, and in an instant of time yield them up again, so that you may know that it matters with what others the first-beginnings of things are bound up and in what position and what motions they mutually give and receive, and may not think that what we see floating on the surface of things or at times coming to birth, and on a sudden passing away, can abide in the possession of eternal first-bodies. Nay, indeed, even in my verses it is of moment with what others and in what order each letter is placed. For the same letters signify sky, sea, earth, rivers, sun, the same too crops, trees, living creatures; if not all, yet by far the greater part, are alike, but it is by position that things sound different. So in things themselves likewise when meetings, motions, order, position, shapes are changed, things too are bound to be changed.

Now turn your mind, I pray, to a true reasoning. For a truth wondrously new is struggling to fall upon your ears, and a new face of things to reveal itself. Yet neither is anything so easy, but that at first it is more difficult to believe, and likewise nothing is so great or so marvellous but that little by little all decrease their wonder at it. First of all the bright clear colour of the sky, and all it holds within it, the stars that wander here and there, and the moon and the sheen of the sun with its brilliant light; all these, if now they had come to being for the first time for mortals, if all unforeseen they were in a moment placed before their eyes, what story could be told more marvellous than these things, or what that the nations would less dare to believe beforehand? Nothing, I trow: so worthy of wonder would this sight have been. Yet think how no one now, wearied with satiety of seeing, deigns to gaze up at the shining quarters of the sky! Wherefore cease to spew out reason from your mind, struck with terror at mere newness, but rather with eager judgment weigh things, and, if you see them true, lift your hands and yield, or, if it is false, gird yourself to battle. For our mind now seeks to reason, since the sum of space is boundless out beyond the walls of this world, what there is far out there, whither the spirit desires always to look forward, and whither the unfettered projection of our mind flies on unchecked.

First of all, we find that in every direction everywhere, and on either side, above and below, through all the universe, there is no limit, as I have shown, and indeed the truth cries out for itself and the nature of the deep shines clear. Now in no way must we think it likely, since towards every side is infinite empty space, and seeds in unnumbered numbers in the deep universe fly about in many ways driven on in everlasting motion, that this one world and sky was brought to birth, but that beyond it all those bodies of matter do naught; above all, since this world was so made by nature, as the seeds of things themselves of their own accord, jostling from time to time, were driven together in many ways, rashly, idly, and in vain, and at last those united, which suddenly cast together, might become ever and anon the beginnings of great things, of earth and sea and sky, and the race of living things. Wherefore, again and again, you must needs confess that there are here and there other gatherings of matter, such as is this, which the ether holds in its greedy grip.

Moreover, when there is much matter ready to hand, when space is there, and no thing, no cause delays, things must, we may be sure, be carried on and completed. As it is, if there is so great a store of seeds as the whole life of living things could not number, and if the same force and nature abides which could throw together the seeds of things, each into their place in like manner as they are thrown together here, it must needs be that you confess that there are other worlds in other regions, and diverse races of men and tribes of wild beasts.

CATULLUS, THE VOICE OF PASSION

The poet Gaius Valerius Catullus was hardly more than thirty when he died in about 54 B.C. Working in the tradition of the Hellenic poets of Alexandria, but with great originality, he produced lyric poems and epigrams as self-revealing and as biting as any in Roman literature. A wellborn gentleman from Verona, Catullus lived the life of a playboy in Rome, where he formed a liaison with Clodia, the wife of a consul-elect and one of the more spectacular femmes fatales of her era. That love affair and its painful aftermath were the fuel that gave substance to many of his most ecstatic and sardonic verses. These poems (in which the name Lesbia cloaks the identity of Clodia) form the greater part of the selection on this and the following two pages.

LXXXV (translated by Horace Gregory)

I hate and love.
    And if you ask me why,
I have no answer, but I discern,
can feel, my senses rooted in eternal torture.

XI (translated by Gilbert Highet)

You, my two old friends, who remain my comrades
whether I may journey to furthest India,
where the sea-beach booms to the pounding monsoon's
    thunderous combers,
or among Hyrcanians, supple Arabs,
fierce Sacae, or dangerous Parthian bowmen,
or to where seven mouths of the Nile, debouching,
    darken the azure,
or perhaps may travel the Alpine passes
towards the new-won triumphs of mighty Caesar,
Rhine, the Gauls' frontier, and the terrifying
    outermost British,
you whom I know willing wherever heaven
sends me forth, to share my adventures with me,
take for me these words to my girl, a message
    short and unpleasant.
Give her my good-bye, her and all her lovers,
whom she hugs so close to her in their hundreds,
loving not one, yet with her constant lusting
    leaving their loins limp.
Gone is all my love, which she once respected—
murdered through her guilt, as a flower blooming
out upon the edge of the meadow, falls when
    touched by the ploughshare.

LXXII (translated by Eric A. Havelock)

Once you would say to me: "Your heart has found me
    And yours alone.
I would not have the arms of Jove around me
    More than your own."
Saying it, you became no more the fashion
    Of cheap desire,
But wife and child and home, loved with the passion
    Of life-long fire.

I know you now. Yet my soul goes on burning,
    As burn it must,
When you and all I gave to you are turning
    To death and dust.
Strange, do you say? How strange that love should cherish
    Light that is gone!
That every kindly thought of you should perish,
    Yet love last on.

CI (translated by Robert Fitzgerald)

By strangers' coasts and waters, many days at sea,
    I came here for the rites of your unworlding,
Bringing for you, the dead, these last gifts of the living,
    And my words—vain sounds for the man of dust.
        Alas, my brother,
You have been taken from me. You have been taken from me,
    By cold Chance turned a shadow, and my pain.

Here are the foods of the old ceremony, appointed
    Long ago for the starvelings under earth:
Take them; your brother's tears have made them wet; and take
    Into eternity my hail and my farewell.

LI (*translated by Lord Byron*)

Equal to Jove that youth must be—
Greater than Jove he seems to me—
Who, free from Jealousy's alarms,
Securely views thy matchless charms.
The cheek, which ever dimpling glows,
That mouth, from whence such music flows,
To him, alike, are always known,
Reserved for him, and him alone.
Ah! Lesbia, though 'tis death to me,
I cannot choose but look on thee;
But, at the sight, my senses fly;
I needs must gaze, but, gazing, die;
Whilst trembling with a thousand fears,
Parched to the throat my tongue adheres,
My pulse beats quick, my breath heaves short,
My limbs deny their slight support,
Cold dews my pallid face o'erspread,
With deadly languor droops my head,
My ears with tingling echoes ring,
And life itself is on the wing;
My eyes refuse the cheering light,
Their orbs are veiled in starless night;
Such pangs my nature sinks beneath,
And feels a temporary death.

VIII (*translated by Horace Gregory*)

Poor damned Catullus, here's no time for nonsense,
open your eyes, O idiot, innocent boy, look at what has happened:
once there were sunlit days when you followed after
where ever a girl would go, she loved with greater
love than any woman knew.
Then you took your pleasure
and the girl was not unwilling. Those were the bright days, gone;
now she's no longer yielding; you must be, poor idiot,
more like a man! not running after
her your mind all tears; stand firm, insensitive.
Say with a smile, voice steady, "Good-bye, my girl," Catullus
strong and manly no longer follows you, nor comes when you are
calling
him at night and you shall need him.
You whore! Where's your man to cling to, who will praise your
beauty,
where's the man that you love and who will call you his,
and when you fall to kissing, whose lips will you devour?
But always, your Catullus will be as firm as rock is.

LXX (*translated by Robinson Ellis*)

Saith my lady to me, no man shall wed me, but only
    Thou; no other if e'en Jove should approach me to woo;
Yea; but a woman's words, when a lover fondly desireth,
    Limn them on ebbing floods, write on a wintry gale.

IN SEARCH OF CATULLUS

The task of recapturing in English the essence of a poem by Catullus has always been a most difficult one for translators. Almost always something of the original—its literal meaning, its economy of form, or its emotional power—must be sacrificed. Reproduced below, at left, is one of the most famous of his poems. To its right is a literal prose translation; on the opposite page are two verse renditions—one by a seventeenth-century Englishman, the other by a present-day American—that show what different results may be achieved by poets of different eras and dispositions.

Poem V

Vivamus, mea Lesbia, atque amemus,
rumoresque senum severiorum
omnes unius aestimemus assis.
soles occidere et redire possunt:
nobis cum semel occidit brevis lux,
nox est perpetua una dormienda.
da mi basia mille, deinde centum,
dein mille altera, dein secunda centum,
deinde usque altera mille, deinde centum.
dein, cum milia multa fecerimus,
conturbabimus illa, ne sciamus,
aut nequis malus invidere possit,
cum tantum sciat esse basiorum.

(*translated by Leonard C. Smithers*)

Let us live, my Lesbia, and let us love, and count all the mumblings of sour age at a penny's fee. Suns set can rise again: we when once our brief light has set must sleep through a perpetual night. Give me of kisses a thousand, and then a hundred, then another thousand, then a second hundred, then another thousand without resting, then a hundred. Then, when we have made many thousands, we will confuse the count lest we know the numbering, so that no wretch may be able to envy us through knowledge of our kisses' number.

LXXVI (*translated by William Walsh*)

Is there a pious pleasure that proceeds
From contemplation of our virtuous deeds?
That all mean sordid actions we despise,
And scorn to gain a throne by cheats and lies?
Thyrsis, thou hast sure blessings laid in store,
From thy just dealing in this curst amour:
What honour can in words or deeds be shewn,
Which to the fair thou hast not said and done?
On her false heart they all are thrown away;
She only swears, more eas'ly to betray.
Ye Powers! that know the many vows she broke,
Free my just soul from this unequal yoke!
My love boils up, and, like a raging flood,
Runs through my veins, and taints my vital blood.
I do not vainly beg she may grow chaste,
Or with an equal passion burn at last:
The one she cannot practise, though she would:
And I contemn the other, though she should:
Nor ask I vengeance on the perjur'd jilt;
'Tis punishment enough to have her guilt.
I beg but balsam for my bleeding breast,
Cure for my wounds, and from my labours rest.

XLVI (*translated by William A. Aiken*)

How rapidly the iron gales of March
are melted in the crucible of spring!
Away, Catullus! Swift as swallow, fly
from breathless summer when the sun will parch
Nicaea's fields; fly without faltering
to where in fame and foam great seaside cities lie.

To yearning heart of wanderer give rein
with fervid foot; so bid a long farewell
to that fond band of friends, who once left home
together, but who must return again
from separate paths, through mottled scenes to swell
the ranks that sway along the spidered roads to Rome.

XCII (*translated by Jonathan Swift*)

Lesbia for ever on me rails,
To talk of me, she never fails,
Now, hang me, but for all her art
I find that I have gained her heart.
My proof is this: I plainly see
The case is just the same with me;
I curse her every hour sincerely,
Yet, hang me, but I love her dearly.

(*translated by Richard Crashaw*)

Come and let us live my Deare,
Let us love and never feare,
What the sowrest Fathers say:
Brightest *Sol* that dyes to day
Lives againe as blith to morrow,
But if we darke sons of sorrow
Set; ô then, how long a Night
Shuts the Eyes of our short light!
Then let amorous kisses dwell
On our lips, begin and tell
A Thousand, and a Hundred, score
An Hundred, and a Thousand more,
Till another Thousand smother
That, and that wipe of another.
Thus at last when we have numbred
Many a Thousand, many a Hundred;
Wee'l confound the reckoning quite,
And lose our selves in wild delight:
While our joyes so multiply,
As shall mocke the envious eye.

(*translated by Horace Gregory*)

Come, Lesbia, let us live and love,
nor give a damn what sour old men say.
The sun that sets may rise again
but when our light has sunk into the earth,
it is gone forever.
        Give me a thousand kisses,
then a hundred, another thousand,
another hundred
        and in one breath
still kiss another thousand,
another hundred.
        O then with lips and bodies joined
many deep thousands;
    confuse
their number,
        so that poor fools and cuckolds (envious
even now) shall never
learn our wealth and curse us
with their
evil eyes.

CICERO AND THE
REPUBLICAN CONSCIENCE

Latin prose comes of age with Cicero, the orator, philosopher, and politician, who in retrospect seems to dominate Roman letters in the middle of the first century B.C. *So much of his work was preserved and so much of it read in later ages that some of his admirers have gone so far as to call the Renaissance a renaissance of Cicero and to cast this ancient Roman as the father of the democratic constitutions under which we live today.*

To his contemporaries Cicero was a master orator whose arguments were always respected but seldom decisive. Somewhat irresolute in politics, he was never to repeat the glory of his one year as consul (63 B.C.*), but he ended his career with a gallant gesture of defiance against the blind forces that were destroying his beloved republic. In the fourteen* Philippics, *published in 44 and 43* B.C., *he brought his rhetorical gifts to bear against Marcus Antonius (Mark Antony), who was contending for power with Octavian, the nephew of the slain Julius Caesar. In late 43, when a temporary truce between these military strongmen left their critics unprotected, Cicero was one of the first to be tracked down and killed by Antony's agents. The peroration, or summation, of the* Second Philippic *is considered an extraordinary example of political argument.*

from the SECOND PHILIPPIC
(*translated by Norman J. DeWitt*)

Therefore, call before your mind, Marcus Antonius, that glorious day on which you abolished the dictatorship; keep before your eyes the joy of the Senate and the Roman people, compare it with this monstrous marketing which you and your friends have conducted; then you will understand how great is the gulf between gain and glory. But truly, just as certain people, under the effects of some illness and because of some numbness of the senses, do not appreciate the pleasant flavors of their food, so lustful men, greedy, criminally inclined, do not have the capacity to enjoy the taste of true fame. But if the prospect of true fame cannot lure you to right action, cannot fear, either, distract you from conduct of the foulest sort? You do not fear the courts of law. If this is because of your innocence, I compliment you; but if it is because your position rests on force, don't you understand what a man really ought to fear when his lack of fear of the courts is on that basis? But if you are not afraid of brave men and fine citizens because they are kept from your person by an armed bodyguard, your own partisans, believe me, will not put up with you very long. More-

over, what kind of a life is it to be afraid of something from your own followers day and night? Unless, of course, you have men bound to you by stronger obligations than Caesar had in the case of some of these by whom he was killed, or unless you are to be compared to him in any respect. In him there was a great mind, a powerful brain, logical ability, a tenacious memory, literary talent, capacity for taking pains, power of reflection, application; he had accomplished feats in war, however disastrous to the constitution, that were still great; having planned for many years for absolute rule, he accomplished what he had in mind through great exertion and at great hazards; by public shows, by public works, by bonuses to veterans, by public feasts, he used to woo popularity with the unlettered populace; he had bound his own followers to his side by gifts, his opponents by a show of forgiveness—in short, he had already brought to a free community the habits of slavery, partly out of fear, partly out of passivity.

I can compare you with him on the basis of your passion for power, but in other respects you are not in any way comparable. But out of the many evils which he has branded upon the republic, there has arisen this much good: he has taught the people of Rome how far to trust each man, to whom they may entrust themselves, and against whom they should be on guard. Don't you reflect upon these troubles and don't you perceive that it is enough for resolute men to have learned how fair an enterprise it is, how welcome an achievement, how glorious in name, it is to strike down a tyrant? Or do you suppose that when men would not put up with Caesar, they will put up with you? Believe me, they will compete with one another hereafter as they run to do this work, and no opportunity that is slow to come will be waited for.

Come back to your senses sometime, I beg of you; think of those from whom you have sprung, not those with whom you live. Deal with me as you will, but come back into the good graces of the republic. But take thought for your own future; I will publish my own manifesto. In my youth I defended the republic; I shall not desert it in my age; I scorned the swords of Catiline; I shall not be in dread of yours. What is more, I would cheerfully offer my body if by my death the state can recover its liberty, so that at long last the pangs of the Roman people may bring to birth that with which it has so long been in labor. Indeed, if in this very temple some twenty years ago I said that death could not come out of due season to a man who had been consul, how much more truly do I say that it cannot come out of season to an old man! Yes, to me, gentlemen of the Senate, today death is even something to be wished for, now that the honors I have won and the services I have performed are things of the past. Two things only do I pray for: one, that at my death I may leave the Roman people free—no greater boon than this could be given me by the immortal gods; second, that the outcome of life may be for each man as each man deserves of the republic.

The treatise De officiis (On Duty) *is another product of Cicero's late years. It is addressed to his only son Marcus, who thereby received the perhaps unsolicited gift of a set of moral principles to live by. Whatever its effect on Marcus,* On Duty *was eventually to become one of the most influential and most quoted of Cicero's works. It stands as a masterly summing up of the philosophies that supported Cicero's Stoicism and serves as an excellent foundation on which to build a political ethic. The following excerpt deals with the obligation to seek public office.*

from ON DUTY
(*translated by Paul MacKendrick*)

Now there are many at present, and there have been many in the past, who in pursuit of this peace of mind that I have been talking about have withdrawn from affairs of state and fled to the refuge of retirement, among them the best-known and by far the most distinguished philosophers and numbers of men of high seriousness who have not been able to stand the conduct either of the people or of princes, and have lived in the country enjoying their estates. Their aim was like that of kings: to lack nothing, to obey no one, to live independently, the essence of independence being to live as you please.

Therefore, though men eager for power have this desire for independence in common with these men of leisure whom I have mentioned, the former think they can acquire independence by having great wealth, the latter by being satisfied with the little they have. On this subject we ought not to scorn completely the opinion of either side, but the life of the men of leisure is easier, safer, and less annoying or overbearing toward others, while the life of those who adapt themselves to public affairs and the carrying on of important business is more profitable to the human race and better calculated to attain fame and distinction.

Therefore we ought perhaps to yield a point to those who do not take part in affairs of state, provided they devote their extraordinary talent to philosophy, and to those who have withdrawn from public affairs because of the impediment of poor health or some other quite serious reason, since such men hand over to others both their right to office and their credit for holding it. But if those who have no such motive allege that they despise the power and titles that the majority admire, in my opinion their attitude deserves not only no credit, but even positive condemnation. Insofar as they despise fame and think it nothing worth, it is hard not to approve of them, but the ground of my criticism is that they seem to regard the trouble and inconvenience of political life in general, and defeat and failure at the polls in particular, as a disgrace of some kind, and beneath their dignity. For some people, when things go wrong, are not consistent: they condemn pleasure with the utmost strictures, but are too weak in the face of pain; quite inconsistently, they are careless of fame but crushed by gossip.

But those to whom nature has granted what it takes for a public career ought to cast aside all hesitation, run for office, and administer the government, for there is no other way for the city to be ruled or a man's magnanimity to be made manifest. Men embarking on public careers no less than philosophers, and perhaps even more, must cultivate magnificence and that scorn of human vicissitudes which I talk about so often, as well as peace of mind and freedom from worry, at least if they are going to live without anxiety and in a dignified and consistent way. This is easier for the philosophers, since there are fewer things in their lives open to the blows of fortune, since their needs are less, and since if any misfortune befalls them, their fall cannot be so heavy. Therefore not without reason greater emotions of the soul are aroused in public men than in those who lead lives of retirement, which is all the more reason that the former must practice magnanimity and free themselves from anxiety. Moreover, a man who embarks upon a public career should be careful not to consider merely how honorable an action is, but also whether he has an opportunity of carrying it out; and in this connection he must take care not to let laziness lead him to premature despair, nor eagerness to overconfidence. Finally, before you tackle a job of any kind, you must prepare yourself for it diligently.

THE LETTERS OF CICERO

The image of Cicero the man—with his vanity and pettiness as much in evidence as his wit and wisdom—appears most clearly in the pages of his voluminous correspondence. (Surprisingly an age within which Lucretius disappeared with hardly a trace preserved for posterity about eight hundred of Cicero's letters.) Some of the most candid of these messages were addressed to Atticus, a friend from student days who had settled into a life of commerce and cultured ease in faraway Athens. Requiring no elaborate flattery and representing no political threat, Atticus was obviously one of the few people to whom Cicero could vouchsafe his innermost thoughts and his most honest reports of the events taking place in Rome. These missives are among the most valuable historical documents of the late republican era.

In one of the earliest of the surviving letters, the forty-one-year-old Cicero informally describes the Roman political scene as he speculates about his own chances as a consular candidate. His judgment was fairly accurate. Mark Antony's uncle, Lucius Julius Caesar, did in fact become consul in 64 B.C. and Cicero won his consulship for 63. Catiline did not win and later conspired unsuccessfully to overthrow the republic. Cicero, as consul, exposed him before the Senate and the public in four famous orations, thus achieving the high-water mark of his public career.

CICERO TO ATTICUS, *July,* 65 B.C.
(translated by Arthur Patch McKinlay)

You are eager to know how my candidacy is coming on. As far as I can make out, the situation is this: The only one as yet to come out openly is Publius Galba. He gets an outright, old-fashioned *no*. Gossip has it that his premature announcement has made capital for me. For most persons in denying him declare themselves as my supporters; and so my expectations are aroused somewhat as the rumor gets around that my friends are in the majority. I shall probably start my canvass at the election for tribune, July seventeenth. My competitors who seem most certain of running are Galba, Antonius, and Cornificius. At this news, no doubt, you have either smiled or groaned. It will be enough to make you tear your hair out to hear that in some quarters Caesonius is regarded as likely to run. Aquilius will hardly be a candidate, for he has issued a denial in which he pleads as excuses ill health and his position in the courts. Catiline is sure to compete unless in his coming trial for embezzlement the jury shall decide that the sun does not shine at midday. As for Aufidius and Palicanus, I fancy you will hardly wait for me to write.

Of the candidates for this year's election, Caesar (Mark Antony's uncle) seems sure of winning. According to report, the race for the other seat will be between Thermus and Silanus. They have so few friends and are so little known that I imagine that Curius could be brought in as a dark horse. No one, however, thinks so but me. It seems to suit my interest best that Thermus should be elected, for since he has gained some prominence as commissioner for the repair of the Flaminian Way, there is none of the present candidates who if left over till next year would be a more formidable rival. Such in brief is about the way I am able to size up the political situation thus far.

Early in 49 B.C. Gaius Julius Caesar crossed the Rubicon and marched on Rome with his legions, in direct defiance of the Senate. His rival Pompey withdrew to Brundisium in southern Italy, from which place he later sailed to Greece in search of the support of the eastern provinces. There was soon to be civil war between the two surviving partners of the First Triumvirate. The two letters that follow show Cicero in the depths of despair. He had seen the breakdown of republican government and was witnessing the retreat of Pompey, who in Cicero's eyes was the less objectionable of the two autocrats who could fill the vacuum. The first letter is a diatribe against Pompey (who hardly merited this much criticism, since he had little choice but to abandon Italy). In the second letter Cicero becomes a Hamlet, seeking relief from his preoccupation with painful alternatives by considering the larger philosophical questions that they imply.

CICERO TO ATTICUS, *February* 24, 49 B.C.
(translated by E. O. Winstedt)

What disgrace, and therefore what misery! For I feel disgrace to be the crown of misery, or indeed the only real misery. Pompey treated Caesar as his protégé, began suddenly to fear him, declined terms of peace, made no preparation for war, quitted Rome, lost Picenum by his own fault, got himself blocked in Apulia, went off to Greece without a word, leaving us in ignorance of a plan so important and unusual. Then all of a sudden Domitius' letter to Pompey and Pompey's letter to the consuls. It seemed to me that the Right had flashed upon his gaze, and that he, the old heroic Pompey, cried:

> *What subtle craft they will, let them devise,*
> *And work their wiliest in my despite.*
> *The right is on my side.*

However Pompey bids a long farewell to honour and away for Brundisium. They say that Domitius and those with him surrendered on receipt of the news. What a doleful business! Grief prevents me writing more. I await a letter from you.

Though now I rest only so long as I am writing to you or reading your letters, still I am in want of subject matter, and feel sure that you are in the same position, for the present crisis debars us from the free and easy topics of friendly correspondence, and the topics connected with the present crisis we have already exhausted. However, not to succumb entirely to low spirits, I have taken for myself certain theses, so to speak, which deal with *la haute politique* and are applicable to the present crisis, so that I may keep myself from querulous thoughts and may practise the subject. Here are some:

Whether one should remain in one's country, even under a tyranny. Whether any means are lawful to abolish a tyranny, even if they endanger the existence of the State. Whether one ought to take care that one who tries to abolish it may not rise too high himself. Whether one ought to assist one's country, when under a tyranny, by seizing opportunities and by argument rather than by war. Whether one is doing one's duty to the State, if one retires to some other place and there remains inactive, when there is a tyranny; or whether one ought to run every risk for liberty. Whether one ought to invade the country and besiege one's native town, when it is under a tyranny. Whether one ought to enrol oneself in the ranks of the loyalists, even if one does not approve of war as a means of abolishing tyranny. Whether one ought in political matters to share the dangers of one's benefactors and friends, even if one does not believe their general policy to be wise. Whether one who has done good service for his country, and by it has won ill-treatment and envy, should voluntarily put himself into danger for that country, or may at length take thought for himself and his dear ones and avoid struggles against the powers that be.

By employing myself with such questions and discussing the pros and cons in Greek and Latin, I divert my thoughts a little from my troubles and at the same time consider a subject which is very pertinent. But I fear you may find me a nuisance. For, if the bearer makes proper headway, it will reach you on the very day you have your attack of ague.

Shortly after composing the reflective letter that appears above, Cicero directed a message to Caesar, one of many that are known to have passed between the two men. By offering himself as peacemaker, he sought to avoid a commitment to Caesar's cause. A week later, in a face-to-face meeting with the future dictator, he reiterated his refusal of support. In the following month Caesar, who was in the process of eliminating Pompey's allies in Spain, wrote to Cicero, hoping by this time for nothing more than the latter's neutrality. Despite professions of friendship, these prominent Romans were in fact political enemies bound by little more than a mutual respect for each other's abilities. Caesar's letter is typically the more terse and direct of the two.

CICERO TO CAESAR, *March 19, 49 B.C.*
(*translated by Michael Grant*)

When I read your letter—passed to me by our friend Furnius —in which you requested me to come near Rome, it did not surprise me that you wanted to utilize my 'advice and position'. But I asked myself what you meant by also referring to my 'influence' and 'support'. However, my hopes—and I based them on your outstanding and admirable statesmanship—made me conclude that what you aimed at was peace, and agreement and harmony among Romans: and for that purpose I felt that both my character and my background suited me well.

If I am right in my interpretation, and if you are at all disposed to protect our friend Pompey and reconcile him to yourself and the state, you will certainly find no one better adapted to that aim than myself. In speaking both to him and to the Senate I have always advocated peace ever since I first had the opportunity of doing so; and I have taken no part in the hostilities from their outset. My considered opinion was that the war involved an infringement of your rights in view of the opposition by unfriendly and envious persons to a distinction the Roman people had conferred on you. But in just the same way as at that time I upheld your rightful position myself and also urged everyone else to help you, so now I am deeply concerned for the rightful position of Pompey.

A good many years have passed since I first chose you and him as the men whom, above all others, I proposed to support and have as my friends—as I do. So I ask you, indeed I pray and entreat you with all urgency, to spare some time—among your many grave cares—to consider this problem: how, by virtue of your kindness, can I best be enabled to behave decently, gratefully, and dutifully to Pompey, so as not to be oblivious of his great kindness towards myself? If this was a matter relating to myself alone, I should still hope that you would grant my request. However, I suggest that your honour and the national interest are also at stake; and what they demand is that I, who am a friend of peace and of you both, should receive every protection from you in my efforts to achieve a reconciliation between yourself and Pompey, and peace for the people of Rome.

I thanked you on another occasion for saving Lentulus, as he had saved me; and now, when I read the truly thankful letter in which he told me of your generosity and kindness, I feel that in rescuing him you rescued me at the same time. If you appreciate the reasons why I am under a grateful obligation to him, I beg you to give me the opportunity of fulfilling my obligation to Pompey as well.

CAESAR TO CICERO, *April 16, 49 B.C.*
(*translated by Michael Grant*)

Although I was convinced that you would take no rash or ill-judged action, nevertheless my anxiety about what people are saying has impelled me to write to you and urge, in the name of our friendship, that you should not make any move, now that things have gone my way, which you did not see fit to make while matters were undecided. For, everything having manifestly turned out to our advantage and the disadvantage of the other side, you will have seriously damaged the good relations between our two selves—as well as acting against your own interests—if you display resistance to the trend of events. It would then be evident that your action resulted not from support of a cause, since the cause is the same as it was when you decided to hold aloof, but from your objection to something that I have done. And that would be the severest blow you could inflict on me.

Our friendship entitles me to ask you not to do it. Besides, what could be more appropriate for a man of peace and integrity, and a good citizen, than to keep out of civil disturbance? There were many who felt that to be so, but were prevented from acting as they wished because of the dangers that would have been involved. Weigh up the evidence provided by my career and by your own assessment of our friendly relations, and you will find abstention from the quarrel the safest and most honourable course.

The warning implied in Caesar's letter did not prevent Cicero from joining Pompey's forces in Thessaly. After Pompey's defeat, the dictator drew from Cicero a grudging approval of his regime.

Late in 45 B.C. Cicero entertained Caesar in one of his country villas. One can hardly miss the sense of awe that creeps into his wry description of the event in a letter to Atticus (right). In three months Caesar was murdered. Cicero, though not involved in the conspiracy, had nothing but praise for the assassins. To them he owed his last brief chance to dream of a restored republic in which his voice would no longer be drowned out by the din of clashing armies and marching bodyguards.

CAESAR, AUTHOR AND ENGINEER

from THE GALLIC WAR
(translated by H. J. Edwards)

The Meuse flows from the range of the Vosges, in the territory of the Lingones, and, receiving from the Rhine a certain tributary called the Waal, forms the island of the Batavi; then, no more than eighty miles from the Ocean, it flows into the Rhine. The Rhine rises in the land of the Lepontii, who inhabit the Alps; in a long, swift course it runs through the territories of the Nantuates, Helvetii, Sequani, Mediomatrices, Triboci, and Treveri, and on its approach to the Ocean divides into several streams, forming many large islands (a great number of which are inhabited by fierce barbaric tribes, believed in some instances to live on fish and birds' eggs); then by many mouths it flows into the Ocean.

When Caesar was no more than twelve miles away from the enemy, the deputies returned to him as agreed: they met him on the march, and besought him earnestly not to advance further. When their request was not granted, they asked him to send forward to the cavalry in advance of his column and to prevent them from engaging, and to grant themselves an opportunity of sending deputies into the land of the Ubii. They put forward the hope that, if the chiefs and the senate of the Ubii pledged their faith on oath, they (the Germans) would accept the terms which Caesar offered; and they asked him to give them an interval of three days to settle these affairs. Caesar supposed that all these pleas had the same object as before, to secure by a three days' interval the return of their absent cavalry; however, he said that on that day he would advance no further than four miles, in order to get water. He instructed them to meet him there next day with as large a number as they could, in order that he might take cognisance of their demands. Meanwhile he sent instructions to the commanders who had gone forward with all the cavalry not to provoke the enemy to an engagement, and, if provoked themselves, to hold their ground until he himself with the army had come up nearer.

The enemy had no more than eight hundred cavalry, for the party which was gone across the Meuse to get corn was not yet returned. Our own men, five thousand strong, had nothing to fear, for the deputies of the Germans had left Caesar but a short while before, having asked for a truce that day. However, directly they saw our cavalry, the enemy charged, and speedily threw our men into confusion. When our men turned to resist, the enemy, according to their custom, dismounted, and, by stabbing our horses and bringing down many of our troopers to the ground, they put the rest to rout, and indeed drove them in such panic that they did not desist from flight until they were come in sight of our column. In that engagement were slain seventy-four of our cavalry, and among them the gallant Piso of Aquitania,

(translated by Michael Grant)

A formidable guest, yet no regrets! For everything went very pleasantly indeed. However, when he reached Philippus on the evening of the 18th, the house was so full of soldiers that there was hardly a room free for Caesar himself to have dinner. Two thousand men! I was distinctly alarmed about what would happen the next day, but Cassius Barba came to my rescue with a loan of some guards. A camp was pitched on my land and the house was put under guard. On the 19th he stayed with Philippus until one o'clock and let no one in—I believe he was doing accounts with Balbus. Then he went for a walk on the shore. After two he had a bath. . . . Later he had an oil-massage and then sat down to dinner.

He was following a course of emetics, so he ate and drank without *arrière-pensée* and at his ease. It was a sumptuous dinner and well-served. . . . His entourage were very lavishly provided for in three other rooms. Even the lower-ranking ex-slaves and the slaves lacked for nothing; the more important ex-slaves I entertained in style.

In other words, we were human beings together. Still, he was not the sort of guest to whom you would say "do please come again on your way back." Once is enough! We talked no serious politics, but a good deal about literary matters. In short, he liked it and enjoyed himself. He said he was going to spend one day at Puteoli and the next in the neighbourhood of Baiae. There you have the story of how I entertained him—or had him billeted on me; I found it a bother, as I have said, but not disagreeable. Now I am going to stay on here for a little and then go to my place at Tusculum.

As Caesar passed Dolabella's house on horseback his whole guard paraded under arms to the right and left of him, which they did nowhere else, so I heard from Nicias.

Gaius Julius Caesar, while climbing to unprecedented heights of political power, found time to achieve literary distinction with a remarkable series of accounts of his military campaigns, written in a restrained, documentary style much admired for its clarity. These self-serving memoirs, through which Caesar parades in the third person like a modest god, color the truth by omitting details uncomplimentary to the author, but they seldom stray far from the facts. Excerpted here is a section from Book IV of De bello Gallico *(The Gallic War), describing a lightning attack on the Germans and the first Roman crossing of the Rhine in 55 B.C. It portrays Caesar as the brilliant, unpredictable strategist and the imaginative military engineer that he undoubtedly was, and it presents him at his lucid best as a writer.*

the scion of a most distinguished line, whose grandfather had held the sovereignty in his own state, and had been saluted as Friend by the Roman Senate. Piso went to the assistance of his brother, who had been cut off by the enemy, and rescued him from danger, but was thrown himself, his horse having been wounded. He resisted most gallantly as long as he could; then he was surrounded, and fell after receiving many wounds. His brother, who had escaped from the fight, saw him fall from a distance; then spurred his horse, flung himself upon the enemy, and was slain.

After this engagement was over, Caesar felt that he ought no longer to receive deputies nor to accept conditions from tribes which had sought for peace by guile and treachery, and then had actually begun war. Further, he judged it the height of madness to wait till the enemy's forces should be increased and their cavalry returned. Knowing as he did the fickleness of the Gauls, he apprehended how much influence the enemy had already acquired over them by a single engagement; and he considered that no time to form plans should be given them. Thus determined, he communicated to the lieutenant-generals and the quartermaster-general his purpose not to lose a day in giving battle. Then, most fortunately, a certain thing occurred. The next morning, as treacherous and as hypocritical as ever, a large company of Germans, which included all the principal and senior men, came to his quarters, with a double object—to clear themselves (so they alleged) for engaging in a battle the day before, contrary to the agreement and to their own request therein, and also by deceit to get what they could in respect of the truce. Caesar rejoiced that they were delivered into his hand, and ordered them to be detained; then in person he led all his troops out of camp, commanding the cavalry, which he judged to be shaken by the recent engagement, to follow in the rear.

Triple line of columns was formed, and the eight-mile march was so speedily accomplished that Caesar reached the enemy's camp before the Germans could have any inkling of what was toward. They were struck with sudden panic by everything—by the rapidity of our approach, the absence of their own chiefs; and, as no time was given them to think, or to take up arms, they were too much taken aback to decide which was best—to lead their forces against the enemy, to defend the camp, or to seek safety by flight. When their alarm was betrayed by the uproar and bustle, our troops, stung by the treachery of the day before, burst into the camp. In the camp those who were able speedily to take up arms resisted the Romans for a while, and fought among the carts and baggage-wagons; the remainder, a crowd of women and children (for the Germans had left home and crossed the Rhine with all their belongings), began to flee in all directions, and Caesar despatched the cavalry in pursuit.

Hearing the noise in rear, and seeing their own folk slain, the Germans threw away their arms, abandoned their war-standards, and burst out of the camp. When they reached the junction of the Meuse and the Rhine, they gave up hope of escaping further; a large number were already slain, and the rest hurled themselves into the river, there to perish, overcome by terror, by exhaustion, by the force of the stream. The Romans, with not a man lost and but few wounded, freed from the fear of a stupendous war—with an enemy whose numbers had been 430,000 souls—returned to camp. Caesar gave to the Germans detained in camp permission to depart; but they, fearing punishments and tortures at the hand of the Gauls whose land they had harassed, said that they would stay in his company, and he gave them liberty so to do.

The German campaign thus finished, Caesar decided for many reasons that he must cross the Rhine. The most cogent reason was that, as he saw the Germans so easily induced to enter Gaul, he wished to make them fearful in turn for their own fortunes, by showing them that a Roman army could and durst cross the Rhine. Moreover, that section of the cavalry of the Usipetes and Tencteri which, as I have mentioned above, had crossed the Meuse to get booty and corn, and had taken no part in the battle, had now, after the rout of their countrymen, withdrawn across the Rhine into the territory of the Sugambri, and joined them. To them Caesar sent envoys to demand the surrender of the men who had made war upon himself and Gaul. They replied that the Rhine marked the limit of the Roman empire: if he thought it unfair that the Germans should cross into Gaul against his will, why did he claim any imperial power across the Rhine?

The Ubii, on the other hand, the only tribe beyond the Rhine which had sent deputies to Caesar, made friendly terms, and given hostages, earnestly besought him to assist them, as they were grievously hard pressed by the Suebi; or, if the urgent concerns of state prevented that, only to transport his army across the Rhine: that would suffice for their present help and future hope. So great, they said, even among the farthest tribes of Germany was the renown and reputation of his army, after the defeat of Ariovistus and the success of this last action, that their own safety was secure in the prestige and the friendship of Rome. They promised . . . boats for the transport of his army.

For the reasons above mentioned Caesar had decided to cross the Rhine; but he deemed it scarcely safe, and ruled it unworthy of his own and the Romans' dignity, to cross in boats. And so, although he was confronted with the greatest difficulty in making a bridge, by reason of the breadth, the rapidity, and the depth of the river, he still thought that he must make that effort, or else not take his army across. He proceeded to construct a bridge on the following plan. He caused pairs of balks eighteen inches thick, sharpened a little way from the base and measured to suit the depth of the river, to be coupled together at an interval of two feet. These he lowered into the river by means of rafts, and

set fast, and drove home by rammers; not, like piles, straight up and down, but leaning forward at a uniform slope, so that they inclined in the direction of the stream. Opposite to these, again, were planted two balks coupled in the same fashion, at a distance of forty feet from base to base of each pair, slanted against the force and onrush of the stream. These pairs of balks had two-foot transoms let into them atop, filling the interval at which they were coupled, and were kept apart by a pair of braces on the outer side at each end. So, as they were held apart and contrariwise clamped together, the stability of the structure was so great and its character such that, the greater the force and thrust of the water, the tighter were the balks held in lock. These trestles were interconnected by timber laid over at right angles, and floored with long poles and wattlework. And further, piles were driven in aslant on the side facing down stream, thrust out below like a buttress and close joined with the whole structure, so as to take the force of the stream; and others likewise at a little distance above the bridge, so that if trunks of trees, or vessels, were launched by the natives to break down the structure, these fenders might lessen the force of such shocks, and prevent them from damaging the bridge.

The whole work was completed in ten days from that on which the collecting of timber began, and the army was taken across. Leaving a strong post at either end of the bridge, Caesar pressed on into the territory of the Sugambri. Meanwhile from several states deputies came to him, to whose request for peace and friendship he replied in generous fashion, and ordered hostages to be brought to him. But from the moment when the bridge began to be constructed the Sugambri, at the instigation of the Tencteri and Usipetes among them, had been preparing for flight; and now they had evacuated their territory, carried off all their stuff, and hidden themselves in the remote part of the forests.

Caesar tarried for a few days in their territory, until he had burnt all the villages and buildings, and cut down the corn-crops. Then he withdrew into the territory of the Ubii; and, after a promise of his help to them, if they were hard pressed by the Suebi, he received the following information from them. The Suebi, when they had discovered by means of their scouts that a bridge was being built, held a convention according to their custom, and despatched messengers to all quarters, ordering the people to remove from their towns, to lodge their children and all their stuff in the woods, and to assemble in one place all men capable of bearing arms. The place chosen was about the middle of the districts occupied by the Suebi; here they were awaiting the approach of the Romans, having determined to fight the decisive battle on this spot. By the time when Caesar learnt this he had accomplished all the objects for which he had determined to lead his army across the Rhine—to strike terror into the Germans, to take vengeance on the Sugambri, to deliver the Ubii from a state of blockade. So, having spent in all eighteen days across the Rhine, and advanced far enough, as he thought, to satisfy both honour and expediency, he withdrew into Gaul and broke up the bridge.

1. Earliest known written Latin, Greek letters

2. Latin letters, late 7th century B.C.

3. Detail of inscription on Trajan's column, c. A.D. *114; perfect lettering*

5. Geometric analysis, 17th century

6. Illuminated G, late 9th century

4. Gothic S, Germany, 13th century

P. TERENTII

A N D R I A.

PROLOGUS.

POETA cum primum animum ad scribendum ap-
Id sibi negoti credidit solum dari,   [pulit,
Populo ut placerent, quas fecisset fabulas.
Verum aliter evenire multo intelligit.
Nam in prologis scribundis operam abutitur,
Non qui argumentum narret, sed qui malevoli
Veteris poetæ maledictis respondeat.
Nunc, quam rem vitio dent, quæso, animum advortite.

*S OROREM falso creditam meretriculæ,
Genere Andriâ, Glycerium vitiat Pamphilus:
Gravidaque facta, dat fidem, uxorem sibi
Fore hanc: nam aliam pater ei desponderat
Gnatam Chremetis: atque ut amorem comperit,
Simulat futuras nuptias; cupiens, suus
Quid haberet animi filius, cognoscere.*

7. 3rd-century Roman square capitals

8. Type by Baskerville, 1772

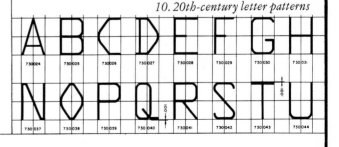

ABCDEFGH IJKLMNOP

9. Standardized Baskerville capitals, 19th-20th centuries

10. 20th-century letter patterns

ABCDEFGH
730024 730025 730026 730027 730028 730029 730030 730031
NOPQRSTU
730037 730038 730039 730040 730041 730042 730043 730044

THE RISE OF LATIN LETTERS

Though the Romans derived their alphabet from the Greeks, the shape of their letters was their own. A radical process of evolution led from the first crude Latin scratchings to the stately splendor of the letters on Trajan's column. Every age since has drawn, according to its own lights, on the Roman designs, adapting, decorating, or twisting them, but remaining under their spell.

SIR JOHN EDWIN SANDYS, *A Companion to Latin Studies*; ANDERSON; ANDERSON; THE PIERPONT MORGAN LIBRARY; BIBLIOTHEQUE NATIONALE; THE PIERPONT MORGAN LIBRARY; VATICAN LIBRARY; ALEXANDER NESBITT, *The History and Technique of Lettering*, DOVER PUBLICATIONS, INC.; IBM

THE
PUBLIC LIFE
OF ROME

Though many wellborn individuals shared Horace's delight in a country retreat, the Romans as a people were hardly given to lives of seclusion or contemplation. Their disposition was gregarious, their pleasures were urban, and their political and business lives centered in the open meeting and the market place. Processions—religious, civil, or triumphal—fascinated them. Romans flocked to the circus and the arena in unbelievable numbers, and they congregated in smaller but no less noisy crowds at theatres, at public baths, and even at the law courts, where their boisterous appreciation of the oratory of advocates did little to expedite the administration of justice. Citizens of means could spend long hours in the city's expensive barbershops or at lavish, all-night banquets. The typical patrician had a lively interest in politics and considered the Senate a club of the elect; the plebeian artisan valued the fellowship in his guild.

For more than five hundred years, the hub of Rome's public life and the mecca of its populace was the Roman Forum, whose ruins are viewed at left through the arch of Septimius Severus. This great open area, lined with shops, temples, and government buildings, daily attracted hordes of merchants, buyers, speculators, and politicians, as well as the idle and curious. By the time of Julius Caesar, it was often so congested that the first of several additional forums was begun in order to accommodate the overflow.

In the relief at right, a magistrate is attended by lictors and servants who carry his sedan chair; the mule-drawn chariot in which this distinguished Roman rides would not have been permitted to enter the Forum, which was normally barred to all but pedestrian traffic. Below, at left and at right, coins minted in the second century B.C. celebrate the most fundamental rights of citizenship under the republic: suffrage and the right of appeal. A later coin (center) bears an impression of the Curia Julia, built under Caesar. There the Senate met in imperial times.

ALL THREE: BRITISH MUSEUM

STATESMEN AND CITIZENS

A major officeholder was a much-revered figure in Rome, but he was seldom a law unto himself. A consul of the republic often felt compelled to repeat for the benefit of the crowd in the Forum the speech that he had delivered in the Senate, and an emperor seldom dared to suspend expensive entertainments and grain distributions expected by his subjects. Neither could afford to neglect the claims of the citizenry, for Romans were keenly aware of the rights conferred upon them by law and tradition. Even after such basic privileges as *provocatio*, the right of appeal to the assembly, and *suffragium*, the vote in that assembly, had lost their meaning, and even after the exalted Senate had lost its power to control political events, the lowliest Roman citizen could still claim—if not always enforce—the right of appeal to the highest Roman magistrate, the emperor himself.

Every Roman city had its forum. In the mural above, a painter has conveyed in rough strokes the restless commercial activity of the forum at Pompeii in the first century A.D. Prospective customers mill around a vendor of crockery who is displaying his wares (left) and a shoe peddler attempting to make a sale (right).

THE WORKING POOR

Much of Rome's manual labor was performed by slaves, but the city also harbored a large class of artisans, who either sold their services or manufactured and traded goods in the urban market. They ranked low on the Roman social scale, worked long hours, and seldom grew rich. The professional guilds to which they often belonged were more like clubs than modern trade unions, offering companionship but no economic gains.

The wall painting at left depicts a master carpenters' festival; the paraders carry a carved exhibit that illustrates their craft. The goatherd pictured in the relief above was either a slave or a member of the class of landless rural inhabitants who lacked even the advantages enjoyed by the urban poor. The reliefs at right represent (from top to bottom) a workshop in which a cobbler and spinner practice their trades; a goldsmith's shop; a towboat of the kind that carried wine along Italy's waterways; and a typical Roman open-air market stall, at which a woman is selling such produce as fruit and game.

THE ROMAN FEAST

For most Romans, the morning was devoted to work, the afternoon to exercise or recreation at the public baths. And for the well-to-do Romans the evening often signaled the beginning of many hours of prodigious banqueting. Men feasted at parties enlivened by entertainments no less exotic than the rich foods, and very often they brought along their wives. At major feasts, a bath and a massage after the first round of courses sometimes served to refresh diners' appetites.

A Pompeiian painting depicting a banquet shows several guests dining in typical reclining positions. At left, a servant removes the shoes of a late arrival while another servant (right) supports a diner who may have over-indulged. Stories of self-induced vomiting as a means to further eating are much exaggerated; there were very few Romans who did anything quite so repulsive.

PLEASURES OF THE THEATRE

Romans enjoyed considerable variety in their stage fare, though most of what they saw derived from the Greeks. This was true even of the comedies of Plautus and Terence, who were among the very few major playwrights that Rome produced. Eventually mimes—topical farces performed without masks—and pieces featuring music drew the largest audiences.

In the painting on the opposite page, a character in a comedy, possibly by Plautus, makes the traditional gesture of the horns to ward off the evil eye. Above, a Pompeiian mosaic shows a rehearsal of a Greek satyr play, which included dancing. Carved discs (left and opposite) served as theatre tickets in Rome.

VI

THE COMING OF CAESAR

Therefore, my lords, strain every nerve for the preservation of the state, look in every quarter for the storms, which will burst upon you, if you do not see them in time.

Cicero, fourth oration against Catiline, 63 B.C.

The Romans never forgot the despotic reign of Sulla when the streets ran with blood and strange portents darkened the sky. His rule, however, was mercifully brief; for after two years of it, in 79 B.C., he abruptly stepped down, abandoned Rome to its fate, and retired to his estate at Puteoli, near Naples. He offered no explanation. The historian Appian says that Sulla was "weary of war, weary of power, weary of Rome." He spent his remaining days fishing, hunting, talking with his friends, and writing his memoirs —which have perished. A cultivated voluptuary, he gave himself up to a life of pleasure. He had written comedies, and it amused him to see them performed by actors and actresses who flocked to his court. He was well guarded by the Cornelii, who had followed him into retirement. He died in the following year and received a tyrant's funeral. The Romans, having feared him during his reign, in retrospect regarded him as a man of vast audacity, worthy of their respect. His body was carried to Rome on a golden bier preceded by horsemen and trumpeters, his battle standards, and the twenty-four lictors who had attended him. When the bier reached Rome, the senators came to pay homage and carried it to the Campus Martius, the traditional burial ground for kings. For the cremation of the body, the women of Rome provided immense quantities of spices, and there was enough left over to make a large statue of him from frankincense and cinnamon.

Sulla left no successor, only a number of ruthless and audacious followers who were determined to advance themselves. His desire to strengthen the Senate as a stabilizing force was frustrated by the rise of military chieftains and adventurers, whose rivalry led to further conquests, internecine struggles, heightened social tension, and finally to the collapse of the republic.

The era that saw the emergence of Pompey and Crassus and the ultimate triumph of Gaius Julius Caesar was not, however, one of aggrandizement and brutality only. The pursuit of wealth and power was accompanied by a rapid growth of cultivated life, literary expression, and intellectual enquiry. Although dominated by men of the sword, it was also the time of the poet-philosopher Lucretius, the lyric poet Catullus, the encyclopedist Varro, with his studies of Roman history, customs, agronomy, and the Latin language, and the versatile Cicero, who embodied the culture of the final decades of the republic at its best.

Even before Julius Caesar emerged to enlarge the Roman world, it had become far flung. By about 60 B.C. Rome ruled over northern Italy up to the Alpine passes; over southern France; over the Iberian peninsula save for its northwestern corner and part of what is now Portugal; over the Dalmatian coast, Thrace, and

Greece; over a broad belt of Asia Minor fronting on the Black and Mediterranean seas and including such ancient seats of power as Ephesus, Antioch, Sidon, and Tyre; and over such North African coastal centers as Cyrene, Leptis, and the remnants of Carthage. Raw materials, together with tribute and tax money and slaves from the conquered provinces, added to Roman wealth—as did the gain of the rapacious governors whom Rome sent out.

The influx of slaves, though profitable, was not entirely a blessing. It brought in men and women alien to the old Roman stock and thereby led to its dilution. The slave population of Rome in the late republic may have numbered two hundred thousand. Of these, all were by no means farm workers or domestic servants; many of the educated slaves became tutors, secretaries, librarians, and physicians. Few passages in Roman writing are more handsome than Cicero's affectionate correspondence with his own secretary Tiro, who helped him with his writings and was given freedom, becoming after Cicero's death the guardian and editor of his literary estate. Yet the foreign slave also brought with him social unrest. In 73 B.C. Spartacus, a Thracian gladiator, fomented and led a mass revolt of slaves, including Celts, Germans, and tribesmen from his own rough country northwest of Greece. Some ninety thousand in number, these desperate men vanquished several Roman armies and threatened much of central and southern Italy before they were brought to bay by Marcus Licinius Crassus, a praetor appointed to take over the command of this newest civil war from the defeated consuls.

Despite all political and social uncertainties, life in and around the city of Rome flourished. Early in the first century B.C., the senatorial class as well as the leading equites had begun to build, on the Palatine and other heights, great mansions complete with coffered ceilings, mosaics, wall paintings, libraries, sculpture-courts, and surrounding gardens. The urban poor, their number swelled by masses of dispossessed peasants, were quartered in lodging-houses or in multistoried tenement blocks known as *insulae*, some of which lined the slopes leading down to the Forum. The Forum served as a year-round center not only of oratory but of every kind of daily commerce—buying and selling houses, produce, livestock, slaves, ships, cargoes. Since Rome was approaching a population of one million, a habit arose among the rich of erecting country retreats—villas surrounded by parks and ponds. Cicero had eight villas. Clodia, the sensual wife of consul Metellus Celer and the woman whom Catullus loved as the "Lesbia" of his lyrics, was known for holding extravagant garden and boating parties that were filled with music, gaiety, and frivolity.

In a copy of a contemporary statue, a benign Julius Caesar steps forward as if to offer Romans the gift of his wisdom and strength. The formula SPQR (senatus populusque Romanus), recalling the ancient authority of the Senate and the people, survived the fall of the republic and its institutions.

Greek influence stood very high in Rome. Lucretius expounded to a Latin audience the teachings of the Greek philosopher Epicurus, with his argument that the universe consists of random atoms over which the gods themselves have no control, and that man can best overcome his fears of death and godly vengeance by equipoise and contemplation of the "majesty of things." Catullus, though trained in polished alexandrine meter, harked back to the impassioned style of Sappho of Lesbos as he pursued his beloved "Lesbia" in Rome. Cicero as orator took the Athenian Demosthenes as his model, and as moralist leaned heavily on both the conservative idealism of Plato and on the Stoics' emphasis on practical social virtues. Men like Catullus and Cicero spoke Greek as well as Latin, and their houses were filled with Greek books and works of art. The thought and style of Greece were commingling with the practical intelligence and verve of the Romans to produce an eclectic yet increasingly polished civilization.

Though the Romans were philhellenes in their acquisition of ideas and tastes, they still adhered to many of their own. Not all the influence of Athens altered, for instance, the position of Roman women—particularly the Roman matron of the upper classes, proud, dignified, often a participant in her husband's public affairs, and free from the seclusion that had shut in the Athenian wife. She was the object of high matrimonial alliances between clans; she accompanied her husband to banquets and often made her voice heard in politics. Cicero's wife Terentia, a particularly gifted woman, appears to have been highly skilled at handling her husband's property and accounts.

The high role of the Roman leader's lady—one to become even more important amid the strategic marriages and divorces of Caesar and thereafter—stood in contrast to the low role of the courtesan, one very different from the part played by the gifted *hetaira* in Athenian Greece. Liaisons outside of marriage were at best furtive; and as for the prostitute, there was no talk of obliging temple hostesses such as those at Corinth. Prostitutes took out licenses at the aediles' office and thereupon donned their distinctive dress and boldly dyed their hair to denote their calling.

In this mixed and increasingly literate society, a major cultural pursuit emerged—that of oratory, which became perhaps the most characteristic vehicle of Roman self-expression. Greek manuals of oratory and Greek teachers had been known in Rome since Cato's time, and had helped to mold the style of many leading statesmen. The first Latin-speaking school of rhetoric was opened in 95 B.C.; and as political competition intensified, oratory became even more important. Studies in gesture, delivery, diction, and the effective

A marble relief pictures a small Italian city as it looked in the days of the early Caesars. Blocks of two- and three-storied tenements congest the area enclosed by the ancient (and by that time superfluous) town wall. At right, the country villas of the wealthy, with their colonnades and gardens, sprawl across nearby hillsides.
MUSEO TORLONIA, ROME; ALINARI

marshaling of argument were regarded as essential training for aspiring, young men. Cicero won his consulship chiefly by dint of his marvelously sonorous and rhythmic utterances, and Julius Caesar himself was regarded as second only to Cicero in his command of speechmaking.

Barring mighty Caesar, Marcus Tullius Cicero was the most characteristic and brilliant personage of the era—and moreover the one who most staunchly defended traditional republican ideas against the swordsmen who finally destroyed him. Not of patrician birth, but rather the son of an equites who had devoted himself to literature, he began life as one of the *novi homines* of the times; he was schooled by Greek tutors and dedicated himself to law. A brilliant young advocate, pleading criminal and civil cases before senatorial courts, including a brave and winning defense of a victim of the rapacity of one of Sulla's henchmen, he attracted so much attention that he was elected quaestor in 76 B.C., at the age of thirty, and thus entered the Senate; seven years later he became an aedile; then he won a praetorship, which permitted him to preside over the highest civil court of Rome; finally in 63 B.C.—a year that was to see renewed domestic tumult—he was chosen consul.

Witty, urbane, always graced with style and courage, Cicero comes down to us as the most articulate and comprehensive figure of late republican Rome. Fifty-eight of his speeches survive along with seven works on oratory, and nearly twenty on philosophy, and over eight hundred personal letters on topics ranging from high affairs of state to details of his personal life. He had no single predominant style, but wrote in many different manners, each suited to the occasion and to his audience. The gay informality of many of the letters to his friend Atticus, the vigorous clarity of his narrations in criminal proceedings, and the elegant and subtle dialogue of his books on rhetoric and philosophy stand in contrast to the orotund magnificence in which, for a denunciation or a peroration, he summons up full powers of the Latin language. His prose became a model for cultivated speech for a thousand years and more after his death.

Cicero was to defend to the death a republican system based on an alliance of his own mercantile class and the aristocracy against strong dictators above and dissatisfied masses below. But other leaders and forces attractive to the people were rising. Among Sulla's ill-assorted crowd of adventurers one stood out: Gnaeus Pompeius, who was known as Pompey. He was a brilliant and impressive cavalry officer. He had a broad head, large nose, and athletic body and was skilled in running, leaping, riding, and fencing. He was popular with his soldiers and ferociously ambitious. Born in 106 B.C., the same year as Cicero, Pompey was twenty-three when under Sulla he successfully led an army against the followers of Marius. After notable victories in Sicily and Africa, he returned to Rome and demanded from Sulla the right to enter the city in triumph, although only consuls were permitted to enjoy triumphs, and no one could become a consul until the age of forty-two. Pompey was adamant: "More people worship the rising than the setting sun." Sulla, surprised by the remark, said: "Then let him triumph!" So, he triumphed and was thereafter called Pompeius Magnus, Pompey the Great. When Sulla died, Pompey expected to be appointed the dictator's successor, but when the will was read he was not mentioned in it at all. Sulla, who had wearied of Rome, had finally wearied of Pompey.

For the next five years Pompey fought in Spain. He returned to Rome in 71 B.C. to assist Crassus in crushing the slave revolt led by Spartacus. When he arrived in the city, the Senate's two most influential men were Crassus and Cicero. Crassus, like Pompey, had been a faithful follower of Sulla and had amassed a great fortune during the time of the proscriptions by buying up cheaply the estates of the proscribed and then selling them dearly. Shrewd, affable, a skilled intriguer in the inner councils of the Senate, he was also a capable and ruthless general, tracking down the Spartacists with unexampled ferocity, crucifying the slaves who fell into his hands. He left only fugitives to be mopped up by the returning Pompey the Great.

When Pompey presented himself to the Senate he expected to hear his own praises spoken by Crassus. Instead he heard a panegyric honoring Cicero. The affront was deliberate and demonstrated that the two soldiers were now rivals for power, and that Crassus was seeking to win the great orator to his side. At the head of their armies they cowed the Senate, suspending their enmity long enough to be made joint consuls for the year 70 B.C., during which they managed to undo much of Sulla's constitution, reducing the Senate's powers and restoring those of the tribunes. Then Pompey won a sweeping command at sea and in the east, and distinguished himself by putting down pirates, by vanquishing King Mithridates of the Black Sea realm of Pontus, and by founding colonies, while jealous Crassus in Rome worked to strengthen his own position against Pompey's return. Immensely rich, he bought the voters while Cicero swayed them with oratory; Pompey, on the other hand, by nature scrupulous and lacking a faculty for intrigue, had little to recommend him but his generalship.

Having successfully completed his tasks abroad, Pompey returned to Italy in 62 B.C., prepared to play the role of another Sulla.

Mithridates the Great, king of Pontus in northern Asia Minor, was the most resilient opponent of Rome's expansion during the first half of the first century B.C. He fought sporadic wars against Roman armies for more than two decades, before suffering a final defeat at the hand of Pompey in 66 B.C.
LOUVRE; GIRAUDON

Completely fearless, he dramatized his return by leaving his army at Brundisium and entering Rome accompanied only by a small staff. But Rome was in no mood to receive another Sulla. Only a few months earlier one of Sulla's lieutenants, Lucius Sergius Catilina, known to history as Catiline, had made a terrifying bid for power with a plan to seize the city with the help of Gauls from the north and of a fifth column that would fire the public buildings and create panic. The conspiracy of Catiline might have succeeded if it had not been for some Gallic informers in Rome. Catiline's agents were exposed by Cicero and were arrested and sentenced to death; shortly afterward, a Roman army defeated the forces of Catiline and killed him. The horror of those days when the fate of Rome hung in the balance was vividly remembered on Pompey's return.

After Pompey's arrival in Rome the possibility of a violent clash between him and Crassus grew more imminent. It was averted, however, by the intervention and mediation of an extraordinary young leader who returned in 60 B.C. from a successful command in Spain. Gaius Julius Caesar brought together the two statesmen to form with himself the triple alliance known as the First Triumvirate. This was a fateful moment in Roman history, for it marked Caesar's first bid for power.

Before the legends accumulated around his name, Caesar was not a man who inspired any particular confidence. He was a gallant, a spendthrift, and a born conspirator, who carefully covered his traces. It was rumored and widely believed that he had been in secret correspondence with Catiline and would have been among those to seize power if that man's rebellion had been successful. He had held some minor positions in government, and in 63 B.C., at the age of thirty-seven had secured the position of *pontifex maximus*, the ceremonial head of the state clergy. Yet in that year he was still not widely known. He had not commanded any large armies—nor indeed any armies at all. Apart from a daring, youthful exploit on the island of Lesbos—he had saved the life of a fellow soldier—and a punitive expedition that he had subsequently led against pirates, he had taken no leading part in wars. At an age when young soldiers had been covering themselves with glory, he had been busily engaged in seducing the wives of politicians and practicing law. He was deeply in debt to Crassus, for with his help Caesar had been sent to Spain, where he had shown himself to be a brilliant and unorthodox general, careless of danger, restless and violently ambitious, driving his men hard and himself harder. In 60 B.C. he was back in Rome, hungry for power.

His appearance suggested much, but not all, of the inner man. The few surviving portraits in bronze and marble show an ideal-

A gifted soldier and a key protagonist in Rome's civil wars, Pompey (shown in a late portrait) rose to prominence under Sulla and was ultimately driven from power by a former ally, Caesar. Unlike the latter, Pompey revealed his genius early in life, but grew increasingly ineffectual during his final years.
NY CARLSBERG GLYPTOTEK, COPENHAGEN

A crucial event of the Gallic war was Caesar's victory, in 52 B.C., over a huge army assembled by Vercingetorix, the only leader who succeeded in uniting the fiercely independent Gallic tribes. Likenesses of the bearded chieftain and of an attacking Gallic war chariot appear on a Roman denarius.
BOTH: BRITISH MUSEUM

ized Caesar, lean and suave, with high cheekbones and a mouth like a trap. Yet the coins struck in his lifetime show a thin, craggy face, a thin nose, a thin neck, set lips, knit brow, and large deep-set eyes, which we know were black and very piercing. He became bald at an early age and was particularly sensitive about this condition. His skin had a curious marble-like pallor, and there is some evidence that he suffered from a mild form of epilepsy. He had an intensity that appealed to women and made some men afraid.

According to Suetonius, Caesar claimed descent from the goddess Venus and from one of the legendary kings of Rome. But in fact, his family was not a very distinguished one, though it achieved one socially important marriage when his aunt Julia wedded Marius, the sworn enemy of Sulla. During the Sullan proscriptions young Caesar had fled to save his life. Friends had pleaded for him, and Sulla was supposed to have remarked: "In that boy there are many Mariuses," suggesting that an eye might well be kept on him. Yet at another time Sulla supposedly dismissed Caesar with the remark: "He wears his girdle too loosely." Wearing a loose girdle was accounted as a sign of effeminacy.

At the age of forty, still wearing his girdle loosely, dressing with exquisite taste, brushing his few remaining hairs forward, Caesar set about to conquer Rome with the same cold intelligence and thrust that had brought about his victories in Spain. The First Triumvirate had introduced a new and hitherto untried form of dictatorship, one that could remain stable only so long as the three men's interests coincided. The triumvirs held absolute power, though the fictions of republican rule were being maintained. Consular elections were held, and Caesar became consul for the first time in 59 B.C.; his colleague the conservative Marcus Calpurnius Bibulus served as co-consul.

Also in the year 59 B.C. Pompey was given Caesar's daughter Julia in marriage. Crassus, who had offered the state a vast sum for the privilege of collecting public revenues in the eastern provinces of Asia, found the revenues disappointing and he asked the Senate for relief. The Senate refused. Caesar obligingly arranged to have a law passed requiring the Senate to offer remission to Crassus, the richest man in Rome. Pompey, in turn, was rewarded with the ratification of his eastern conquests. He had promised his veterans large areas of land, and these were now set aside for them. For himself, Caesar demanded that at the end of his consular year he obtain the governorship of Cisalpine Gaul, and when the newly appointed governor of Transalpine Gaul conveniently died Caesar asked that this province also be given to him. He raised three legions in preparation for assuming his new post and then carefully arranged to station them near Rome, ringing the city with his soldiers. The hint was not lost on anyone—certainly not on Cicero, who had declined to join the coalition of the generals. Caesar had observed that Sulla's abdication had only shown that Sulla did not know the first thing about the nature of dictatorship. A dictatorship is not something that can be put aside lightly; it must be held with all the force and all the stratagems at the leader's disposal. In stepping down from the consular office Caesar was not yielding his power. He was simply preparing for greater power—a more absolute rule over a larger empire. On a far more massive scale he was employing the ruse first attempted by Catiline: in alliance with the Gauls and with his own agents in the city he would become the undisputed master of Rome.

Caesar emerged from his year as consul with immense powers. He could select his own commanders, found colonies as he wished, push back the frontiers wherever it served his purpose, and employ the treasure of conquered peoples for his own ends. His governorship of Gaul was to last for five years, but it was renewable. The army that was entrusted to him was so powerful that it could survive any enemy. With the Gallic levies that he intended to raise, he foresaw that in a very short space of time he would accumulate more power in the form of treasure and men-at-arms than any Roman before him had been able to amass.

He spent the following nine years carving out an empire in Gaul as more and more opportunities for conquest and enrichment presented themselves to him, and thereby delayed his threatened return to Rome. He was constantly on the march, constantly putting down rebellions and extending his dominions. The poet Lucan speaks of him as a man *in arma furens* ("furious for war") and impatient to cut bloody swathes through the enemy: "He would rather burst open the city gates than have them opened for him. He preferred to ravage the land with fire and sword than to receive the farmer's permission to cross it peacefully. He detested an unguarded road, or to parade like a peaceful citizen." Caesar would have disagreed with that verdict. He would have said that he waged war in a spirit of analytic enquiry, without rage, his sole object being to bring greater glory to Rome by force of arms. In *De bello Gallico*, his commentaries on the Gallic war, he presents himself as a man of single-minded purpose, who regards war as an exercise of the mind, with Roman brain power pitted against that of the barbarians. Above all else, Caesar was interested in the mechanics of conquest—the unrelenting march of the war machine once its precise purpose had been established and its goal had been calculated.

A fourth-century copy of a portion of Cicero's De republica *can be clearly discerned (in double columns) on parchment that was re-used in the eighth century* A.D. *The treatise was one of many works of Cicero, which survived to exert a greater influence in later ages than they did during his own lifetime.*
VATICAN LIBRARY

Caesar's commentaries do not reveal the whole man. His hesitations, doubts, and complexities are glossed over. The report is written in a style so plain that it seems to be without art; no rhetorical devices are employed. Sallust, on the other hand, in describing the Jugurthine war, gives the hot breath of the campaign, the rush and roar of the cavalry, the sense of human beings engaged in dubious conspiracies and hand-to-hand combat. Caesar describes his stratagems or battle plans in stark and precise terms. His crowning achievement was the defeat, in 52 B.C., of the Gallic army led by the chieftain Vercingetorix. Caesar appears on the scene wearing his blood red cloak:

> *His coming was known to the enemy by the color of his cloak—that cloak which he was accustomed to wear as his distinguishing mark in battle—and then they saw the cavalry squadrons and the cohorts, which he had ordered to follow behind him, these being plainly visible from the heights: so they joined the battle. From both sides came battle cries, which were taken up by the men on the rampart and along the whole length of the entrenchment. Our men threw down their spears and got to work with their swords. Suddenly the enemy saw the cavalry in their rear; fresh cohorts were coming up. They turned and fled, and the cavalry cut off their flight. There was great slaughter. . . . Seventy-four standards were presented to Caesar; only a few of that great army succeeded in reaching their camp safely. When they saw from the town the slaughter and flight of their countrymen, they surrendered to despair and recalled their troops from the entrenchments. As soon as they heard what had happened, the Gauls fled from their camp. . . . Our cavalry pursued them and caught up with them about midnight; a large number were taken and killed; the survivors made for their towns.*
>
> *The next day Vercingetorix addressed his war council. "I have not undertaken this war for my own ends," he said, "but for our common freedom. Since I must accept my fate, I freely offer myself to you. If you want to kill me in order to make amends to the Romans, do so, or surrender me alive." A deputation was sent to Caesar to decide what should be done. He ordered them to lay down their arms and surrender their chiefs. He sat down at the fortifications in front of the camp, while the chiefs were brought to him. Vercingetorix surrendered, and the arms were laid down.*

In this terse, compact way, never raising his voice, Caesar describes the fall of the fortress town of Alesia, which brought to an end his long battle with Vercingetorix. The most remarkable qualities of the description are a certain suavity and ease. He was not writing for schoolboys, but for the men of his own class—the aristocracy of generals who were the real rulers of Rome. His deliberate understatements, the sense of order that he quietly imposes on chaos, and the calm superiority that he displays throughout the passage arise from a peculiar attitude of mind that is proud, austere, and intensely ambitious.

Caesar's ruthlessness is barely masked by the restrained tone of his memoirs. He sometimes reports not only the slaughter of enemy warriors but the systematic butchering of their families to the last man, woman, and child. On one occasion he had his legionaries cut off the right hands of several thousand rebellious Gauls. Vercingetorix, whose nobility in defeat Caesar makes no effort to disguise, was kept imprisoned for six years to serve as a living exhibit at Caesar's triumph, and after being paraded through the streets of Rome, was put to death.

Cicero, who was always uncomfortable in Caesar's presence, called him "an instrument of wrath, terrifying in his vigilance, swiftness, and energy." What was most terrifying was Caesar's insatiable appetite. Not content with conquering Gaul, he went on to attack large areas of what is now Flanders; he crossed the Rhine and went into Germany; and twice he invaded Britain, though these brief campaigns were scarcely more than reconnaissances in depth. The final conquest by Rome was still to come.

The triumvirate had long since collapsed. In 53 B.C. Crassus had led an army against the Parthians of the east only to suffer the loss of seven legions in the greatest Roman defeat since the battle of Cannae, and to meet death himself; his severed head and right hand were presented to the Parthian king. With Crassus gone, Caesar prepared to confront Pompey. The ties that had bound them had been broken in 54 B.C. after the death of Caesar's daughter Julia, wife of Pompey. The two men had no love for one another, though they protested their friendship. "When the clash comes," wrote Cicero, "every man on earth will be involved." Pompey was serenely unconscious of danger: "I have only to stamp my feet, and armed men will start from the soil of Italy," he is said to have declared. In January, 49 B.C., contrary to the wishes of the Senate, Caesar and his troops crossed the flooded Rubicon —the frontier between Cisalpine Gaul and Italy—and all of Pompey's and Caesar's protestations of friendship were seen to have been merely the preparations for a duel to the death.

Pompey with his troops slipped across the Adriatic to Illyria while Caesar stormed into Rome and seized the state treasury. Pompey's generals were in command in North Africa and Spain, and in addition Pompey had command of the seas. Caesar decided to strike first at Spain, where he quickly defeated an army loyal to Pompey. Then he turned to the east, and in August, 48 B.C., at the battle of Pharsalus, in Thessaly, a heterogeneous force supporting Pompey was decisively defeated; over a hundred standards were captured and Pompey fled. Appian gives a hair-raising account of how the opposing armies, after invoking the gods and sounding their trumpets, marched toward each other "in stupor and deepest silence." Lucan tells the story that on the following morning Caesar ordered a luxurious breakfast to be prepared for him on the battlefield, and as the sun was rising he calmly contemplated the faces of the dead around him.

The triumph of Caesar was not complete, for Pompey had escaped. Caesar was determined to rid the world of him, and three days later, having learned that Pompey was making his way toward Egypt, he set out in pursuit. Pompey could have gone to North Africa, where there were armies loyal to him, but he seems to have chosen Egypt quite deliberately in the hope of raising an Egyptian army to protect himself against Caesar. In the past he had shown many favors to the Egyptian royal house; he knew the country well; and its capital, Alexandria, was regarded as impregnable. He made a mistake by sending heralds to announce his arrival, for the Egyptians were in no mood to receive a defeated Roman general. He had scarcely set foot on the sandy shore when he was stabbed in the back. His head was cut off and removed to a safe place; his body was stripped and left lying on the sand until someone thought of providing a funeral pyre by setting fire to an abandoned fishing boat.

When Caesar reached Alexandria he was civilly received. Shown the head of Pompey, he wept; it was one of his rare moments of sentiment. But Egypt only awakened his appetite for conquest, and soon there was war between his small army of some three thousand and a much larger Egyptian force. He first seized the city's famed lighthouse on the strategic island of Pharos, opposite the harbor, thus giving his ships access to the port; but Alexandria remained in Egyptian hands, confining him. For six months he was in deadly peril. The conqueror of Gaul, the master of the Roman empire, found himself in command of some fifty houses along the seacoast, and nothing more.

At some time during this period Caesar encountered the princess Cleopatra, who was a member of the house of the Ptolemies and a descendant of the half brother of Alexander the Great. As Plutarch recounts the story, the beautiful princess sailed secretly to Pharos during the night and was carried into Caesar's presence wrapped in a carpet. She stepped out from the carpet and announced that she had come both as a friend and an ally. He was immediately captivated by her. "By this ruse," says the historian

The town gate of Glanum, a Roman colony in what is now French Provence, was built about 40 B.C. Figures of captive Celts (between the columns on either side of the arch) celebrate the conclusion, some ten years earlier, of Caesar's campaigns in Transalpine Gaul. His success in the north removed an ancient threat to towns, some of which had been Roman since the period of the Second Punic War, in the Rhone valley and along the Mediterranean.
JEAN ROUBIER

Plutarch, "Cleopatra caught Caesar in her toils."

It is possible that he had been captivated by her long before; they appear, at least, to have been in correspondence. Caesar was fifty-four, Cleopatra was nineteen. They were well matched in cunning, and both possessed an imperial manner, sharing a common belief in their divine ancestry—Cleopatra believed herself to be the incarnation of the goddess Isis, as Caesar held himself to be descended from Venus. The alliance they formed was to have an incalculable effect on the destiny of Rome.

For all her youth Cleopatra had the instincts of a veteran. Her beauty was one of the weapons she employed with consummate skill. To charm Caesar she gave magnificent banquets at which she appeared splendidly caparisoned, and even after Roman reinforcements came and Alexandria finally fell, he stayed at her side in Egypt. She appears to have induced him into taking a long journey with her up the Nile as far as the borders of Ethiopia. Altogether he spent nine months in Egypt. A few weeks after he left her, she gave birth to his son Caesarion.

More fighting was still to be done. In 47 B.C. he marched northward through Syria to Pontus on the Black Sea. Near Zela he destroyed the army of King Pharnaces, the son of Mithridates the Great, four hours after sighting it. After this battle Caesar sent to Rome the words that were later displayed on the banners at his triumphs in Rome: *Veni, vidi, vici* ("I came, I saw, I conquered").

In Roman Africa there remained an army of Pompey's followers, allied with the forces of the kings of neighboring Numidia and in open resistance to Caesar. After a brief stay in Rome, early in 46 B.C. Caesar sailed for the Carthaginian coast to put down their rebellion. A story was told that when he came ashore he slipped and fell, and a cry of horror went up from the soldiers, who thought the fall of their commander could only presage defeat; but he had the presence of mind to say: "So I possess thee, Africa!" There were continual skirmishes, but few pitched battles. Though superior to his own veterans in number, the enemy mass of Gallic, Spanish, and African cavalry was elusive. Provisions threatened to run out. Caesar himself was ill, suffering, according to Plutarch, an epileptic attack. Yet the outcome, given his brilliance and aura, was never in doubt, and Numidia, too, now fell into his hands. He returned to Rome in 45 B.C. to receive a greater triumphal celebration than any Roman general had ever known. He had conquered Gaul, Egypt, the Pontic realm, and much of North Africa, and there was a triumph for each victory. Four days of celebrations followed: carts were overflowing with booty, and huge paintings were carried aloft depicting the scenes of his battles and the conquered towns in flames. Wearing a gold helmet and the robes of Jupiter, carrying the eagle-topped ivory scepter, his face glowing with red paint, he presented himself as triumphator to the multitude.

Almost every power that Caesar could desire was now bestowed on him by an obedient Senate. In 46 B.C. he was made dictator for a ten-year term—with command of all armies, sole control of all public monies, and authority to determine the lists of senators, equites, and the citizenry as a whole. Immune from veto of the tribunes, he could issue decrees without consulting the public assembly. He could afford to ignore that assembly; his vast personal power rested on the solid base of his mass of legionaries, each of whom, on his return from his quadruple triumph, was awarded a grant of 20,000 sesterces (with benefits reaching as high as 200,000 sesterces for individual officers). By this time the revenues of the Roman state and Caesar's own immeasurable spoils from his conquests—including as a major item the sale of innumerable captives —had become so intermixed that the great mass of Romans saw him as their personal benefactor.

Thus armed, he devoted the second half of 46 B.C. to a phenomenal exercise of civil leadership. He settled a great number of veterans on lands in Italy and outside. He revived Corinth and Carthage as commercial centers and sent experts to Corinth to plan a canal across the isthmus. With the dictator's affection for vast building schemes, he redesigned the Forum and drew plans for new suburbs, new temples, new libraries; and because there were areas where the Tiber overflowed its banks, he decreed that the river's course be altered. In his priestly role as *pontifex maximus*, which gave him authority over the calendar and festivals, he decreed a massive reform of the calendar Romans had lived by for centuries, but which had fallen far out of step with the solar year. The new Julian calendar, introduced in January, 45 B.C., was based on the studies made by Egyptian astronomers and has survived, with only slight modifications, to our own day.

In December of 46 B.C., however, when Caesar's triumph was complete and when civil strife had ended at last, news came of a revolt in Spain. Many survivors of the defeats in Africa had found refuge there, and Pompey's sons had marshaled still another force seeking to overthrow Caesar. Hurrying to Spain, the dictator defeated the rebels at Munda, near Cordova, in a battle which he very nearly lost. For a moment his troops panicked, and Caesar, who only a few months before had the world at his feet, gave way to terror at the thought of dying on some remote Spanish battlefield. Men remembered that he had "the look of death on his face" as he

Though the Romans learned more and more about the lands whose shores were washed by mare nostrum, *there were always realms beyond their easy reach which they could know only through the often conflicting accounts of a few travelers. There is both fact and fantasy in a Pompeiian painting that shows pygmies combating a flesh-eating hippopotamus on the Upper Nile.*

plunged into battle; his sudden appearance stemmed the rout. "On other occasions I fought for victory," he said, "but today I fought for my life." The Roman historian Velleius Paterculus writes that the battle was the bloodiest and most perilous Caesar had ever fought. It was also to be his last.

Either before or after the battle, Caesar was joined by his eighteen-year-old grandnephew Octavian. The youth had risen from sickbed, and Caesar appears to have been deeply moved by his courage. They traveled together by carriage through Spain. Mark Antony claimed they were lovers; Caesar certainly felt a greater affection for his sister's grandson than for anyone else. Soon after this when he was writing his will, Caesar named Octavian as the principal heir to his fortune, his honors, his title, and his power.

Caesar was back in Rome at the beginning of October, 45 B.C., celebrating his fifth triumph. In theory it was a triumph over Spain; in fact it was a triumph over the followers of Pompey, who were Romans. Among the crowds watching the procession were many who had lost fathers and sons in Spain.

Once more the senators vied with one another in heaping new honors upon the conqueror. He was given the right to wear the purple toga of the Roman kings, to appear everywhere in a laurel crown, and to sit in a gold chair. His image was to be borne in procession among the images of the gods and set up in a prominent place in the temple of Jupiter. He was hailed as the Father of the Country, and a statue of gold was erected to him on the speaker's platform in the Forum. An order was given that in every temple in Rome and in all the towns of the empire there should be statues of him. The anniversaries of his birth and his major victories were to become holidays. His likeness appeared on coins in 45 B.C. and 44 B.C.; also in 44 he was made dictator for life, and his person was declared sacrosanct and inviolate. Senators swore to defend him at the cost of their own lives. Caesar accepted the new honors as his right, but seems to have been unconvinced that his person was sacrosanct, for in December when he went to visit Cicero in his villa at Puteoli, near Naples, he was surrounded by a guard of two thousand men.

As the days passed Caesar became increasingly remote, arbitrary, and authoritarian. Once, holding court in the portico of the temple of Venus Genetrix—erected to honor his adopted ancestor —before the gilded statue of the goddess modeled on the body of Cleopatra, he failed to rise when the senators presented themselves. Toward the end of January, 44 B.C., a crowd meeting him on the Appian Way cried, "*Rex!*" He replied that he was not a king but Caesar, but when the ringleaders among the crowd were

Shortly before 100 B.C., Marius ordered a likeness of the eagle—admired by the Romans as the strongest of birds—to be affixed to the standard of each legion. The onyx relief above was executed less than a century later, by which time the eagle had come to symbolize the power and majesty of imperial Rome.
KUNSTHISTORISCHES MUSEUM, VIENNA

A profile of Brutus on a silver denarius commemorates one of the most famous of political assassinations. The reverse of the coin bears the legend "Ides of March," a pair of daggers, and a cap of liberty, which symbolizes the ostensible goal of the conspirators who murdered Caesar.

arrested, he was incensed and ordered the arresting officers removed from their posts. In February, at the ceremony of the Lupercalia, the consul Mark Antony laid a crown of laurels interlaced with the white ribbons of the royal diadem at his feet. The laurel crown was lifted to his head. Few applauded then, but there was deafening applause when Caesar removed the crown. He asked that the crown be taken to the temple of Jupiter and that there should be inscribed in the public records the following words: "At the bidding of the people, Antony, the consul, offered to Caesar, the perpetual dictator, the kingship, which Caesar refused."

Yet during the following days a statue of Caesar was crowned by his supporters, and it became known that he had consulted the sacred books. Caesar had been planning the conquest of Parthia, and the sacred books said the Roman army could conquer Parthia only if commanded by a king. By this time there were few who had any doubt that Caesar intended to become king and to found a dynasty. Cleopatra, whom he had brought to Rome with their son Caesarion, was living in a villa on the bank of the Tiber. The Romans despised Cleopatra and were irked by the presence of the statue modeled after her in the temple of Venus Genetrix. They may have wondered whether Caesarion might not inherit the throne. Caesar knew he was in danger, but perhaps he was too ill, or too tired, or too proud, to care.

The plot to murder Caesar was devised by men he favored and to whom he had granted high positions. Gaius Longinus Cassius was a veteran who had been named praetor in 44 B.C.; Gaius Trebonius had been approved as consul the previous year; Decimus Junius Brutus was about to take command of Cisalpine Gaul; Lucius Tillius Cimber had been promised the government of Bithynia; Marcus Junius Brutus had fought for Pompey, but had been pardoned by Caesar. Most of the conspirators belonged to patrician families—the Old Guard of the perishing republic. Their motives were mixed. They feared his plays for popularity among the masses and the soldiery, handing out enormous sums as doles and veterans' benefits; they were repelled by the venality of some of his favorites, fatting on his spoils; they longed for the liberty and class order of past days; above all, most of them being senators, they were affronted by his claim to absolute and arbitrary power, reducing the Senate to an ignominious servant of his will.

Altogether some sixty men were involved in the plot, and inevitably rumors reached Caesar's ears, but he dismissed them haughtily. On the evening of March 14, he dined with Marcus Aemilius Lepidus, the commander of the armed forces, and possibly they discussed the rumors, for when the conversation turned to the best way in which to die, Caesar is said to have answered: "Suddenly."

During that night he was restless, and once all the doors and windows burst open in a gust of wind. His wife Calpurnia begged him not to leave the house next morning for the meeting of the Senate. He laughed at her fears, but to please her he called in the diviners, who performed their solemn rites. The omens were unfavorable. Yet he was looking forward to the Senate meeting to be held in the portico of Pompey's theatre on the Campus Martius —a meeting that was to ratify his use of *rex* as his title when he was outside of Italy. In three days he intended to leave for Apollonia, on the Illyrian coast, where a vast camp had been prepared for the veterans who would take part in the Parthian campaign. There, too, he would be able to see Octavian, whom he now regarded as his adopted son.

It was just after eleven o'clock in the morning when he stepped into the portico to receive the salutes of the senators, who rose to greet him. A moment later Lucius Tillius Cimber approached him to plead that his brother be recalled from exile. Caesar refused to listen to him; Cimber insisted, and as he did so the other conspirators gathered round, pressing themselves against Caesar, completely surrounding him. Twenty-three dagger thrusts felled him at the foot of Pompey's statue.

Borne to his house by slaves, the body of Caesar remained there for several days, while the conspirators debated what should be done and made speeches in self-justification, calling upon the gods to witness that tyranny was dead and the republic would be restored. They had planned to throw the body into the Tiber, but Mark Antony had taken possession of it, along with Caesar's treasure and private papers, including the will, and thereby made his own claim for power. In the famous speech he delivered over Caesar's body when it was placed in the Forum, he brought the crowds to such a pitch of excitement that they took possession of the body and insisted that it be burned in the Forum before their eyes. Women tossed their jewelry into the pyre, musicians and actors who had taken part in his triumphs removed the embroidered costumes they wore for the occasion, tore them to ribbons, threw their shields and swords into the fire, which burned all night. It was such a funeral as might be given a barbarian chieftain.

A day or two before the funeral, the mother of Octavian sent a letter to her son in Apollonia. "The time has come when you must play the man, decide, and act," she is said to have written him, "for no one can foretell the things that may come about." No one, least of all the conspirators, could have foretold that power would soon pass into the hands of Octavian—the emperor Augustus.

Impressions from Caesar's supposed death mask give the best evidence as to his personal appearance in his late years, when he achieved the pinnacle of political power. His head was longer and his face more cavernous than they were portrayed to be by the flattering artists of his day.
MUSEUM OF ANTIQUITIES, TURIN

HOUSE OF CEII, POMPEII; ALFREDO FOGLIA

THE
DOMESTIC
LIFE OF ROME

From its beginnings and throughout its course, Roman civilization was strongly rooted in the family or clan. In early centuries the head of the family, the paterfamilias, exerted total, patriarchal control over the family's women, but by the time of the Caesars this control had become a fiction. The Roman matron of imperial times had achieved a position of dignity and influence, often owning and administering property and in some instances making her voice heard in her husband's political affairs.

Girls were often taught with boys; some women received higher education and achieved a true intellectual rapport with their men. Increasing affluence and slaves to tend to household chores gave the Roman upper-class woman the freedom to pursue her own interests, sometimes artistic, sometimes frivolous. Morality grew lax under the empire; many people took lovers, and divorce became fairly common in some upper-class circles. But even the changing attitudes toward morals did not undermine the basic, proud cohesion of the family group.

The house as the center of family life became increasingly luxurious as fortunes grew. Though Romans spent much of their time outside the house—in the forum, at baths, arenas, or theatres—great attention was given to making it a handsome center for living. The wall painting opposite—astonishingly modern in design—from a villa at Pompeii conveys a Roman's desire for domestic elegance.

THE FAMILY CIRCLE

Like all peoples, the Romans marked the important steps of life with ritual and celebration. An engaged man gave his fiancée an iron or gold ring, and the young woman was showered with gifts. The wedding was an elaborate affair; after the ceremony itself, friends attended a feast at the bride's home; then, singing and shouting, they accompanied the couple to their new house, where the groom whisked his wife into his arms and carried her over the threshold. When the couple had a baby, he was ritually purified and bestowed with a name; another religious ceremony took place when a boy reached sixteen and donned the toga of manhood.

A detail (opposite) of a first-century A.D. *relief depicts the moment in a wedding when the couple join hands to symbolize their union. The relief below (from one of the Gallic provinces) illustrates an infant's growth into boyhood. At left, the father gazes with pride as his wife feeds their new-born son; soon the baby is old enough to be dandled. Short years remain for him to play with his donkey and cart before he has to cope with the problems of life: inevitably that day arrives—he must recite his lessons.*

THE LEISURE OF LADIES

Throughout the history of ancient Rome, plebeian women lived in much the same way: they married young, bore children, and ran the household with little time to indulge in immorality or play. But the growth of fortunes in the late republic gave patrician women the time for frivolity. "And all the news of the world she knows," Juvenal wrote scornfully of the Roman wife, "The secrets of the step-dame and the son;/Who speeds and who is jilted; and can swear/ Who made the widow pregnant, when, and where." Indeed while politics and philanthropy became the concern of some, gossip and entertainment became most ladies' main preoccupations; when they were not attending social functions with their husbands, they liked to play games, shop, or go to the theatre.

One of the most popular amusements among the Romans amounted more to a passion than a pastime; they were fanatic gamblers. They wagered on everything, and any game of chance appealed to them. The ladies in the marble monochrome below are playing knucklebones (an uncomplicated game based on odds and evens) and are probably betting heavily. During the empire dilettantism became quite fashionable among the women, who prided themselves on such accomplishments as writing little poems, declaiming in public, and playing musical instruments. The lady at right, ensconced in the bronze chair, was obviously so impressed with her talents that she asked to be pictured with her cithara.

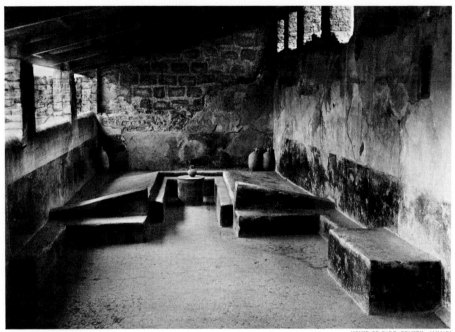

HOUSE OF CARO, POMPEII; ALINARI

ELEGANCE AT HOME

The vast majority of urban Romans lived in squalid, many-storied apartment buildings, which did not even have such amenities as a place for a fire for cooking and heat. Some middle-class families occupied luxurious duplex apartments with balconies and little gardens, and the wealthy few had fine town houses and sprawling country villas. Villas had their own baths, and the grandest of them boasted running water and swimming pools. Indeed, the younger Pliny's house, seventeen miles from Rome, was apparently unpretentious as villas went—it had at least twenty-five rooms, including a glassed-in arcade and two dining rooms, yet he described his home only as "enough for my needs, but not expensive to keep up."

At left is the atrium, or reception hall, of a Herculaneum villa. The pool catches water from an opening in the roof. A plan of a villa is shown at top right: a. entrance; b. atrium; c. winter dining rooms; d. reception room; e. atrium; f. baths; g. kitchen; h. courtyard; i. summer dining rooms; the many small rooms are bedrooms. Below the floor-plan is a Pompeiian dining room. Diners reclined on the couches while entertainers performed in the open space. Murals and mosaics graced most houses, but furnishings, though elegant, were usually few and often uncomfortable. Smoky light glimmered from oil lamps like that at right, and although only the most elaborate homes had heated floors, all had braziers that provided warmth, and some like the one at bottom right heated water also.

LOUVRE; ARCHIVES
PHOTOGRAPHIQUES

MUSEO NAZIONALE,
NAPLES; ANDERSON

181

The Pompeiian artists, who were masters of still life, particularly delighted in a beautifully appointed table or an arrangement from a well-stocked kitchen, as is demonstrated in this mural depicting eggs and game.

THE DINNER HOUR

In Petronius' satire, the banquet guests of the vulgarian Trimalchio gobbled up a course including in small part roast beef, testicles, kidneys, virgin sow bellies, cheesecake, lobster, goose, and mullets, only after whetting their appetites with olives, dormice dipped in honey and poppy seeds, sausages, and pomegranates. Petronius was exaggerating, but it has been recorded that at least at one banquet twenty-two courses, accompanied by vintage wines, were featured. A meal *en famille* was, of course, less elaborate, but every wealthy family had one or more cooks, who even on simple occasions prepared the spicy dishes that the Romans loved.

In each wealthy household a vast number of servants was commonly employed to get a meal on the table. The relief below depicts a provincial couple (center) waited upon by two servitors as others (left) pour wine; the slaves at right will soon bring on another course. The scene at bottom shows dinner preparations in the kitchen. The slaves at left are bringing flour and water to the man in the middle who kneads them into dough. At right two other servants get the oven ready to bake the bread.

VII

THE TRIUMPH OF AUGUSTUS

The day of Octavian began when he received his mother's letter informing him of his great-uncle, Caesar's, death; he was eighteen and studying in Apollonia, in Illyria. It ended fifty-eight years later when, revered as Father of his Country, he died after a reign of four and a half decades that far surpassed in political accomplishment, in the accumulation of national wealth, and in the flowering of the arts any period the Romans had known before. At the time Octavian received his mother's message, Rome was in a state of civil disarray. Caesar had failed to unite his people and to bring them lasting order. But when Octavian, under the title of Augustus, reached the end of his years, a great national revival had come about, imbued under his leadership with the spirit of patriotism and of return to the virtues of republican ancestors. In the outcome, the republic itself finally vanished, giving way to the personal rule of a long line of emperors, of whom he was the first and one of the most enlightened. Under him, institutions were both altered and stabilized; imperial boundaries were extended and secured. Above all, as a sovereign artist of politics, he laid the basis of a structure of power and relative concord that was to make possible a century and more of *pax Romana*.

Sculptors portrayed young Octavian as having grave nobility and calm. With his broad, unfurrowed brow, high cheekbones, finely chiseled lips, and determined chin, he resembled those young princes among the successors of Alexander the Great who carved out kingdoms for themselves in the east and minted coins showing their almost too-perfect profiles.

To the end of his life there was a strange remoteness about him, as though he held himself deliberately apart and never quite fitted into the Roman scene. Possibly there was Greek blood in him, for some of his ancestors supposedly lived in the Greek colony of Thurii, in southern Italy. His tutors were Greeks, and throughout his life he was devoted to Apollo, the god of light and lucidity. Saturated in Greek culture, Octavian wrote plays in Greek. His weapons, too, were the Greek weapons of guile and the sudden, oblique thrust—though in his mastery of organization and in his ruthlessness he was thoroughly Roman.

When Octavian set out from Apollonia for Rome in 44 B.C. he knew what had to be done: he would avenge Caesar, and he would go about it cautiously, stubbornly, with the sobriety of a man possessing a single purpose. He crossed the Adriatic Sea in a small boat and landed in an obscure port not far from Brundisium. There he learned that Caesar had named him his adopted son and the inheritor of three-fourths of a vast estate and of a name that was a title to power. Calling himself Gaius Julius Caesar Octavianus, he presented himself to the garrison at Brundisium, where he was received with acclamation. Then with a small armed guard he continued on his way to Rome.

Near Naples Octavian met his mother and stepfather, who were all for abandoning his enterprise of claiming his patrimony, for they were fearful of Mark Antony's power in the capital. There, too, he met Cicero, who found him friendly and deferential, though Cicero complained that the companions of Octavian kept addressing the young man as Caesar and were breathing slaughter against the conspirators, who were Cicero's friends. Octavian was a remarkable visitor, well mannered, but absolutely determined. Cicero, who was soon to be publicly complimenting the youth, appears, at this first meeting, to have reacted to him with suspicion. His fears, though premature, were to prove justified.

The distinguished band of conspirators had failed to make concerted plans for succession to the rule after the assassination; there was still a party and an army that had been loyal to Caesar—and Mark Antony, the surviving consul and self-proclaimed guardian of Caesar's legacy, had strong appeal to it, as did Octavian. Soon after Octavian's arrival in Rome, the conspirators were either in hiding or in full flight, leaving the city to the mercy of the two men about to become deadly rivals. A third contender for power was Marcus Aemilius Lepidus, whose positions as Caesar's master of the horse and as *pontifex maximus* gave him an official rank next to Antony's, and who as governor of Narbonese Gaul and Hither Spain controlled a body of troops in the provinces.

Antony and Octavian were utterly contrasting figures. Antony, at the age of thirty-nine, was a man in the prime of life. He had powerful shoulders and a bull-like neck, and his strong jaw, fine forehead, and aquiline nose made him look like a matinee idol, and there was much of the actor in him. He had high coloring and drank heavily; drink seems to have been the stimulus that aroused him to action. He was brave and immensely ambitious, and he claimed to be descended from Hercules. He amused himself by walking about the streets of Rome naked to the waist, a broadsword at his side, talking to all he met. His soldiers adored him, for he was always generous to them and seemed to enjoy their company. He liked making grand gestures. Once he ordered his steward to pay twenty-five "myriads" of money to a friend. The steward thought that if he piled the coins in a great heap Antony would be ashamed of his liberality. Instead, Antony took one look at the mountain of coins and said: "It is such a little pile! Give him twice as much!" But his bluster and posturing were the mask of a man beset by uncertainty.

The idealized portrait of the emperor Augustus, above, captures the godlike qualities attributed to him by his subjects. Control of the military, a vast fortune, and brilliant statesmanship enabled him to bring a long-lasting peace to Rome, which in turn fostered prosperity and the expansion of the empire.

When Octavian and Mark Antony became allies in the struggle for Caesar's throne they chose Lepidus (depicted on the coin above), a general whom Caesar had appointed pontifex maximus, *as the third member of the triumvirate that they established in 43* B.C. *Seven years later, Octavian forced the ineffectual Lepidus to retire from public life.*

Octavian, on the other hand, was a pale and sickly youth. When he presented himself to Antony to claim his inheritance, he was so reserved he could barely bring himself to speak in public. At first Antony would have nothing to do with Caesar's callow grand-nephew, who had only a small following. Although Octavian claimed a proud lineage, Antony spread the rumor that he was descended on his mother's side from a great-grandfather of African birth, who had kept a perfumery and then a bakery at Aricia, and that his paternal great-grandfather had been only a humble rope-maker. It may have been true, but to despise Octavian was folly in view of Caesar's will. A few days after the meeting, Antony complained that some of the followers of Octavian had attempted to murder him. This, too, may have been true. Octavian, quiet but steely-eyed, may have been readying his sword.

The duel between Antony and Octavian would last for thirteen years. It would be fought across the length of Europe with no quarter given. But there were long periods of truce when the adversaries were too exhausted or too comfortable to fight.

Octavian had begun raising a private army by paying many of Caesar's veterans the amounts promised them in the dictator's will. Then he placed himself and his forces at the disposal of the Senate against his rival and made overtures to Cicero, who was convinced that Antony was more dangerous to Rome than Octavian. In a remarkable speech known as the *Second Philippic* Cicero attacked Antony with astonishing force, describing him as a forger, an embezzler, a lecher, and a drunkard who consorted with criminals and actresses and spent his days and nights in orgies. According to Cicero, Antony was responsible for all Rome's troubles because he had offered the crown to Caesar, and his death would be a suitable offering to the shades of Caesar. Cicero called the senators to witness that not even Catiline had been so menacing to the Roman state. For a few more weeks the civil war was fought in words, and passions mounted. Octavian, by his mere presence in Rome, demonstrated his confidence in ultimate victory.

In the winter of 44 B.C., at the end of his consulship, Antony slipped out of Rome, raised an army of his own, and marched northward in the hope of raising an even larger army in Cisalpine Gaul, to which he had laid claim. A series of confused struggles followed between Antony and Octavian and their partisans. The Senate, which under republican influence had declared Antony a public enemy, became alarmed by the energy of the young man whom it had pitted against him. Cicero declared that Octavian should be "flattered, used, and pushed aside." But in 43 B.C. Octavian shrewdly countered: he marched on Rome with his army of eight legions to support his demand for the consulship for the following year (42 B.C.)—an office that was promptly awarded him. It was to be the first of his thirteen consulships, which formed the basis of his power, and it gave him a strong position from which to continue his struggle for power with Antony.

In the midst of the rivalry, however, there was Lepidus, who was able to swing his force of some seven legions to either contender. The Senate had hoped to use him against Antony as it had used Octavian, but Lepidus decided to join Antony's side, for which he in turn was proscribed. Then, rather than fight intramural contests among themselves, with republican enemies ready to take advantage of them, Antony, Octavian, and Lepidus decided they had better suspend their differences as Pompey, Crassus, and Caesar had done before them, and accordingly they formed a triumvirate, claiming supreme power over public affairs. A cowed Senate confirmed their status in late 43 B.C. for a period of just over five years, thereby abdicating what little power it still possessed. On a small island near present-day Bologna, under conditions of extraordinary secrecy, Antony, Octavian, and Lepidus met and entered upon a compact to divide the Roman world among them. They were alone except for their legions, which lined the banks of the river; they could surrender to whatever impulses they pleased, and for three days and three nights they indulged themselves by drawing up harsh laws and engaging in sophisticated intrigues. Finally they were able to announce that Transalpine and Cisalpine Gaul would go to Antony; Spain, to Lepidus; Africa, Sardinia, and Sicily, to Octavian. Since the state treasury was empty and they needed bounties for their troops, they drew up lists of proscriptions: the rich were to be killed and their estates confiscated; old debts were to be paid off, and the slates wiped clean.

Among those whose names were on the death lists was Cicero, who had exulted over the death of Caesar, attacked Antony, and sought to undermine Octavian. He could expect no mercy. He was in his litter, not far from one of his villas near the seashore, when the assassins caught up with him. For a few moments he gazed at them keenly, leaning his chin on his left hand, and then calmly bared his throat to their swords. His head and hands were hacked off and presented to Antony, who ordered them nailed to the speaker's platform in the Forum as a warning to others. Plutarch says the Romans shuddered: "And they believed they saw there, not the face of Cicero, but the image of Antony's own soul."

Octavian was to regret his connivance in this crime against one of the greatest of Romans. One day, many years later, he found one of his grandsons reading a book by Cicero. On seeing Octa-

Although the triumvirate was not reinstalled when its term expired in 33 B.C., neither Antony nor Octavian would relinquish control; instead, each prepared for war to determine who was to be the sole leader of Rome. They met in the sea battle of Actium in 31 B C. The cast of a gem carved to commemorate his victory shows Octavian as Neptune.
MUSEUM OF FINE ARTS, BOSTON; FRANCIS BARTLETT DONATION

189

vian the boy did his best to hide the book, but it was taken from him. For a long time Octavian pored over the pages, and at last he handed the book back, saying gravely: "My son, he was a learned man, and he loved his country."

Here and there resistance flared up against the triumvirs. The conspirators Cassius and Brutus were raising armies in the East, marching through Asia Minor, and ordering every city they entered to surrender its treasure so that they could pay bounties to their troops. But in 42 B.C., a year after the meeting on the island, the forces of Antony and Octavian met the forces of Brutus and Cassius at Philippi, in northern Greece, and under Antony's leadership defeated them; both Brutus and Cassius committed suicide. The republican cause finally perished.

Once again there was a division of the spoils. Italy was to be ruled in common; Transalpine Gaul and all the lands east of the Ionian Sea were to go to Antony; and Octavian was to receive Dalmatia, Sicily, Sardinia, Africa, and Spain. (Lepidus was ignored until Octavian ceded Africa to him in the year 40 B.C.) The twenty-one-year-old heir was sometimes reminded that he owed his vast realm to the generalship of Antony.

The next years saw efforts to stabilize a system of joint leadership and division of rule, but also the gradual heightening of the tension between Octavian and Antony that was to lead to their climactic clash at Actium. A new, disturbing element appeared in the person of Sextus Pompeius, a son of Pompey the Great, who had been outlawed by the triumvirs after raising his own army in Spain and briefly holding fleet command under the divided Senate's orders, only to re-emerge as chief of a piratical force that raided the commerce of the Italian coast. His success at this was such (he had moreover seized Sicily and Sardinia) as to force the triumvirs to come to terms with him and treat him almost as an equal, awarding him the islands he had occupied, and Corsica as well. Amid this accommodation Lepidus virtually vanished. Then in 38 B.C., a year that saw Rome in straits of confusion, Octavian took up arms against Sextus, whom he accused of violating agreements, and asked Antony for support in putting down the intruder.

Antony and Octavian failed to meet in time, and the latter was alone when he was defeated by Sextus—a humiliation that cast a pall of doubt over the year 37 B.C., in which Antony's and Octavian's joint supreme powers were renewed for another five years. In 36, the pall was seemingly lifted when Sextus was beaten at sea by Octavian's lieutenant Agrippa and forced to flee to the east, where he was put to death by one of Antony's commanders. Upon Sextus' defeat, Octavian proclaimed a new era of peace and pros-

This basalt head is thought to represent Octavian's third wife Livia, who became one of her husband's political confidants as well; he often sought her advice about his plans. Livia's wisdom, virtue, and dignity made her the personification of an ideal toward which he wanted all Roman women to strive.
LOUVRE; GIRAUDON

perity, and the day of the victory was made an annual religious holiday. The person of Octavian himself—*divi filius*, or "son of a god," ever since Caesar had been deified in 42 B.C.—was declared sacrosanct and inviolable. But despite Octavian's claim that he had brought peace and order to the empire, the final act in the drama of rivalry was still to come, shaped in large part by the matrimonial alliances and sexual interests of its chieftains.

To pacify Antony, Octavian in 40 B.C. had promoted a marriage between his sister Octavia and his rival. At about the same time, he himself wedded a twice-married woman related to Sextus—Scribonia, who gave him little joy. On the day of their daughter Julia's birth, he divorced her—"because," as he wrote, "I could not bear the way she nagged at me." Octavian then fell in love with Livia Drusilla, the nineteen-year-old wife of Tiberius Claudius Nero, a republican leader and veteran soldier who had fled to Greece after attempting to raise an army of former slaves against Octavian. Livia was pregnant by her middle-aged husband. Nero, however, complacently divorced her, and she married Octavian and remained faithful to him all the years of their marriage, dying in extremely old age in the reign of her son Tiberius Claudius Nero Caesar.

What had attracted Octavian to Livia was her serene, aristocratic beauty and perhaps a certain loftiness of manner. She had, if one can trust the statues, a commanding presence, features of perfect regularity, enormous eyes, and thick, wavy hair. She practiced the old republican virtues of chastity, obedience, and silence, though she could sometimes unbend: when Octavian heard that she had seen some men parading naked in the street, he flew into a rage, only to soften when she answered that to a woman like herself naked men were no different from statues. No one else had so great an influence on Octavian, who carefully made notes on the subjects he wanted to discuss with her—a remarkable tribute to her critical intelligence. She gave him no children, but he never divorced her for a more fertile bride. After Octavian's death she was pronounced *mater patriae*, the Mother of her Country, and when temples were erected to honor her husband she was invariably honored by being included in the dedication. Her greatest service to the Romans lay in her devotion to Octavian and in the civilizing influence she brought to bear on him.

Meanwhile Antony, too, had come under the influence of an extraordinary woman—Cleopatra. She had escaped from Rome in 44 B.C., after the murder of Caesar, and returned to Egypt. In 41, before his marriage to Octavia, Antony had summoned Cleopatra to Tarsus to answer a charge of aiding the republicans: the penalty for such a crime was death. When she presented herself to him, she

Above is the frescoed tablinum, *or reception room, of Octavian's and Livia's unostentatious house on the Palatine. Two of the projects most important to the ruler—moral reform and the preservation of tradition—were among his least successful, despite the example of sobriety that he set in his own life.*
HOUSE OF LIVIA, ROME; PINO BRESCIA

Having started to bring some order to the chaos caused in Italy by the civil wars, in 30 B.C. Octavian set off for Egypt; a detail (above) of a mosaic found near Rome depicts life along the Nile. (At lower left Roman soldiers gather for a party.) Egypt was quickly conquered, adding greatly to Octavian's ability to carry out his policies, since he regarded the new province, which was rich in crops and treasures, as his own domain.

was attended by all the seductive panoply of an actress in full command of the stage. "She came sailing up the river Cydnus," wrote Plutarch, "in a ship with a golden stern and outspread sails, while silver oars beat time to the music of flutes and fifes and harps. She lay under a canopy of gold cloth, dressed as Venus in a picture, while beautiful boys like painted cupids stood on each side and fanned her. Her maids were dressed like sea nymphs and graces, and some were steering the rudder while others worked the ropes. All manner of sweet perfumes were wafted ashore." Such is the description that Shakespeare was to adapt into the most splendid passage of his *Antony and Cleopatra*.

Whether Antony fell under her spell at that meeting or at subsequent ones remains a matter of conjecture. The impulses of Cleopatra, having been Caesar's mistress and having perhaps entertained a hope of becoming his wife, appear to have been to make a matrimonial and dynastic alliance with this new powerful man of Rome and thereby preserve her kingdom. She succeeded. The Romans learned in 37 B.C. that Antony, who had been living openly with Cleopatra, had married her, divorcing Octavia to do so. Moreover, he had given her as a wedding present much of the eastern half of the empire that was under his dominion and legitimized the children she had borne him. It was an affront to Rome and to Octavian in particular because Octavia was his sister.

After campaigning victoriously against the Parthians, Antony returned from Armenia in 34 B.C. for a curious triumphal procession through the streets of Alexandria. In triumphs held at Rome, it was customary for the conqueror to lay his laurels on the lap of the great statue of Jupiter on the Capitoline hill. Antony, however, placed his on the lap of Cleopatra as she sat on a golden throne, wearing the robes of the Egyptian goddess Isis. On that same evening there occurred a solemn celebration of the self-proclaimed divine rulers, Cleopatra-Isis and Antony-Osiris. This, an outrage to Roman ideas, served to emphasize the new division of the empire that Antony announced to the Egyptians. Cleopatra was declared queen of kings and of the sons of kings, and the fourteen-year-old Caesarion, her son by Caesar, was awarded the title of king of kings.

In 32 B.C. Antony committed a fatal error. He sent Octavia formal letters of divorce, and a messenger was despatched to Rome with instructions to deposit his will in the temple of the vestal virgins. Once deposited, such wills were sacrosanct, and only at the writer's death could the seals be removed. Yet Octavian seized the will and read it to the Senate. The senators noted its provision that if Antony died in Rome, he desired his body to be taken to Alexandria and given to Cleopatra. The implications were clear. He had turned his back on Rome, which had brought him to power, and had become so infatuated with Cleopatra that he no longer had a mind of his own. Octavian was determined on war, and Antony's perverse affection for an oriental princess provided a suitable excuse. At a ceremony in the temple of Bellona war was formally declared.

Romans would have preferred to fight on Italian soil, and they even suggested that Antony ferry his troops from the East to Italy. The coast would be cleared, and he would be given time to regroup his forces. Antony, suspecting that such a chivalrous offer concealed treachery, refused, but agreed to fight in Greece and set up his headquarters near Actium. Octavian ferried an army across the Ionian Sea and landed it close to Antony's. Antony may have had over five hundred ships, including one of Cleopatra's squadrons. At noon, on September 3, 31 B.C., the two fleets met and there was some desultory skirmishing, with the lighter Roman ships buzzing around the slow-moving, heavily armored ships of Antony, while the two armies took up their positions along the shore. Several of Antony's squadrons surrendered, and Cleopatra precipitously sailed away, abandoning Antony to his own resources. When Antony saw the purple sails of her flagship vanishing into the distance, he did what no other commander had ever done before—he fled from his army and fleet to run after a woman.

Before he made his decision to follow Cleopatra, Antony had the destiny of the world in his hands. He commanded nineteen legions on the shore, twelve thousand horse, a mighty navy, provinces with inexhaustible supplies of treasure and manpower, and a capital in Egypt that rivaled Rome in wealth and splendor. By the time he climbed on her flagship he had lost them all. We are told that he made his way to the prow and sat there for three days, his hands covering his face—possibly he was drunk.

The collapse at Actium was followed by the suicides of Antony and Cleopatra when the victor eventually reached Alexandria. Italy and the western provinces had already sworn allegiance to Octavian in 32 B.C.; now the entire eastern empire fell into his hands as well, rich Egypt becoming a domain that he ruled as the successor of the Ptolemies. He was virtually the master of the Mediterranean world, and all that was left for him to do was to put down surviving resistance among Antony's followers and to consolidate a new order in divided Rome. The first task was readily accomplished; the second he had set for himself was more difficult, however, and his solution revealed all his artistry of power.

When he returned to the capital in the summer of 29 B.C. to

The head at top may represent Cleopatra, Egypt's ambitious queen. Below it, is a contemporary marble portrait of Antony, the lover whom she acquired with a view to a possible personal gain from the inevitable conflict between him and Octavian. Cleopatra was with Antony at the battle of Actium. When their defeat became apparent they returned to Egypt, where, on Octavian's arrival, they committed suicide.

celebrate a three-day triumph, parading the spoils of Egypt through the streets, he was greeted as peacebringer by a war-weary people whose economy and very city had become badly run down. He immediately suggested measures of encouragement and reform. Rome's huge army of some sixty legions was slashed in half, and Octavian's income from Egypt was applied to settle veterans on plots of land. Unpaid back taxes were forgiven and records were burned. A general amnesty for Antony's followers was declared. The Senate, swollen by Julius Caesar's liege men, was judiciously cleansed and cut back in size. All this—along with the start of a vast program of urban renewal and rebuilding that was to change the face of Rome—was accomplished on the basis of Octavian's commanding prestige and presence, though he held no regular office other than that of annual consul, with the additional title of princeps, or first citizen. In effect, he controlled the state through his money and his well-rewarded soldiery. Yet ostentation and the trappings of power had no interest for a man so absorbed with the substance of power. In a time of self-indulgence he set an example of a return to republican austerity, living in a small house on the Palatine, his bedroom hardly larger than a cell, and wearing simple robes woven by his wife. Deliberately he presented himself as a man utterly without vanity, even without ambition, who remained at his post only because he regarded it as his duty to impose order on the empire.

In theory his power reposed in the fiction that he had restored the republic. Coins were struck honoring him as LIBERTATIS P[*opuli*] R[*omani*] VINDEX ("vindicator of the liberty of the Roman people"). Although he also proclaimed himself to be that, he had not the least intention of restoring the republic, and he was to destroy the vestiges of its liberties by reducing its governmental forms to mere extensions of his authoritarian rule. In one of the craftiest moves ever made by a statesman, he appeared before the Senate in 27 B.C. to announce that he wished to relinquish his power, having led his people to peace and well-being: "I shall lead you no longer, and no one will be able to say that it was to win absolute power that I did whatever has hitherto been done. . . . Receive back also your liberty and the republic; take over the army and the subject provinces, and govern yourselves as has been your wont." He was careful to remark, however, that "nothing in the world would deter me from aiding you when you were in danger . . . I gave myself to you unstintingly . . ."

The Senate was filled with Octavian's adherents and they became his willing accomplices. His seeming self-denial was actually a bid for the confirmation of even further power, backed by his

194

prestige or what he was to refer to in his memoir, the *Res gestae*, as his *auctoritas*. Almost everything a chief of state could desire was granted him by the listening Senate. He was to hold a ten-year proconsular imperium over Gaul, Spain, Syria, and Egypt; this involved control of the bulk of Rome's army. To consul and princeps, a third title was added—*augustus*, or "worshipful"—suggesting an exalted, priestlike presence and indicating prophetical knowledge and divine favor; its connotations dated back to Romulus, who had established Rome *augusto augurio* ("under the most favorable augury"), so the chronicler Ennius said. The Senate also voted to place laurels and a wreath of oak leaves on the door of his house, and to hang in the Senate a gold shield inscribed with a tribute to his valor, clemency, justice, and piety.

Though Augustus—this being the name under which he was from then on to be known—refused such titles of majesty as king and emperor and shrewdly preferred the simple one of princeps, he found in 23 B.C. that to run the vast affairs of Rome efficiently he needed even more power than he had already obtained. Refusing what would have been his twelfth consulship, he was given overriding proconsular power throughout the empire and was named tribune for life, a position that gave him power of veto. This was the highest peak of unchallenged authority yet reached in Rome.

Though chilly and reserved, Augustus did not exercise his principate in lofty isolation. He had close and gifted advisers—none more influential than Marcus Vipsanius Agrippa, who was his faithful deputy, and Gaius Cilnius Maecenas, who never held public office, but who was a trusted counselor, diplomatic agent, and friend of many years, besides being, with his wealth and culture, a patron of the arts, which Augustus was anxious to further as a reflection of his regime.

Born of an obscure family, Agrippa had been Augustus' boyhood friend; he was in Apollonia when news came of Julius Caesar's murder and was one of the first to advise the young man to make a bid for power. Then he had distinguished himself against Sextus Pompey and at Actium and had put down uprisings in Augustus' behalf in Gaul and Spain. Surviving portraits show his rugged, strong-jawed, granitic features. "In him," says the historian Velleius Paterculus, "there was no difference between thought and action." We are told that he was utterly impervious to danger and absolutely loyal to Augustus. An outstanding general and a man of considerable learning, he was also a brilliant administrator, organizing cities such as Heliopolis in the East, constructing a vast new water-supply system for Rome, and supervising the building of a road network in southern Gaul. When in

Agrippa, seen at left, served the emperor Augustus well as general, adviser, and associate in the work of rebuilding Rome. He oversaw great public improvement programs and personally paid for the erection of the original Pantheon, along with aqueducts and baths. Augustus chose Agrippa as his successor, but outlived him and had to name Livia's son Tiberius to be the next ruler. Below is an onyx cameo honoring Tiberius' victories in Pannonia. He is shown at left stepping from a chariot to be received by Augustus, who is being crowned by the goddess Roma at right; below them a victory monument is being raised.

195

18 B.C. the Senate renewed Augustus' extraordinary powers for five years, Agrippa was named his co-regent, sharing his tribunicial authority. There was no question, to be sure, as to who the actual ruler was; but Agrippa was both the second man in Rome and probably first in line for a dynastic succession, since Augustus himself had produced no male heirs and had given his daughter Julia to him in marriage. When Agrippa (born in the same year as Augustus) died at the age of fifty-one, he left a great gap in the life and surroundings of the emperor, who was to survive him by a quarter of a century.

Maecenas differed sharply from Agrippa in background and personality. Descended from a noble Etruscan clan, he was a patrician of great charm and style, calm and gentle, and particularly bent on exerting a restraining influence on Augustus, in whom he had detected a streak of unnecessary cruelty. Tolerant, urbane, brave, he was a liberal in an authoritarian age. If Agrippa was all for action, Maecenas was for caution and moderation, and so they admirably complemented one another. Gathering poets around him at his country estate, Maecenas encouraged Vergil and Horace to place their talents at the service of Augustus. Vergil, the elegiac writer raised in the Mantuan countryside, became through Maecenas' sponsorship a confidant of Augustus, who asked him on occasion to accompany the imperial household on trips abroad and at one point appears to have suggested that he might write an epic on the late wars. Instead, Vergil wrote the *Aeneid*—the epic purporting to describe the finding and conquest of Italy by Augustus' ancestor Aeneas, but also intended to celebrate Rome's illustrious destiny and the moral foundations of the peace and order Augustus had achieved. The triumph of Aeneas was the triumph of Augustus, who appears in the poem in a prophetic vision of his great ancestor. In this vision Augustus is seen enthroned within the temple of Apollo as he inspects the tribute offered him by all the peoples of the world, and these gifts are hung on the gleaming white temple gates. Again and again Vergil insists that it was not for plunder or lust of battle that the Romans came to dominate the world; they were to dominate it because the gods had decreed that rule should be given to the righteous, the just, and the blessed.

Once in a mood of despair Vergil wrote to Augustus to complain of the difficulties of composing the *Aeneid*. "It is so shapeless a thing," he wrote, "that I think myself mad to have embarked on it." It is true that it lacks the clear contours of the *Iliad* and was evidently written with immense difficulty by a poet burdened by the magnitude of his theme and its demands of style. He was con-

The reliefs that adorn the Ara Pacis (shown at top), the altar of the Augustan peace, are among the greatest works of art produced in the early empire. In a detail (above) from the shrine are the portraits of some of Augustus' family and officials, shown in calm and dignified—but unidealized—poses. The Roman Senate had the altar erected on the Campus Martius to commemorate Augustus' return from Gaul, where he had been living for three years, so important to him was the administration of that province.

tinually rewriting, "licking it into shape," Suetonius remarked, "as the she-bear does her cubs." Even with the epic completed, except for the finishing touches, he was so dissatisfied that he begged his friends to burn the manuscript when he died. However, Augustus ordered that Vergil's wish be disregarded, and the epic was published as it was left, with half-lines uncompleted and awkward passages unchanged. Vergil had claimed that he needed three more years to perfect it, and it is possible that if he had been given those years he would have ruined it.

What survives is the proudest literary monument ever offered to an emperor. Although Vergil celebrates the noble achievements of Aeneas, he has a quite un-Roman pity for Aeneas' fallen enemies. Indeed, pity and terror are major themes in the epic. It is almost as though Vergil had been granted prophetic powers, seeing Rome as both conqueror and victim, tyrant and slave. Augustus looked outward at the world at peace. Vergil looked inward and saw that the peace was delusory and impermanent and at the mercy of dark forces.

Horace, both a witty amorist and a traditional moralist, exquisitely deft in the use of his words, was invited to compose a hymn for the secular games announced for 17 B.C. to celebrate the first ten years of Augustus' principate. This he did in the form of the celebrated poem *Carmen saeculare,* which opens with an invocation to Apollo and his sister goddess Diana to keep Rome under their protection. Addressing them, the poet proclaims: *"Roma vestrum est opus* (Rome is your handiwork)." He was undoubtedly writing in praise of Augustus, who had taken Apollo for his special patron.

For three days and three nights the games were held, with vast processions moving through the city; at night, under the full moon, there were torchlight marches; finally, a choir of youths and maidens sang Horace's hymn outside Apollo's temple on the Palatine. All classes gave homage to the durable victor and leader who had brought peace, prosperity, and a wiser distribution of the spoils or rewards of growth to Rome.

Augustus, both in his early and later years, was aware of the far boundaries of his empire, advancing some, consolidating others. In 19 B.C. he organized campaigns to subdue what remained of resistance in Spain; he spent some three years in Gaul, organizing it and making Lugdunum (Lyons) its capital; he advanced Roman power across the Alps into the Bavarian plain and along the Danube to Vindobona (Vienna) and the Hungarian grassland; he sought for a stable northeastern border along the rivers Weser and Elbe, but was finally stopped in A.D. 6 by Teuton tribes. In the east, meanwhile, he had reached a settlement with Parthia whereby the Euphrates was recognized as the border between two empires.

In 18 and 17 B.C. Augustus instituted reform legislation at home that was designed to improve morals and restore republican virtues, though he had no intention of restoring republican institutions. Laws against adultery, coupled with restrictions on luxury and ostentation, emanated from him. In order to stabilize marriage and promote offspring, benefits were bestowed upon the parents of large families, and a candidate for public office could win precedence because of the sheer number of his children. Ancient rites and domestic rituals that had fallen into decay in a time of Roman absorption with cults of the east were restored. Augustus is described as having been particularly engaged in reviving respect for the lares and penates and for the vestal virgins. Though he had shown favor to Ovid, the liveliest and naughtiest poet at his court, this puritan emperor eventually banished him. Augustus' vast public works program—restoring old temples and providing a new forum—was in large part an effort to provide work for the unemployed.

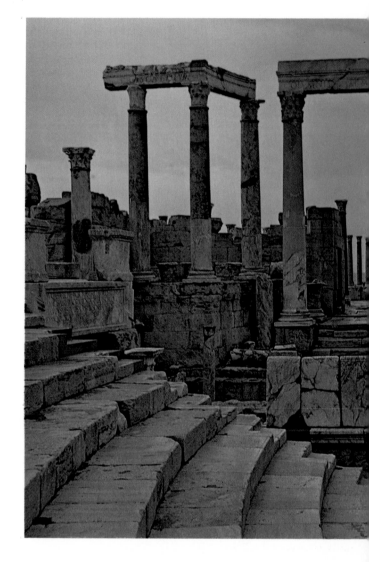

During the rest of his reign Augustus ruled in austere majesty, his powers being periodically renewed by a compliant Senate. He was the fount of honor, the chief magistrate, the commander of all armies (which had taken an oath of personal allegiance to him), the holder of the treasury, and after 12 B.C. when he became *pontifex maximus* after the death of Lepidus (previous holder of the office), the head of the state religion as well. He could issue edicts and judicial decisions without review. He had been given the right to make treaties and thus conduct foreign affairs as he saw fit. His personal income was immeasurable, drawn in great part from revenues from various parts of the empire that he governed through his deputies as provinces of his own. As in the case of Caesar before him, his own treasury and that of the state were intermixed. His power of patronage, of appointment, and of reward was oriental in its extent.

Yet with this vast concentration of might in his person, he was wise enough to see that he would do well to share it or delegate a considerable part of it to others. A great empire could not be well managed by a supreme potentate alone. It needed the skillful and devoted hand of men who would share the responsibility for it. It needed, in short, a high administrative class. One aspect of the genius of Augustus lay in recognizing in the humbled Senate, now no longer the lofty and contumacious arbiter of Roman fortunes, the basis of collaboration with himself. He paid courtly deference to the senators, rising in their presence and repeatedly referring matters to them for further consideration. Anxious to secure

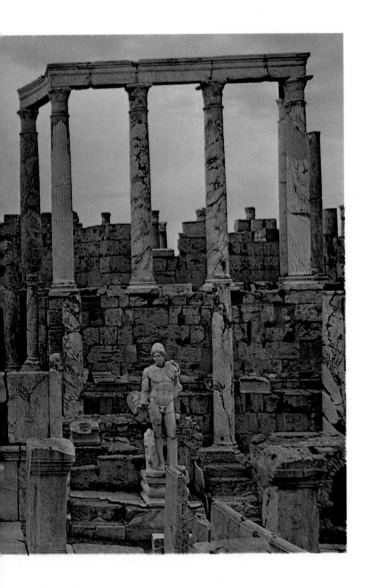

Above is a view of Leptis Magna, located on the coast of Libya; it was built on a former Phoenecian site and was developed at the behest of Augustus. The emperor was responsible for the modernization of many towns in areas that had bowed to Rome, and he set up an efficient bureaucratic system to administer them. In fact, consolidation was an important facet of Augustus' program to strengthen the empire; another was to gain more territory, and although he did not win as much as he wished, by the time he died Rome had eleven more provinces than when he came to power.

both their loyalty and their talents, he extended their functions, encouraging them to take over legislative and judicial roles from the popular assemblies, the tribunes, and the judges, and to share with him the burdens of imperial management—all subject, to be sure, to his final veto. Some laws were left to the Senate to promulgate; many provinces were left to it to administer; and the basis of membership in the Senate was broadened to attract promising young men of the class of equites whom he wished to recruit for careers in public office. Augustus was in need of trained men to serve as quaestors, aediles, praetors; all positions from which they could rise to become legion commanders, governors, and prefects. Using the Senate as his base, he offered long-term, salaried appointments to such men, as against the volunteer and amateur system of the republic. In effect, the Senate and the senatorial order became his administrative right arm. He himself, both magisterial and deft, combined the ways of a dictator, a constitutional monarch and an American President calling upon the "advice and consent" of the Senate, while building a formidable bureaucracy.

Almost uninterrupted peace under Augustus led to even greater prosperity. Rome, which had previously resembled a large sprawling village, became amid his rebuilding of temples and monuments a splendid city, and the wealth of the empire flowed into it. Not long before his death Augustus remarked: "I found Rome built of sun-dried bricks; I leave it clothed in marble."

In 9 B.C., midway in his reign, the Ara Pacis, an altar to the Augustan peace, was dedicated on the Campus Martius. Augustus, who had built numerous large temples to the gods, could no doubt have raised one in his own honor; instead he allowed the Senate to erect a rather modest shrine less than forty feet long to commemorate his greatest achievement. Although richly decorated with symbolic friezes and carved portraiture (one can recognize Augustus and Agrippa, Livia and Augustus' daughter Julia) the altar reflects a certain restraint—a quality lacking in many of Rome's later emperors.

When he died at seventy-six in A.D. 14, having also outlived Maecenas, Vergil, Horace, and his only two grandsons—his daughter Julia's children by Agrippa—no further memorial in marble was needed. The empire itself, unchallenged, masterful, and bearing the imprint of Augustus' firm and lucid mind stood there for all to see. For centuries the Romans were to look back on the Augustan age as a period when their world was divinely blessed, when peace was as familiar as daily bread, and hope was the commonplace of daily lives.

THE ROMAN FACE

The art of the Romans is often scornfully referred to as derivative and sterile; ironically some of the outstanding achievements of their civilization are artistic. The Romans perfected satire; they were superb painters of still life; they erected buildings of a scale and design undreamed of before their time. One of their greatest accomplishments was portrait sculpture, which began to emerge in the third century B.C. As a further irony, the busts and statues produced were usually the work of sculptors from Greece and the East. The portraits those artists carved, however, were basically Roman, for the characteristics of the Roman patrons themselves supplied the inspiration that resulted in a gallery of faces of startling candor and lasting vitality.

Roman tradition and outside influences combined to create what in effect was a new art form. Romans were familiar with the idealized sculpture of Periclean Attica, and more so with the sentimentalized realism of Hellenistic art. They well knew Etruscan funerary sculpture which, though stylized, did not hesitate to show extra flesh where it had been added or the wen where it grew. Their practice of making death masks had also accustomed them to seeing in portraits the sags and lines of age. But most importantly, it was the Roman's insistent individualism, his matter-of-factness, his interest in the here-and-now that made him demand utter truthfulness in images of himself and those surrounding him—as in the gravestone of a citizen and his wife opposite.

The gravitas of age and the pensiveness of youth mark the faces of these Roman citizens.

203

*Since sculptors usually worked on commission, most Roman portraits are of wealthy patrons or public leaders.
But artists used everyday people as models too, and thereby left to posterity an intimate view of Roman citizens
of every class and age. At top (from left to right) are the emperor Decius, a charioteer, and a youth; at
bottom, a little boy, a young woman, a senator; opposite, an aristocratic lady displays a stylish coiffeure.*

OVERLEAF: *Two portraits unsparingly suggest the toll that Rome's strenuous life took of its citizens.*

MASTERS

OF THE

GOLDEN AGE

... quin aspera Iuno,
quae mare nunc terrasque metu caelumque fatigat,
consilia in melius referet, mecumque fovebit
Romanos, rerum dominos, gentemque togatam.

Vergil, Aeneid
(translation on page 210, column two, lines 20–24)

Exegi monumentum aere perennius
regalique situ pyramidum altius,
quod non imber edax, non Aquilo impotens
possit diruere...

Horace, Odes, III: 30
(translation on page 218, lines 1–3)

Like the Periclean Athens that preceded it and the Elizabethan England that came later, Augustan Rome was fortunate in breeding in its time of triumph a brilliant generation of poets and chroniclers to celebrate it and to pursue the study of man, his passions and condition. Rome produced neither an heir to Aeschylus and Socrates nor a precursor of Shakespeare; yet, wedded to the written word as Athens had been to the spoken one, it brought forth, with the gift of its marvelously concise and resonant language, some of the most accomplished men of letters of all time.

In Vergil, Rome produced something more than a man of letters; it reared a major poet whose *Aeneid* gave to his patron Augustus and to posterity a proud national epic, built on Homer, a poem so lyrical and compassionate as to enrapture Dante. Imitation of Greek models went hand in hand with intense individuality. Propertius adapted the traditional elegy to tell intimately of his amours and explore the nature of those whom he had loved and lost. Horace turned the ode into the instrument for his exquisite urbanity and wit. Ovid, playboy of Augustan writing, was both its leading amorist and master storyteller, presenting in his *Metamorphoses* in effect a mock epic on sporting gods and ancestors. Livy, the greatest patriotic historian of the Romans, produced in prose a rich chronicle compounded of fact and fable. Chaucer, Petrarch, Shakespeare were among those who leaned on Ovid and Livy as particular sources for their knowledge of antiquity. Seldom, in fact, have so few authors influenced so many great ones of later times.

Between the muses of epic and tragedy, Vergil reads from his Aeneid.

THE SPLENDOR OF VERGIL

from the AENEID
(*translated by Rolfe Humphries*)

Arms and the man I sing, the first who came,
Compelled by fate, an exile out of Troy,
To Italy and the Lavinian coast,
Much buffeted on land and on the deep
By violence of the gods, through that long rage,
That lasting hate, of Juno's. And he suffered
Much, also, in war, till he should build his town
And bring his gods to Latium, whence, in time,
The Latin race, the Alban fathers, rose
And the great walls of everlasting Rome.

Help me, O Muse, recall the reasons: why,
Why did the queen of heaven drive a man
So known for goodness, for devotion, through
So many toils and perils? Was there slight,
Affront, or outrage? Is vindictiveness
An attribute of the celestial mind?

*The opening lines above herald the action. Aeneas, son of Venus
by Anchises of the Trojan royal house, is so hounded by Juno,
consort of Jupiter and hater of Trojans, that when seeking to
find a new home for himself and his followers after Troy's fall,
he finds himself a shipwrecked wanderer. His mother Venus,
seeing his sufferings, pleads with Jupiter to succor him and to
remember the promise that Trojans would one day found a
realm in Italy. The god reassures her:*

He smiled, in answer,
The kind of smile that clears the air, and kissed her.
"Fear not, my daughter; fate remains unmoved
For the Roman generations. You will witness
Lavinium's rise, her walls fulfill the promise;
You will bring to heaven lofty-souled Aeneas.

There has been no change in me whatever. Listen!
To ease this care, I will prophesy a little,
I will open the book of fate. Your son Aeneas
Will wage a mighty war in Italy,
Beat down proud nations, give his people laws,
Found them a city, a matter of three years
From victory to settlement. His son,
The boy Ascanius, named Ilus once,
When Troy was standing, and now called Iulus,
Shall reign for thirty years, and great in power
Forsake Lavinium, transfer the kingdom
To Alba Longa, new-built capital.
Here, for three hundred years, the line of Hector
Shall govern, till a royal priestess bears
Twin sons to Mars, and Romulus, rejoicing
In the brown wolf-skin of his foster-mother,
Takes up the tribe, and builds the martial walls
And calls the people, after himself, the Romans.
To these I set no bounds in space or time;
They shall rule forever. Even bitter Juno
Whose fear now harries earth and sea and heaven
Will change to better counsels, and will cherish
The race that wears the toga, Roman masters
Of all the world. It is decreed. The time
Will come, as holy years wheel on, when Troy
Will subjugate Mycenae, vanquish Phthia,
Be lord of Argos. And from this great line
Will come a Trojan, Caesar, to establish
The limit of his empire at the ocean,
His glory at the stars, a man called Julius
Whose name recalls Iulus. Welcome waits
For him in heaven; all the spoils of Asia
Will weigh him down, and prayer be made before him.

The achievement of Roman peace by means of the victory at Actium (31 B.C.), after a century of strife, gave Augustus' friend Vergil the impetus to crown his career as a writer of pastorals and idylls with a vast poem recounting the myths that surround Rome's origin and proclaiming the grandeur of its destiny. Noble Aeneas, survivor of the holo- caust at Troy, described by Homer, proceeds on an odyssey that leads him through many perils into the arms of Dido of Carthage and finally to the promised land where he is to sire a race. Cast in lines of stately eloquence, the twelve books of the Aeneid range over wars and romance with a haunting sense of the tragedy that often results from the gods' commands. Here are some central passages in a recent translation by an American scholar.

Then wars will cease, and a rough age grow gentler,
White Faith and Vesta, Romulus and Remus,
Give law to nations. War's grim gates will close,
Tight-shut with bars of iron, and inside them
The wickedness of war sit bound and silent,
The red mouth straining and the hands held tight
In fastenings of bronze, a hundred hundred."

Seeking refuge on Africa's shore, Aeneas is made welcome at the court of beautiful Dido, widowed queen of splendid Carthage, whom Venus with her wiles has attracted to him. Stirred, Dido asks the voyager to tell his story. Recounting his ordeals, he narrates a climactic moment at Troy—King Priam's death:

Just then through darts, through weapons, came Polites,
A son of Priam, fleeing deadly Pyrrhus,
Down the long colonnades and empty hallways,
Wounded, and Pyrrhus after him, vicious, eager
For the last spear-thrust, and he drives it home;
Polites falls, and his life goes out with his blood,
Father and mother watching. And then Priam,
In the very grip of death, cried out in anger:—
"If there is any righteousness in heaven,
To care about such wickedness, the gods
Will have the right reward and thanks to offer
A man like this, who has made a father witness
The murder of his son, the worst pollution!
You claim to be Achilles' son. You liar!
Achilles had some reverence, respected
A suppliant's right and trust; he gave me back
My Hector's lifeless body for the tomb,
And let me go to my kingdom." With the word

He flung a feeble spear, which dropped, deflected
From the rough bronze; it had hung there for a moment.
And Pyrrhus sneered: "So, go and tell my father
The latest news: do not forget to mention,
Old messenger-boy, my villainous behavior,
And what a bastard Pyrrhus is. Now die!"
He dragged the old man, trembling, to the altar,
Slipping in his son's blood; he grabbed his hair
With the left hand, and the right drove home the sword
Deep in the side, to the hilt. And so fell Priam,
Who had seen Troy burn and her walls come down, once
                                              monarch,
Proud ruler over the peoples and lands of Asia.
He lies, a nameless body, on the shore,
Dismembered, huge, the head torn from the shoulders.

Dido tries to calm her rising passion for Aeneas, recalling her oath of faithfulness to her dead husband:

But the queen finds no rest. Deep in her veins
The wound is fed; she burns with hidden fire.
His manhood, and the glory of his race
Are an obsession with her, like his voice,
Gesture and countenance. On the next morning,
After a restless night, she sought her sister:
"I am troubled, Anna, doubtful, terrified,
Or am I dreaming? What new guest is this
Come to our shores? How well he talks, how brave
He seems in heart and action! I suppose
It must be true; he does come from the gods.
Fear proves a bastard spirit. He has been

So buffeted by fate. What endless wars
He told of! Sister, I must tell you something:
Were not my mind made up, once and for all,
Never again to marry, having been
So lost when Sychaeus left me for the grave,
Slain by my murderous brother at the altar,
Were I not sick forever of the torch
And bridal bed, here is the only man
Who has moved my spirit, shaken my weak will.
I might have yielded to him. I recognize
The marks of an old fire. But I pray, rather,
That earth engulf me, lightning strike me down
To the pale shades and everlasting night
Before I break the laws of decency.
My love has gone with Sychaeus; let him keep it,
Keep it with him forever in the grave."
She ended with a burst of tears.

Their love consummated, Dido and Aeneas look forward to happiness together; but Jupiter, through Mercury, commands Aeneas to tear himself away and proceed with his mission to found Rome. There is no choice but to obey. Caught in the conflict between divine will and human emotion, Dido upbraids her sadly departing lover and prepares for self-inflicted death:

She looked him up and down; then blazed out at him:—
"You treacherous liar! No goddess was your mother,
No Dardanus the founder of your tribe,
Son of the stony mountain-crags, begotten
On cruel rocks, with a tigress for a wet-nurse!
Why fool myself, why make pretense? what is there
To save myself for now? When I was weeping
Did he so much as sigh? Did he turn his eyes,
Ever so little, toward me? Did he break at all,
Or weep, or give his lover a word of pity?
What first, what next? Neither Jupiter nor Juno
Looks at these things with any sense of fairness.
Faith has no haven anywhere in the world.
He was an outcast on my shore, a beggar,
I took him in, and, like a fool, I gave him
Part of my kingdom; his fleet was lost, I found it,
His comrades dying, I brought them back to life.
I am maddened, burning, burning: now Apollo
The prophesying god, the oracles
Of Lycia, and Jove's herald, sent from heaven,
Come flying through the air with fearful orders,—
Fine business for the gods, the kind of trouble
That keeps them from their sleep. I do not hold you,
I do not argue, either. Go. And follow
Italy on the wind, and seek the kingdom
Across the water. But if any gods
Who care for decency have any power,
They will land you on the rocks; I hope for vengeance,

I hope to hear you calling the name of Dido
Over and over, in vain. Oh, I will follow
In blackest fire, and when cold death has taken
Spirit from body, I will be there to haunt you,
A shade, all over the world. I will have vengeance,
And hear about it; the news will be my comfort
In the deep world below."

Reaching Italy and the prospect of his realm, Aeneas asks to be led to the underworld to visit the shade of his dead father Anchises. Guided by the sibyl, he crosses the river Styx, sees many ghastly shapes and the spirits of famous evildoers suffering tortures. Then he reaches the Elysian fields, where his father welcomes him and shows him the multitude of souls waiting beside the river Lethe, where they must drink forgetfulness:

He saw, in a far valley, a separate grove
Where the woods stir and rustle, and a river,
The Lethe, gliding past the peaceful places,
And tribes of people thronging, hovering over,
Innumerable as the bees in summer
Working the bright-hued flowers, and the shining
Of the white lilies, murmuring and humming.
Aeneas, filled with wonder, asks the reason
For what he does not know, who are the people
In such a host, and to what river coming?
Anchises answers:—"These are spirits, ready
Once more for life; they drink of Lethe's water
The soothing potion of forgetfulness.
I have longed, for long, to show them to you, name them,
Our children's children; Italy discovered,
So much the greater happiness, my son."
"But, O my father, is it thinkable
That souls would leave this blessedness, be willing
A second time to bear the sluggish body,
Trade Paradise for earth? Alas, poor wretches,
Why such a mad desire for light?" Anchises
Gives detailed answer: "First, my son, a spirit
Sustains all matter, heaven and earth and ocean,
The moon, the stars; mind quickens mass, and moves it.
Hence comes the race of man, of beast, of wingèd
Creatures of air, of the strange shapes which ocean
Bears down below his mottled marble surface.
All these are blessed with energy from heaven;
The seed of life is a spark of fire, but the body
A clod of earth, a clog, a mortal burden.
Hence humans fear, desire, grieve, and are joyful,
And even when life is over, all the evil
Ingrained so long, the adulterated mixture,
The plagues and pestilences of the body
Remain, persist. So there must be a cleansing,
By penalty, by punishment, by fire,
By sweep of wind, by water's absolution,

Before the guilt is gone. Each of us suffers
His own peculiar ghost. But the day comes
When we are sent through wide Elysium,
The Fields of the Blessed, a few of us, to linger
Until the turn of time, the wheel of ages,
Wears off the taint, and leaves the core of spirit
Pure sense, pure flame. A thousand years pass over
And the god calls the countless host to Lethe
Where memory is annulled, and souls are willing
Once more to enter into mortal bodies."

*Strengthened by Anchises' prophecy that the Romans of times
ahead are destined to be rulers of the world, Aeneas wages fierce
wars to gain mastery over native tribes, his chief foe being young
Turnus, leader of the Rutulian clan and a favorite of Juno.
After great slaughter, in the course of which Turnus kills Aeneas'
young friend and ally Pallas, a single combat between Turnus
and Aeneas is proposed. At this point Jupiter, aroused by Juno's
continuing intervention against Aeneas, orders her to cease, and
she replies with an extraordinary formula of accommodation.
Their dialogue follows:*

                    And Juno, gazing
From a golden cloud to earth, watching the duel,
Heard the all-powerful king of high Olympus:—
"What will the end be now, O wife? What else
Remains? You know, and you admit you know it,
Aeneas is heaven-destined, the native hero
Become a god, raised by the fates, exalted.
What are you planning? with what hope lingering on
In the cold clouds? Was it proper that a mortal
Should wound a god? that the sword, once lost, be given
Turnus again?—Juturna, of course, is nothing
Without your help—was it proper that the beaten
Increase in violence? Stop it now, I tell you;
Listen to my entreaties: I would not have you
Devoured by grief in silence; I would not have you
Bring me, again, anxiety and sorrow,
However sweet the voice. The end has come.
To harry the Trojans over land and ocean,
To light up war unspeakable, to defile
A home with grief, to mingle bridal and sorrow,—
All this you were permitted. Go no farther!
That is an absolute order." And Juno, downcast
In gaze, replied:—"Great Jove, I knew your pleasure:
And therefore, much against my will, left Turnus,
Left earth. Were it not so, you would not see me
Lonely upon my airy throne in heaven,
Enduring things both worthy and unworthy,
But I would be down there, by flame surrounded,
Fighting in the front ranks, and hauling Trojans
To battle with their enemies. Juturna,
I urged, I own, to help her wretched brother,

And I approved, I own, her greater daring
For his life's sake, but I did not approve,
And this I swear by Styx, that river whose name
Binds all the gods to truth, her taking weapons,
Aiming the bow. I give up now, I leave
These battles, though I hate to. I ask one favor
For Latium, for the greatness of your people,
And this no law of fate forbids: when, later,
And be it so, they join in peace, and settle
Their laws, their treaties, in a blessèd marriage,
Do not command the Latins, native-born,
To change their language, to be known as Trojans,
To alter speech or garb; let them be Latium,
Let Alban kings endure through all the ages,
Let Roman stock, strong in Italian valor,
Prevail: since Troy has fallen, let her name
Perish and be forgotten." Smiling on her,
The great creator answered:—"You are truly
True sister of Jove and child of Saturn, nursing
Such tides of anger in the heart! Forget it!
Abate the rise of passion. The wish is granted.
I yield, and more than that,—I share your purpose.
Ausonians shall keep their old tradition,
Their fathers' speech and ways; their name shall be
Even as now it is. Their sacred laws,
Their ritual, I shall add, and make all Latins
Men of a common tongue. A race shall rise
All-powerful, of mingled blood; you will see them
By virtue of devotion rise to glories
Not men nor gods have known, and no race ever
Will pay you equal honor." And the goddess
Gave her assent, was happy, changed her purpose,
Left heaven and quit the cloud.

*In a sense, then, Juno wins. Though the Trojans are to conquer,
their very identity is to be extinguished in the creation of a
combined people to be called the Latins. Aeneas, as instrument
of gods and destiny, is agreeable to this resolution of the strife.
But there is one final thrust. On the field he encounters Turnus,
a foe misguided only in that he did not see the forces of destiny.
Aeneas would have spared him out of sheer humanity had he not
seen Turnus wearing dead Pallas' sword belt. In rage, therefore,
Aeneas kills him—and on this tragic and equivocal note the great
epic poem of the Romans ends:*

And on Aeneas presses: the flashing spear,
Brandished, is big as a tree; his anger cries:—
"Why put it off forever, Turnus, hang-dog?
We must fight with arms, not running. Take what shape
You will, gather your strength or craft; fly up
To the high stars, or bury yourself in earth!"

And Turnus shook his head and answered:—"Jove,
Being my enemy, scares me, and the gods,
Not your hot words, fierce fellow." And his vision,
Glancing about, beheld a mighty boulder,
A boundary-mark, in days of old, so huge
A dozen men in our degenerate era
Could hardly pry it loose from earth, but Turnus
Lifts it full height, hurls it full speed and, acting,
Seems not to recognize himself, in running,
Or moving, or lifting his hands, or letting the stone
Fly into space; he shakes at the knees, his blood
Runs chill in the veins, and the stone, through wide air going,
Falls short, falls spent. As in our dreams at night-time,
When sleep weighs down our eyes, we seem to be running,
Or trying to run, and cannot, and we falter,

Sick in our failure, and the tongue is thick
And the words we try to utter come to nothing,
No voice, no speech,—so Turnus finds the way
Blocked off, wherever he turns, however bravely.
All sorts of things go through his mind: he stares
At the Rutulians, at the town; he trembles,
Quails at the threat of the lance; he cannot see
Any way out, any way forward. Nothing.
The chariot is gone, and the charioteer,
Juturna or Metiscus, nowhere near him.
The spear, flung by Aeneas, comes with a whir
Louder than stone from any engine, louder
Than thunderbolt; like a black wind it flies,
Bringing destruction with it, through the shield-rim,
Its sevenfold strength, through armor, through the thigh.

PROPERTIUS IN LOVE

DEATH AND TRANSFIGURATION
from the Elegies
(*translated by Gilbert Highet*)

Ghosts do exist. Death does not finish everything.
    The pale phantom lives to escape the pyre.
Yes: bending over my pillow, I saw Cynthia—
    interred that day beside the highway's roar.
Still sleepless, brooding on my mistress' funeral,
    I loathed the chilly empire of my bed.
Her hair was just the same as at her burial,
    her eyes the same; her dress scorched down one side;
the fire had eaten at her favourite beryl ring;
    her lips had tasted Lethé, and were pale.

She spoke, in a voice panting with life and passion: her hands
    quivered meanwhile, the frail knuckles snapped.
"Cheat! Liar! false to me and every other girl,
    can sleep have any influence on you?
Can you forget those wakeful nights in the Subura?—
    the well-known window, open for my escape,
through which I dropped the rope, night after night, and dangled,
    climbing down hand by hand into your arms?
Even at street-corners Venus brought us together: often
    we warmed the paving-stones as we embraced.

Gone now, gone, our secret promises! The wind,
    deaf and unfeeling, scattered all our vows.
Yet, as my eyes were closing, no one spoke my name:
    I could have gained, at your call, one more day.
No watcher sat beside my body with his rattle;
    my head was gashed, propped on a broken pot.
Then were you seen sadly stooping above my coffin
    and sobbing passionately, clothed in black?
If you would not escort my bier beyond the gates,
    you might have made it walk slowly till then.
And why, ungrateful dog, did you not call the winds
    to fan my flames, perfume my pyre with spice?
Was it too much to break a jar of wine upon
    my ashes, strew them with cheap hyacinths?
Lygdamus must be burned: that slave needs white-hot iron:
    I saw his treachery in my pale wine.
Or else let cunning Nomas hide her secret potions—
    the glowing pot will soon convict her hands.

And she who once was cheap for public sale each night
    but now trails gold embroidery in the dust—

Turnus is down, on hands and knees, huge Turnus
Struck to the earth. Groaning, the stunned Rutulians
Rise to their feet, and the whole hill resounds,
The wooded heights give echo. A suppliant, beaten,
Humbled at last, his hands reach out, his voice
Is low in pleading:—"I have deserved it, surely,
And I do not beg off. Use the advantage.
But if a parent's grief has any power
To touch the spirit, I pray you, pity Daunus,
(I would Anchises), send him back my body.
You have won; I am beaten, and these hands go out
In supplication: everyone has seen it.
No more. I have lost Lavinia. Let hatred
Proceed no further."
Fierce in his arms, with darting glance, Aeneas

Paused for a moment, and he might have weakened,
For the words had moved him, when, high on the shoulder,
He saw the belt of Pallas, slain by Turnus,
Saw Pallas on the ground, and Turnus wearing
That belt with the bright studs, of evil omen
Not only to Pallas now, a sad reminder,
A deadly provocation. Terrible
In wrath, Aeneas cries:—"Clad in this treasure,
This trophy of a comrade, can you cherish
Hope that my hands would let you go? Now Pallas,
Pallas exacts his vengeance, and the blow
Is Pallas, making sacrifice!" He struck
Before he finished speaking: the blade went deep
And Turnus' limbs were cold in death; the spirit
Went with a moan indignant to the shadows.

In contrast to the sage and serious Vergil, laureate of Rome, his contemporary and admirer Sextus Propertius was a man of fire, concerned with his personal tragedies of love's pursuit and not with the weal and dignity of the state. Equal in feeling to his predecessor Catullus, Propertius found himself both master and slave of women and was seized by an urge to understand their nature and his thralldom. In one of his elegies (which won him admittance to the circle of the patron Maecenas) he wrote of the ashes of his love for his mistress known as Cynthia, who visits him in death after they have betrayed each other in their lives of love. As its most recent translator (whose version appears below) remarks, this astonishing work is "a macabre elegy worthy of Poe or Baudelaire."

who gives the servant-girls cruel new loads of spinning
    if any chance to chatter about my face—
(because old Petalé hung garlands on my tombstone
    she lies imprisoned in the filthy stocks;
Lalagé was hung up by her twisted hair and beaten
    because she asked a favour in my name)—
that woman now has melted down my golden statue,
    to get a dowry from my blazing pyre!

Propertius, you deserve it, yet I shan't reproach you.
    I was the queen for long years in your books.
I swear, by the irrevocable spell of Destiny
    (and so may Cerberus let me gently past!),
I kept my faith to you. If not, let hissing vipers
    slide through my grave and coil upon my bones....

But now, hear my injunctions—*if* you can still obey
    and are not all benumbed by Chloris' magic.
First, let my nurse, Parthenié, in trembling age
    lack nothing: in your need, she was kind to you.
And let my darling Latris, named for faithful service,
    not hold the looking-glass for your new love.

All the remaining poems you have made for me,
    burn them; and henceforth praise my name no more.
Tear off the ivy from my tomb when its fighting tendrils
    twist softly with their tresses round my bones.
Where fruitful Anio broods among its branchy fields,
    where Hercules' power keeps the ivory white,
there on a pillar write a phrase worthy of me,
    but short, to catch the Roman traveller's eye:
Here in the earth of Tibur golden Cynthia lies,
    a glory added, Anio, to your banks.

Remember, do not scorn dreams from the gates of the good:
    when good dreams visit this world, they have weight.
At night we fly up, phantoms released from prison,
    and Cerberus himself wanders unchained;
at dawn the law compels us to revisit Lethé,
    all counted by the ferryman while we cross.
Though others may possess you, later I shall hold you
    alone and clutching closely, bone to bone."

After this speech of harsh complaint and anger ended,
    the ghost melted away from my embrace.

THE ELEGANCE OF HORACE

from the ODES

I:5
(translated by John Milton)

What slender Youth bedew'd with liquid odours
Courts thee on Roses in some pleasant Cave,
   Pyrrha for whom bind'st thou
   In wreaths thy golden Hair,
Plain in thy neatness; O how oft shall he
On Faith and changed Gods complain: and Seas
   Rough with black winds and storms
   Unwonted shall admire:
Who now enjoyes thee credulous, all Gold,
Who always vacant, always amiable
   Hopes thee; of flattering gales
   Unmindfull. Hapless they
To whom thou untry'd seem'st fair. Me in my vow'd
Picture the sacred wall declares t' have hung
   My dank and dropping weeds
   To the stern God of Sea.

I:22
(translated by John Quincy Adams)

The man in righteousness arrayed,
   A pure and blameless liver,
Needs not the keen Toledo blade,
   Nor venom-freighted quiver.
What though he wind his toilsome way
   O'er regions wild and weary—
Through Zara's burning desert stray,
   Or Asia's jungles dreary:

What though he plow the billowy deep
   By lunar light, or solar,
Meet the resistless Simoom's sweep,
   Or iceberg circumpolar!
In bog or quagmire deep and dank
   His foot shall never settle;
He mounts the summit of Mont Blanc,
   Or Popocatapetl.

On Chimborazo's breathless height
   He treads o'er burning lava;
Or snuffs the Bohan Upas blight,
   The deathful plant of Java.
Through every peril he shall pass,
   By Virtue's shield protected;
And still by Truth's unerring glass
   His path shall be directed.

Else wherefore was it, Thursday last,
   While strolling down the valley,
Defenseless, musing as I passed
   A canzonet to Sally,
A wolf, with mouth-protruding snout,
   Forth from the thicket bounded—
I clapped my hands and raised a shout-
   He heard—and fled—confounded.

Tangier nor Tunis never bred
   An animal more crabbèd;
Nor Fez, dry-nurse of lions, fed
   A monster half so rabid;
Nor Ararat so fierce a beast
   Has seen since days of Noah;
Nor stronger, eager for a feast,
   The fell constrictor boa.

Oh! place me where the solar beam
   Has scorch'd all verdure vernal;
Or on the polar verge extreme,
   Block'd up with ice eternal—
Still shall my voice's tender lays
   Of love remain unbroken;
And still my charming Sally praise,
   Sweet smiling and sweet spoken.

Suave and sardonic, always shrewd in his awareness of human ways, Horace is the arch-poet of foibles, friendships, and country pleasures, writing of them with jewellike preci-sion—and possibly a barb. What he says is often less absorbing than the way he says it, as in the odes below as well as in his satires and letters. His ideas, revolving about those of aurea mediocritas *("the golden mean") and* carpe diem *("enjoy the pleasures of the day"), were hardly lofty, yet his attachment to traditional virtues and simplicities moved many a man in his day, and his exquisite style, brevity, and wit have challenged genera-tions of translators, a number of them adapting him freely for the sheer pleasure of it.*

I:23
(translated by Louis Untermeyer)

You shun me Chloë, like a fawn
    That, frightened, seeks its timorous mother,
    Running this way and the other,
When familiar paths are gone;
Starting at the lightest breeze,
    Or a bush stirred by a lizard,
    Or when Spring, the gentle wizard,
        Trembles in her knees.

Chloë, do not fear me so—
    I am not a beast to scare you,
    Not a lion that would tear you;
Do not treat me as a foe.
Chloë, leave your mother's side;
    Come, you are a child no longer.
    Make your faint desires stronger—
        Be a bride.

I:25
(translated by Robert Fitzgerald)

The young men come less often—isn't it so?—
To rap at midnight on your fastened window;
Much less often. How do you sleep these days?

There was a time when your door gave with proficiency
On easy hinges; now it seems apter at being shut.
I do not think you hear many lovers moaning

"Lydia, how can you sleep?
"Lydia, the night is so long!
"Oh, Lydia, I'm dying for you!"

No. The time is coming when you will moan
And cry to scornful men from an alley corner
In the dark of the moon when the wind's in a passion,

With lust that would drive a mare wild

Raging in your ulcerous old viscera.
You'll be alone and burning then

To think how happy boys take their delight
In the new tender buds, the blush of myrtle,
Consigning dry leaves to the winter sea.

I:38
(translated by Eugene Field)

Boy, I detest the Persian pomp;
    I hate those linden-bark devices;
And as for roses, holy Moses!
    They can't be got at living prices!
Myrtle is good enough for us,—
    For *you*, as bearer of my flagon;
For *me*, supine beneath this vine,
    Doing my best to get a jag on!

HORACE   III:9
(translated by Robert Herrick)

While, Lydia, I was loved of thee,
Nor any was preferred before me
To hug thy whitest neck: than I,
The Persian King lived not more happily.

LYDIA

While thou no other didst affect,
Nor Cloe was of more respect;
Then Lydia, far-famed Lydia,
I flourish't more than Roman Ilia.

HORACE

Now Thracian Cloe governs me,

Skillful with the Harpe, and Melodie:
For whose affection, Lydia, I
(So Fate spares her) am well content to die.

LYDIA

My heart now set on fire is
By Ornithes sonne, young Calais;
For whose commutuall flames here I
(To save his life) twice am content to die.

HORACE

Say our first loves we showed revoke,
And severed, joyne in brazed yoke:
Admit I Cloe put away,
And love again love-cast-off Lydia?

LYDIA

Though mine be brighter than the Star;
Thou lighter than the Cork by far;
Rough as the Adratick sea, yet I
Will live with thee, or else for thee will die.

III:30

(*translated by William Ewart Gladstone*)

Now have I reared a monument more durable than brass,
And one that doth the royal scale of pyramids surpass,
Nor shall defeated Aquilo destroy, nor soaking rain,
Nor yet the countless tide of years, nor seasons in their train.
Not all of me shall die: my praise shall grow, and never end
While pontiff and mute vestal shall the Capitol ascend,
And so a mighty share of me shall Libitina foil.
Where bellows headstrong Aufidus, where, on his arid soil,
King Daunus ruled a rural folk, of me it shall be told
That, grown from small to great, I first of all men subtly wrought
Aeolian strains to unison with our Italian thought.
So take thine honours earned by deeds; and graciously do thou,
Melpomene, with Delphic bays adorn thy poet's brow.

IV:7

(*translated by Samuel Johnson*)

The snow dissolv'd no more is seen,
The fields, and woods, behold, are green,
The changing year renews the plain,
The rivers know their banks again,
The spritely Nymph and naked Grace
The mazy dance together trace.
The changing year's successive plan
Proclaims mortality to Man.
Rough Winter's blasts to Spring give way,
Spring yield[s] to Summer['s] sovereign ray,
The Summer sinks in Autumn's reign,
And Winter chils the World again.
Her losses soon the Moon supplies,
But wretched Man, when once he lies
Where Priam and his sons are laid,
Is naught but Ashes and a Shade.

Who knows if Jove who counts our Score
Will toss us in a morning more?
What with your friend you nobly share
At least you rescue from your heir.
Not you, Torquatus, boast of Rome,
When Minos once has fix'd your doom,
Or Eloquence, or splendid birth,
Or Virtue shall replace on earth.
Hippolytus unjustly slain
Diana calls to life in vain,
Nor can the might of Theseus rend
The chains of hell that hold his friend.

HORACE AND THE BORE *from the* Satires
(*translated by Franklin P. Adams*)

I'm ankling, as I do, one day
Along the good old Sacred Way,
Thinking of business or some dame—
A guy comes up; I know his name
And nothing else. He grabs my hand
With nerve to beat the well-known band,
And says to me: "Hello, old kick!
And How is every little trick?"
"I'm well," I say. "There's nothing new;
I can't complain; the same to you."

He sticks, and so I say: "Good-by!
Don't take any wooden denarii."
"Surely you know me," says the bore,
"I've got a lot of learned lore."
"Well, that's just dandy," I reply,
"That makes your average pretty high."
Faster I walk upon the pave
And see my valet, the lucky slave,
I wish I had his temper quick
So I could brain these bores who stick.

This cluck keeps talking Jove knows what
But do I answer? I do not.
So he says: "Listen, I'm aware
You're anxious to give me the air.
No use. I'll stick around all day.
I'll foot your dogsteps. Whither away?"

I say: "Don't let me spoil your plan;
I'm going far to see a man
Whose name is F. O'Brien Schreiber;
He's sick, and lives across the Tiber."
"Oh, that's all right," goes on his talk,
"I've lots of time, and I love to walk . . ."
So there I am, like some young jack
With a load too heavy for his back.

He starts again: "Believe me or not,
Viscus and Varus aren't so hot,
For where's the lad can make more rhyme

Than I in the same amount of time?
Who dances better? And I sing
About as well as anything."
I sneak a word in: "Listen, brother:
Got any family? Got a mother,
An aunt, or anyone who'd give
One damn whether you die or live?"

"Not one; all, all are laid away."
(The lucky stiffs! Oh, happy they!
But I'm alive. That is my lot.
Why don't you put me on the spot?
Into my coffin by a bore cast,
My epitaph the Sabellian forecast:
"Here lies a boy whom guns can't kill,
Whom no disease has e'er made ill.
But oh, this boy will perish young,
Done to his death by a babbling tongue.
Be warned, my son, when talkers harry you,
Run off as fast as your feet will carry you.")

Well, when we come to the Vestal Shrine—
It being then 10:39—
He says he has to go to court
Or lose his case. "OK, old sport,"
I say. But he says: "Listen, please,
Wait here, I beg you on my knees."
"I know no law," I say, "good-by.
You know I've got to see this guy."

He says: "I don't know what to do:
Give up my law case, Quint, or you?"
"Oh, give me up!" I say. "Oh no,"
Says he. So on and on we go.
And then he says: "Say, just between us,
What is your contract with Maecenas?"
"He picks his friends; wise in his dome;
No better, finer man in Rome."
"Why not give me a recommend?
You'd be supreme with *me* as friend."

"It's different over there," I said,
"From how you've got it in your head.
There's not a house whose life is cleaner,
No home where everything's serener.
Let one be wealthier than I or wiser,
Nobody cares—nor he nor I, sir."
"Almost too good," says he, "for truth."
"Well, so it is," I tell the youth.
"Aha!" says he, "in me you rouse
A wish to know your patron's house."
"Just try it," I say, "he's quite a guy.
He's hard to know, but just you try."
"I'll bribe the slaves, and if the door
Slams in my face, I'll ask for more;
And if I can't get in, I'll meet

Maecenas somewhere on the street.
I'll meet that man if but to bow to.
You can meet kings if you know how to."

As chatters on this boring Babbitt,
We meet, as Ol' Gal Luck would have it,
Fustus Aristius. "Hello, old goat!"
"Hello, yourself!" I pull his coat,
I wink, I sigh. See him pretend
To get me wrong! A hell of a friend!
I say, trying to get him to connive at
My lie, "You want to talk in private?"

"Sure, any time," I hear him say,
"But this is a Jewish holiday."
"What of it?" I ask. "Well, I refuse,"
He says; "why scandalize the Jews?
Some day we'll try again," says he.
Why should this day be dark for me?
For off the ragged rascal ran
And left me with that terrible man.

But ha! The plaintiff meets this fellow
And sees him and begins to bellow:
"Where are you going, you crook? Come here,
You dog, you swine, you racketeer!"
Off goes the bore to court. How loud
The yelling of the gathering crowd!
And did I join that mob, or follow?
No. I genuflected to Apollo.

TO MAECENAS *from the* Letters
(*translated by Gilbert Highet*)

I promised I should spend only a week in the country—
liar! now you have missed me all through August. Yet
if you wish me to remain healthy, thoroughly fit,
Maecenas, please give me (afraid of illness) the leave
which you would give me were I ill. Let the first fig
and autumn heat bring out the slow black funerals,
while every father and mamma worries about the children,
while business occupations and social observances
result in burning fevers and quick obituaries.
Later, when winter plasters snow on the Alban fields,
your poet will come down to the seashore, watch his health,
keep warm, and read; and, my dear friend, revisit you
(if you permit) with the warm west winds and the first
swallows.

You made me rich, Maecenas, but not like the southern farmer
feeding his guests on pears, urging them "Eat up!"
"I've had enough." "Take more; take all you want." "No, thanks."
"Surely your children will enjoy a few presents?"
"Your kindness means as much as though I'd gone home loaded."
"Very well. What you leave will go straight to the pigs." . . .

THE DIVERSIONS OF OVID

*Born in time to be a friend of Horace and a kindred spirit of Propertius, the aristocratic Ovid (43 B.C.–A.D. 17) was trained in law only to become the most engaging hedonist in Roman letters. His lexicons of amorous pursuit—*Amores (Loves) *and* Ars amartoria (Art of Love)*—were so explicit that he ran afoul of Augustus' efforts to improve the moral climate of the state and died in banishment. Wry, frivolous, ever-ready with epigram and sardonic comment on the sexes, he lacked probity; but he excelled in retelling old stories in a way that reduced the gods and their favorites to human dimensions. In his tales and satires, combining fable, romance, and searching comedy, he left a lasting image of the most polished attitudes of Rome in the era of the emperor Augustus.*

HELEN TO PARIS *from the* Letters
(translated by John Dryden)

How dares a stranger with designs so vain,
Marriage and hospitable rights profane?
Was it for this, your fleet did shelter find
From swelling seas, and ev'ry faithless wind...
Does this deserve to be rewarded so?
Did you come here a stranger or a foe? ...
I keep my honor still without a stain,
Nor has my love made any coxcomb vain.
Your boldness I with admiration see;
What hope had you to gain a queen like me? ...
Sure 'tis some fate that sets me above wrongs,
Yet still exposes me to busy tongues.
I'll not complain; for who's displeas'd with love,
If it sincere, discreet, and constant prove?
But that I fear; not that I think you base,
Or doubt the blooming beauties of my face;
But all your sex is subject to deceive,
And ours alas, too willing to believe.
Yet others yield; and love o'ercomes the best:
But why should I not shine above the rest? ...

Your letter fill'd with promises of all,
That men can good, and women pleasant call,
Gives expectation such an ample field,
As wou'd move goddesses themselves to yield....
For oh! your face has such peculiar charms,
That who can hold from flying to your arms!
But what I ne'er can have without offence,
May some blest maid possess with innocence.
Pleasure may tempt, but virtue more should move;
O learn of me to want the thing you love.
What you desire is sought by all mankind:
As you have eyes, so others are not blind.
Like you they see, like you my charms adore:
They wish not less, but you dare venture more.
Oh! had you then upon our coasts been brought,
My virgin love when thousand rivals sought,
You had I seen, you should have had my voice;

Nor could my husband justly blame my choice.
For both our hopes, alas you come too late!
Another now is master of my fate.
More to my wish I cou'd have liv'd with you,
And yet my present lot can undergo.
Cease to solicit a weak woman's will,
And urge not her you love, to so much ill....

My hand is yet untaught to write to men:
This is th' essay of my unpractis'd pen:
Happy those nymphs whom use has perfect made;
I think all crime, and tremble at a shade.
Ev'n while I write, my fearful conscious eyes
Look often back, misdoubting a surprize.
For now the rumour spreads among the crowd,
At court in whispers, but in town aloud.
Dissemble you, what e'er you hear 'em say:
To leave off loving were your better way;
Yet if you will dissemble it, you may.
Love secretly: the absence of my lord
More freedom gives, but does not all afford:
Long is his journey, long will be his stay;
Call'd by affairs of consequence away.
To go or not when unresolv'd he stood,
I bid him make what swift return he cou'd:
Then kissing me, he said, "I recommend
All to thy care, but most my Trojan friend."
I smil'd at what he innocently said,
And only answer'd, you shall be obey'd.
Propitious winds have borne him far from hence,
But let not this secure your confidence.
Absent he is, yet absent he commands:
You know the proverb, Princes have long hands....
Our flames are mutual; and my husband's gone:
The nights are long; I fear to lie alone.
One house contains us, and weak walls divide,
And you're too pressing to be long denied:
Let me not live, but every thing conspires
To join our loves, and yet my fear retires.

You court with words, when you should force imploy:
A rape is requisite to shamefac'd joy.
Indulgent to the wrongs which we receive,
Our sex can suffer what we dare not give.
What have I said! for both of us 'twere best,
Our kindling fires if each of us supprest. . . .

You boast the pomp and plenty of your land,
And promise all shall be at my command:
Your Trojan wealth, believe me, I despise;
My own poor native land has dearer ties.
Shou'd I be injur'd on your Phrygian shore,
What help of kindred cou'd I there implore?
Medea was by Jason's flatt'ry won:
I may, like her, believe, and be undone.
Plain honest hearts, like mine, suspect no cheat,
And love contributes to its own deceit. . . .
Yet fears like these, shou'd not my mind perplex,
Were I as wise as many of my sex.
But time and you may bolder thoughts inspire;
And I perhaps may yield to your desire.
You last demand a private conference,
These are your words, but I can guess your sense.
Your unripe hopes their harvest must attend:
Be rul'd by me, and time may be your friend.
This is enough to let you understand;
For now my pen has tir'd my tender hand:
My woman knows the secret of my heart,
And may hereafter better news impart.

NARCISSUS *from the* Metamorphoses
(translated by F. A. Wright)

There was a pool with silvery water bright,
  To which no neat herd e'er his cattle drave;
No she-goats feeding on the mountain height,
  Nor wandering sheep disturbed the unruffled wave.
No bird or beast came near its thirst to fill,
No falling branches broke the mirror still.

Worn with the chase, Narcissus laid him down
  In the lush grass that grew along the brink,
Beneath the shadow by cool poplars thrown,
  And stooping o'er the spring prepared to drink.
When lo! another beauty met his gaze
That did another thirst within him raise.

For as he bent a wonder came to view:
  An imaged face that set his heart on fire;
An incorporeal hope, a joy untrue,
  Shadow of substance, phantom of desire.
Entranced he lies in ecstasy alone
Like some slim statue carved of Parian stone.

Flung down he marvels at those stars, his eyes,
  And at his locks than Bacchus' own more fair;

He sees the roses and the ivories
  Of neck and cheek and lips beyond compare.
Now loves he that which others in him love,
And on himself his passion fain would prove.

How often did he stoop to kiss the pool
  That mocked his lips; how often with his arm
Seek in the depths beneath the surface cool
  To draw towards his lips the shadowed charm.
He knows not what he sees; but still he burns,
And to the fond illusion still returns.

O foolish boy, why seek to clasp in vain
  A fleeting image! Nowhere wilt thou find
Thy heart's desire; nothing will remain
  Shouldst thou endure to leave the pool behind.
'Tis but a shade reflected thou dost see,
And if thou turnest 'twill return with thee.

Yet naught could draw him from that lonely place,
  No thought of food, or sleep at eventide.
Ever he gazed upon the mirrored face
  And with the vision ne'er was satisfied.
Until at last he rose, and to the trees
Bewailed his mournful fate in words like these:

"Ye woods, where lovers ever shelter find,
  Have you a grief than mine more cruel known,
Or found a heart so vexed by fate unkind
  In all the long years that you here have grown?
I see—yet what I see may not obtain.
I love—and yet deluded love in vain.

And still—O grief!—we are not parted now
  By roads or hills or walls with close shut gates.
If but the water passage would allow
  He too expectant on my coming waits.
For when I stretched my lips towards the spring
He strove to mine his upturned face to bring.

So slight the barrier that between us lay
  I almost might have touched his rosy cheek.
Come, my beloved, come to me, I pray:
  Fly not from me when I your presence seek.
You need not shun me. I am young and fair
And nymphs have begged me oft their couch to share.

Your kindly looks have hope within me bred.
  I stretch my arms; and you stretch yours to mine.
I weep; you seem at once to droop your head.
  I smile; your eyes with laughter gayly shine.
And in the movements of your lips I guess
And answer to the words that I address.

Ah! now I know the truth. I, I am he!
  It is my very self that I desire,
And my own image in the fountain see.

I lit the flame that burns me with its fire;
What can I do? Be lover now or loved?
Beggared by my own wealth, yet helpless proved.

O would that from myself I might escape—
    Strange, strange petition!—Would he were not here,
That love of mine, and had another shape
    From that which to my eyes now seems so dear.
Full soon, methinks, from this sore load of grief
My very agony will bring relief.

For I must die: and then my pain will end.
    Only I wish that he might longer live.
Two deaths in this one blow will Fortune send
    And to two loving hearts destruction give.
Alas, alas! I cannot bear my doom:
My life is done ere it had reached its bloom."

SPORT WITH CORINNA *from the* Loves
(translated by Christopher Marlowe)

'Twas noon when I, scorch'd with the double fire
Of the hot sun and my more hot desire,
Stretch'd on my downy couch, at ease was laid,
Big with expectance of the lovely maid.
The curtains but half-drawn, a light let in,
Such as in shades of thickest groves is seen;
Such as remains when the sun flies away,
Or when night's gone, and yet it is not day.
This light to modest maids must be allow'd,
Where shame may hope its guilty head to shroud.
And now my love, Corinna, did appear,
Loose on her neck fell her divided hair;
Loose as her flowing gown, that wanton'd in the air.
In such a garb, with such a grace and mien,
To her rich bed came the Assyrian queen.
So Lais look'd when all the youth of Greece
With adoration did her charms confess.
Her envious gown to pull away I tried,
But she resisted still, and still denied;
But so resisted that she seem'd to be
Unwilling to obtain the victory.
So I at last an easy conquest had,
Whilst my fair combatant herself betray'd.
But when she naked stood before my eyes,
Gods! with what charms did she my soul surprise!
What snowy arms did I both see and feel!
With what rich globes did her soft bosom swell!
Plump as ripe clusters rose each glowing breast,
Courting the hand, and suing to be prest!
What a smooth plain was on her belly spread!
Where thousand little loves and graces play'd!
What thighs! what legs! but why strive I in vain,
Each limb, each grace, each feature to explain?
One beauty did through her whole body shine;
I saw, admir'd, and prest it close to mine.

The rest, who knows not? Thus entranc'd we lay,
Till in each other's arms we died away;
O give me such a noon (ye gods) to ev'ry day.

ADVICE TO MEN *from the* Art of Love
(translated by Rolfe Humphries)

So, you need have little doubt when it comes to winning them
                                                        over;
    Out of the many there are, hardly a one will refuse.
If they say Yes, or say No, they're pleased with the invitation:
    Even suppose you guess wrong, it costs you nothing to try.
But why should you be wrong? Untried delights are a pleasure:
    Those which we do not own tempt with attraction and charm.
In the fields of our neighbor the grass forever is greener;
    Always the other man's herd offers the richer reward.
Take some trouble, at first, to make her handmaiden's
                                                        acquaintance:
    She, more than anyone else, really can lighten your way.
She must be one you can trust, if she knows of the tricks you are
                                                        playing,
Confidante, wise and discreet, high in her mistress' regard.
Spoil her by promising much, and spoil her by pleading a little,
    What you seek you will find, if she is willing you should.
She will choose the right time—a maid is as good as a doctor—
    When she is in the right mood, all the more ripe to be had.
When she is in the right mood, you will know it because she is
                                                        happy,
    Like the flowers in the field, seeming to burst into bloom.
When the hearts are glad, and sorrow does not confine them,
    Then they are open wide, and Venus steals coaxingly in.

ADVICE TO WOMEN *from the* Art of Love
(translated by Rolfe Humphries)

What we cannot resist is elegance: don't let your hair blow
    Wild in the wind, employ just the right touch of the hand.
There are, of course, many styles and pleasing ways of
                                                        adornment;
    Look in your mirror and choose which is most seemly to use.
If your face is long, you should part your hair in the middle;
    If your features are round, then let your hair be a crown. . . .
Here is a girl who should run her hands through her hair, keep it
                                                        fluffy;
    There is another whose style calls for the plain and severe.
One might do well with her combs mottled with tortoise-shell
                                                        markings,
    Others do equally well using a wavy design,
But it is foolish to count the acorns that hang on the oak-tree,
    Count the bees in the hive, number the fish in the sea,
So I cannot keep track of the vagaries of fashion,
    Every day, so it seems, brings in a different style.
Even neglected hair might prove becoming to many,
    Something of yesterday's charm contradicting the comb.

LIVY, TELLER OF TALES

The historian Livy, writing at the same time as Ovid (both men died in A.D. 17), spoke in dramatic and rhetorical prose quite different from the verse of his witty contemporary. His topic, like Vergil's, was Rome's origin and destiny. His technique was a mixture of drawing on the few records that existed and adding to them such stories as he thought enlivening. His immense talent lay in narration, combining the credible and the all but incredible, and in his brilliance at embellishment and dramatic effect. If he was not one of the world's great historians, he was one of the great storytellers of history.

from A HISTORY OF ROME
(translated by Moses Hadas and J. P. Poe)

HORATIUS AT THE BRIDGE

As the enemy drew near, everyone from the surrounding countryside fled into the city, which was then encircled with guards. Some areas of the city seemed well protected by the city walls and by the barrier of the Tiber river; but the Sublician Bridge would have afforded the enemy access to the city if not for one man, Horatius Cocles. His strength was the final rampart which fortune provided the city. He happened to be stationed on guard at the bridge when he saw the Janiculum suddenly taken by attack and the enemy rush down from it at full speed. His own men, when they saw this, threw down their arms and fled from their posts in panic and confusion. Seizing one after another, he tried to stop them, crying to them and swearing by the faith of the gods that they were deserting their posts in vain. If they crossed the bridge and abandoned it, there would soon be more of the enemy on the Palatine and Capitoline than were now on Janiculum. He admonished them to destroy the bridge with their swords or with fire, or any way possible, while he withstood the enemy's attack, as long as he was able, alone. With that he marched resolutely to the head of the bridge.

There he stood with his sword in his hand, a stirring sight among the fugitives who had turned their backs upon the fight. When the enemy caught sight of him, they were astounded at his audacity. Two men were shamed into remaining with him, Spurius Larcius and Titus Herminius, both men of high birth and great personal reputation. With their help Horatius repulsed the first and most violent assault; but he ordered them to retreat when only a small part of the bridge remained and those who were cutting it down shouted to them to go back. Then, looking round at the Etruscan leaders with fierce and menacing eyes, he challenged each one. He taunted them all with being slaves of tyrants and with attacking the liberty of others while being unconcerned for their own. For a moment they hesitated, each looking to the others to begin the battle; but at length, shame compelled them to attack. Raising the battle cry, from all sides they threw their spears at their single opponent. But all of them stuck in his shield, and Horatius remained unmoved, with feet firmly planted at the head of the bridge. They were about to dislodge him with a concerted charge, when the loud crash of the falling bridge and the Romans' shout of exultation announced that their work was completed. As the Etruscans hesitated in dismay, Horatius cried, "Father Tiber, I beseech you to receive these arms and this soldier in safety in your stream." With that, still wearing his armor, he dived into the river and with missiles falling all around swam safely to the shore.

HANNIBAL ATTACKS WITH ELEPHANTS

Hannibal's light-armed Balearics began the battle, but when they were confronted with legions who were more heavily armed they were quickly withdrawn and sent to the wings. This immediately endangered the weary Roman cavalry. These numbered only four thousand, and even before had hardly been able to withstand the ten thousand horsemen of the enemy, most of whom were still fresh. Now they found themselves almost buried under a cloud of javelins thrown by the Balearics. Moreover the unaccustomed odor as well as the sight of the monstrous elephants stationed on the wings caused the horses to panic and break. As for the infantry, although they were equal to the Carthaginians in courage, they were not so in strength. For the enemy was fresh and had prepared their bodies for battle, while the Romans were hungry, exhausted, and stiff with cold. They might still have successfully resisted by dint of courage alone if they had been opposed only by infantry; but soon the Balearics had routed the cavalry and were directing their missiles upon the infantry's flanks, while the elephants charged into the middle of their line. Meanwhile Mago and the Numidians, as soon as the Romans had passed their hiding place, attacked their rear and created great panic. But despite these dangers from every side, the infantry held steady for some time—best of all, surprisingly, against the elephants. Light-armed soldiers posted for that purpose turned them aside by throwing javelins, then struck them under the tail where the hide is soft.

CORIOLANUS SPARES ROME

A large number of matrons gathered about Venturia, the mother of Coriolanus, and Volumnia, his wife. It is uncertain whether this was inspired by the women's fear or was contrived by government officials; in any case, they succeeded in obtaining the assistance of mother and wife. Venturia, then a very aged woman, and Volumnia, carrying her two small sons, accompanied them into the enemy camp. With tears and prayers the women defended the city which the arms of men could not protect.

When they reached the camp it was reported to Coriolanus that a large number of women were present. Previously the majesty of the state, personified in its envoys, had failed to move him, as well as the religious awe which the sight of its priests had inspired. Now he resolved to be even more inflexible against women's tears. However, the excessive grief of Volumnia, who stood weeping between her daughter-in-law and her grandsons, soon attracted the attention of one of his friends, who said to him, "Unless my eyes deceive me your mother and wife and children are here." Coriolanus sprang from his seat like a madman and tried to embrace his mother; but she, abandoning her tears for words of anger, said, "Tell me before I suffer your embrace: Have I come to see my son or an enemy? Am I a captive in your camp or your mother? Is it for this that I have struggled through a long life and an unhappy old age—in order to see my son first an exile, then an enemy? Could you really devastate this land which gave you birth and nurtured you? However hostile and vengeful your coming, did not your anger subside when you crossed your country's borders? When you came in sight of Rome, did not this thought occur to you, 'Within those walls are my home and the gods of my family, my mother, wife and children?' But for me, Rome would not be besieged: If I had never had a son I should have died a free woman in a free country. I am able now to suffer no greater misery, and you no greater disgrace. But, miserable as I am I shall not be for long: It is these you must consider; for if you continue, only an untimely death or long slavery remains for them."

With these words his wife and children embraced him; at the same time a great wail arose from the crowd of women lamenting their own fate and that of their country. At last he relented;

after embracing his family he sent them away, and withdrew his army from before the city.

CINCINNATUS DROPS HIS PLOW

For those who are disdainful of all human values except riches and who think that high position and excellence are impossible without great wealth, it is worthwhile to listen to the following story.

The one hope of the people and the empire of Rome, Lucius Quinctius, cultivated a farm of four acres on the other side of the Tiber. It was directly across from the spot where the dockyard now is situated and to this day is called the Quinctian meadows. There he was found by the deputation from the senate, either bent over his spade as he dug a ditch or plowing—at any rate, as historians agree, occupied with the work of his farm. After greetings had been exchanged, they expressed the wish that "it might turn out well for both him and his country" and requested that he put on his toga and hear the mandate of the senate. Crying out in surprise, "Is everything all right?" he called to his wife to hurry and bring the toga from the cottage. There, after wiping off the dust and sweat, he put it on and came forward to the deputation, who hailed him dictator and summoned him into the city. When they had explained the army's alarming situation he crossed over the Tiber in a boat provided by the state. On the other side he was greeted by his three sons, who had come out to meet him, followed by other friends and relatives, and by most of the senators. Accompanied by this gathering he was conducted to his house by the lictors. A great crowd of plebeians also collected, not at all overjoyed to see Cincinnatus' selection; they considered the office too powerful and the man himself even more relentless and uncompromising. For that night no precautions were taken, aside from posting a watch in the city.

The next morning Cincinnatus arose and went into the Forum before daybreak, where he named Lucius Tarquitius as master of horse. This man was a patrician by birth, although he had been forced by poverty to serve in the infantry, and was considered the finest soldier in Rome. Accompanied by Tarquitius, the dictator went into the assembly of the people, where he proclaimed a suspension of all civic affairs, ordered shops to be closed throughout the city, and forbade the transaction of all private business. He then issued an order that everyone of military age should report in arms at the Campus Martius before sunset, carrying rations for five days and twelve stakes for palisades. Those too old for military duty he ordered to prepare rations for their neighbors serving in the army while these were preparing their arms and looking for stakes. Immediatley the young men ran to collect stakes, taking the first they came to, with no one stopping them, since everyone was eager to carry out the orders of the dictator. At the appointed time the line was drawn up in an order adapted for battle as well as marching, in the event that the occasion should arise; the dictator led the infantry in person, with Tarquitius at the head of the cavalry.

THE ROMAN ART OF LAW

To the claim that Roman arms conquered the world, one may add that Roman law accomplished no less a task. Wherever they went, the Romans took with them the legal concepts and procedures they had developed over centuries, implanting these among barbarian tribes as well as older civilized societies, so that their law survived the empire itself. The evolution of a body of civil law, with its rules of evidence and of the rights of a defendant (innocent until proven guilty), was a product of Roman thinking.

At the core of this thought lay the concept of natural law. Originating in Greece, this doctrine held that a sense of reason flowing from man's own nature and soul imposed on him the duty to mirror such reason in his dealings under law with others; then right would ensue. Men could ill afford to make arbitrary rules and judgments; a fair standard had to prevail. Moreover, following the rule of reason, sound law could be made equally applicable to men everywhere. It was such thinking that encouraged Roman legislators to broaden what had originally been *ius civile*, or law for Roman citizens only, into *ius gentium*, or law governing all inhabitants of the empire and their contractual agreements. Modern international law derives directly from the Romans because they applied the principle of natural law to relations between states, believing that under it, differences between contrasting legal systems could be resolved.

The true genius of Roman law lay in its flexibility. The guiding idea that emerged was that if law was to remain viable in the changing conditions of Rome's complex society, it must be subject to continuing adaptation. A wise judge, the Romans believed, should be bound by precedent established in the body of written law but also be free to make his own interpretation in the light of the case in hand.

In the twentieth century, the renowned Justice of the United States Supreme Court, Oliver Wendell Holmes, was to make the observation that "The life of the law has not been logic; it has been experience," adding that "the necessities of the time, the prevalent moral and political theories, institutions of public policy, avowed or unconscious, even the prejudices which judges share with their fellow men" have a good deal to do with determining the rules by which men should be governed. In this he was in effect echoing the thinking of the jurists of Rome.

The result of the Roman jurists' concentration both on continuity and elasticity is that much of their law survives in many adaptations in the western world today. Here are some instances of their principles and procedures:

THE ROLE OF LAWYERS

After an era of early priestly administrators of Roman law, a caste of aristocratic and learned laymen arose under the late republic to function as advisers to everyone needing legal aid in legislation or litigation. These men, known as *prudentes* or *jurisprudentes*, foreshadowed the professional bar. Their *communis opinio* could, in fact, determine the interpretation of the law.

TRIAL BY JURY

Though widely practiced among the Greeks, the Romans gave it their own form. At times as many as seventy-five citizens sat on the juries that considered only criminal cases. Majority votes determined the verdict, after the defense had exercised its right to challenge and cross-examine witnesses.

RIGHTS IN THE FAMILY

Roman law, as it grew, overcame the ancient custom of allowing only men to own property. By the time of the empire a woman could receive an inheritance and control her own dowry. Laws of inheritance also permitted a man to choose an heir from outside his family, although a blood heir could not be altogether disinherited without good reason. The making of a will was an act of considerable solemnity. A Roman enjoyed the right of testament only if he was a citizen or had acquired a special dispensation from the state; in either case, the validation of the will required sworn witnesses.

RULES OF CONTRACT

The earliest Roman contracts were verbal; later, property was transferred by means of witnessed entries into the account books of both parties. Commercial law bound the parties both to the implicit as well as the explicit stipulations of contracts. Civil suits were brought either before judges appointed from lists of citizens of standing (judicial service was considered a civic duty) or before arbiters agreed to by both parties. Judgments could be appealed to higher courts; litigation might even go on for several years.

VIII

ARCHITECTS
OF
EMPIRE

Fare thee well, Tiberius, most charming of men, and success go with you, as you war for me and the Muses. Fare thee well, most charming and valiant of men and most conscientious of generals, or may I never know happiness.

Emperor Augustus, in a letter to his
adopted heir, as reported by Suetonius

The coming of the emperors brought profound and cumulative changes in the institutions, the mores, and the very physical appearance of Rome. Many old public organs, along with many old buildings, survived. But new structures of power were overtaking the former, while vast new undertakings in stone overshadowed the latter. The Senate survived in its ancient dignity, but its authority was much altered and diminished. Tiberius, Augustus' successor, sought in his reign (A.D. 14—37) to continue his stepfather's policy of encouraging the Senate to collaborate with the ruler in the management of the empire; but with the disappearance of political parties, and thereby of public debate, the Senate's old role as the vital center of Roman statecraft was gone. Great, new speakers' rostra were erected, but under the new order there was no Cicero to exhort the citizens from them.

The consuls were still annually elected, but they were hardly more than ceremonial relics of the past, their powers long superseded by those gathered into the hands of a single head of state, who ruled by virtue of a grant of tribunicial authority (*tribunicia potestas*) and through his control of the army and of political patronage. The civil service, which Augustus had founded on the basis of the senatorial class and the equites, was to be developed by Tiberius and to be organized into a great imperial bureaucracy by the brilliant though sickly Claudius, who as emperor (A.D. 41—54) established three or more executive bureaus and went so far as to invite freedmen rather than aristocrats to head them. In 27 B.C. Augustus had created, from among the bodyguards that had surrounded individual generals during the republic, a corps of soldiers that was to enjoy special status as protectors of the emperor, his clan, and the imperial order of rule. These picked professionals, the Praetorian Guard, rapidly became a formidable new power in the state—one that on occasion could be decisive. Claudius owed his accession as emperor to them, at a time when the Senate was debating whether or not the republic should be restored. As Edward Gibbon remarked succinctly, "While the Senate deliberated, the Praetorian Guards had resolved." In years to come, the protectors of emperors sometimes became their captors.

Such shifts in power affected the whole character of the age. Political interest, once so broad and intense, now tended to become narrow, if not passive, and to concentrate on the ways of emperors and on the rise and fall of their favorites. Cornelius Tacitus, the historian of the new era, was in large part a chronicler of court intrigues and imperial eccentricities, of which there were many. It was a time of decline of popular participation in government (elections were taken out of the hands of the assemblies and placed in those of the compliant Senate, possibly at about the time of Augustus' death) and of the rise of great imperial monuments and gifts to the people that were very often provided from the emperor's own treasury.

Of the major rulers who followed Augustus in the first century A.D.—Tiberius, Claudius, Nero, Vespasian, Titus, Domitian—each set his individual seal upon the development of the state and upon the face of Rome itself. The physical transformation of the capital, begun by Caesar, was only a part—though the most spectacular part—of that astonishing flowering of architecture and engineering that studded the empire near and far with aqueducts, bridges, paved highways, ceremonial arches, stadiums, open-air theatres, and large public halls, or basilicas. If Romans no longer expressed themselves individually in politics, they did so collectively and magnificently in stone.

By Caesar's time the Roman Forum, wedged in among the hills, had become so crowded that he had ordered the building of a new one to the northwest of the old. He had also chosen the area known as the Campus Martius, beyond the Capitoline hill and beside the river's bend, as the site for future public buildings; and on this land were to rise the Pantheon, the baths of Agrippa, the mausoleum of Augustus, the baths of Nero, and the stadium of Domitian. Caesar had also enlarged the Circus Maximus, between the slopes of the Aventine and Palatine hills, into an immense stadium some two thousand feet long and able to accommodate two hundred fifty thousand people, who came to watch chariot and horse races and gladiatorial shows. But the spaciousness and splendor begun by Caesar still left most quarters of Rome a nest of old and narrow streets jammed with traffic and so short of living space as to result in the construction of tenements for the poor—rabbit warrens consisting of six and seven stories of cubicles that were usually rented out by the room at exorbitant rates. Augustus wisely limited the height of these *insulae*, as they were called, to seventy-five feet, since they were firetraps and collapsed frequently.

It was not until after the great fire of A.D. 64, which leveled many parts of the city, that what we might term a program of general urban renewal was begun. Tacitus, recounting the disaster, speaks of "those narrow winding passages and irregular streets, which characterized old Rome"; but he adds that some citizens did not like the cutting of new and broader ways through the rubble nor did they like the creation of open spaces, and thought the old order "had been more conducive to health, inasmuch as the narrow streets with the elevation of the roofs were not equally penetrated by the sun's heat, while now the open space, unshel-

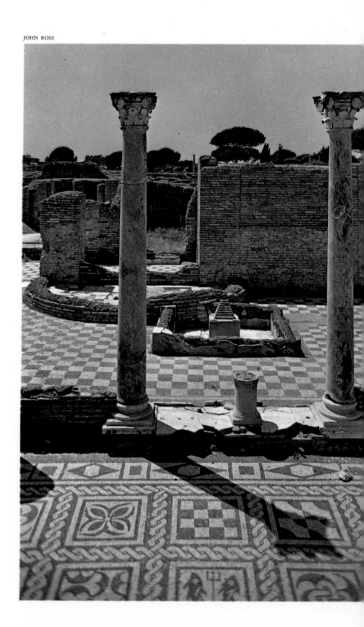

JOHN ROSS

The fall of the republic doomed Roman democracy, but it ushered in two centuries of unparalleled growth. The empire expanded, new towns flourished, and magnificent structures arose to attest the glory of Rome. A mosaic floor in Ostia recalls the wealth of Rome's seaport at the mouth of the Tiber.

tered by any shade, was scorched by a fiercer glow."

Though Augustus himself has been estimated to have either built or rebuilt over one hundred public buildings, his interests did not lie in the direction of devising a new city plan. He did, however, reorganize the city's management in a manner that again revealed his administrative mastery. He divided the sprawling metropolis into fourteen *regiones*, or wards, and over two hundred fifty precincts. To maintain public order he set up a police force of three cohorts of a thousand men each, reporting to the city prefect. To guard against fires, Rome's greatest daily hazard, he established a corps of seven cohorts of professional firemen, or *vigiles*, who also had the power to make arrests. To maintain its public buildings, to safeguard its water supply, and to oversee the maintenance of the roads, he appointed separate boards of commissioners known as *curatores*.

In its new and refurbished buildings, the Rome of the Augustan age reflected the character of Augustus, who was determined that his city should tower over all others in the world. All authority came from there; it was to be the visible center of all men's loyalties, the lodestar by which they lived, the place of ultimate judgment and reward. At the same time, because Augustus considered himself to be a man of studied moderation, wearing homespun and living in his small villalike mansion on the Palatine, there had to be a limit to ostentation. Stateliness rather than opulence was his theme, and he liked to stress the utilitarian nature of his improvements. This the architect Vitruvius did also, and he dedicated to Augustus the ten books of his *De architectura*. After acknowledging the superhuman intelligence of Augustus, Vitruvius goes on to remark that the emperor had embarked on a program of general welfare, the establishment of public order, and the provision of public buildings intended for practical use.

To accomplish his aim, Augustus enlarged Rome's central meeting area by adding a third forum next to the one built by Caesar. He turned his attention to an important element in "useful" building—the basilica, or the assembly hall, of which a number had been rising in Rome as well as in other cities of importance. These halls were usually roofed and offered far greater protection against weather than did the open colonnades that surrounded public squares in Greece, though the design of the basilicas may have been of Greek origin. Usually they were rectilinear, with lines of columns within their walled enclosure, and with a raised platform at one end on which the presiding official sat, often against the background of a tall, curved apse. They were both governmental and social meeting places, protected against summer's heat

The architect of the so-called temple of Vesta (right) employed the cylindrical shape commonly used for the house of the sacred flame. The temple is in one of the many forums built near the original Roman Forum, which, though never abandoned, underwent numerous alterations. Augustus, who had repaved and otherwise improved the Roman Forum and had completed a forum begun by Caesar, eventually built one of his own (below); the three columns are from the temple he raised to Mars the Avenger.

and winter's storms; in time the Christians would adapt the design of the basilica, transforming the hall into a church and placing an altar where the dais had been. Augustus, for his part, rebuilt for the second time the Basilica Aemilia, after Caesar's reconstruction of the even earlier building had been damaged by fire. On a far larger scale Augustus rebuilt Caesar's Basilica Julia, on the south side of the Forum, giving it a long central space that has been calculated at about two hundred seventy by fifty feet, with lines of interior columns on all four sides. All but the foundations of Augustus' basilicas have disappeared; one can only speculate as to what Pliny meant when he wrote that the reconstructed Basilica Aemilia was one of the three finest buildings in the empire.

In the eyes of Augustus, temples were useful too: their building or rebuilding was an act of piety to the gods who had granted him victory, but it was also an affirmation of national faith in the divine protectors. He was not deeply religious in the spiritual sense; but it was practical to favor the gods who had favored him. Since he believed that he was protected by Apollo and that the god had presided over his victory at Actium, he built on the Palatine a temple of Carrara marble, dedicated to his tutelary god, with pillared portico and inlaid ivory doors, with a statue of Apollo, and equipped with two libraries—one of Greek books, the other of books in Latin, as if to symbolize a marriage between the two cultures.

In support of the oath he had sworn at Philippi in 42 B.C. that he would build a great temple to Mars the Avenger if he won the battle, he raised a shrine to the god of war in his forum, and with wings that contained not books, but military relics. Among the noblest relics was the sword of Julius Caesar. Augustus no doubt planned that the temple of Mars should assume many of the functions previously fulfilled by the great temple of Jupiter on the Capitoline, across the way. In this new temple the conquering general would deposit his laurel wreath after his long triumphal procession; here was to be the center where the record of Roman valor and glory under arms would forever be preserved. Only three columns and a fragment of architrave survive.

Other temples were to come forth in profusion, such as those of Concord and of Castor, rebuilt from a decayed state by Tiberius after he became Augustus' heir. At the base of the Capitoline, in an area which Augustus is thought to have given over to the arts, a great theatre was completed, with two tiers of arcades and a seating capacity of some twenty thousand. Dedicated to Augustus' young son-in-law Marcellus, this open-air auditorium was a vast improvement over early Roman theatres, which were built of wood. Spectators had been offered little in the way of comfort in

To make an arch engineers built a wooden framework on which ribs of flat bricks were laid to reinforce the concrete, which would be poured into the intervening spaces. Because the thrust of the vaults in larger buildings was excessive and the erection of heavy framework was expensive, the Romans learned to make a strong, but lightweight concrete that relieved both problems.

The Romans constructed probably the finest paved roads in antiquity, some of which lasted hundreds of years. The diagram shows a cross section of a typical major highway. A deep trench was dug into which was laid a layer of flat stones; next, stones in mortar, topped by concrete or sand and stones; and finally, there were cobbles set in mortar. The unpaved edges made a sidewalk.

The Romans knew the mechanics of the water wheel from early in their history, but because of the abundance of slave labor and the paucity of water power in Italy, they generally declined to use it. However, in about A.D. 200 they set up the complex above, in Gaul. Water dropped onto sixteen wheels, which turned thirty-two mills, which produced twenty-eight tons of meal a day.

those earlier structures; they were forced to stand before a wooden stage to watch a play. The theatre of Marcellus was revolutionary in other ways, too, for it greatly exceeded in size what was probably the first masonry theatre in Rome, built only forty-two years earlier by Pompey.

Augustus and Agrippa, his adopted son and right-hand man, together had presided over the centennial games that marked the city's dedication to Apollo in 17 B.C., and together they had planned the city's rebuilding. Livy spoke of Augustus as "the founder or restorer of all the temples of Rome"; yet a great deal of the practical work lay in the hands of Agrippa, a brilliant organizer who was also a great engineer. He built aqueducts, erected one of Rome's major public baths, and provided the city with one of its most extraordinary temples—the stately Pantheon. After two ruinous fires, the Pantheon was to be rebuilt by the emperor Hadrian as a lofty, domed, circular shrine; it has survived as one of antiquity's most noble buildings, and to this day no one can be certain how much or little of Agrippa's own work was preserved in its stones. Hadrian, in any event, must have felt deep respect for what his predecessor had wrought when he set his own architects to work on it, for he caused an inscription to be carved in huge letters running almost the entire length of the pediment: M · AGRIPPA · L · F · COS · TERTIUM · FECIT—meaning that Agrippa had made this edifice in his third consulship. Such tribute to an earlier designer was indeed unique. Hadrian, possibly one of the most thoughtful and accomplished of Romans, evidently realized that he was in the presence of a master builder.

Agrippa was, in fact, one of the major practical geniuses of Rome. The city's needs for a sure water supply for its fast-growing citizenry were immense, and they had been ably met before his time by four aqueducts that brought in a constant flow from watersheds in the Alban hills. Under Augustus, Agrippa added two more and united and administered the whole system, which has been estimated to have provided some three hundred million gallons for the city every day, or about one hundred fifty gallons for each man, woman, and child. These aqueducts were the life-bringers to a metropolis unable to rely on the muddy Tiber for cleansing and recreational baths, and Romans regarded them as their supreme engineering achievement. Above all, they were practical—not simply ornamental. As Sextius Julius Frontinus, the governor of Britain who became a prominent engineer, remarked: "Will anybody compare the idle pyramids, or those other useless though renowned works of the Greeks with these aqueducts, these many indispensable structures?"

Under Augustus and his successors, the engineers came into their own, developing three major architectural elements that were to become distinctive of Roman architecture—the arch, the vault, and the dome. These forms were not original to Rome; Egyptians and Mesopotamians had raised arches and vaults, and small clay domes may have been built in the Near East from early times. But the Greeks, for their part, relied almost entirely on the post-and-lintel system of construction, and it remained for the Romans to exploit arched forms as the means of spanning large spaces. That they were able to accomplish this was due largely to their innovation in the making of concrete: they used lime mortar, a far stronger binding material than the traditional clay. This was a revolutionary departure in building techniques. Using temporary wooden supports, curved brickwork mixed with liquid mortar could be laid aloft, to become as secure as any masonry when the mixture set, and much lighter. Though huge stone blocks were still generally used in erecting a wall, it was also found that a wall could be just as strong and much less bulky and costly in carrying the thrust from above if composed of courses of broken stones and brick fragments bound with the new mortar. All that remained was to mantle the walls for appearance's sake with ornamental glass, stucco, or face-brick, and coffer the interiors of arches and ceilings with ingenious designs.

Yet the great buildings, erected with extraordinary skill and attention to balance and detail, were the product of a somewhat limited background. There is no evidence that the architects and engineers were trained in mathematics; they worked, as Vitruvius says, *ex fabrica et ratiocinatione*, which may be translated as "on the job and with hard thinking." They used models extensively, drew levels with plumb lines, and employed simple surveying instruments, together with huge wooden cranes worked by treadmills and pulleys. But their equipment was not notably superior to that used centuries earlier by Assyrian kings, who also built roads, aqueducts, and buildings that created awe in the minds of their subjects. The Roman contribution to architecture was expressed mainly in a dramatic magnification of scale, made possible by the most imaginative use of forms and materials. Near the end of the first century A.D., a palace was built on the Palatine for the emperor Domitian; it contained a lofty hall with a lengthy barrel vault more than one hundred feet in span—the precursor of the colossal vaulted enclosures of the baths of the later emperors Caracalla and Diocletian. Agrippa's Pantheon, moreover, when it was rebuilt and possibly enlarged by Hadrian early in the second century A.D., was roofed by a dome almost one hundred fifty feet

A first-century A.D. tomb relief depicts a huge crane operated by slaves in a treadmill. Because the Romans had armies of slaves, few time limits, and a large treasury, the idea of inventing a machine to get more done faster (with a few exceptions like the grape press) seldom occurred to them; they built bigger, better versions of fairly simple devices borrowed from other civilizations.
VATICAN; ANDERSON

in diameter—an engineering feat that pointed the way to the ever-greater experiments that were to culminate in the vast dome of the church of Hagia Sophia, in Constantinople.

The new order of building spread rapidly across the empire as an embodiment of Roman strength and leadership. Soon every major provincial capital had its basilicas, its roofed baths, its monumental arches, its paved roads, and often its aqueducts too. The Romans also inspired their allies to emulate them. When Herod the Great of Judaea determined to found a new seaport on the barren coast of Palestine, to which he had fallen heir as head of the Hyrcanian dynasty, he decided to show his friend Augustus that he, too, could build a city on the Roman scale. Enormous blocks of limestone, fifty feet long, were lowered into twenty fathoms of water, to provide a sea wall. The new city's public buildings included a theatre, an amphitheatre, and a hippodrome; aqueducts brought water from a distant river; there was a large and complex drainage system operated by tidal power. Here is the Jewish chronicler Josephus' description of Herod's seaport, which was to become the administrative capital of Judaea under Roman rule and to maintain that role during the three centuries and more that saw the Romans in power there.

> *At the harbor mouth there rose three colossal statues supported on pillars on both sides, and the pillars on the left of the ships entering the harbor were supported by a massive tower, and those on the right by two upright blocks of stone clamped together, even higher than the tower on the other side. Adjoining the harbor were houses, also of limestone, and the streets of the city, which were laid out at equal distances apart, led to the harbor. On rising ground, facing the harbor mouth, stood Caesar's temple, which was of exceptional size and beauty, containing a colossal statue of the emperor, not inferior to Olympian Zeus, and there was another statue dedicated to Roma, comparable with the Hera of Argos. Herod dedicated the city to the province, the harbor to those who sailed the sea, and to Caesar went the glory of the new creation; therefore he called it Caesarea.*

A chief uniting element of the empire was, of course, the complex road system radiating from Rome and begun centuries earlier with the building of the Appian Way, which crossed the Pontine marshes on an embankment as it headed in a straight line to Capua, in Campania. By Augustus' time the network had been extended as far as the Rhine and Danube frontiers; mileposts marked the distance from Rome, or within the provinces, the distance from the nearest provincial city. A road had been pushed on

232

The port of Ostia had been pillaged by pirates in 68 B.C.; Augustus made it one of his many rebuilding projects, and it began to flourish again. Many emperors after him left their mark there, too, so that by about A.D. 150 the large cosmopolitan city boasted two new harbors, fine public buildings, airy apartments, and it had become the largest receiving port in Italy. The sesterce opposite, struck by Nero, depicts boats in the harbor that Claudius had built in about A.D. 50. Below are the ruins of a block of Ostian apartments.

from southern France across the Pyrenees to the river Ebro; the greater and lesser St. Bernard passes, in the Alps, had been opened for traffic to Switzerland and the Rhine, and to the highlands of Provence. Whether Romans carved out entirely new routes or adapted earlier tracks, surfacing and ballasting them, remains a matter of some debate. In any case Roman roads were built very straight and often they measured three feet in depth, consisting of a foundation of rubble supporting tiers of stone and concrete and topped by a pavement to support heavy-wheeled traffic.

The accession of Tiberius, in A.D. 14, upon Augustus' death at the age of seventy-six, brought to the principate another man of brilliant military background, who under the tutelage of his imperial stepfather had become a builder of provinces as well as of great architectural structures. Yet Tiberius, fifty-five when he came to the throne, was a soured person, having lived perhaps too long in the shadow of Augustus, who had shown him little affection. Son of the republican officer Tiberius Claudius Nero and of Livia (who divorced Nero to marry the rising emperor), Tiberius accompanied Augustus on campaigns in the east. In 11 B.C. he had subdued the Pannonian tribes along the Danube; he had also distinguished himself in the fighting in Germany. But Augustus, after the death of his son-in-law Agrippa and of his own grandsons, chose Tiberius as his successor only with reluctance. To cement the family bond, he had required that Tiberius divorce his wife and marry Agrippa's widow Julia. A hesitant man, forced into an unhappy marriage, now came to power.

Tiberius immediately disclaimed any desire to receive the same sweeping authority that Augustus had enjoyed, by telling the senators that he was unequal to the whole burden of the state. Furthermore, he told them: "A well-disposed and helpful princeps should be the servant of the Senate. I have looked upon you as just, kind, and indulgent masters, and so regard you." Tacitus thought Tiberius was hypocritical in making these obeisances to the senators, who at the same time were making obeisances to him in their search for a leader. He may have been sincere in his protestations, however, sensing only too well that he could not carry the full responsibilities of Augustus. But the reluctant new princeps, who finally accepted all the titles and honors of office, including a lifelong proconsular imperium, was not to view the senators in such a self-effacing way for long.

In his first years he gave Rome a civil rule of high quality, appointing men of merit to key posts, awarding the Senate increased administrative functions in line with Augustus' scheme, and ensuring freedom for the little public debate that remained. In his

233

later years, however, his troubles accumulated, exacerbated by his lack of public appeal, his failures in tact when dealing with the Senate, his growing indifference to public affairs, and his involvement with dynastic rivalries and household favorites. Augustus was so popular that he could walk about Rome unprotected; Tiberius feared for his life. Augustus chose to live in an unassuming private house; Tiberius, for all his professions of humility, built himself a sumptuous palace on the Palatine, along with a huge barrack to house his Praetorian Guard.

There are few Roman emperors stranger than Tiberius, for he was endowed with high qualities, and might but for some flaws of character and wounds of experience have continued the tradition of his stepfather. Outwardly his reign was a period of prosperity and generally prevailing peace. The empire continued along the course mapped out by Augustus, with the momentum the great princeps had given it. Trade flourished, especially with the east. More and more roads were built across North Africa, a vast program of city planning was begun in Antioch, and wealth flowed from the silver mines in Spain into the hands of their owner, the emperor. Tiberius' nephew Germanicus, campaigning beyond the Rhine frontier, restored among the German tribes the prestige that had been lost by the defeat of Varus' legions in the Teutoburgian Forest. Minor rebellions in Africa and Gaul caused barely a ripple on the surface of the imperial order.

Yet in the emperor's own household and in his own person there was increasing disarray. Young Germanicus, whom he had made his son by adoption, caused him trouble through unruliness and ambitious seeking of popularity; Germanicus' death under mysterious circumstances while he was in the East raised unanswerable questions. Tiberius' only son, Julius Caesar Drusus, died suddenly in A.D. 23, leaving him no recourse but to hunt for heirs in the family of the late Germanicus. A miserable family feud broke out in which Agrippina, the headstrong widow of Germanicus and mother of three sons, became the center of intrigues against the emperor. By this time Tiberius had fallen under the sinister influence of Lucius Aelius Sejanus, the prefect commanding the Praetorian Guard, who promoted the quarrel, and with his men concentrated in the permanent barrack near Rome's gates, plotted to win the succession for himself. It was Sejanus who, evidently aware of Tiberius' increasing melancholy and instability, persuaded the emperor to withdraw his seat of residence to the island of Capri, while he himself would oversee affairs in Rome— a division of actual and seeming power that led to the tragic dissolution of Tiberius' once-promising reign.

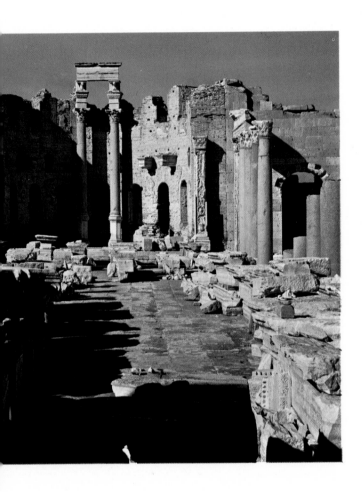

What was to become the usual layout of a Roman forum began to evolve in the second century B.C. The idea of an open area surrounded by colonnades was basically Greek, but the sealing off of one side of that area with a basilica wall was Roman. The long, enclosed basilicas, usually vaulted, served as law courts, meeting halls, and business offices. Opposite, the plan of a typical basilica is that of Septimius Severus at Leptis Magna. Although it is in ruins, above, it still conveys a sense of its original vast size.

By nature studious, tolerant, and lethargic save for the pursuit of military affairs, Tiberius did not have in him the qualities of a tyrant. Yet he became a tyrant in spite of himself, turning with brutal force against Agrippina and her sons and finally against his favorite Sejanus too, and invoking the law of high treason against his enemies or suspected enemies until there were few people in the empire who trusted him or whom he could trust. Much of this he accomplished from his southern island retreat, a haven into which he disappeared only to emerge from it on occasion with corrosive and unpredictable force. In his Villa Jovis, perched high on the cliffs of Capri, he secluded himself from the world as he presided from a distance over his dominions. Suetonius observed that no magnificent architectural works marked Tiberius' reign. He left unfinished his effort on two major monuments that might have commended him to posterity, the great temple to Augustus the Divine in Rome and the restoration of Pompey's theatre. Yet his eyrie on Capri was one of the most spectacular constructions of the age—a sprawling, fortresslike mass built about a central courtyard with four rain-catching cisterns, with reception rooms and galleries arranged in a semicircle fronting on the sea, with baths and libraries in the wings. In the most remote section of the villa were the emperor's private chambers, reached through labyrinthine corridors beyond the quarters of members of his court. Kitchens were relegated to still a different wing to avoid the intrusion of cooking odors, and in a remote terrace annex there was still another set of living quarters—perhaps the most private of imperial chambers.

The emperor possessed other villas as well on the island of Capri, which became his private domain, with no one permitted to land on it without his express permission. In summer he would retreat to a cool grotto on the mainland overlooking the Gulf of Amyclae—in itself a small palace with its marble basins, fountains, pools, and collection of statuary. As Suetonius recalls, "But after the loss of his two sons, of whom Germanicus died in Syria and Drusus at Rome, he [Tiberius] withdrew into Campania; at which time opinion and conversation were widespread that he would never return and would soon die. And both turned out to be nearly true. For, indeed, he never returned to Rome, and a few days after leaving it, when he was at a villa of his called 'The Cave' near Terracina, during supper a number of stones fell from above killing many of the guests and attendants, but he almost miraculously escaped." Several more years were given to him, but the empire had all but lost sight of him when he died in A.D. 37.

Augustus, for all his wise statecraft, had produced no clear-cut

A coin honors Tiberius, Augustus' successor, for his aid to earthquake-stricken cities in Asia Minor. The emperor continued the tradition of public building started by Caesar, although he did so sparingly, being one of Rome's most economy-minded sovereigns.

program for the succession, with the result that an emperor could choose an heir according to whim, trusting in the Praetorian Guard to assist the changeover when the moment came. From the offspring of Germanicus, Tiberius had picked Gaius, who was to become a disaster for Rome. Gaius, who was known as Caligula—Little Boots—from the child's version of soldier's boots he had sported as a youngster, was a handsome man of twenty-five, popular with the soldiery, and the hope of a people weary of Tiberius' ways when he was acclaimed princeps in A.D. 37 with Guard support. For a short while he ruled ably; then for three years he ruled like a madman until he was stabbed to death by a Praetorian officer, the prefects of the Guard being party to the murder plot.

In his early months he seemed the bringer of a new, liberal dispensation. He recalled political exiles, suspended treason trials, banished informers from his court, made public the accounting of the empire's finances (a practice instituted by Augustus but abandoned by Tiberius), held games, and launched a large building program. Then, from a model prince, he quite abruptly changed into an autocrat of exceptional cruelty and irresponsibility, moreover desiring that he receive the honors accorded to a god. A severe illness, which he is known to have suffered, may have deranged him; or it may have been his high office that caused him to fall victim to delusions of grandeur. No previous princeps had permitted a cult of emperor worship; Caesar and Augustus had been deified only after their deaths. Caligula, however, erected a temple to himself with a life-sized statue of himself in gold, and every day the statue was dressed in the clothes identical with those he was wearing on that day. He formed his own priesthood, which offered prayers and performed the appropriate sacrifices—for which he had a nice taste, urging those who wished to worship him to offer up flamingos, peacocks, woodcocks, and pheasants on certain days. According to Suetonius, he communed with his fellow gods: "When the moon shone full and bright he always invited the Moon-goddess to his bed; and during the day would indulge in whispered conversations with Capitoline Jupiter, pressing his ear to the god's mouth and sometimes raising his voice in anger. Once he was overheard threatening the god: 'If you do not raise me up to Heaven I will cast you down to Hell.'"

Meanwhile he resorted to indiscriminate murder. On a whim he caused his father-in-law to slit his own throat. He was suspected of incest with his sister Drusilla. He squandered state funds: Tiberius had left the state a fortune of twenty-seven million gold pieces, but Caligula spent it all and left the treasury bankrupt.

Abroad, his perversities and follies were also notorious—misman-agement and oppression brought Mauretania and Judaea to the brink of revolt. He lined up a great array of his troops on the Channel coast to invade Britain, but changed his mind and marched them away again. The news of his death, in a capital seething with humiliation and indignation, was greeted with relief.

What Caligula had undermined was more than restored by his successor, Claudius, during the thirteen years of his rule. The new emperor was physically handicapped. Early in life he may have suffered many illnesses; he walked with a tottering gait, trembled continually, slobbered, and spoke in a manner that was difficult to understand. A nephew of Tiberius (Caligula himself had left no heir), he had long been overlooked for the succession because of his infirmities, and his elevation was largely a matter of chance. Following Caligula's assassination, members of the Praetorian Guard had found him in hiding in the Palatine palace, and its chiefs had decided that this all but forgotten man could serve them well as an emperor beholden to them. Thus Claudius, with his weak chin, weak knees, and shaking head, became at fifty-one the successor of the line of the handsome Augustus. But though his body was weak, his mind was not, and his intellect overcame his limitations. Suetonius remarked that for all his infirmities, he "possessed majesty and dignity of appearance." Claudius was an intellectual and indeed a scholar. He had written voluminously on Etruscan history, and he composed forty-one "books" or chapters on the reign of Augustus. No other Roman emperor ever knew so much about the Roman past, and Claudius' love and respect for it made him, in turn, a follower of Augustus' aim of judicious dis-tribution of functions in an imperial state, as against Caligula's oriental despotism.

Pursuing a policy of measured growth, he was able to add five provinces to the empire: Mauretania (once a satellite kingdom, later split into two); Thrace, Lycia, and Britain. Almost a century had passed since Julius Caesar's first assault upon England. But Rome's foothold in the distant island had remained tenuous since that time, while on the other hand the emerging Britons had con-siderably advanced themselves, setting up small tribal kingdoms, trading with Gaul, attracting Gallic settlers, and absorbing Gallic influences as well. In A.D. 43, responding to an appeal from the Kentish chieftain Verica, who had long lived in Rome and pro-fessed to be friendly to the empire, Claudius dispatched four legions numbering some forty thousand men to put down the local rulers and organize their territories into a major province. A legion commander named Vespasian distinguished himself

Claudius (at top) ruled ably despite many personal weaknesses. He was responsible for adding several provinces to the empire, for strengthening the bu-reaucracy needed to administer it, and for under-taking a vast public works program. He had been preceded by Caligula (at bottom), who did little but bankrupt the treasury and attempt to deify himself.

At top is Agrippina, Caligula's mother and Nero's grandmother. Her daughter inherited her love for conspiracy; the younger Agrippina successfully plotted to have her son Nero named as successor to Claudius and then, it was said, fed the emperor poisoned mushrooms. Five years after Nero acceded, she in turn became victim; her son was tired of her meddling. The mad emperor is portrayed at bottom.

against the British tribesmen, and Claudius arrived in time to lead the final assault and accept their submission, permitting some of their petty kingdoms to survive within the imperial boundary he had set up between the river lines of the Severn and the Humber.

In his governing Claudius tried to follow Augustus' method of accommodation and balance, seeking to befriend the Senate. Intent on public improvements, he instituted a building program that was not as decorative as Augustus', but considerably more utilitarian. A new harbor was built at Ostia, north of the Tiber's silted mouth. Two aqueducts were completed for Rome. In many parts of the empire major roads were added to the existing system, some running to the Channel coast, and one of them extending for three hundred fifty miles from the Adriatic across the Brenner Pass to the Danube in Germany. Most ambitious of all among his engineering projects was that of reclaiming valuable farm land south of the capital: thirty thousand men were employed for eleven years in draining the Fucine Lake and in driving a tunnel three miles long to carry off the surplus water.

Yet, for all his merits, Claudius had shortcomings in leadership. Of necessity, because of the increasing complexity of the empire's business, he developed the bureaucracy begun by Augustus to the extent of setting up a group of private secretaries, who conducted themselves virtually as ministers of state and vastly enriched themselves in the process. He failed to impose a restraining hand on them and let himself be unduly guided by them; the fact, moreover, that these palace favorites were non-Roman freedmen was not reassuring to the Senate. And, most tragically for himself, he lived under the influence of two ill-chosen wives. The first was the promiscuous Messalina; the second was the imperious Agrippina, daughter of Germanicus and the elder Agrippina, who persuaded him to adopt Nero, her young son of an earlier marriage. In A.D. 54 Claudius was murdered by his ambitious second wife, who thus cleared the way for Nero and for herself as matriarch.

No novelist could have invented Nero; as an emperor he all but exceeds the bounds of credibility. Yet in his virtues and vices he was typical of his age, brilliant and decadent, elegant and gross. In his youth he was conspicuously handsome, with his finely chiseled nose, square chin, thick curls powdered with gold, and a physique well made except for his thin short legs. In time he would become a travesty of himself, grown fat, pot-bellied, thick-lipped with self-indulgence. The beginnings of his reign were promising. After the years of the physically grotesque Claudius, the young Nero, coming to the throne at seventeen, appeared to be one of those youthful rulers who ushers in a new age. He was burning with the desire to please and delighted in his popularity. Schooled by his tutor Seneca, the philosopher, he was well read and intelligent; moreover he was a gifted lyre player, a poet, and a singer. (The word *Nero* is derived from a Sabine word meaning "valiant" or "manly.") In the first years of his reign he was prodigal of his good behavior and showed a proper respect for the opinion of others, being especially attentive to the Senate. There was nothing to suggest that he would soon demonstrate massive incompetence, a passion for self-worship, and unbridled cruelty, becoming the murderer both of his mother and of his wife, along with countless others.

Some of the evil in this unstable man can probably be traced back to his domineering mother, a lecherous woman so spoiled by wealth and high position that she regarded her slightest impulse as a command to be obeyed, even if it meant that the entire resources of the state must be placed at her disposal. Agrippina amused herself by liquidating personal enemies and corrupting her son, and she succeeded so well that Nero lost respect for everyone, most of all for his mother. She is shown beside him on one of the first coins struck during his reign, and she made efforts to sit beside him in state on public occasions. Nero, however, grew resentful of her domination at court and had her banished from it, and in A.D. 59 had her put to the sword, declaring that she had planned his assassination. He received the congratulations of the Senate and the Roman people.

For a certain period the people had reasons for applauding him: he fed them well from his own grain ships, he entertained them with his own songs and by taking part in chariot races, and he refused to engage in unnecessary wars. Some virtuous Romans objected to the fact that the emperor made a public display of himself, performing in the theatre, dressing as a racing-chariot driver, and surrounding himself with singularly unpleasant companions —but there were not many virtuous Romans left. For a time he rode the tide of popularity.

Soon, however, there were wars in Britain and Armenia, and Nero began to debase the currency in order to pay for them. Wealthy nobles were put to death on suspicion of opposition, while the emperor relaxed among Greek and oriental favorites of low birth. By A.D. 64, virtually all elements in Rome were united in enmity for him—so much so that when a ruinous fire broke out that year, he was accused of setting it. All the buildings on the Palatine were destroyed; of the fourteen wards or districts of Rome, three were burned to the ground and seven were largely destroyed. Suetonius reports that "pretending to be disgusted by

Nero was genuinely interested in the arts, but when his interest manifested itself, an egoistical rather than a creative act always seemed to take place. Above is a corridor in the Domus Aurea, built to be Nero's palace. Situated in a mile-square park in central Rome, the building itself covered over twenty acres; descriptions of its sumptuous and often very vulgar decorations defy belief.
FOTOTECA UNIONE

the drab old buildings and narrow, winding streets, he [Nero] brazenly set fire to the city." But he appears, in fact, to have been absent from Rome at the time, and hurrying back when the disaster struck, to have directed the firefighting. The story of his fiddling or singing while Rome burned is most dubious. What remains, however, is the fact that in order to divert suspicion of arson from himself he caused it to be cast upon a sect of Jewish heretics who had been holding secret services in the city and who were already the object of enmity. As Tacitus puts it, "Nero fastened the guilt and inflicted the most exquisite tortures on a class hated for their abominations, called Christians by the populace. Christus, from whom the name had its origin, suffered the extreme penalty during the reign of Tiberius at the hands of one of our procurators, Pontius Pilatus . . ." The "exquisite tortures" included being thrown to wild beasts in the amphitheatre or smeared with pitch and used as living torches to illuminate Nero's nocturnal festivals.

The emperor at one time or another took to identifying himself with various gods—Apollo, Hercules, and Helios, deity of the sun —and coins were struck depicting him with a radiating crown. He did, to be sure, order the rebuilding of the ruined areas on new and open lines, with greater protection against fire hazard, and paid for much of this out of his own imperial purse. But he also squandered incalculable sums on the creation of a sumptuous palace and pleasure ground for himself between the Esquiline and Caelian hills. Known as the Domus Aurea because of its rich decorations, it was an immense complex centering about a vestibule lofty enough to house a gilded bronze statue of Nero himself, one hundred twenty feet high, and surrounded by parks, artificial lakes, and colonnades, one of which was reportedly a full mile in length. One of its banqueting halls was circular and equipped with a revolving ceiling; its rooms were richly painted and set with jewels and mother-of-pearl; the ceilings of ivory were pierced with pipes that sprayed perfume upon the banqueters. Tacitus described Nero as a man who desired the impossible—*incredibilium cupitor*—and it was clearly Nero's aim to stagger men's imaginations by the sheer immensity of his performance. But the spell was already broken. Incompetent in the face of a revolt in Judaea, despised by the army, abandoned by his provincial administrators, hated by all classes, he stood virtually alone. A Gallic governor named Julius Vindex got in touch with other commanders and raised revolt against Nero, denouncing him among other things as a bad lyre player. The Senate roused itself to declare him a public enemy. Beset by fears, he killed himself in A.D. 68.

Nero's successors, some of whom shared his grandiose tastes,

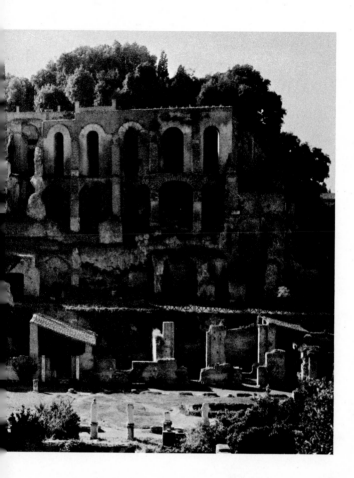

Many Roman building projects were the result of the contributions of several emperors. At times a program was undertaken too late to be completed during one emperor's reign; or a ruler might wish to impose his own touch to a construction he admired or to change it to meet his needs. Tiberius, Caligula, Domitian, and Hadrian all shaped the so-called Palace of Caligula, overlooking the Roman Forum, to suit themselves.
GABINETTO NAZIONALE FOTOGRAFICO

lacked his mania for self-indulgence. The Domus Aurea became the victim of the wreckers, who set about leveling it. Where the private palace had been, there arose public bathhouses and a circus; where Nero had built an artificial lake, there stood the Colosseum. Nothing made by Nero was permitted to remain; and the ancient rite of *damnatio memoriae* was invoked to remove any lingering respect for his memory: his images were destroyed or mutilated, his name was erased from inscriptions, and his public acts were rescinded. Nevertheless for nearly two thousand years his memory has remained fresh as the epitome of the tyrant ready to waste the wealth of an empire for his own pleasure.

His suicide left the succession in doubt. Through maternal lineage he was the great-great-grandson of Augustus; but he had left no heir. The line of emperors known as Julio-Claudian, rulers of a century of glory mixed with perfidy and disaster, had reached its end; the field was now wide open for new candidates for the principate to stake their claims—by force. After a brief period of anarchy, power fell into the hands of Vespasian, the legion commander who had distinguished himself in Britain and who was proclaimed emperor after his troops in the east had hailed him as such. Vespasian was not a man of Julio-Claudian refinement or learning; born of an obscure plebeian family, he had risen in the army through sheer ability and native intelligence, and he disliked the aristocrats. A friendly, down-to-earth man of simple tastes, bullnecked, thickset, he was adored by his soldiers because he spoke their language, and the plebs of Rome liked him for the same reason. Rising to his responsibilities he became, as princeps, one of the major builders of Rome and its empire.

His armies fought successfully both to expand and to consolidate the empire's frontiers. The revolt that had broken out in Gaul upon Nero's death was put down. Roman power was advanced to Scotland and Wales. The rebellion in Judaea, also provoked by Nero's mismanagement, was broken by a 139-day siege of Jerusalem that resulted in the city's surrender to Vespasian's able son Titus. In A.D. 70 Vespasian could claim that peace had been restored along the far-flung borders of the empire. The gates of the temple of Janus were closed to celebrate this, and a new temple to peace was erected, recalling in purpose Augustus' altar of peace, the Ara Pacis.

Only three columns of Vespasian's temple survive. In its time it was apparently the largest of all Roman temples and the most skillfully designed. And this was only one of the magnificent new buildings provided for Rome by an emperor who was frugal in his own tastes, scrupulous, honest, and anxious to restore both

Rome's fortunes and its morality. The temple of Jupiter on the Capitoline had burned down; Vespasian rebuilt it along more sumptuous lines than it had possessed before. He also built most of that barbarous masterwork, the Colosseum, though he himself had no particular liking for gladiatorial displays. The structure had been planned originally by Augustus, and Vespasian simply carried out the intentions of an earlier age.

Though Rome had its Circus Maximus—essentially a long race track—it lacked, until Vespasian's time, an amphitheatre large enough to give many tens of thousands of spectators a good view of the spectacle in the arena. The form of the Colosseum was not new to Rome—there had been other circular or oval structures in Italy—but its dimensions and its engineering were unprecedented. Three steeply rising tiers of seats, capable of holding perhaps forty-five thousand people, were raised by an intricate system of piers, arches, vaults, and cross vaults, with surrounding corridors. A top-story colonnade, added under Titus and Domitian, brought the oval to an outside height of nearly one hundred sixty feet. As we see it today, a ruin that seems to be sinking deeper into the ground, its travertine facing in most part removed long ago, its archways bare, its pilasters crumbling, the floor of the arena broken up to reveal the network of subterranean passages and pens for wild animals, the Colosseum still suggests some of the savage grandeur it once possessed. Its high walls, once topped by masts, shut out the world. Vast and brilliantly colored awnings, scarlet, blue, and yellow, stretched across the auditorium and held off the glare of the sun. Gilded bronze statues stood in the archways. The colored light, passing through awnings, cast a theatrical gleam upon the spectacle; the shouts of the audience echoed off the stone galleries.

Though not an intellectual, Vespasian furthered the arts and education, establishing, for instance, chairs of Greek and Latin rhetoric in Rome. His urge to found his own family dynasty, with his sons Titus and Domitian next in line, brought him into collision with a group of agitators who identified themselves with the Stoic and Cynic philosophers and who accused him of autocratic intentions. This led to some cruel meting out of punishment on the part of a man who had otherwise shown himself tolerant.

There was to be a dynasty known as the Flavian from Vespasian's family name, but it was short-lived. Titus, the handsome, popular conqueror of Jerusalem, had been made virtual co-regent by his father in preparation for the succession; but when he came to power in A.D. 79, he was to have only two years of rule. As openhanded as his father was parsimonious, his liberality and

Above is a bakery in Pompeii, a wealthy community that was destroyed by the volcanic eruption of Vesuvius in A.D. 79. At left are the ovens and at right is a row of mills. Grain was poured into the top of the hourglass-shaped stone that was turned by mules or slaves; the flour fell onto the cylindrical platform below.
MRS. WILHELMINA JASHEMSKI

242

pleasant ways delighted all classes. When he died at the age of forty-two, he left a triumphal arch of modest but exquisite proportions, a new public bath, a record of great aid to the sufferers of a new fire and plague in Rome, and a memory that caused him to be deified alongside Caesar, Augustus, and his father. Suetonius spoke of him as the "darling of the human race." No one was to say the same of his brother Domitian, who came to the throne to be the last of the Flavian line.

The second great fire in Rome, however, was preceded by the eruption of Vesuvius, which buried the prosperous city of Pompeii under some thirty feet of lava and volcanic ash in the first year of Titus' reign. Suddenly overwhelmed, the city was preserved as though in amber for the spades of archaeologists. As a result we know more about the day-to-day details of the lives of Roman citizens in the years of Vespasian and Titus than in any other period of the empire. When Vesuvius erupted, the shops were open, and children in school were scribbling their letters on wax tablets. We can visit the slaves' dormitories, the stockyards, the prostitutes' quarters, the shops of butchers, bakers, jewelers, and dyers, and if we want to know how cloth was dyed, we have only to look at the wall paintings showing dyers at work.

Pompeii, first settled by descendants of neolithic people of Campania, had come under the influence of the nearby Greek colonies along the coast; this no doubt accounts for the early refinement of its arts. Etruscans and Samnites had in turn occupied it, each contributing their strains of culture and growth. Finally came the Romans, under whom it became an important port, trading center, and resort, combining a certain Greek delicacy in its villas with Roman weight in its baths and other civic buildings.

There were paintings everywhere—on store fronts, inside factories, and in private houses, where they sometimes decorated the rooms from floor to ceiling. Ubiquitous, lively, and devoted to even the frankest personal detail, these tell of a population in love with color, amusements, and self-representation. Many of the Pompeiian paintings have been regarded as provincial in execution and as many were also coarse in theme; but great Rome itself left no comparable array neither in quality nor quantity.

In individual buildings, too, there was evidently much originality and vigor in this mixed community. The small Pompeiian temple of Apollo, an adaptation of Hellenistic design, was one of the most exquisite of Italian constructions. The Stabian baths, dating back to perhaps 120 B.C., included what may have been the first dome erected on Italian soil, roofing its *frigidarium*. The dome did not converge on a point at its apex, but left a large circular open-

Pompeii abounds with examples of non-state-supported building. The temple of Apollo above, raised on ancient, sacred ground, was restored in the time of Nero with funds contributed by private citizens. The many luxurious, lavishly decorated houses there also attest to the Roman's desire for individual grandeur.
ACE WILLIAMS, SHOSTAL

approx. 141'

ing at the top to admit light and air—thus prefiguring the much vaster dome, with a similar opening, that the emperor Hadrian was to mount on Rome's Pantheon.

Domitian, who came to power in A.D. 81, was as taken up with great building as his late father and brother had been, laying out a new stadium in the Campus Martius, commencing a new forum that was to become known by the name of his successor, Nerva, and raising on the Palatine a vast palace of his own with walls ten feet thick, topped, it may have been, with a colossal barrel vault. Yet Domitian, unlike the other Flavians, was a singularly forbidding figure. In foreign matters he conducted himself ably, intent on strengthening, and where possible, advancing frontiers. In Britain he pushed them ahead, chiefly through a five-year campaign led by Gnaeus Julius Agricola, father-in-law of the historian Tacitus. In central Europe he improved the Danube boundary by establishing advanced outposts along its tributary river Main. In eastern Europe, along the lower reaches of the Danube, in what is now Rumania, he faced and withstood the threat of Dacian tribes, though not without paying them a bounty for peace. In his choice and control of provincial officials, he appears to have been astute; in his administration of revenues and taxes, demanding but fair. In his everyday confrontations with leaders and the public at home his performance became disastrous.

Embittered perhaps by jealousy of Titus and his own wait for power, he turned to tyrannical arrogance and display. He demanded of his subjects the subservience due to an oriental monarch: they were to revere him as a god and on one occasion he held out his hands for a kiss. He degraded the Senate in particular by assuming the role of *censor perpetuus*, thereby making himself master of its composition, and requiring it to endorse all his actions. As these became increasingly capricious and cruel, conspiracies formed against him, and his own wife took part in a palace plot that in A.D. 96 did away with him. He left no children.

So passed the second dynasty to rule over imperial Rome. Both had brought forth highly gifted men as well as unstable ones; both had seen the brilliant use of power as well as the abuse of it. Cruelty and at times venality had played their familiar parts. Yet, amid many occasions of disorder, all the major emperors save Nero had contributed in one way or another to the enlarging and strengthening of the imperial structure. All saw themselves as builders in both the governmental and the physical sense; even Nero, public disaster that he was, was too alert to public building and rebuilding to be entirely despised. The satirists Juvenal and Martial mocked the ways of Domitian, and pockets of republican opposition to the trend toward absolute monarchy persisted. But the centers of agitation were now confined to a small group of intellectuals who claimed for themselves the mantle of the Stoic tradition of thought, and both Vespasian and Domitian had virtually silenced them by banishment. By and large, the people seemed to feel that their emperors, for all their faults and favorites, had served to restore confidence in Rome as a permanent institution, not just the plaything of contending generals, and that one would do best to trust in their foresight, or *providentia*. The true Stoic, meanwhile, could draw strength from the memorable lines that Horace had written:

Not the rage of the million commanding things evil,
Not the doom frowning near in the brows of the tyrant,
Shakes the upright and resolute man
In his solid completeness of soul.

With the Flavians extinct, a new line of leadership was to arise, and it was to be Rome's good fortune that a new century brought with it two such wise and spacious statesmen as the emperors Trajan and Hadrian. The foundations for their rule, for all the cracks in the wall, had been generally well laid. Trajan was to increase the size of the empire by his victories over the Dacians and Parthians and others; Hadrian was to consolidate it further by his administrative mastery.

The success of their reigns was to be made immediately visible to all citizens of the city, for it was demonstrated by structures that were in themselves the culmination of the greatest art of the Romans, their architecture. Trajan, in addition to completing a new forum and erecting new baths, was to supervise the design of the spectacular column that celebrates his campaigns by means of a winding, carved scroll some six hundred twenty-five feet long. Hadrian, in addition to building his famous villa at Tivoli—a complex employing domes and vaults around a central mansion beside a miniature lake—was to order a marvelous new temple to be erected on or beside the foundations of Agrippa's burnt-out Pantheon. Perfectly round, of unprecedented proportions for such a shape, its internal diameter is precisely equalled by its height. Its interior is fitted with marble panels, niches, and alcoves; its coffered vault is pierced at the top by a great circular "eye." It was perhaps the most brilliant building erected since the Parthenon in Athens had brought the building program of Pericles to its peak. One of few Roman structures to be preserved without any appreciable loss or fault, the Pantheon was to remain an embodiment of Rome's highest imagination and triumph.

Cutaway views of two of the most magnificent edifices produced by Rome's talented architects are shown opposite. The Pantheon (at bottom) was designed to be as wide as it is high. That the Roman engineers could leave hollows in the walls indicates their facility with concrete. At top is a drawing of the Colosseum, built in the reigns of Vespasian and Titus, and restored by Nerva and Trajan. The huge amphitheatre, which seated forty-five thousand, was divided into four tiers. A view inside the Colosseum (above) shows that the cellars were actually made up of dozens of rooms; there gladiators and wild animals were housed. Before the contests animals were placed in cages that could be lifted by block and tackle to the mouth of a tunnel that led to the arena.

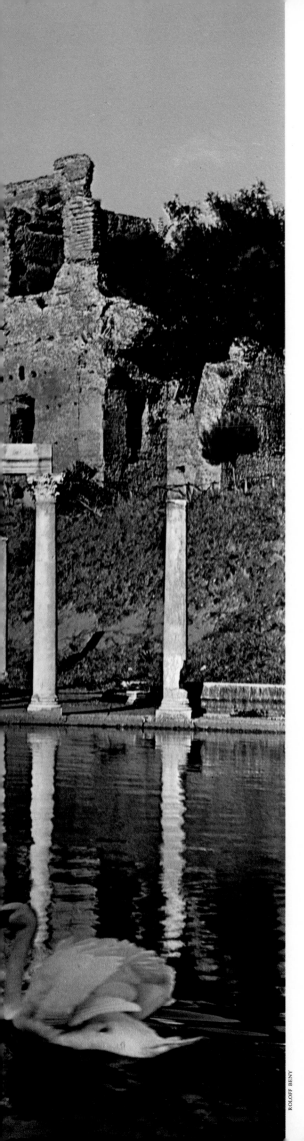

THE MASTER BUILDERS

The Romans might be called the greatest architects of antiquity. They borrowed almost all their architectural forms and building techniques, but wrought such changes on them that by the first century A.D. they had created a daring and unique style that was profoundly to influence the western world. The style was based on the arch and its extensions, the vault and dome, thitherto little used, and it was made possible by a Roman innovation—concrete that did not buckle under the stresses of the huge structures.

Civil engineering became another of Rome's highly developed skills. City planners laid out town after town, formal but pleasant, endowed with baths, forums, and theatres, and supplied with elaborate systems of aqueducts and sewers. To connect the cities the Romans stretched out a vast network of solidly constructed roads along which traveled the fastest post the world would know until the advent of the railroad.

A far less tangible but equally important Roman contribution to the West is the conception of a building as a conscious means of shaping space to affect the emotions of the people inside it. The gigantic enclosure of the Colosseum heightened the drama of brute sports; the lofty Pantheon conveyed a commanding sense of awe. An atmosphere of relaxation and enjoyment was attained in the design of Roman villas—none more imaginative than Hadrian's (opposite), with its pools, ornaments, and vistas.

TRIUMPHANT ARCHES

Many ancient peoples had employed the arch in construction, but its full potential was not realized until the time of the empire when the Romans made an exhaustive exploration of the uses of the form, which they had adopted from their Etruscan forebears. The Romans were the first to create a concrete that was able to withstand outward thrust without much additional buttressing, and by the middle of the first century A.D. the concrete and brick arch had become not only the means for erecting larger buildings than ever before but an expression of beauty; its extensive use turned Roman architecture into art.

Even before the Romans knew about concrete, they had constructed arches for purely decorative purposes; and large arches with legends and reliefs remained a way of commemorating an emperor. Above is the gigantic arch of Septimius Severus, erected in A.D. 203. At right is a detail of the smaller and far more elegant archway of Titus. Greek orders were added to such arches for the sake of form rather than function; the decorative carving shown here is of the finest.

HARBOR AND HIGHWAY

One of the greatest feats of ancient engineering and planning was the vast system of roads and harbors built by Rome to maintain its far-flung empire. Roads were mainly for official use, but private citizens were granted passports to use them. They found posthouses about every ten miles, and every thirty, inns sold food, lodging, and carnal pleasure. Thus encouraged, many set out to see the world, doing much to unify the empire's disparate peoples. But the system's greatest importance was the speed with which troops could be deployed and information relayed over the roads. Julius Caesar once went 800 miles in eight days, and postriders could move twice as fast. Almost as important was the effect on Rome's flourishing trade: harbors were lined with quays, warehouses, gear and men to unload goods, sometimes into wagons waiting to transport them anywhere along the 180,000 miles of paved roads that stretched across Rome's domain from Spain to Asia.

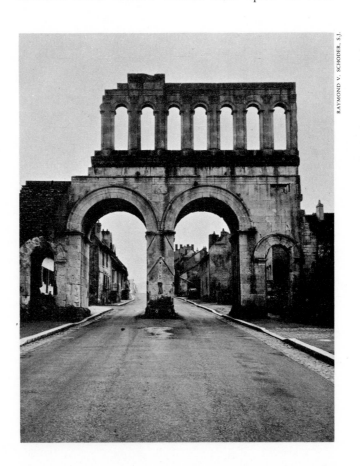

The painting at left probably represents Stabiae, one of the three ports that served Rome; at upper right four boats are anchored in the beautifully decorated and well-equipped harbor. Above, the gateway to Autun, France, is typical of hundreds erected on Roman roads to announce to the traveler that he had reached a town.

PLANNERS OF CITIES

For military and economic reasons, in imperial times Rome built numerous towns throughout its empire, and city planning became one of its major civil engineering projects. Planners borrowed their idea from the Greeks, even to the regular intersection of streets, but they imposed on it much that was characteristically Roman. The rigid layout was ameliorated by arches and colonnades; and some avenues were lengthened to accommodate grand public buildings and forums. In addition there were fresh running water, public latrines, sewer systems, police and fire brigades, and strict traffic laws to make Roman cities among the most livable in the world.

The checkerboard pattern of a Roman town is clearly visible below, in an airview of Thamugadi (Timgad), in Algeria, founded in about A.D. *100 by Trajan. Rome, with its winding labyrinth of streets, had grown up over the centuries, presenting a complete contrast to the "new" cities. Opposite is a view of the oldest Roman forum; the emperors superimposed only a certain amount of order on it.*

ROLOFF BENY

252

THE NOBLEST DOME

The Romans' mastery of building techniques and the manipulation of space reached its summit in the Pantheon; it is the masterpiece of Roman architecture, aesthetically and structurally. The architect who built it for Hadrian in about A.D. 125 found the ideal form for a temple dedicated to the gods of the cosmos. It is not known exactly how the building was erected, but like most Roman edifices its basic ingredients are brickwork and concrete; hidden inside the walls is an elaborate framework of brick arches to support the weight of the dome, and that, too, is presumed to be structured on rows of small arches

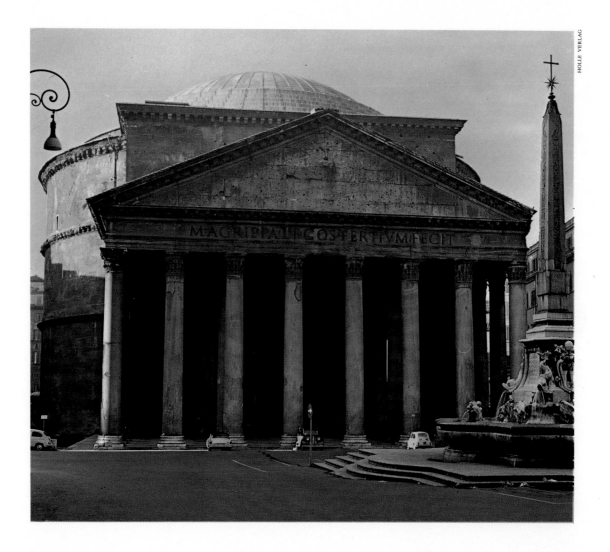

The Pantheon is thought by many to represent near perfection in interior design. Opposite, light pours through the aperture in the coffered dome, helping to create the mystical atmosphere of the windowless building. The temple was not built to be imposing from the outside (above). The Greek-style porch, strangely appended to it, is perhaps from Agrippa's temple, the structure that Hadrian's Pantheon (later restored by Septimius Severus) replaced.

ARTIFICIAL RIVERS

By 300 B.C. the population of Rome had grown so large that its sources of fresh water were no longer adequate, and the censor Appius Claudius had built the city's first aqueduct. It was an underground conduit as the major part of every Roman aqueduct was to be, despite the occasional need for soaring "bridges" and open concrete canals. After choosing a spring or river to be tapped, an engineer designed the straightest channel that would ensure a gradual downhill run of water into cisterns, whence it was piped to users. There were leakage problems, but Rome could amply supply public baths and private consumers from its many aqueducts.

Their facility with the arch enabled the Romans to span almost any river or gorge; the bridges and aqueducts they built, although meant to be functional, are also among the most beautiful of their constructions, for they are usually devoid of superimposed decoration, and their proportions are often superb. An excellent example is the three-tiered Pont du Gard (right) in Nîmes, France. Because of the great expense of such high-flown aqueducts, wherever possible, open channels (like the one above) or underground runs were built instead.

ULTIMATE GRANDEUR

Monumentality rather than innovation marked the architecture of the third century A.D. The builders had complete confidence in their materials and their ability to use them, and easily erected ever-larger and more complex buildings. But with few exceptions (like a domed bath with buttressed walls, erected in about 250) the enormous baths, palaces, and basilicas that were being raised throughout the empire, in a final spurt of energy, were based on centuries-old ideas.

A plan of the gigantic baths of Caracalla and its surrounding libraries (1), gymnasiums (2), stadium (3), and shops and offices (4) is shown opposite, above a view of the hotroom (5). The complex, which covered about thirty-three acres, was splendidly decorated throughout. Above, the plan of a huge villa near Piazza Armerina, Sicily, indicates its well-integrated design. The villa's famous hunt mosaics, at right, still have their brilliance.

LEONARD VON MATT

OVERLEAF: *Though much of its façade has fallen, the Colosseum, built around A.D. 90, survives as the most imposing structure of ancient Rome, brilliant in engineering and shapely in design. It dwarfs the fourth-century arch of Constantine in the foreground.*

HERSCHEL LEVIT

IX

THE ROMAN PEACE

For some two hundred years following the accession of Augustus, the Mediterranean world was virtually at peace. War, when it was waged at all, was confined almost entirely to frontier areas. Never in human history had there been so long a span of general tranquility, and never again was peace to be maintained so steadily among so many people. One mighty state seemed almost to embrace the world, with only the savage tribes of northern Europe and of central Africa and the mysterious nations of the Orient living beyond the pale. The *pax Romana*, the Roman peace, extended from Scotland to the vast Sahara Desert, and from Portugal to the borders of Persia. Throughout much of the empire, men lived out their lives in quiet contentment, safe from marauding armies, going about their affairs in the knowledge that they were sheltered by Rome, a stern but generous master that demanded unyielding obedience to its laws, at the same time granting to each community the right to adapt those laws to local circumstances. Under Roman protection trade flourished, cultivation was extended, and prosperity was brought to regions that had never before progressed beyond mere subsistence.

There were times when Romans appeared to be awed by the scope of their success. Pliny the Elder speaks of the immense majesty of the Roman peace (*immensa Romanae pacis maiestas*) as though he could scarcely bring himself to believe that so great a thing had been accomplished. He was, after all, contemplating a world in which Britons and Africans were speaking the language of Cicero and Vergil, a world in which Spaniards and Syrians were building Roman roads, using Roman weights and measures, and swearing allegiance to a Roman emperor. On a continent lacerated for centuries by local and general wars, there was suddenly peace.

The legions that had imposed Roman rule were not, of course, gone or forgotten. Few Roman subjects dared to break the peace for fear of punishment almost too severe to contemplate. Those who did revolt—such as the hapless nationalists of Judaea—served as a terrifying example for any others who might be so inclined. Rebels could hope for no outside help, for as yet there existed no military power that could seriously challenge that of Rome. Although the empire was anything but an armed camp, the element of compulsion was never entirely absent.

And the peace was by no means a perfect one. Occasionally some mad emperor—a Nero or a Domitian—would grope his way to the throne, create sudden confusion at the heart of the imperial complex, and send a succession of shudders through the Roman world. But the administrative machinery was well oiled; the civil services continued to function, and the very immensity of the empire ensured that it could not all come apart at once. To the mass of Romans the occasional murders in the imperial palace, the sporadic uprisings in Britain, Gaul, or Africa, the revolts of the Jews were little more than ripples on the surface of a peaceful lake. With the advantage of hindsight, historians have been fond of comparing this era—and particularly the quiet years of the mid-second century A.D.—to a sunny afternoon in late summer during which storm clouds are gathering ominously on the horizon. To many Romans, however, it must have seemed that Vergil's dream of a world of plenty, in which men went about unarmed, was about to become a reality.

The Mediterranean had become a Roman sea, its shores white with Roman temples and crowded with Roman *municipia*. Roman ships patrolled the Atlantic and roamed the Black Sea. Since all roads ended in Rome, the Romans were able to buy silk from China, spices from the East Indies, perfume from Arabia, glass-ware from Tyre and Sidon, marble from Greece, porphyry from Egypt, tin from Britain and Spain, and furs from the far north. Epicures had their choice of figs and dates from Syria, tunny from the Black Sea, oysters from Britain, and sausages from Gaul.

For two centuries the lands bordering the Mediterranean were intensely cultivated. The Sea of Galilee, today surrounded by a half-moon of scalded rocks and another half-moon of patchy fields, was then green with the reflections of innumerable trees. The forests of cedars in Lebanon ranged for mile upon mile and were carefully guarded since they provided timber for the Roman fleet. The Fens of England were cornfields; so, too, were the plains of La Camargue, in southern France. Spain, which Pliny the Elder described as overflowing with silver and gold mines, exported not only precious metals but lead, iron, and copper in addition to tex-tiles, wine, olive oil, and the celebrated fish sauce known as garum. From the many cities of Asia Minor and Syria came a con-stant supply of luxury clothing and linens, leather products, drugs, perfumes, spices, and dyes.

By enriching the empire, trade provided a cement that bound the provinces together. Generally the expense of transporting goods over long distances did not prevent a growing exchange of products. But when it did discourage trade, it also fostered local self-sufficiency and prosperity by stimulating the development of manufactures in areas where such industries might not otherwise have developed. Thus, glassmaking centers arose in Europe to compete with Sidon (where the art of glass blowing was invented during the early Roman empire), and Gaul became the foremost producer of the pottery known as *terra sigillata*, once a specialty of

Of the enlightened rulers who guided Rome during most of the second century A.D., Marcus Aurelius was the last. An emperor skilled in the manage-ment of both civil and military affairs, he was also a philosopher, leaving, in his Meditations, *a rec-ord of the Stoic principles by which he lived.*

263

the Etruscan city of Arretium. Ironically, prosperous Italy was among the least self-sufficient regions, for it depended on huge imports of grain from Egypt, Africa, Sicily, and other provinces to feed its growing population.

The exchange of goods between neighboring provinces and localities was immensely facilitated by the proliferation of paved roads. The Roman highway system grew steadily during the first and second centuries A.D., its tentacles extending to the borders, and sometimes beyond the borders, of the empire. The Romans were so addicted to roadmaking that they even built a highway along the Nile River from Alexandria to what is now the Aswan area, in southern Egypt, although the Nile itself constituted a more practical artery of transportation. The roads were extremely well constructed originally and were kept in constant repair by the cities and provinces that they served. Not until the fall of the empire were they left to decay. Some, crumbling and overgrown, were rediscovered centuries after they were built, by peoples who attributed them to giants or the devil or gnomes. Other roads were attended to through the ages, and a few of them are still in use today. The breadth and solidity of these roads, and the frequency with which they were repaired in some parts of the empire, hint at the volume of the traffic that they must have accommodated during the time of the Roman empire.

Although the Romans did not have a seafaring temperament, and their ships and sailing methods did not match their other accomplishments, there was nevertheless a development of sea traffic, for transport by sea continued to be the most practical means of moving bulky quantities of goods over great distances. Some of the vessels plied regular routes through the Mediterranean—particularly those that carried grain from Alexandria to Ostia. Trade was not confined within the imperial borders. Hoards of Roman coins found in Scandinavia, India, and Ceylon testify to the initiative of the merchants of that era. Trade with the Orient became a significant source of wealth for such Syrian cities as Palmyra and Bostra, to which caravans brought silks, spices, and other goods from ports on the Persian Gulf and the Red Sea. Roman gold and art objects are known to have moved eastward into India and the lands beyond. In the late second century A.D., Greco-Roman merchants presented themselves at the court of the Chinese emperor, claiming to be envoys from the Roman emperor.

Provincial life during the first and second centuries A.D. was generally calm and orderly. Civic affairs were conducted with a degree of independence that no one could have hoped for at the time of the conquests. At the head of the administration in each province was a governor, issuing orders in the name of the emperor, protected by a personal guard, and assisted by a staff of civil servants that, from the time of Vespasian, was often recruited from among the most gifted provincials rather than exclusively from Rome's aristocracy. Most of the provincial governors seem to have been well chosen. Though occasionally rapacious, they were seldom tyrannical, and as a rule, respected both the rights of the people they governed and the customs of the ancient cities where they had their headquarters.

When the governor sat in judgment, local assessors would often sit beside him to explain the customs of the land and to advise him on native law, for the provincial laws were still operative where they did not conflict with Roman ones. In the western provinces, general assemblies met once a year in the provincial capital to offer sacrifices to Rome and the emperor; those formal ceremonies were followed by debates and discussions on the state of the province, after which complaints and suggestions might be handed to the governor. This was not democracy, for only the leading members of the provincial communities attended the one-day parliament, but the process may at least have served to persuade Rome's subjects that the empire was not merely a tyranny devoted to the glorification of Roman power.

Because the Romans urgently wanted peace, they were prepared to offer to the subject peoples the gift of Roman citizenship as the supreme reward for good behavior. Provincials who served in the army would receive the citizenship upon discharge, and whole cities might receive citizenship from the hands of a grateful governor or from a general who wanted to reward a city that had placed its resources at his disposal. The gift of citizenship was not lightly regarded. When Saint Paul claimed Roman citizenship he was claiming the full protection of Roman law over the local law of the province of Judaea; and his cry "I appeal to Caesar" was the cry of a provincial who knew himself to be especially favored and protected by the emperor. He claimed the right to be tried by the emperor or by a judge responsible to the emperor, and his person was inviolate until the trial had taken place.

Cities had always served, in fact, as the basic political building blocks upon which the Roman administrative pyramid rested, and for many years, the granting of citizenship to non-Roman municipalities was one of the major tools by which the Romans established consent among the governed. Under the republic, the franchise was extended to colonies that had been established by Roman citizens on foreign soil. After the creation of the empire, it became the practice to "colonize" by granting citizenship to

Trade flourished throughout the empire during the long era of the Roman peace. Although the Romans did not have the same genius for shipbuilding as they did for roadbuilding, the merchant fleet was a very important means of moving goods from one part of the empire to another. The relief shows a transport ship sailing into Ostia's harbor, which is guarded by Neptune. A lighthouse flame rises in the background.

One result of peace and good rule was an ever-growing number of wealthy individuals throughout the empire; seaside villas like the one below, in the Pompeiian wall painting, multiplied. Despite the importance of manufacturing and the cultural supremacy of cities, the economy was based on agriculture, and many fortunes were made from the produce of great estates. The mosaic represents a villa in North Africa, a fertile area in the empire.

foreign communities in return for services rendered or for conspicuous progress toward Romanization. This approach was especially effective during the first hundred years of the empire, and it was an important part of the emperor's political arsenal during the second. As time passed, however, the Romans became less discriminating in their application of this policy, with the result that the number of citizens increased enormously. In A.D. 212, remarkably soon after the collapse of the Roman peace, the emperor Caracalla granted citizenship to all of the inhabitants of the empire but the slaves. By that time, the burdens of citizenship—and particularly, heavy taxes—had begun to outweigh its advantages.

The penetrating power of Roman civilization in any given province—the degree to which the Romans succeeded in stamping their own political and social brand upon a subject people—was largely determined by the characteristics of the society that they conquered. The essential differences between the western and eastern provinces were so marked that it seems that there were two empires long before any formal division into eastern and western branches took place. In Britain and Gaul and in parts of Spain and North Africa, civic life itself might have been described as a Roman invention. Many of the major cities had started their histories as Roman colonies, and the Romans could claim, with some justice, that they had brought the blessings of civilization to the land. Latin was the lingua franca in all European lands that were situated to the west of the Illyrian shore of the Adriatic and in that part of Africa that extended westward from Cyrenaica.

East of this line Latin never replaced Greek. There lay the Hellenistic world, an incredible complex of ancient lands and peoples, a world united briefly under Alexander of Macedonia, imbued with Greek learning, and tinctured by Greek institutions. To these lands—to Greece, to Egypt, to Asia Minor, to Syria, and to Judaea—the Romans came not as civilizers but as soldiers and representatives of a rude young culture. This was a world of cities, many of them prosperous, some of them several centuries older than Rome. Administration of the eastern provinces, with their various ethnic groups and their strange but sophisticated religions and their ancient customs, took all of the political acumen that Rome could muster. At times, as in Judaea in both the first and second centuries A.D., the task proved too much even for Roman administrative genius. Roman hegemony was to survive in these regions long after it had been expunged in the West; yet the several centuries of Rome's eastern rule were to produce, in the Byzantine empire, a world that was not truly Roman, but an amalgam of Rome, Greece, and all that had gone before.

There were also great differences in the treatment of specific provinces, and there seems to have been a strong tendency to allow early precedents to guide subsequent policy. For example, the inhabitants of Narbonensis, the most Romanized of the Gallic provinces, enjoyed the special favor of Augustus and consequently found themselves in possession of certain extraordinary rights. These rights were seldom abridged by later rulers. In the middle of the first century A.D., the emperor Claudius, praising the people of Vienna (Vienne), spoke of a long-established right of the citizens of "this most ornate and worthy colony" to appoint their own senators to Rome—a privilege that raised provincial Vienna to the status of a Roman city.

Other provinces seem to have borne for decades and even centuries the marks of imperial disfavor. Egypt was exploited unmercifully, being regarded merely as a granary that must produce sufficient corn to feed the Romans. Later imperial policy followed that of Augustus, who treated the province as his own preserve to be mulcted of all its wealth and treasure as he pleased. Only Alexandria, the second city of the empire and the only major city in Egypt, escaped the crushing weight of Roman exploitation largely by virtue of its importance in trade. The province itself experienced an inevitable economic and social decline. An Egyptian in the third century A.D. wrote an anguished protest against the slow destruction of his country, crying out that the gods had deserted it and that soon "this most holy land, the very seat of shrines and temples, will be full of the graves of men."

Many provinces, of course, were governed without any particular evidence of favor or disfavor, and there were also some that suffered briefly under a hostile emperor or enjoyed temporary advantages under a friendly one. Hadrian's special love for Greece, for instance, resulted in great benefits to this highly regarded but somewhat impoverished realm.

Of the histories of the provinces during these relatively placid centuries, Judaea's must stand out. Because the religious nationalism of the Jews presented a peculiarly difficult problem, the country was permitted to retain a high degree of independence under the leadership of an aristocratic priestly caste; its Roman governors, however, were not loath to assume full military powers and rule by martial law at the first sign of intransigence. Judaea was to serve as an example of both Roman liberality and Roman severity. Although the Judaean rebellions are often attributed to the peculiarly virulent nature of the Jewish nationalism of that time, there may have been other, equally important reasons. Josephus remarks in his introduction to *The Jewish War* that the Romans

A faïence relief from Hildesheim, Germany, depicts a Roman official and his wife. Under the emperors from Nerva to Marcus Aurelius provincial administration was strengthened. Capable and honest men, who could work closely with local leaders were often sent to govern the provinces.
RICHARD ERDOES

feared the Jews would make common cause with the Parthians, Rome's hereditary enemies in the east, and that Rome was prepared to go to any lengths to safeguard its foothold in Palestine. Whatever the causes, Judaea was racked by great revolts, which were followed by exceptionally ruthless repressions. Jerusalem was captured, looted, and razed in A.D. 70 by legions under the future emperor Titus. An even more brutal clash occurred between A.D. 131 and 135. A widespread rebellion provoked the Romans to wage a war of annihilation in which the land was devastated and a large part of the Jewish population was put to the sword. This slaughter was carried out at the order of the emperor Hadrian, who, but for this, is remembered as one of the most generous and enlightened of Roman rulers.

The Roman army went about its work of destroying Judaea like a pitiless machine, and there is no doubt that it wielded terrible powers. Yet it was rarely used as a suppressor of rebellion within the empire during that era. It was not, in fact, the least admirable of Roman institutions. Largely recruited from the provinces, it was pervaded with democratic feeling. As a rule, men rose by merit, not by special influence, and the accidents of birth had little to do with advancement. Because the legions were often rotated a soldier at the end of his career might find that he had served in most of the provinces of the empire. We hear of Spaniards serving in Lower Moesia (northern Bulgaria), of Carthaginians serving in Britain, of Germans serving in Palestine, and of Gauls serving in Italy. Provincial differences tended to disappear within the overwhelming uniformity of army life, and the contact of the legions with the people of the many provinces helped knit the empire together, although in later times each legion was almost entirely comprised of men from the province in which it was stationed.

The camps and fortresses followed an unchanging pattern: vast, drab, walled-in squares with watchtowers. One large building was reserved for the camp commander, and nearby there would be the heavily guarded treasury and shrine of the standards. There were long lines of wooden barracks, but the grim uniformity of the camp was broken by the presence of granaries, kitchens, ovens, horse-lines, latrines, punishment cells, the surgery and the hospital block, the armorer's and the leather-worker's shops, and perhaps a building for the veterinary. There was a parade ground, and somewhere outside the camp there were baths, an amphitheatre, and merchants' booths. Often there was an underground Mithraic temple where devotees were initiated in a small cramped pit as they were "cleansed" in the dripping blood of a bull that had been butchered on an iron grating above their heads.

Despite the new wealth, the masses remained impoverished; under Trajan at least a third of Rome's people lived on public grain doles. Ironically, lavish fun was provided for the poor, too. They cavorted in elegant baths and cheered in great arenas. A mosaic from the baths of Caracalla pictures four gladiators.

These permanent camps, however, represented only one aspect of Roman military might. There were also veterans' organizations, which could be called upon to serve when danger threatened. In the provinces these auxiliaries formed a reserve of trained men that could be thrown into battle at the bidding of the prefects, who served as chief officers in the district camps. In the city of Rome there was the Praetorian Guard, several thousand strong. In theory it was the bodyguard of the emperor, but in reality it constituted a force that discouraged raids upon the city from without and revolutionary uprisings from within. The Praetorian Guard was an elite corps, well paid and granted special privileges. On occasion it had the power to bring to office the emperors it was designed to serve; the rest of the time it remained a decorative but effective discouragement to troublemakers.

The legions were stationed along the frontiers at the extreme limits of Roman power. Through the first and second centuries A.D., except during a few brief intervals of anarchy, these units were entirely responsive to the will of the reigning emperor. Twenty-five legions existed at the death of Augustus. As the empire became larger, their number increased, but the rate of increase was not precipitous. Because these units were rarely at full strength (a full complement consisting of about 5,000 men), the standing army of Augustus amounted to little more than 115,000 men and that of Trajan to perhaps no more than 150,000. The task of defending so vast an empire would have been impossible without the use of provincial auxiliaries, local militias, and the armies of the vassal states. Yet even when all these are included, it would appear that Rome never had more than 350,000 armed men at its disposal. The cost of maintaining such an army was not generally a prohibitive burden on the treasury of the early empire; the *pax Romana* released the latent wealth of the world, and in order to maintain itself in a position of overwhelming power, Rome needed to appropriate only a fraction of the emerging riches. With this modest portion, it was not only to support an army but was also to become wealthier than any city that had ever existed.

The new riches, however, proved to be inducements to luxury; indeed luxury had become a way of life. It was not unusual for a rich man to possess four or five country retreats and a town house in Rome. But there was nothing new in luxurious living. Under the republic Cicero had collected country houses as other men collected Greek sculptures, and he showed no notable signs of decadence. Pliny the Younger, the inheritor of three fortunes, possessed a country villa as large as a palace, but lived a life of exemplary dedication. Luxury, such as it was, was often the in-

Oceanus
Germanicus

SARMATIA

HIBERNIA

Oceanus Atlanticus

Amber, Furs,

Amber

Albis

EBORACUM

GERMANIA
INFERIOR

GERMANIA

BRITANNIA • CAMULODUNUM

DEVA

ISCA SILURUM

LONDINIUM

VETERA
CASTRA
COLONIA
AGRIPPINENSIS
GESORIACUM

Rhenus

BONNA

DUBRIS
PORTUS

Mosa

Mosella

MAGUNTIACUM

Danubius

CARNUNTUM

AQUINCUM

TROESMIS

BELGICA

AUGUSTA
TREVERORUM

ARGENTORATUM

VINDOBONA
(Vienna)

BRIGETIO

DACIA

APULUM

LUGDUNENSIS

LUTETIA

Sequana

GERMANIA
SUPERIOR

RHAETIA

AUGUSTA
VINDELICORUM

NORICUM

VIRUNUM

PANNONIA

SISCIA

SIRMIUM

SINGIDUNUM

VIMINACIUM

Ister (lower Danube)

NOVAE

DUROSTORUM

MOESIA

THRACIA

LUGDUNUM

VIENNA (Vienne)

Liger

AQUITANIA

BURDIGALA

Rhodanus

MEDIOLANUM

Padus

PLACENTIA

GENUA

VERONA

AQUILEIA

RAVENNA

ARIMINUM

ANCONA

ARRETIUM

DALMATIA

SALONAE

Metals, Timber

Mare

Adriaticum

NAISSUS

PHILIPPOPOLIS

MACEDONIA

THESSALONICA

DYRRHACHIUM

Mare Aes

NARBONENSIS

ARELATE

MASSILIA

NARBO MARTIUS

Tiberis

Pottery, Wine, Grain, Meat

ALERIA

CORSICA

Rhodanus

OSTIA

ROMA

I T A L I A

MISENUM

PUTEOLI

BRUNDISIUM

TARENTUM

Wine

EPIRUS

ACHAIA

ATI

CORINTHU

SPARTA

BRIGANTIUM

LEGIO

Iberus

TARRACONENSIS

CAESAR AUGUSTA

BRACARA AUGUSTA

Textiles, Grain, Oil, Wine, Metal

TARRACO

SARDINIA

Grain

Grain, Wine, Sulphur

RHEGIUM

Marble, Honey

Textiles, Marble, Leph

LUSITANIA

TOLETUM

VALENTIA

CARALES

PANORMUS

MESSANA

SYRACUSAE

SICILIA

AGRIGENTUM

Grain, Marble, Ivory, Slaves

Grain, Papyrus, Drugs, Granite, A

OLISIPO

EMERITA AUGUSTA

CORDUBA

CARTHAGO NOVA

Copper, Silver, Fish Sauce

CARTHAGO

Mare   Internum

BAETICA

GADES

TINGIS

CAESAREA

MAURETANIA

CIRTA

LAMBAESIS

THAPSUS

NUMIDIA

SABRATA

AFRICA

LEPTIS MAGNA

CYREN

Ivory

HADRIAN'S EMPIRE

Early Second Century A.D.

———— MAJOR ROMAN HIGHWAYS

Products → PRINCIPAL PROVINCIAL EXPORTS

Products → PROVINCIAL IMPORTS FROM
AREAS OUTSIDE THE EMPIRE

■ LEGION HEADQUARTERS

▲ NAVAL BASES

▪▪▪▪ FORTIFIED WALLS AND EARTHWORKS

THE BUSY WORLD
OF THE ROMANS

In the second century of the Roman peace, the Mediterranean area was a scene of endless commercial activity. With Roman armies guarding the frontiers, Roman navies keeping the sea lanes free of pirates, and Roman roads linking the major centers of population, the empire was experiencing a great expansion of production and trade. As the agricultural base was extended, increasing quantities of grains and other produce moved from province to province. The practice of manufacturing specifically for foreign trade was also becoming widespread. Prosperous Italy, seat of the imperial capital and the imperial treasury, was the major market for provincial exports, but in a larger sense, the empire itself was a vast market, attracting trade goods from lands as distant as India and China.

PRINCIPAL PRODUCTS OF ITALY
AND THE PROVINCES

Italy
> Manufactured products, woolen goods and clothing, wine, olive oil, grain, marble

Sicily and Sardinia
> Grain, wine, sulphur

Spain
> Gold, silver, copper, zinc, lead, tin, flax, wool, textiles, rope, fish products, wine, fruit, grain, olive oil, salt

Gaul and the German Provinces
> Pottery, wine, textiles, glass products, gold and silver manufactures, brass, wool, cheese, hams, olive oil, grain

Britain
> Iron, tin, hides, grain, coal, lead

Central Europe and Dalmatia
> Iron, timber, gold, silver

Eastern Europe
> Iron, gold, grain, fruit, fish, salt

Macedonia and Greece
> Wine, honey, marble

Asia Minor
> Textiles, leather, pottery, marble, parchment, timber, drugs, wine, olive oil, horses, cattle, carpets, jewels

Syria, Judaea, and Arabia
> Timber, dye, glass products, textiles, leather goods, asphalt, perfume, drugs

Egypt
> Grain, textiles, papyrus, drugs, granite

North Africa
> Grain, olive oil, figs, marble

evitable corollary of peace. Satirists made much of the vulgar and ostentatious feasts given by a certain kind of intemperate Roman, and there are some accounts of women wearing fabulously costly gowns and of entertainments so expensive that they would have beggared anyone less wealthy than a millionaire, but history has also recorded great benefactions to worthwhile projects by men aware of the obligations of wealth.

Wealth under the empire was not limited to the senatorial class and the equites, nor even to Romans and Italians. It could be found in all the parts of the Mediterranean. (The names of Greeks, particularly, appear with monotonous regularity in imperial inscriptions relating to wholesale dealers in various seaside cities.) And, to some degree, luxury had seeped down even to the lowest of the urban classes, who were entertained by free games supplied by the state and fed on the free wheat granted to them by the emperor from the government granaries.

At the beginning of the empire Agrippa had built the first free baths. Soon there were hundreds of public baths scattered across the empire. The gift of a bathhouse, with money for its upkeep, came to be expected from the citizen who had amassed wealth and wished to be remembered by his fellows. These buildings were monuments to leisure. They were to be found in remote towns on the borders of the empire, and even in villages. In Rome itself they came to be as large as palaces and as sumptuously adorned. The baths of Diocletian covered about thirty-two acres, those of the emperor Caracalla were spread over thirty-three acres.

The baths were more than buildings; they were whole cities dedicated to the principle that many forms of leisure could be housed in a single setting. The bathhouses became a center of Roman social life. The Roman who visited one of these establishments went first to the *apodyterium*, where he undressed; his body was rubbed with oil in the *unctorium*; a warm bath called the *caldarium* was followed by a stay in the *laconicum*, or steam room; the visitor then cooled off in the *tepidarium* and had his plunge in the *frigidarium*. Such was the ritual of the citizen intent only on the bath, but other forms of amusement were offered, too. There were gardens, courtyards, colonnades, shops, restaurants, reading rooms, libraries, art galleries, debating halls, rest rooms, gymnasiums, massage rooms, and promenades. There were wrestling rooms and swimming pools. Sometimes there were gambling rooms and clusters of rooms set apart for prostitutes. Very often— and this was true particularly in the provinces—the baths served also as lodginghouses, and a man who wished to could spend most of his life under that welcome roof.

THE RESONANT NAMES OF THE LEGIONS

As military men generally do, Roman legionaries counted pride in their unit as among the most valuable of their assets. If the tangible sign of a legion's honor was its eagle, the chief symbol of its individuality was its designation. Under the empire, this included both a number, often dating from republican times, and a title, which might allude to the emperor who had founded the legion (Claudia, Trajana), to a place where it once campaigned (Scythica, Macedonica), to some military exploit (Valeria Victrix), or to the circumstances under which it was formed (Gemina, for example, indicated that a pair of legions had been joined to form one). Legions that suffered humiliating defeat were usually dissolved; thus the very fact of survival was testimony of a distinguished history. Below are the names of legions posted abroad in Hadrian's time (see map on preceding pages); many traced their titles to the reign of Augustus more than a century earlier.

IN SPAIN

VII Gemina

IN BRITAIN

II Augusta, VI Victrix, XX Valeria Victrix

IN THE GERMAN PROVINCES

I Minervia, XXX Ulpia Victrix, XXII Primigenia, VIII Augusta

IN EASTERN EUROPE

X Gemina, XIV Gemina, I Adiutrix, II Adiutrix, IV Flavia, VII Claudia, I Italica, XI Claudia, V Macedonica, XIII Gemina

IN THE NEAR EAST

XV Apollinaris, XII Fulminata, XVI Flavia, IV Scythica, III Gallica, X Frentensis, VI Ferrata, III Cyrenaica

IN AFRICA

II Trajana, III Augusta

Although the public bath was dedicated to leisure and cleanliness, it could, and often did, become a noisy, squalid, and debilitating place abounding with cutthroats and catamites. Seneca, who once lodged above a bathhouse, was appalled by the continual noise, and in his puritanical fashion wondered why people wanted to bathe in hot water. "Do they want to parboil themselves?" he asked. Yet, like the Greek gymnasium, a bathhouse could also serve as a place of spiritual refreshment, and a man with a scholarly turn of mind could enjoy the museums, the art galleries, libraries, and lecture halls without once encountering a bather. The great palaces of entertainment served all tastes and admitted almost anyone.

The Roman taste for grandeur found its perfect embodiment in the immense and splendidly decorated baths, with broad colonnades, pleasant gardens, and a welter of statues and paintings. Here the extremes of luxury were cultivated with fastidious taste. Marble-encrusted columns reached dazzling heights, and gilding was extensively employed.

The public bath was a benefit of Roman affluence that was not denied to the poor. An ill-paid workman living in a hovel on the top floor of an overcrowded *insula* might spend the afternoon splashing in the water beside the aristocrats. Senators frequented the public bathhouses, and sometimes in a show of democratic feeling the emperor might bathe with the citizens, over whom he had the power of life and death. A kind of democracy existed among the citizens of all classes; emperor and workman saw themselves as belonging to the same *communitas*. But that sense of equality extended only to citizens and freedmen. Outside of this society, and in a somewhat ambiguous relationship to it, were the masses of slaves.

At the end of the first century A.D., there must have been nearly four hundred thousand slaves in Rome, constituting about a third of the city's population, but their number was declining. The great wars were over, and slaves no longer marched into Rome in vast processions to be sold, one by one, to the highest bidders. Slave-capturing expeditions patrolled the Barbary Coast, and slaves could still be bought in adequate numbers in the slave markets at Alexandria and on the Aegean island of Delos, but generally the price of purchase was high.

The character of slavery was changing with the times. Slaves were often brutalized, but far more often they were treated with respect and consideration, and sometimes almost seemed to be members of the families who owned them. Under Hadrian a law was passed forbidding the master to kill, torture, or mutilate a

At top, an Augustan relief depicts a naked slave being auctioned by a Greek slave trader (left). Infrequent warfare in the second century A.D. resulted in marked diminution in the number of slaves, and those available were undoubtedly expensive. Consequently the economy began to return to a system of tenant farming, but slavery never completely died out in the empire. Although the influence of Stoicism evoked more humane laws, they did not much help slaves laboring in mines and on farms. Household slaves, however, often gained the affection of their masters and were freed. The relief at bottom shows a manumission ceremony.

A statuette found in modern Algeria represents the Roman goddess Victoria, a deity sacred to soldiers. By the second century A.D. *entire cities were being built in Roman North Africa for legionary veterans who were settled there to cultivate newly irrigated lands not included in large patrician and imperial estates upon which the African economy was based.*

slave. As late as the time of Nero, the Senate had seen fit to sentence to death all the slaves of an official murdered by only one of them—a form of punishment with ancient precedents—but for the most part, those days had passed. The slave was coming to be regarded as a human being whose dignity was to be respected. This change was due, in part, to the Stoic doctrine that all men were equal before God; by the second century that doctrine had become an article of faith among the educated.

But even before this liberal trend in private and official attitudes had made itself felt, the increasing influence of the slaves had introduced a disturbing element into the larger society of free Roman citizens. Pliny the Elder uttered a great cry that reverberated through the long years of the Roman peace: *"Vincendo victi sumus; paremus externis* (By conquering we are conquered; we are servants to foreigners)."* That dependence, that sense of gradual loss of power to a foreign element, was felt strongly during the first century when there were more slaves than in later times. Although many slaves labored in mines and factories or on the great estates, a few achieved exalted status as imperial secretaries or advisers. Juvenal complains bitterly against slaves who were the great officials' doorkeepers and who had to be bribed to permit a supplicant to enter. Such slaves did not remain slaves for long; after a year of doorkeeping they were usually wealthy enough to buy their freedom.

In fact enough slaves bought their freedom to cause Tacitus to remark ruefully that if freedmen were regarded as a separate class, they would outnumber the freeborn. So many freedmen rose to positions of wealth and power that they actually did form a special group. They were the new blood pouring into the veins of the citizenry, causing its gradual and subtle transformation.

Freedmen were everywhere, in all the trades, in all the professions, in all the armies on all the frontiers. By A.D. 200 many who were Roman citizens were the descendants of former slaves. The bloodlines of Europe, Africa, and Asia fed the mainstream. The process had been at work for centuries, and the poet who spoke of "the Orontes flowing into the Tiber" was hardly overstating the case. Rome was indeed a great melting pot.

By the time of Domitian's assassination, in A.D. 96, Rome had become quite a different place from what it was when Augustus had established the principate. Not only had the city itself changed almost beyond recognition, but the temper and character of the Romans had changed too. They demanded more luxuries, and were avidly searching for new experiences. The threat of war and the tumult of political upheaval were largely absent; Romans could now expect to die in their beds. To them the empire seemed secure. There were in fact many pressing problems; among the most important were the growing restlessness of the people and the absence of a common faith, a common purpose. Oriental religions were proliferating on Roman soil. New and startling divinities were being worshiped. For many Romans, apparently, the joy had gone out of life, and the long peace had become unendurable without the consolation of religion. The empire had certainly not reached the point of becoming politically unmanageable, but there was no Augustus to give it grace and distinction, and no philosopher-king had arisen to give it meaning.

The post-Augustan emperors of the first century A.D. were rarely imaginative rulers. It is doubtful that they speculated about the possible connections between the triumph of imperial absolutism and the paralysis of the popular will. They tended to believe that bread and circuses answered the people's needs, and indeed there was ample bread, and the circuses grew more splendid every year. In fact these emperors needed little sophistication. They reigned during a magical era in the empire's history, an era when prosperity was increasing, when taxes were relatively light, and the civil service was small, efficient, and staffed by able men who needed little guidance. What was perhaps most important was that they reigned at a time when no great enemies or powerful hordes of barbarians were pressing against the frontiers. It was not surprising then that the terror of a Domitian had little effect outside the capital and that it failed to shake the imperial foundations. And because the emperor who followed Domitian initiated a process of adopting a successor without regard to blood relationship, there was no recurrence of such terrors for the better part of a century; Rome entered a prolonged period of good government such as a few other states have enjoyed.

The beginning of this era was signaled by the Senate's election of one of its own—the sixty-six-year-old Marcus Cocceius Nerva —to the vacant imperial throne in A.D. 96. The aging senator reigned less than two years, but instituted some much-needed reforms including the new "law" of succession that resulted in the elevation to the throne of the four able rulers who were to guide Rome's fortunes through the succeeding eighty-three years—years that saw the empire reach its height. These four men—Trajan, Hadrian, Antoninus Pius, and Marcus Aurelius—were of markedly varying temperaments, but all of them possessed *gravitas* and *aequanimitas*, the qualities of dignity and authority and of calm impartiality that were traditionally associated with enlightened leadership. They cared deeply about the welfare of the people

A funerary stele illustrates the mingling of Roman and Carthaginian conventions in African provincial art. The dedicant appears at center; one of her attendants (right) sacrifices a ram, an animal sacred to Saturn, a god identified with the Punic divinity Baal. Castor and Pollux, usually shown on horses in Roman steles, are mounted on dolphins (top).
ROGER WOOD

Above, from top to bottom, are contemporary busts of Trajan, Hadrian, and Antoninus Pius, three emperors whose successive reigns spanned sixty-three years (A.D. 98–161). Under Trajan, the empire reached its greatest size. Hadrian's administrative genius and Antoninus' beneficence secured for their subjects a prolonged period of almost undisturbed prosperity and peace.

they ruled and were serenely aware of their responsibilities. The general tone of their administrations was anticipated by Nerva during his brief reign.

With his withered skin, enormous beaked nose, and firm, pointed chin, Nerva did not look like a Roman emperor; he looked like an eminent jurist, which is what he was. As a youth he acquired a reputation as a poet. But it was not his poetry that commended him to the Romans when they decided to grant him supreme power. They wanted another Numa, a stern and kindly judge, a man who would represent sanity in a world that had been ruled disastrously by the morbidly insane Domitian. They chose Nerva because he seemed incorruptible and yet very human and because he was a distinguished lawyer and the scion of a family steeped in the traditions of imperial service.

Nerva accomplished all that the Romans could have expected of him. He confirmed the senators in their powers, forbade statues of himself, restored the estates confiscated by Domitian, and allotted lands to poor peasants. Detesting the gladiatorial shows, he issued an edict restricting the amount of money that could be spent on them, and revived the theatre. Because Domitian had raided the treasury and the empire was nearly bankrupt, Nerva embarked on a campaign of retrenchment, selling many of the imperial estates to the highest bidders. Similarly he ordered the auctioning of the hoards of jewels, vestments, and furniture that his predecessors had collected.

The most notable of the emperor's innovations was a scheme for the support of poor children at public expense. This grant, known as the *alimenta*, was financed by the interest from government loans to landowners and municipalities. The *alimenta* amounted to sixteen sesterces a month for boys, twelve for girls. Nerva hoped by means of the program to relieve poverty, to encourage the peasants to remain on the land, to increase the birthrate, and to eliminate the wild bands of waifs that roamed the countryside. He succeeded to a considerable degree.

In October, A.D. 97, in a formal ceremony at the temple of Jupiter, Nerva adopted Marcus Ulpius Trajanus, the military commander on the Rhine, as his son and successor. The emperor died three months later. Shortly before his death he said: "I have done nothing in my life which prevents me from retiring and living in safety the life of a private citizen." Tacitus, who admired the man warmly, said: "He combined two things once irreconcilable—the authority of the prince and the freedom of the people."

Trajan, a Spaniard, was the first provincial to occupy the Roman throne. He was in Colonia Agrippinensis (Cologne) when he learned of his succession, and months passed before he journeyed south. When he reached Rome he entered the city on foot, with only a small escort. He had no use for the grand gestures. He took command of the empire unobtrusively, like an experienced engineer who slips quietly into the cab of a giant locomotive.

Trajan was a progressive ruler. He was a professional soldier and the son of a professional soldier, a broad shouldered man, powerfully built, with finely shaped features, a look of keen intelligence, an easy smile, and furrowed brows. The Middle Ages were to regard him as the perfect emperor. His portraits are rarely idealized. We see him—in the sculptures on Trajan's column and on the triumphal arch at Beneventum—moving quietly among the soldiers, with no flamboyance, no hint of any great enjoyment of his exalted status. Like many emperors he enjoyed building, and the ruins of the gigantic forum of Trajan, with its libraries, its basilica, its famous column, its shops, and its colonnaded square, testify to his determination to build on as large a scale as possible. These vast architectural schemes, however, did not take the form of private indulgence; he built no Domus Aurea nor Hadrian's villa for himself. He liked the ordinary things of life.

Trajan's military campaigns were the last by which the Romans appreciably extended the geographic limits of their empire. Twice the emperor led his armies against the Dacians, a powerful tribe of cattle breeders who lived in the inaccessible highlands of Transylvania and were in the habit of demanding tribute to keep the peace. The Dacians, defeated in A.D. 102, were granted liberal terms, which they soon broke. A second campaign, four years later, ended with the destruction of the Dacian army and the incorporation of Dacia into the empire as a province. Trajan was granted a sumptuous triumph, and for a brief time, the silver and gold found in the Dacian capital flooded Rome, and Dacian prisoners of war flooded the slave markets and the gladiatorial games. Toward the end of his life Trajan led successful expeditions against Parthia and Arabia and looked at last upon the Persian Gulf, as Alexander the Great had done centuries before. The *pax Romana* had reached its furthermost bounds.

These eastern conquests, however, had brought the Romans into a new and unfamiliar world, a world in which even Hellenic influences were negligible and in which the Roman presence was regarded as utterly alien. No firm or lasting Roman administration was ever to be established in such lands as Mesopotamia and Armenia. Even as the conquest of Parthia was being completed, revolts occurred among the recently subjected peoples to the rear of Trajan's advancing legions. About the same time, there were

After his sudden death in the Nile, Antinoüs, the young Bythinian who was a favorite of Hadrian, became an object of worship by many eastern religious cults and the subject of numerous portraits. The likeness of the youth (above), dressed in the Egyptian manner, was found at Hadrian's villa near Tivoli.
VATICAN; ANDERSON

uprisings of the Jewish communities in Syria and Egypt. These disturbances forced Trajan, who may have been contemplating an invasion of India along the route once followed by Alexander, to retrace his steps and recapture several cities that he had taken only a few months earlier. During this campaign he fell ill. He was apparently on his way back to Rome when he died in Asia Minor.

Though remembered for his military exploits (he was the first outstanding Roman general to occupy the throne), Trajan was no less impressive as a political administrator. He probably gave more attention to the details of government operations than had any emperor before his time. Within a context of humanitarian aims, he concerned himself above all with the efficiency of administrative processes and bequeathed to Hadrian, his brilliant successor, a tradition of excellence both in the conduct of government and in the staffing of the most important positions in the imperial civil service, whether in Italy or in the provinces.

As a personality Trajan disarms us by his simplicity and honesty. These qualities are in evidence in a famous letter to Pliny the Younger, who, as the governor of Bithynia, had sought the emperor's advice about measures to be employed against Christians. Trajan wrote, in part: "If a Christian offers prayers to our gods, he must be pardoned, however suspect his past conduct may have been. Anonymous pamphlets must not be used as a basis for accusation, for they create the worst kind of precedent and are entirely out of keeping with the spirit of the age."

Trajan died in A.D. 117 at the age of sixty-four, after having ruled for nearly twenty years. Hadrian, whom he had adopted on his deathbed, was another Spaniard and another soldier, a relative, and trusted lieutenant who had assisted the emperor in both military and political capacities. Hadrian was fair-skinned, with bluish-grey eyes, thick curly hair, and a well-trimmed beard—he was the first emperor to wear a beard. He was, like Trajan, scrupulous, adventurous, and curiously modern, but it cannot be said that simplicity was one of his virtues.

Hadrian possessed all of the talents and was one of the few supremely cultivated men who had ever occupied a throne. He had an expert's knowledge of painting and sculpture, spoke Greek and Latin with equal proficiency, and to the end of his life remained boundlessly curious about everything. Tertullian, a Latin ecclesiastical writer, called him *omnium curiositatum explorator*. He was a scholar, philosopher, poet, aesthete, and architect, and yet he appeared to enjoy sharing his meals with common soldiers and could walk with them twenty miles a day in full armor. Above all, he was an exceptionally gifted administrator, blessed with an extraordinary memory, boundless energy, a subtle imagination, excellent judgment, and great decisiveness.

Hadrian's first important act was to abandon Trajan's conquests east of the Euphrates on the sound theory that the administration of such realms as Parthia, Armenia, and Mesopotamia would overtax imperial resources. He spent the better part of his twenty-one-year reign traveling restlessly through his newly consolidated empire, applying his genius for government to the drafting of countless reforms in the provinces. No less expert in military matters, he improved the discipline of the army, invented new tactics, and studied the economics of camp life, reducing unnecessary expenses. In about A.D. 122 he crossed to Britain and personally surveyed the line from the Tyne to the Solway Firth, establishing the seventy-three-mile Wall of Hadrian as a defense against the wild tribes of the north. He revised the system of tax collection, and his reign saw the completion of a great codification of the Roman law. He was responsible for few wars, the fierce uprising and destruction in Judaea representing one of his rare failures to control the flow of events by peaceful methods.

The glory of Hadrian's building program was the Pantheon, a miracle of symmetry, composed entirely as an interior and designed to capture, through the circular aperture in the dome, the golden rays of the sun and the pale glow of the moon. If the Pantheon expresses the subtlety of Hadrian's imagination, the villa at Tibur (Tivoli) hints at his refinement and complexity, and his gigantic mausoleum, completed during the reign of his successor, reveals that he could be grandiose. He clearly intended that this huge tomb on the right bank of the Tiber should be even larger and more imposing than that of Augustus. It was in fact so massive that it served as a fortress in the Middle Ages. The huge, cylindrical structure is known today as the Castel Sant' Angelo.

The last few years of Hadrian's reign were not his happiest. Pederasty was not an unusual vice among the Romans, but Hadrian's love of a particularly charming and handsome Bithynian youth named Antinoüs appears to have been obsessive. When the boy drowned in the Nile, probably by suicide, the emperor seemed shaken to the point of madness, ordering that a great city (Antinoopolis) be built at the site of the drowning and commissioning innumerable art works in memory of his favorite. There are indications also that the emperor's late years were marred by disease, that he grew increasingly severe and intolerant, and that he tried to take his life. The great Judaean war belongs to these years. Hadrian died at last in A.D. 138, but not before he had composed a peculiarly delicate little poem of farewell. Its lines, which commit his

An equestrian statue of Marcus Aurelius on the Capitoline hill shows him returning the salute of his legions. The reign of this emperor was troubled by an outbreak of the plague and by numerous military invasions that signaled the end of the Roman peace and the beginning of the empire's long decline.
LEONARD VON MATT

"gentle, wandering little soul" to the underworld, are like the plaintive song of a lonely shepherd.

Some months before he died, Hadrian chose as his successor a tall, thin, courteous man who was to reign for twenty-three years —Antoninus Pius. On coins, his ravaged face is oddly disturbing, for he looks like a Christian saint. He was gentler than Hadrian, more of the scholar, less of the adventurer. He quoted the words of Scipio that it was preferable to save a single citizen than to slay a thousand foes. He would have thought a triumph a mockery of everything he stood for. The historian Julius Capitolinus said: "He looked after all things and all men as if they were his own." He was passionately addicted to good works, with the result that "the provinces all prospered under him, informers were abolished, and only one man was condemned to death for aspiring to seize the throne." However, he seems to have taken few measures to stave off future troubles other than building a new defensive wall in Britain. Historians are inclined to regard him with a kind of lurking disfavor, for it seemed as though history stood still during the years when he occupied the throne. There were minor uprisings in Britain and North Africa, the Tiber flooded, and parts of Antioch and Rome burned down, but this seems to have been the limit to the excitement that can be discovered in his reign.

Before he died at seventy-five, Antoninus heeded Hadrian's decree that he adopt both Marcus Aurelius (a young favorite of Hadrian's) and Lucius Verus (Antoninus' nephew), but Antoninus did not make Lucius a co-emperor. Marcus alone succeeded to rule. Marcus possessed Antoninus' equanimity in a more robust body. He was a skilled athlete and hunter and was credited with considerable gifts as a painter. He had the Stoic temperament, and they said of him that neither in grief nor in joy did he change countenance. Such austerity in an emperor would be almost beyond belief if we did not have the testimony of his *Meditations*, a work that celebrates the Stoic virtues and documents his heroic search for self-knowledge. In it we find the man who ruled the greatest empire on earth recording such thoughts as these: "Think of the universal substance, of which thou hast a very small portion; and of universal time, of which a short and indivisible interval has been assigned to thee; and of that which is fixed by destiny, and how small a part of it thou art."

Marcus needed all of his austerity. Soon after his accession, in A.D. 161, the Parthians attacked the eastern frontier. Although this threat was repelled, a more terrible enemy, the plague, accompanied the soldiers on their return to Italy and subsequently raged through the empire for many years. Before the Parthians had been completely pacified, and while wagons carrying the bodies of plague victims clattered through the streets of Rome, hordes of German and Sarmatian tribesmen—pressed from the north and east by Goths and other migrants—broke through Rome's under-manned defenses along the Danube, swept into Italy, and besieged Aquileia, at the head of the Adriatic Sea. The wars against these invaders, notably the Marcomanni and the Quadi, were to continue to take place during most of the emperor's reign. The enemy was driven back, but the victory was a hollow one. Those great movements of northern European and Asiatic peoples that were soon to threaten to engulf the empire were beginning. Marcus died in Vindobona (Vienna) in A.D. 180, at the age of fifty-nine, before he could achieve his dream of securing a more practical line of defense by advancing the imperial frontier northward to the Elbe River and the Carpathians.

Self-knowledge did not make Marcus the best judge of others. As one of his earliest acts, he made his worthless adoptive brother Lucius Verus co-emperor, generously honoring a claim that was of dubious validity. Lucius was a profligate and an incompetent general who might have done much damage to the empire if he had not died in A.D. 169. Far more serious was Marcus' decision to be the good father and to elevate Lucius Aelius Aurelius Commodus, his son, to a share of the government, for he thus turned his back on the adoptive principle that had given Rome its greatest rulers. With Commodus, who became emperor at nineteen, insanity returned to the Roman throne, and the greatest period of *pax Romana* came to an end.

Nerva, Trajan, Hadrian, Antoninus Pius, and Marcus Aurelius had followed one another against all probability. So much intelligence and grace among emperors would have seemed almost too much to hope for at the end of the first century. In about A.D. 150, when it seemed that the peace might continue forever, the Greek rhetorician Aristides declared that the Romans were the only rulers known to history who reigned over free men. "The luster of your rule is unsullied by any breath of ungenerous hostility; and the reason is that you yourselves set the example of generosity by sharing all your power and privileges with your subjects, so that in your day a combination has been achieved which previously appeared impossible—the combination of consummate power and consummate benevolence. Rome is a citadel that has all the people of the earth for its villagers." Marcus Aurelius wrote: "For me as emperor, my city and fatherland is Rome, but as a man, the world." At the death of Marcus, the great dream faded. Commodus stands at the beginning of the empire's long decline.

A relief from Trajan's column in Rome recalls the proudest years of Rome's imperial glory. Against the background of a great bridge—probably the one used by the legionaries to cross the Danube to conquer Dacia—Trajan (fourth from the right) is shown at an altar offering a sacrifice to Rome's benevolent gods.

ROME ABROAD

The second century A.D. found Rome at its zenith, ruling a peaceful Mediterranean empire of seventy to one hundred million people. Less than a half of one percent of the population was under arms, and this relatively small force was concentrated mainly at the frontiers: behind the Wall of Hadrian (left), the formidable barrier that wound across northern Britain; at the great fortified camps that guarded the long Rhine-Danube defensive line; and at the borders of Armenia and Mesopotamia. Within these boundaries, savage Berbers, cultivated Greeks, resourceful Syrians, and stubbornly clannish Gauls were all content to live as Roman provincials. The commonwealth was bonded together by Roman law, by Rome's undisputed military supremacy, by the lure of Roman civilization, and by the economic prosperity and lucrative trade that flowered under the shelter of an almost universal peace.

The balance of forces in the empire was delicate. Ancient eastern lands had proud cultures and ideas that were at variance with those of Rome, and the new masters faced innumerable problems of persuasion, administration, example, and enforcement. But Rome could afford to tolerate diversity, and it governed the provinces with considerable regard for local laws and traditions. The countless roads, aqueducts, bridges, baths, arenas, theatres, and temples that survive from this period in Roman provincial history testify as much to Rome's self-confidence as to its technical prowess.

THE SINEWS OF SPAIN

Rome drew considerable strength from Spain, the land where it had planted some of its earliest overseas colonies. The peninsula, which had supplied the republic with military manpower and wealth, continued to contribute to Roman fortunes during the empire. The Roman treasury normally collected one half of the proceeds from mining operations, and the veins of copper, gold, silver, and other precious metals were exceptionally rich. The Spanish provinces continued also to produce excellent soldiers, two of whom—Trajan and Hadrian—were the first provincials to become Roman emperors. But the benefits were not entirely one-sided. An early imperial census shows that the southern trading center of Gades (Cadiz) rivaled the richest Italian cities in the number of its wealthy citizens. As Spain prospered economically, it also profited by Roman technology, the traces of which are still to be encountered in the Spanish landscape.

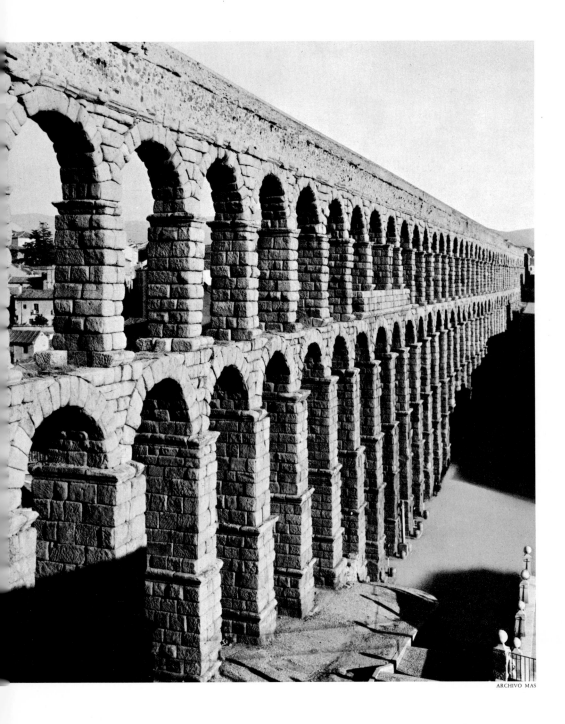

Pictured above is a detail from a second-century A.D. *marble sarcophagus discovered in Cordova; successful merchants frequently made a show of their wealth by preparing elaborate tombs for themselves. At left is the aqueduct at Segovia, in central Spain; the double-tiered structure, towering above the three- and four-storied houses that surround it, is about nine hundred yards long and is still in use. The theatre at right, at Merida, was one of many buildings constructed in Spain at the order of Agrippa during the reign of the emperor Augustus.*

GROWTH IN GAUL

One of the phenomena of the early empire was the rise of Gaul, a region of feuding tribal chieftains that lay to the north of the Latinized Mediterranean coast. It became, within a century of its absorption by Rome, a peaceful country prospering through trade and manufacture. Lugdunum (Lyons), at the confluence of the Rhone and Saône rivers, was its chief city. The Gauls retained their identity to a greater degree than did the inhabitants of most of the other western provinces. Thus, the wedding of Rome and Gaul produced a mixed culture in which the Celtic tongue enjoyed almost equal status with Latin, and the old tribal gods continued to draw devotees. Even some of the old tribal names survived, being retained in the names of cities such as Paris (the Roman Lutetia Parisiorum) and Rheims (the Roman Durcortorum Remorum).

The bronze Apollo at left, found near the Channel coast, indicates the spread of Roman influence to remote areas of Gaul. Above, a votive relief shows the horned, bearded figure of Cernunnos, a Gallic deity, flanked by a pair of Roman gods, Apollo and Mercury, in a group portrait that symbolizes the harmonious association of two dissimilar religious worlds.

The realism that the Romans often strove for in sculpture was achieved in a Gallic work of the Roman period, probably by an artist familiar with Roman techniques. The bronze representation of a cock—a bird which has come to be regarded as a French national symbol—was recovered from the waters of the Rhone River, near the modern Lyons.

RIVER FRONTIERS

From the time of Augustus to that of Diocletian, Rome's natural line of defense in northern Europe followed the Rhine and Danube rivers. Along this frontier much of Rome's military strength was concentrated, and to it the legionaries brought their ancient Roman disciplines, traditions from the provinces where they had been recruited, and religious cults of eastern origin. However, some native peoples of this frontier—such as the Germans or the Illyrian tribesmen of Pannonia—were hardly touched by these eclectic influences and remained resolutely independent in their religions, social customs, and ways of living.

The relief at left was discovered in a subterranean Mithraic sanctuary at the former site of a Roman camp along the Rhine frontier. The largest panel shows the Persian god Mithra in the act of killing a bull; the sacrifice of a bull became a part of the initiation ceremony of this cult. The figure above, with the rooster's head, outfitted for battle in the fashion of a Roman auxiliary, was found in Switzerland. The relief at right, though carved in imperial times, shows its subjects—a Pannonian tribesman and a pair of women—in native costume.

ROLOFF BENY

CITIES
IN THE SUN

In the lands that had been
wrested from Carthage, the Romans built upon the remains
of the Punic civilization. By the
second century A.D.—the gold-
en age of Africa—much land
was under cultivation that had
never before known a plow.
Numidia and Africa Proconsul-
aris, provinces with vast, slave-
worked estates, rivaled Egypt as
producers of grain for export to
Italy. As villages grew into full-
fledged *municipia*, the Romans
constructed theatres, arenas,
and public buildings. They
even built whole cities, most of
which—like Thamugadi in the
eastern part of Algeria—were
eventually to sink into the sands.

*At left, a Roman Diana gazes into
the bright African sky at the coastal
city of Leptis Magna. The theatre
at Sabrata (right), with columns of
red granite imported from Italy,
was "air-conditioned," having been
designed to give audiences the full
benefit of the cooling ocean breezes.*

OVERLEAF: *A triumphal arch and a stubble of broken columns mark the site of Thamugadi, in what is now an Algerian wilderness.*

WEALTH FROM AFRICA

In North Africa the limits of civilization have always been defined by the water supply. The Romans did not fail to exploit areas already favored by nature. Lands watered by the Nile were cultivated to the fullest, ports with good harbors became major cities, and great oases such as the Faiyûm, forty miles south of modern Cairo, became centers of vigorous, new life. But more importantly, Roman techniques of water conservation and irrigation brought agriculture and civilization to the desert. Today, Algerian and Tunisian wastelands are strewn with cisterns that trace the extent of Roman land development.

The second-century A.D. *painting of an Egyptian girl (at left) is one of a group known as the Faiyûm Portraits; it was painted on a wooden panel that was tied over the face of a mummy. Below, a mosaic from a villa on the Tripolitanian coast depicts the threshing of corn on an African estate. At right are the ruins of Leptis Magna, once a great port-city of Roman Africa.*

EAST OF THE AEGEAN

In the East, Rome governed provinces that had once been part of a world united by Alexander the Great and that had been permeated with Hellenizing influences. The Romans looked to prosperous Asia Minor for tax revenues, to the Syrian cities for manufactured goods, to the distant Orient for precious luxuries, and to the Nile basin for grain. But despite their value to Rome, the eastern provinces, in which local and Greek traditions commingled, were never to become as Romanized as were those of the West.

*At left, a relief from a Roman sar-
cophagus discovered in Thessalonica shows the beasts of the field
being enraptured by Orpheus, much
as the ancient lands of the East fell
under the sway of Hellenism. The
bronze statuette above, representing
the Egyptian god Horus, was found
in Pakistan; the work is believed to
have been fashioned in Alexandria
and was probably an item of exchange in the trade with the Orient.
At upper right is a terra-cotta figure of a camel and its driver from
Aphrodisias, in Asia Minor. The
relief at right was found in Palmyra, a Syrian community serving
the camel caravans that carried
goods from the East; it pictures three
local deities whose worship persisted.*

OUTPOSTS IN ARABIA

Perhaps the most extraordinary city in the Roman empire was Petra, conquered during the reign of Trajan and subsequently made the capital of the Roman province of Arabia Petraea, southwest of Judaea. An important station on the caravan route between Syria and Arabia, the city was situated in a deep, narrow valley surrounded by steep hills. Its architectural remains, including a number of edifices that were not so much built as carved out of solid rock, are unlike any in the ancient world. Petra was rediscovered in 1812, after having been abandoned for many hundreds of years.

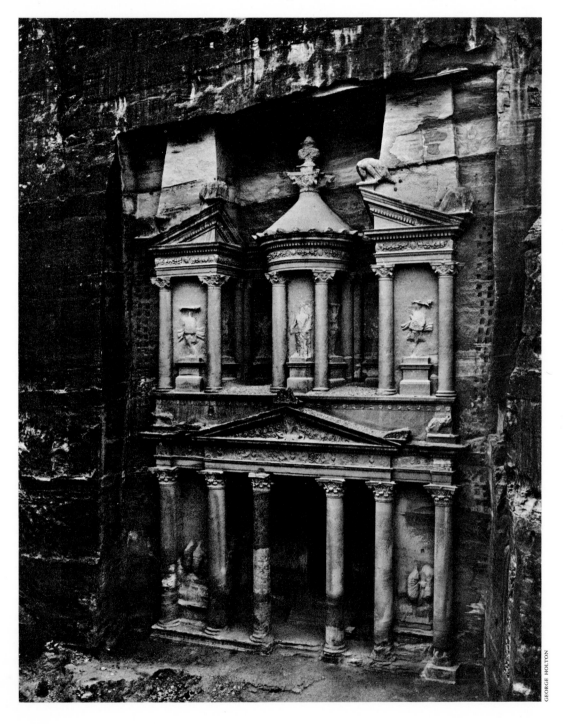

At left, the pale columns of the treasury at Petra are viewed through a deep cleft in the sandstone cliff; it was said that Moses created the crevasse by striking the mountain with his rod. The complete façade of the building, called a treasury by the Arabs, is shown above. It probably served either as a tomb or a temple in Roman times.

OVERLEAF: *A hot sun bakes the ruins of a Roman theatre in the Arabian city of Bostra, another center that, like Palmyra, Petra, and Antioch, profited from the lucrative commerce between the empire and the Far East.*
ROLOFF BENY

X

AN ERA
OF
EXCESS

Nevertheless, this emperor, the most cruel of men, and, to include all in a single phrase, a fratricide and committer of incest, the foe of his father, mother, and brother, was raised to the rank of the gods by Macrinus, his slayer, through fear of the soldiers, especially the Praetorians.
Historia Augusta, *description of the death of Caracalla*

Seldom in history has so speedy and tragic a reversal taken place as that which followed the era of the "good emperors" of second-century A.D. Rome. Despite tensions and wars along its frontiers, the empire of Marcus Aurelius stood at the zenith of stability and liberal order when his death, in A.D. 180, left it in the hands of the gross and dull-witted Commodus. In the next generations it was to decline into a condition approaching disruption. Military adventurers and usurpers followed each other to the throne; civil wars broke out; a police state was established, and political agents and soldiery swarmed like locusts over the land while foot-loose robber bands scoured the countryside. The treasury was looted periodically, trade stagnated, and Goths, Franks, and Persians overran the uncertain frontiers. After the sun of Rome's late summer, storms arose on every side; the signs of decay, corruption, barbarity, and fear lay across the entire Roman world.

At rare intervals an emperor with sufficient strength and intelligence would arise to halt the steady corrosion for a few months or years. New ideas would be brought forth to reconstitute the weakened state. But the process of decomposition was never wholly arrested. At the center of its causes lay the very nature of absolute monarchy, with no remaining civil body able effectively to restrain it: all could be well under a strong and magnanimous emperor; all could go wrong under a venal and predatory one who had been hoisted into power by his soldiery. This was the era that saw a vast increase in the power of the military as a whole, over and beyond that of the emperor's Praetorian Guard. Increasingly massive provincial armies had come into being, permanently stationed in far parts of the empire and composed more and more of non-Roman levies. Each of these armies—the greatest being those in Britain, in the Danube-Balkan area, and in Syria—saw in its successful leader a potential emperor, and on occasion, rival armies would proclaim rival emperors. The result was to be the first steps toward division of the empire on one hand and total militarization on the other.

Commodus, last member of the dynasty founded by Antoninus Pius, made way for this military era by instituting his own regime of terror—one so unconscionable and savage that many leading citizens looked to the armies for relief. Not since Nero had so odious and degenerate a person appeared at the top. Priding himself on his physical prowess, yet without a shred of courage, Commodus found his best friends among gladiators; it amused him to appear in the arena in gladiatorial costume and slay unarmed opponents. He regarded himself as the embodiment of the great Hercules and appeared in the streets with the lion's skin and club—

attributes of the god—borne before him. He slaughtered senators at will and permitted his pampered favorites in the Praetorian Guard to run daily affairs of state as they pleased. He established a large harem for himself, paraded in women's garments, publicly kissed his male favorites, and delighted in inventing degrading punishments for his officials. He even thought of changing the name of Rome to Colonia Commodiana. A palace cabal finally got rid of him by causing Commodus' wrestling partner to strangle him. The Senate, which had lived in mortal fear of him, uttered a unanimous and prolonged curse on his memory:

He who killed all men, let him be dragged by the hook!
He who killed young and old, let him be dragged by the hook!
He who killed men and women, let him be dragged by the hook!
He who set aside wills, let him be dragged by the hook!
He who plundered the living, let him be dragged by the hook!
We were the slaves of slaves!

Commodus was evidently unbalanced and had let matters go too far. He was not exceptional in that age in his wanton love of cruelty. The least attractive trait of the Romans was a traditional blood lust that delighted in witnessing death in the arena and that led, perhaps inescapably, to the murderous excesses of a Nero or a Commodus. The Greeks, though relishing the sight of human combat, had expressly forbidden games involving weapons, and they long refrained from building any amphitheatres in which spectacles of man against beast were to be presented. But the Romans, deriving their interest in bloody exhibitions from Etruscan funeral games, enjoyed the fight to the death. Gladiatorial shows (duels of armed men against men) as well as wild animal shows (hungry beasts pitted against each other or faced by men with spears and dogs) had been familiar in republican times. Even the most civilized emperors had not only continued them but had also enlarged them in scope as entertainment for the public.

Thus Augustus recorded that during his reign he had given the people twenty-seven gladiatorial shows in which 10,000 fighters appeared. He also gave them twenty-six spectacles of African animals in which about 3,500 beasts were killed. Whereas 320 pairs of public duelists had fought to the death during the aedileship of Julius Caesar, no less than 5,000 pairs were put in the ring during a festival celebrating a triumph of the emperor Trajan. Even so calm and civilized a Roman as Pliny the Younger spoke gravely about the necessity of offering gladiatorial displays to the public.

The fighters were in large part prisoners of war, condemned criminals, or slaves bought for the purpose of exhibition. Yet free men sometimes became gladiators for the same reasons that have

A portrait of about A.D. *200 pictures an imperial family that was symptomatic of a troubled age. At top right, flanked by his wife, is the emperor Septimius Severus, who ruled by the sword. Below are his sons: the cruel Caracalla, who succeeded him; and Geta (face obliterated), whom Caracalla murdered.*

Commodus, son and successor of the revered Marcus Aurelius, considered himself the incarnation of Hercules and had himself portrayed (above) with the attributes of that god: a club and a lion's skin. He cared more for the games of the arena than for statecraft; his incompetence and extravagance led to anarchy and ushered in a century of military rule.

prompted adventurers in modern times to find refuge in the French Foreign Legion: they join because they are ruined or desperate or because they want to live the lives of complete dedication and obedience, remote from normal responsibilities. The would-be gladiators were placed into schools run by professional trainers, who were either employed by the state or working on their own as suppliers of arena manpower. When a man entered such a school he lost all claim to life by taking an oath that said he was prepared to be whipped, burned, or killed by his trainers. If he displayed cowardice during his training he was put to death. For minor infractions of the rules he was put in chains. The gladiators' barracks at Pompeii held about a hundred men. Sixty-three were in chains at the time of the eruption of Mount Vesuvius.

Gladiatorial games had their own carefully contrived ritual and routine. There were prescribed methods of killing and being killed. Some men fought with two swords, some with one, some with a trident and a net; some were helmeted, some were not. To a gladiator who had fought bravely there would come the welcome cry from the Colosseum crowd, "*Mitte* (Let him go)!'"; those who had fought less bravely heard the roar, "*Jugula* (Throat)!" According to the accepted routine, the losing gladiator was killed by being stabbed in the throat; even the way in which he would stretch out his neck was taught him in the schools. Later, one of the attendants would come running with a hot poker, prodding him to make sure that he was dead.

Under the emperor Domitian, the last ruler of the Flavian dynasty, the cult of the gladiator had reached a new height of excess. Even women appeared as combatants and dwarfs were made to fight dwarfs. In a travesty of taste, Domitian's gladiatorial school was provided with rich mosaics and marble columns. The time of the mass persecutions of Christians, when believers were sent into the arena to fight each other or face professional killers and hungry beasts, still lay ahead; but this ultimate savagery was simply the result of a brutalizing process that had begun long before.

During early decades of the second century A.D., many distinguished jurists flourished, expounding and developing principles and fine points of Roman civil law and procedure. But laws themselves were being flouted at every turn by the use or the threatened use of the sword. After the liquidation of Commodus, in A.D. 192, near chaos ensued: within three months a successor named Pertinax, who had been installed by the Praetorians, was in turn killed by them (he had shown himself too friendly to the Senate); in another two months, yet another successor died, leaving the way open for the strongest man with the biggest army.

Members of the Praetorian Guard, the elite of the army, drew three times the pay of the legionary and in addition received large handouts, or *donativa*. This led to increasing tension between the Praetorians and the polyglot forces in the provinces, and finally to the overthrow of the Guard when Septimius Severus, the general commanding twelve legions in southeastern Europe, marched on Rome after being acclaimed emperor by his troops at Carnuntum, on the Danube. Reaching the city's gates with a host reinforced along the way, he surrounded and overpowered the Guard. Thereafter, it was no longer recruited from Italy and the thoroughly Romanized provinces, but was diluted with foreign elements; often its men came from the least civilized parts of the empire. The center of power was moved from an elite army to a mass army.

Intelligent, versed in both Greek and Roman literature, the African-born Severus was nevertheless a soldier through and through, incapable of thinking in any but military terms. He had commanded armies in Gaul, Sicily, Pannonia, and Germany, and there was hardly another man in the empire who had so wide a knowledge of military affairs. The government he imposed on Rome was nothing less than a military dictatorship based entirely on the power of his troops. It followed that in order to keep them in hand, very large amounts of money would have to be spent on them and special favors bestowed on them. This led to what was in effect a scheme of mass bribery, with resultant burdens on the state. Severus increased the pay of legionaries by almost a third; great masses were quartered on the land, drawing requisitions of foodstuffs, transport, and housing. Finding the treasury nearly empty, he resorted to confiscations to replenish it. Bands of soldiers acting as policemen searched households for political suspects and stripped them of their possessions; forced military service and ruinous taxes were imposed upon the rich. To add to the troubles of the commercial classes, he debased the silver denarius and started Rome on a disastrous policy of inflation.

Thirsting for more and more loot, the soldiers looked to adventures in the east, and Severus gave them the satisfaction of despoiling the royal Parthian city of Ctesiphon. Death finally overtook the soldier-ruler at his provincial seat of Eboracum (York), in Britain, from which he had conducted a campaign to put down an uprising of British tribes. He died in the presence of his wife, the Syrian princess Julia Domna, and of his sons Caracalla (his successor) and Geta. Some eighty years were to pass before another emperor would die peacefully in his bed.

As he was dying, Severus instructed his sons: "Be united, enrich the soldiers, and scorn the rest." He had already greatly en-

A bronze figurine and a sepulchral relief represent a pair of Roman gladiators, each equipped with distinctive armor. The man at top is identifiable as a mirmillo; *a gladiator thus heavily armed was frequently matched against a* retiarius, *whose only weapons were a net and a trident.*

riched the soldiers and raised their status—arranging, for instance, for the admission of non-commissioned officers into the privileged class of equites. Coming into power in A.D. 211, Caracalla followed his father's advice and raised soldiers' pay by another fifty per cent, thereby inflicting a further drain on the state. He declared openly that he was bent on basing his rule on the support not of the traditional upper and middle classes, but of the soldiery, the representatives of the plebs. Arbitrary capital levies were imposed to further undermine the patricians and merchants.

In his famous edict of A.D. 212 Caracalla granted Roman citizenship to all free persons living within the empire. But the measure, although seemingly magnanimous, was actually demagogic and in its way oppressive. Once everyone was a citizen, the hitherto cherished concept of Roman citizenship, with its rights and rewards for people of Roman or Italian birth, lost its meaning and became a mere word. As the historian Michael Rostovtzeff has remarked, Caracalla's chief purpose "was not so much to raise the lower classes, as to degrade the upper." Moreover, admission to citizenship involved the assumption of heavy taxes by all concerned. In the preamble to the law Caracalla himself remarked that the gods would look with favor on the grateful offerings by the new citizens. Certainly he himself looked with favor on this new scheme of extortion, since money was desperately needed to pay increasing bounties to the soldiers and to buy off the barbarian tribes as well. In fact, the bribes were so costly that they amounted to a sum equal to the entire military budget. There is excellent authority for this statement, for it came from Caracalla himself.

In his brief reign Caracalla amassed many titles. He was Germanicus Maximus, Parthicus, Arabicus, Alamannicus, and he had in fact led expeditions against Germans, Parthians, Arabs, and the tribe of the Alamanni, sometimes purchasing peace with money. The satirical suggestion was once made to him that he might also properly adopt the title of Geticus Maximus, for he had arranged the murder of his brother Geta. In love with grandeur, he built the largest baths in Rome and decorated them with unprecedented magnificence. He thought of himself as another Alexander the Great, destined to bring about a marriage between Rome and the East, but he ended as a travesty of Alexander. His most notorious exploit was a massacre of almost a whole generation of young citizens of Alexandria. He himself died at the hands of the Guard before he could put down the Parthians.

What was left of Roman dignity was mocked by the rule of the next emperor—a mincing, painted boy named Elagabalus. He was related to Caracalla, but had been raised in Syria as a hereditary

Chariot racing, like the gladitorial contests, drew large audiences throughout much of the Roman world. The North African mosaic above shows a charioteer in the pose of a proud victor with the starting gate behind him. As is true of horse racing today, drivers rode under certain colors and only the wealthiest citizens could afford to keep stables of horses (with the attendant trainers, grooms, veterinarians, and chariot makers needed to produce winners). The opportunity to gamble on the races added greatly to the popularity of the sport.

priest of the cult of Baal. Already sexually corrupted, he found pleasure in dressing in women's clothes and posing as a prostitute; he had a fondness for walking on carpets of lilies and roses. According to the historian Herodian, who describes Elagabalus' triumphal progress through Rome, amid a rabble of eunuchs and oriental priests, the fourteen-year-old emperor wore purple silk embroidered with gold, his cheeks were stained scarlet, his eyes were artificially brightened, and pearls hung from his neck.

That a Syrian priest should be invited to occupy the highest position in the empire was not altogether surprising. The Romans were becoming weary of their ancient gods, and for centuries they had been looking toward the East in the expectation of discovering gods more powerful than their own. At the time of the Carthaginian wars they had acquired the black stone of the Phrygian Great Mother, and during the last century of the republic the cult of the Egyptian goddess Isis had flourished even when it was officially proscribed. The Great Mother promised fertility and victory, Isis promised everlasting life. Elaborate and impressive ceremonies attended the worship of these goddesses, and the hymns sung in their honor were far more colorful than the practical pleas addressed to Jupiter. The eastern mystery religions answered the need of a people thirsting for divine revelation. By the end of the first century A.D. Rome was being invaded by a host of divinities from Syria and the neighboring countries as well as by a dawning belief in Christ the Saviour.

Though the Senate showed an intense dislike for Elagabalus, the people briefly showered him with affection and tolerated his strange ways. He summoned them to worship Baal, the unconquered Sun, and they raised no objection when in his newly erected temple of Baal on the Palatine he assembled all the sacred fetishes of the Romans—the vestal fire, the shields of Mars, the black stone of the Great Mother—insisting that the Romans should all bathe in the light of the Sun. From Carthage he imported the worship of the goddess Tanit, the heavenly mother, and celebrated the marriage of Astarte and the sun god. The *pontifex maximus*, the ancient and lofty Roman religious office, was replaced by the high priest.

The stories told about Elagabalus' pleasures exceed everything told about Nero, and sometimes they resemble the tales concerning the caliph al-Rashid centuries later. His couches were made of solid silver; his chariots were studded with jewels and gold. He would only swim in a pool perfumed with saffron or other essences; he strewed showers of roses and other flowers over his banquet hall floors and walked in them. His banquets were sheer fantasies: on one day everything served was blue in color, the next

307

Shown above are front and rear views of a Roman helmet and visor of a kind that soldiers wore on parade. It is not impossible that the bronze head-piece, found in northern England, was displayed during exercises honoring Septimius Severus, who died in A.D. 211 at his seat at Eboracum while campaigning in the province of Britain.

BOTH: BRITISH MUSEUM

day green, and on the following day iridescent. At dinners he was partial to tongues of peacocks and nightingales, and on one occasion had the heads of six hundred ostriches brought in so that their brains could be eaten. He delighted in playing pranks on his courtiers: the cushions on which they sat were first inflated, and at a sign the air was let out. When his guests became drunk he sometimes had them shut in for the night and then let in some of his tamed lions and bears to awaken them into a state of fright. He offered a prize to the servant who could bring him one thousand pounds of spider webs. Sometimes after dark he roamed the streets incognito, slipping gold coins into prostitutes' hands with the whisper, "It is a gift from the emperor"; sometimes he appeared in public in his chariot drawn by four huge stags.

The man was evidently mad. Within a few years, Rome wearied of his outrageous presence, and he was murdered in a latrine and thrown into the Tiber. Yet he left a legacy: within a few decades the worship of the Sun became the official religion of the empire.

A respite from perversity or madness occurred when another boy emperor, Elagabalus' adopted son Alexander Severus, came to the throne in A.D. 222, at the age of thirteen, but there was no restoration of objective government. First under the thumb of his mother as regent and then of the military whose support he needed, Alexander Severus was an honest, well-intentioned, yet vacillating person in a time that cried out for manly leadership. Simple in tastes, well schooled, deeply religious in an eclectic fashion, he is said to have kept in his private shrines images of Abraham, Apollonius of Tyana, Orpheus, and Jesus, along with busts of Vergil and Cicero. The great Roman jurist Ulpian, his close friend and dinner companion, saw in him an excellent administrator of the laws. Learned in Greek philosophy and Roman poetry, he reminded some men of Marcus Aurelius. Yet he remained the prisoner of his armies, by now the outright opponents of the propertied classes, and was committed to more exactions, more requisitions, more forced service, more debasement of currency and consequent inflation, to sustain the tottering empire.

It was his misfortune to be the contemporary of Ardashir, founder of the skillful dynasty of Sassanid rulers of the Middle East who revived Persia from its long decline. Out of the disorder of the Parthian empire—the far-flung and incohesive tribal area south and southeast of the Black Sea—there emerged a vigorous neo-Persia, reminiscent of the time of Darius and Xerxes, and it promptly made war on the Syrian possessions of Rome. Alexander Severus, like Caracalla before him, attempted to model himself on Alexander the Great, "without," as he explained, "imitating him in drunkenness." But in a series of campaigns the new Alexander only demonstrated what everyone already knew: he was an excellent soldier, but he was no Alexander the Great.

His wars against the Persians were indecisive, ending in stalemate, but in order to fight them he was compelled to withdraw troops from the frontiers in Germany, and soon he was hurrying across Europe to halt a threatened German invasion. Somewhere in Germany, perhaps in Mainz, one of his soldiers entered his tent while he was sleeping. The emperor awoke and said: "Comrade, have you brought news of the enemy?" The soldier had come to steal and fearing punishment he called to his companions for help. A moment later the emperor was stabbed to death.

In the chaotic half-century following Alexander Severus' death, in A.D. 235, the distinction between a legitimate emperor and a usurper was all but to disappear. The rise and assassination of emperors of either kind became the order of the day: two reigned for only a month, three for a year, six for just two years. Alexander's successor was a rough Thracian peasant named Maximinus, of phenomenal height and physical prowess, but without other talents. Proclaimed emperor by his soldiers at Mainz, he never went through the formality of asking to be recognized by the Senate and never so much as appeared in Rome. Sometimes there were two simultaneous emperors or would-be emperors, each backed by his own military party, or by a senatorial party. There was no Augustus, no Trajan to command the loyalty of the army as a whole and keep dilution, division, and corruption in check.

Feared as they were, the soldier-emperors of this time were evidently expendable. A popular song concerning Maximinus preserved by the historian Julius Capitolinus suggests that the people were perfectly aware that emperors could be overthrown without too much expenditure of energy:

> He who cannot be killed by one is killed by many,
> The elephant is a large beast, but he can be killed,
> The lion is strong, and he can be killed,
> The tiger is strong, and he can be killed,
> Beware of the many, if you fear not one alone.

We are told that Maximinus was present when the song was sung on stage in Greek. He understood none of it, and when he asked why the people were cheering, he was told that the clown on the stage was merely reciting some old verses against violent men. He seemed content and relapsed into his customary uncomprehending stare. A mutiny did away with him after three years of rule.

Emperors came and disappeared so speedily that people in the

The developing anarchy in Rome was slow to make itself felt in the provinces. There, for many decades, civil government and commercial life went on much as before. Above, a relief discovered near Avignon, in southeastern France, pictures a four-wheeled vehicle identified as a ceremonial coach; it was probably used by a Gallic municipal civil servant.

MUSEUM CALVET, AVIGNON; GIRAUDON

farther provinces often did not know who was in power at a given time, and moreover did not care. In Gaul and Egypt, men scarcely concerned themselves with Rome. Roman order, language, and law had been imposed on them, and the somewhat questionable benefits of Roman citizenship had been extended to them, but with the decline in central leadership, local loyalties grew stronger, presaging the division of the empire into its component parts. In the provinces the Roman administrative machinery went on with decreasing reference to the incumbent in the capital, and office holders were drawn more and more from the provincial populace. The provincial armies themselves were now composed largely of local peasants or mercenaries. Emperors' agents could and often did spread political terror through even the outermost areas; but they could not be everywhere at once, and the violence of power battles in Rome sometimes contrasted strangely with the peaceful quality of life beyond the Alps or the Adriatic.

The social and political fabric of the empire was so weakened as to offer opportunities for outsiders to attack the most vulnerable points. Legions were stationed to stand guard along a European frontier, which ran from the mouth of the Rhine, across southern Germany, down the Danube to the Black Sea. In the best of times this had been a difficult line to hold intact; it could readily be breached by determined tribes. Many of the tribesmen—Goths, Alamanni, and those who were to become known as Franks—were skilled frontier fighters, with intimate knowledge of the terrain, and many, having taken service at one time or another with Rome's armies, were well acquainted with the strengths and weaknesses of the Romans.

Thus in the third decade of the third century A.D. the far-flung barriers of an ill-tended empire began to cave in. The Goths, a Germanic people who had moved southward from Sweden and had established a strong state on the Russian plains, took to harrying and raiding Roman frontiers along the Danube, in the Balkans, and in the Black Sea area as well. The Alamanni, a Suebic tribe reared in the forests and flatlands of eastern Germany, had collided with Caracalla's forces in A.D. 213, and in the 230's they were making inroads into the Rhine valley, Gaul, and Italy. The Vandals, also of Germanic origin, had moved into the Hungarian plains, where they were developing a craft of armed riding that was to make their mailed cavalry the scourge of Europe. The Franks—meaning "freemen"—were not a tribe unto themselves, but rather a combination of tribesmen of Germanic origin, growing in their threat as they massed along the Rhine. In the middle of the third century A.D. the Franks broke through the *limes*, or fortified borders, and streamed across Gaul and over the Pyrenees into Spain; they looked to Mauretania, in North Africa, as their next goal.

In this time of folk wandering and tribal assaults, the Middle East also continued on its course of disaffection from Rome. Forces of Goths sailed across the Black Sea to attack Roman outposts in Bithynia, on its southern shore, and no fleet could be mustered to stop them, so far had Rome's naval power declined.

Meanwhile, in the century's third decade, the new stir in the eastern Parthian empire, always inimical to Rome, set its Persian people on an aggressive course that was to lead to efforts to make common cause with the roaming Goths against Rome's dwindling majesty. Thrusts by tall, blue-eyed, flaxen-haired northerners and lithe, dark-complexioned easterners—men of wholly contrasting racial and cultural backgrounds—were to occur with growing frequency. Against this gathering threat, following an abortive campaign against the reviving Persians by Alexander Severus, Rome put into the field another boy emperor, Gordian III, who was acclaimed in A.D. 238 at about the age of thirteen. In 242 he set out for the East to subdue the Persians and fought valiantly against the Sassanid ruler Shapur I, recovering Antioch and Carrhae. In 244 he was dead—killed at the orders of a palace cabal led by a military official of Arab birth who was known by the Greek name of Philippus, or Philip.

Gordian had been a rare figure. The historian Julius Capitolinus describes him as a lighthearted, handsome, amiable youth, versed in letters and loved by the Senate, the army, and the people as no prince had been loved before. A Persian triumph was decreed for him, but he did not live to enjoy it. Philip the Arab, who had reached the rank of Praetorian prefect, is reported to have diverted supply trains from the young emperor and intrigued with the soldiery for his downfall. This was almost the lowest point of military Rome, an empire now split among factions and armies, ruled by generals, boy emperors, and usurpers, with senatorial and military classes in opposition and disarray, its borders broken, credit undermined, corruption rampant, and no man strong enough for the moment to hold off dissolution and decay. Pirates swarmed across the Aegean; tribes from the Sahara pillaged imperial cities along the North African coast; soon Persians were to overwhelm Syria and there to capture a Roman emperor, Valerian, leading him about in captive bonds.

Great defenders and rebuilders of Rome were still to come, and a line of emperors of east European origin was to succor it; but after the debacle of these decades, the glory of the early empire was never to be recaptured.

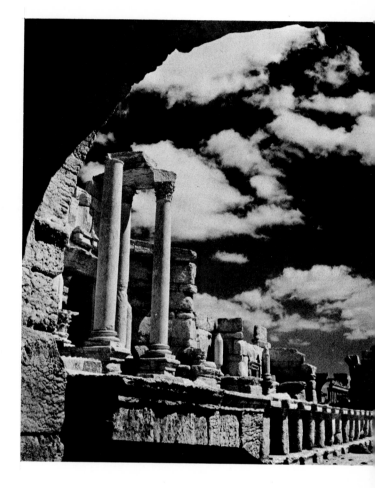

In the early third century, the weakened empire was threatened both by northern tribesmen and by a hostile Persia reviving under its Sassanid rulers. Borders became uncertain. In the East, the Persian impetus caused many cities to grow restive under the Roman yoke. Shown above are the ruins of Palmyra, a Syrian community that broke away from the Roman empire and became a seat of sedition.
ROLOFF BENY

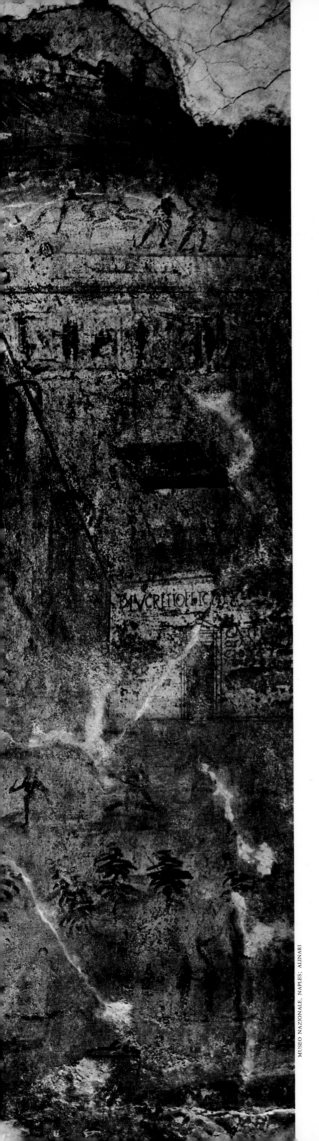

PLEASURES OF THE ARENA

The satirist Juvenal remarked in the second century A.D. that Romans seemed to care about little except bread and circuses. Bread was a necessity, but circuses, especially in imperial times, became more like a mass addiction. The mania for chariot racing knew no geographical limits but those of the empire itself, and the lust to watch gladiators die spread to almost every land except Greece, which never lost its preference for bloodless contests of skill between trained athletes. Roman emperors seemed to sense that the excitement of racing and the spectacle of death in the arenas relieved the frustrations of urban mobs and often served to engender the kind of partisan fervor that had once expressed itself in violent political action. Thus, the number of days devoted to these events was constantly being increased. Eventually citizens in some parts of the empire were spending as many as one hundred and fifty days of the year in stadiums or amphitheatres. There, in perfect safety, often protected even from the glare of the sun by huge awnings (as shown in the Pompeiian painting at left), they watched as charioteers plied their dangerous trade, animals were tortured and butchered, and desperate men—armed with various weapons and pitted against each other in many ingenious combinations —fought without quarter to win a brief moment of popular renown and a chance to live a few more weeks or days.

OVERLEAF: *Carnage in a Roman arena is depicted in a fourth-century* A.D. *mosaic. Two gladiators have already been killed, and another is about to receive a fatal thrust from his adversary.*

313

MAN AGAINST MAN

The Circus Maximus was built in Etruscan times and repeatedly enlarged thereafter. In Trajan's day it could hold at least a quarter of a million spectators, but was still barely large enough to accommodate all of the enthusiasts who flocked to the chariot races to gamble and cheer their favorite colors. Always adding to the excitement was the virtual certainty that on any given day, at least one charioteer, strapped to his reins, would fail to negotiate a turn and either be dragged to his death or precipitate a spectacular chain reaction of accidents.

The ancient reliefs reproduced on these pages communicate some of the frenzy of four-horse chariot racing. Grouped obelisks (to be seen at left and right in both the larger and smaller panels) mark the ends of the spina—the low, central wall around which drivers maneuvered their light chariots. A race usually consisted of seven circuits, a distance of six miles in the huge Circus Maximus (depicted below).

MAN AGAINST BEAST

The *venatio*, an event that featured wild animals, was often a part of the program in the major Roman amphitheatres. Beasts might be pitted against each other or sent into the arena to mangle defenseless humans, but the typical display was a simulated hunt during which animals were stalked by *bestiarii*—specialists armed with spears, bows and arrows, or other weapons. The blood always flowed copiously. As many as five thousand animals may have died during one day of the extended festival that inaugurated Rome's Colosseum in A.D. 80. To keep amphitheatres supplied, a great traffic in wild beasts developed, and as a result, some species (such as the elephant, rhinoceros, and lion) virtually disappeared from familiar North African and Near Eastern habitats.

As slain animals begin to litter the arena the bestiarius *pictured in the mosaic above impales yet another leopard with his spear. In the terra-cotta relief at right, a bear, a lioness, and a lion contend with swordsmen. The Romans endeavored to achieve as much variety as possible in their animal displays in order to keep jaded audiences interested and to whet their appetites for the main attraction—the gladiatorial bouts. At times the blood lust of the crowd was aroused by wholesale butchery such as the slaughter of hundreds of helpless beasts by companies of archers.*

FREE MINDS

OF THE EMPIRE

The term *silver age* is applied to the literature written during the period starting at the beginning of Tiberius' reign (A.D. 14) and ending with the death of Hadrian in 138. But it is a misleading one, implying as it does, an output inferior to the more "classical" works of the time of Vergil and Ovid and Horace that immediately preceded it. The writing of the newer generation is differentiated from the old because it is, indeed, more stylized and epigrammatical, more dependent on artifice and device; it was produced at a time when rhetoric was the all-important scholarly discipline and listening to orators was more popular than theatregoing. At the same time the new writing was more concerned with man and his problems, for the huge influx of foreigners into Rome and Stoic philosophy had broadened the writer's outlook. The empire did not produce such beautiful poetry as the republic had—the times called for stronger stuff. But the writing was more varied in style and genre, and its satire and history were as masterful and passionate as anything produced in the golden age.

Despite some benevolent rulers, it was a time when tyranny and degeneracy were prevalent and the truth was often a dangerous possession. Nero forced the satirist Petronius, the dramatist Seneca, and the poet Lucan to commit suicide. Some, like Juvenal, were exiled for minor offences; Tacitus and Pliny, being more discreet, suffered years of silence waiting for a propitious time to publish their attacks on the evils they had seen.

When the voices of outrage were stilled the last classical literature had been written. Peace took the place of strife in the empire, but no other great Roman writers appeared; nevertheless, the silver age had taught the West the value of wit and satire.

Nothing is left, nothing for future times
To add to the full catalogue of crimes.
The baffled sons must feel the same desires
And act the same mad follies as their sires.
Vice hath attained its zenith! then set sail,
Spread all thy canvas, Satire, to the gale.
But where the powers so vast a theme
                              requires?
Where the plain times, the simple,
                              when our sires
Enjoyed a freedom which I dare not name,
And gave the public sin to public shame,
Heedless who smiled or frowned?

                    Juvenal, Satires
          (translation by William Gifford,
              revised by John Warrington)

An ancient Roman coin is stamped with the profile of the evil and debauched emperor Nero.

THE VENOMOUS VOICE OF JUVENAL

In Juvenal's works satire reached a pinnacle never to be surpassed. The few available details of his life help us to understand the invective and cruel parody in his writing. Juvenal was apparently a dissatisfied government official when he wrote a lampoon that enraged Domitian; he was stripped of his fortune and exiled to Egypt. The penniless satirist was recalled by Nerva to be dependent for many years on the whims of selfish patrons. Feeling himself the victim of a decadent society, he said, "It's hard not to write satire."

Satire III
(translated by John Dryden)

The story of this satire speaks itself. Umbritius, the suppos'd friend of Juvenal, and himself a poet, is leaving Rome, and retiring to Cumae. Our author accompanies him out of town. Before they take leave of each other, Umbritius tells his friend the reasons which oblige him to lead a private life, in an obscure place. He complains that an honest man cannot get his bread at Rome; that none but flatterers make their fortunes there; that Grecians and other foreigners raise themselves by those sordid arts which he describes, and against which he bitterly inveighs. He reckons up the several inconveniences which arise from a city life, and the many dangers which attend it; upbraids the noblemen with covetousness, for not rewarding good poets; and arraigns the government for starving them. The great art of this satire is particularly shown in commonplaces, and drawing in as many vices as could naturally fall into the compass of it.

Griev'd tho' I am an ancient friend to lose,
I like the solitary seat he chose,
In quiet Cumae fixing his repose:
Where, far from noisy Rome, secure he lives,
And one more citizen to Sibyl gives;
The road to Bajae, and that soft recess,
Which all the gods with all their bounty bless.
Tho' I in Prochyta with greater ease
Could live, than in a street of palaces.
What scene so desart, or so full of fright,
As tow'ring houses tumbling in the night,
And Rome on fire beheld by its own blazing light?
But worse than all, the clatt'ring tiles; and worse
Than thousand padders, is the poet's curse;
Rogues that in dog days cannot rhyme forbear:
But without mercy read, and make you hear. . . .
  Then thus Umbritius (with an angry frown,
And looking back on this degen'rate town):
"Since noble arts in Rome have no support,
And ragged virtue not a friend at court,
No profit rises from th' ungrateful stage,
My poverty encreasing with my age,

'T is time to give my just disdain a vent,
And, cursing, leave so base a government. . . .
What's Rome to me, what bus'ness have I there,
I who can neither lie, nor falsely swear?
Nor praise my patron's undeserving rhymes,
Nor yet comply with him, nor with his times . . .
To see the scum of Greece transplanted here,
Receiv'd like gods, is what I cannot bear.
Nor Greeks alone, but Syrians here abound;
Obscene Orontes, diving under ground,
Conveys his wealth to Tiber's hungry shores,
And fattens Italy with foreign whores:
Hether their crooked harps and customs come;
All find receipt in hospitable Rome.
The barbarous harlots crowd the public place:
Go, fools, and purchase an unclean embrace;
The painted miter court, and the more painted face.
Old Romulus, and Father Mars, look down!
Your herdsman primitive, your homely clown
Is turn'd a beau in a loose tawdry gown.
His once unkemb'd and horrid locks, behold
Stilling sweet oil: his neck inchain'd with gold;
Aping the foreigners, in ev'ry dress,
Which, bought at greater cost, becomes him less.
Meantime they wisely leave their native land;
From Sicyon, Samos, and from Alaband,
And Amydon, to Rome they swarm in shoals:
So sweet and easy is the gain from fools.
Poor refugees at first, they purchase here;
And, soon as denizen'd, they domineer;
Grow to the great a flatt'ring servile rout:
Work themselves inward, and their patrons out:
Quick-witted, brazen-fac'd, with fluent tongues,
Patient of labors, and dissembling wrongs.
Riddle me this, and guess him if you can,
Who bears a nation in a single man?
A cook, a conjurer, a rhetorician,
A painter, pedant, a geometrician,
A dancer on the ropes, and a physician.

All things the hungry Greek exactly knows:
And bid him go to heav'n, and heav'n he goes:
In short, no Scythian, Moor, or Thracian born,
But in that town which arms and arts adorn.
Shall he be plac'd above me at the board,
In purple cloth'd, and lolling like a lord?
Shall he before me sign, whom t'other day
A small-craft vessel hither did convey;
Where, stow'd with prunes, and rotten figs, he lay?
How little is the privilege become
Of being born a citizen of Rome! . . .
Call for a fire, their winter clothes they take:
Begin but you to shiver, and they shake:
In frost and snow, if you complain of heat,
They rub th' unsweating brow, and swear they sweat.
We live not on the square with such as these;
Such are our betters who can better please;
Who day and night are like a looking-glass,
Still ready to reflect their patron's face;
The panegyric hand, and lifted eye,
Prepar'd for some new piece of flattery.
Ev'n nastiness occasions will afford;
They praise a belching, or well-pissing lord.
Besides, there's nothing sacred, nothing free
From bold attempts of their rank lechery.
Thro' the whole family their labors run;
The daughter is debauch'd, the wife is won:
Nor scapes the bridegroom, or the blooming son.
If none they find for their lewd purpose fit,
They with the walls and very floors commit. . . .
One drop of poison in my patron's ear,
One slight suggestion of a senseless fear,
Infus'd with cunning, serves to ruin me;
Disgrac'd and banish'd from the family.
In vain forgotten services I boast;
My long dependence in an hour is lost:
Look round the world, what country will appear,
Where friends are left with greater ease than here?
At Rome (nor think me partial to the poor)
All offices of ours are out of door:
In vain we rise, and to their levees run;
My lord himself is up, before, and gone . . .
Swear by our gods, or those the Greeks adore,
Thou art as sure forsworn, as thou art poor;
The poor must gain their bread by perjury;
And even the gods, that other means deny,
In conscience must absolve 'em, when they lie.
    "Add, that the rich have still a gibe in store;
And will be monstrous witty on the poor:
For the torn surtout and the tatter'd vest,
The wretch and all his wardrobe are a jest;
The greasy gown, sullied with often turning,
Gives a good hint, to say: 'The man's in mourning:'
Or if the shoe be ripp'd, or patches put:

'He's wounded! see the plaster on his foot.'
Want is the scorn of ev'ry wealthy fool;
And wit in rags is turn'd to ridicule.
" 'Pack hence, and from cover'd benches rise,'
The master of the ceremonies cries,
'This is no place for you, whose small estate
Is not the value of the settled rate;
The sons of happy punks, the pander's heir,
Are privileg'd to sit in triumph there,
To clap the first, and rule the theater.
Up to the galleries, for shame, retreat;
For, by the Roscian law, the poor can claim no seat.'
Who ever brought to his rich daughter's bed
The man that poll'd but twelvepence for his head?
Who ever nam'd a poor man for his heir,
Or call'd him to assist the judging chair?
The poor were wise, who, by the rich oppress'd,
Withdrew, and sought a sacred place of rest.
Once they did well, to free themselves from scorn;
But had done better never to return.
Rarely they rise by virtue's aid, who lie
Plung'd in the depth of helpless poverty.
    "At Rome 't is worse; where houserent by the year
And servants' bellies cost so dev'lish dear;
And tavern bills run high for hungry cheer.
To drink or eat in earthenware we scorn,
Which cheaply country cupboards does adorn;
And coarse blue hoods on holidays are worn.
Some distant parts of Italy are known,
Where none, but only dead men, wear a gown;
On theaters of turf, in homely state,
Old plays they act, old feasts they celebrate;
The same rude song returns upon the crowd,
And, by tradition, is for wit allow'd. . . .
But here, attir'd beyond our purse we go,
For useless ornament and flaunting show:
We take on trust, in purple robes to shine;
And poor, are yet ambitious to be fine.
This is a common vice, tho' all things here
Are sold, and sold unconscionably dear. . . .
    "Who fears, in country towns, a house's fall,
Or to be caught betwixt a riven wall?
But we inhabit a weak city, here;
Which buttresses and props but scarcely bear:
And 't is the village mason's daily calling,
To keep the world's metropolis from falling,
To cleanse the gutters, and the chinks to close,
And, for one night, secure his lord's repose.
At Cumae we can sleep, quite round the year,
Nor falls, nor fires, nor nightly dangers fear;
While rolling flames from Roman turrets fly,
And the pale citizens for buckets cry.
Thy neighbor has remov'd his wretched store,
(Few hands will rid the lumber of the poor;)

Thy own third story smokes, while thou, supine,
Art drench'd in fumes of undigested wine.
For if the lowest floors already burn,
Cocklofts and garrets soon will take the turn,
Where thy tame pigeons next the tiles were bred,
Which, in their nests unsafe, are timely fled.
 "Codrus had but one bed, so short to boot,
That his short wife's short legs hung dangling out;
His cupboard's head six earthen pitchers grac'd,
Beneath 'em was his trusty tankard plac'd;
And, to support this noble plate, there lay
A bending Chiron cast from honest clay;
His few Greek books a rotten chest contain'd,
Whose covers much of moldiness complain'd:
Where mice and rats devour'd poetic bread,
And with heroic verse luxuriously were fed.
'T is true, poor Codrus nothing had to boast,
And yet poor Codrus all that nothing lost;
Begg'd naked thro' the streets of wealthy Rome;
And found not one to feed, or take him home.
 "But if the palace of Arturius burn,
The nobles change their clothes, the matrons mourn;
The city praetor will no pleadings hear;
The very name of fire we hate and fear,
And look aghast, as if the Gauls were here.
While yet it burns, th' officious nation flies,
Some to condole, and some to bring supplies . . .
 "But, could you be content to bid adieu
To the dear playhouse, and the players too;
Sweet country seats are purchas'd ev'rywhere,
With lands and gardens, at less price than here
You hire a darksome doghole by the year:
A small convenience, decently prepar'd,
A shallow well, that rises in your yard,
That spreads his easy crystal streams around,
And waters all the pretty spot of ground.
There, love the fork, thy garden cultivate,
And give thy frugal friends a Pythagorean treat.
'T is somewhat to be lord of some small ground,
In which a lizard may, at least, turn round.
 " 'T is frequent, here, for want of sleep to die;
Which fumes of undigested feasts deny;
And, with imperfect heat, in languid stomachs fry.
What house secure from noise the poor can keep,
When ev'n the rich can scarce afford to sleep?
So dear it costs to purchase rest in Rome;
And hence the sources of diseases come.
The drover who his fellow-drover meets
In narrow passages of winding streets;
The wagoners, that curse their standing teams,
Would wake ev'n drowsy Drusus from his dreams.
And yet the wealthy will not brook delay,
But sweep above our heads; and make their way,
In lofty litters borne, and read and write,

Or sleep at ease: the shutters make it night.
Yet still he reaches, first, the public place:
The prease before him stops the client's pace.
The crowd that follows crush his panting sides,
And trip his heels; he walks not, but he rides.
One elbows him, one justles in the shole,
A rafter breaks his head, or chairman's pole:
Stocking'd with loads of fat town-dirt he goes;
And some rogue-soldier, with his hobnail'd shoes,
Indents his legs behind in bloody rows.
 "See with what smoke our doles we celebrate:
A hundred guests, invited, walk in state;
A hundred hungry slaves, with their Dutch kitchens, wait.
Huge pans the wretches on their heads must bear,
Which scarce gigantic Corbulo could rear:
Yet they must walk upright beneath the load;
Nay, run, and, running, blow the sparkling flames abroad.
Their coats, from botching newly brought, are torn;
Unwieldy timber-trees in wagons borne,
Stretch'd at their length, beyond their carriage lie,
That nod, and threaten ruin from on high;
For, should their axle break, its overthrow
Would crush, and pound to dust, the crowd below;
Nor friends their friends, nor sires their sons could know:
Nor limbs, nor bones, nor carcass would remain:
But a mash'd heap, a hotchpotch of the slain;
One vast destruction; not the soul alone . . .
 "Return we to the dangers of the night:
And, first, behold our houses' dreadful height;
From whence come broken potsherds tumbling down;
And leaky ware, from garret windows thrown:
Well may they break our heads, that mark the flinty stone.
'T is want of sense to sup abroad too late,
Unless thou first hast settled thy estate.
As many fates attend, thy steps to meet,
As there are waking windows in the street.
Bless the good gods, and think thy chance is rare,
To have a pisspot only for thy share.
 "The scouring drunkard, if he does not fight
Before his bedtime, takes no rest that night;
Passing the tedious hours in greater pain
Than stern Achilles, when his friend was slain:
'T is so ridiculous, but so true withal,
A bully cannot sleep without a brawl:
Yet tho' his youthful blood be fir'd with wine,
He wants not wit, the danger to decline;
Is cautious to avoid the coach and six,
And on the lackeys will no quarrel fix.
His train of flambeaux, and embroider'd coat,
May privilege my lord to walk secure on foot.
But me, who must by moonlight homeward bend,
Or lighted only with a candle's end,
Poor me he fights, if that be fighting, where
He only cudgels, and I only bear.

He stands, and bids me stand; I must abide;
For he's the stronger, and is drunk beside.
" 'Where did you whet your knife tonight?' he cries,
'And shred the leeks that in your stomach rise?
Whose windy beans have stuff'd your guts, and where
Have your black thumbs been dipp'd in vinegar?
With what companion cobbler have you fed,
On old ox-cheeks, or he-goat's tougher head?
What, are you dumb? Quick, with your answer, quick,
Before my foot salutes you with a kick.
Say, in what nasty cellar, under ground,
Or what church porch, your rogueship may be found?'
Answer, or answer not, 't is all the same:
He lays me on, and makes me bear the blame.
Before the bar, for beating him, you come;
This is a poor man's liberty in Rome.
You beg his pardon; happy to retreat
With some remaining teeth, to chew your meat.
"Nor is this all; for, when retir'd, you think
To sleep securely; when the candles wink,
When every door with iron chains is barr'd,
And roaring taverns are no longer heard;
The ruffian robbers, by no justice aw'd,
And unpaid cutthroat soldiers, are abroad,

Those venal souls, who, harden'd in each ill,
To save complaints and prosecution, kill.
Chas'd from their woods and bogs, the padders come
To this vast city, as their native home;
To live at ease, and safely skulk in Rome.
"The forge in fetters only is employ'd;
Our iron mines exhausted and destroy'd
In shackles; for these villains scarce allow
Goads for the teams, and plowshares for the plow.
O happy ages of our ancestors,
Beneath the kings and tribunitial pow'rs!
One jail did all their criminals restrain,
Which, now, the walls of Rome can scarce contain.
"More I could say, more causes I could show
For my departure; but the sun is low;
The wagoner grows weary of my stay,
And whips his horses forwards on their way.
"Farewell; and when, like me, o'erwhelm'd with care,
You to your own Aquinum shall repair,
To take a mouthful of sweet country air,
Be mindful of your friend; and send me word,
What joys your fountains and cool shades afford:
Then, to assist your satires, I will come;
And add new venom, when you write of Rome."

from Satire I
(*translated by L. R. Lind*)

I'll tell you why,
If you have the time and the patience, I've decided to run
The same course that Lucilius ran, in the satire-race.
When soft eunuchs marry, when Mevia sticks a wild boar
And holds a man's hunting spear close to her naked breast,
When a man who used to cut hair in my barber shop
When I was a boy now rivals the richest alone,
When the scum of the Nile, when a slave like Crispinus, who
                                                              comes
From Canopus, can hitch a Tyrian cloak from his shoulder
And wave the gold "summer-ring" on his sweating finger,
Unable to bear the weight of a heavier gem:
It's hard *not* to write satire.

from Satire VI
(*translated by John Paul Heironimus*)

You may give up any hope for harmony as long as your mother-in-law is alive. She teaches her daughter what fun it is to rob her husband of his very shirt; she coaches her, when a letter arrives from a seducer, to write a smart and sophisticated reply. She fools the guards or bribes them. She calls in a doctor when the girl is perfectly well, and heaps the blankets upon her. Meanwhile the lurking lover silently waits in the offing, chafing at the delay. Well, do you expect the mother to impart honorable ways, different from her own? Besides, it's useful to the old hag to have a daughter as bad as herself.

from Satire I
(*translated by William Gifford*)

What! while with one eternal mouthing hoarse,
Codrus persists on my vex'd ear to force
His Theseid, must I, to my fate resign'd,
Hear, ONLY hear, and never pay in kind?
Must this with farce and folly rack my head
Unpunish'd? that with sing-song, whine me dead?

from Satire VIII
(*translated by Gilbert Highet*)

Send down to the docks, your majesty,
send men to find your general in a huge saloon:
you will get him lying near a gangster, cheek by jowl,
mingling with lascars, thieves, and convicts on the lam,
among the undertaker's men and the builders of coffins
and the idle bongo-drums of a lolling eunuch fakir.

TACITUS, THE MASTER HISTORIAN

About all that is known about the life of Cornelius Tacitus, Rome's greatest historian, is that he was a famous orator and was given several important government posts; finally he held the office of proconsul under Trajan. Tacitus had available to him archives, letters of historical importance, and eyewitness reports, and he made good use of all of these in writing his histories. He does not try to hide his disapproval of some of the people he writes about nor his bias about some of the issues, but when that is the case he usually tries to give the other side of the question as well. An absolute master of style, Tacitus is at the same time terse and rhetorical, lean and descriptive, satirical and compassionate, and although completely original he is the epitome of the writers of the silver age.

from the HISTORY
(*translated by Alfred John Church
and William Jackson Brodribb*)

After the conflict at Actium, and when it became essential to peace, that all power should be centered in one man, these great intellects passed away. Then too the truthfulness of history was impaired in many ways; at first, through men's ignorance of public affairs, which were now wholly strange to them, then, through their passion for flattery, or, on the other hand, their hatred of their masters. And so between the enmity of the one and the servility of the other, neither had any regard for posterity. But while we instinctively shrink from a writer's adulation, we lend a ready ear to detraction and spite, because flattery involves the shameful imputation of servility, whereas malignity wears the false appearance of honesty. I myself knew nothing of Galba, of Otho, or of Vitellius, either from benefits or from injuries. I would not deny that my elevation was begun by Vespasian, augmented by Titus, and still further advanced by Domitian; but those who profess inviolable truthfulness must speak of all without partiality and without hatred. I have reserved as an employment for my old age, should my life be long enough, a subject at once more fruitful and less anxious in the reign of the Divine Nerva and the empire of Trajan, enjoying the rare happiness of times, when we may think what we please, and express what we think.

from the GERMANIA
(*translated by H. Mattingly*)

For myself I accept the view that the peoples of Germany have never been tainted by intermarriage with other peoples, and stand out as a nation peculiar, pure and unique of its kind. Hence the physical type, if one may generalize at all about so vast a population, is everywhere the same—wild, blue eyes, reddish hair and huge frames that excel only in violent effort. They have no corresponding power to endure hard work and exertion, and have little capacity to bear thirst and heat; but their climate and soil *have* taught them to bear cold and hunger....

On the field of battle it is a disgrace to the chief to be surpassed in valour by his companions, to the companions not to come up to the valour of their chief. As for leaving a battle alive after your chief has fallen, *that* means lifelong infamy and shame. To defend and protect him, to put down one's own acts of heroism to his credit—that is what they really mean by "allegiance." The chiefs fight for victory, the companions for their chief. Many noble youths, if the land of their birth is stagnating in a protracted peace, deliberately seek out other tribes, where some war is afoot. The Germans have no taste for peace; renown is easier won among perils, and you cannot maintain a large body of companions except by violence and war. The companions are prodigal in their demands on the generosity of their chiefs. It is always "give me that war-horse" or "give me that bloody and victorious spear." As for meals with their plentiful, if homely, fare, they count simply as pay. Such open-handedness must have war and plunder to feed it. You will find it harder to persuade a German to plough the land and to await its annual produce with patience than to challenge a foe and earn the prize of wounds. He thinks it spiritless and slack to gain by sweat what he can buy with blood.

When not engaged in warfare, they spend some little time in hunting, but more in idling, abandoned to sleep and gluttony. All the heroes and grim warriors dawdle their time away, while the care of house, hearth and fields is left to the women, old men and weaklings of the family. The warriors themselves lose their edge. They are so strangely inconsistent. They love indolence, but they hate peace. It is usual for states to make voluntary and individual contributions of cattle or agricultural produce to the chiefs. These are accepted as a token of honour, but serve also to relieve essential needs. The chiefs take peculiar pleasure in gifts from neighbouring states, such as are sent not only by individuals, but by the community as well—choice horses, splendid arms, metal discs and collars; the practice of accepting money payments they have now learnt—from us.

It is a well-known fact that the peoples of Germany never live in cities, and will not even have their houses set close together. They live apart, dotted here and there, where spring, plain or grove has taken their fancy. Their villages are not laid out in Roman style, with buildings adjacent or interlocked. Every man leaves an open space round his house, perhaps as a precaution against the risk of fire, perhaps because they are such inexpert builders. They do not even make any use of little stone blocks or tiles; what serves their every purpose is ugly timber, both unimpressive and unattractive. They smear over some parts of their houses with an earth that is so pure and brilliant that it looks like painting or coloured mosaics. They have also the habit of hollowing out caves underground and heaping masses of refuse on the top. In these they can escape the winter's cold and store their produce. In such shelters they take the edge off the bitter frosts; and, should an invader come, he ravages the open country, but the secret and buried stores may pass altogether unnoticed or escape detection, simply because they have to be looked for.

The universal dress is the short cloak, fastened with a brooch, or, failing that, a thorn. They pass whole days by the hearth fire wearing no garment but this. The richest are not distinguished, like the Persians and Sarmatians, by a long flowing robe, but by a tight one that shows the shape of every limb. They also wear the pelts of wild animals, the tribes near the Rhine without regard to appearance, the more distant peoples with some refinement of taste, for there is no other finery that they can buy. These latter peoples make careful choice of animal, then strip off the pelt and mottle it with patches of the spotted skins of the beasts that live in the outer ocean and the unknown sea. The dress of the women differs from that of the men in two respects only. The women often wear undergarments of linen, embroidered with purple, and, as the upper part does not extend to sleeves, forearms and upper arms are bare. Even the breast, where it comes nearest the shoulder, is exposed too.

from the AGRICOLA
(*translated by Alfred John Church
and William Jackson Brodribb*)

Of this series of events [which led to the defeat of Britain], though not exaggerated in the despatches of Agricola by any boastfulness of language, Domitian heard, as was his wont, with joy in his face but anxiety in his heart. He felt conscious that all men laughed at his late mock triumph over Germany, for which there had been purchased from traders people whose dress and hair might be made to resemble those of captives, whereas now a real and splendid victory, with the destruction of thousands of the enemy, was being celebrated with just applause. It was, he thought, a very alarming thing for him that the name of a subject should be raised above that of the Emperor; it was to no purpose that he had driven into obscurity the pursuit of forensic eloquence and the graceful accomplishments of civil life, if

another were to forestall the distinctions of war. To other glories he could more easily shut his eyes, but the greatness of a good general was a truly imperial quality. Harassed by these anxieties, and absorbed in an incommunicable trouble, a sure prognostic of some cruel purpose, he decided that it was best for the present to suspend his hatred until the freshness of Agricola's renown and his popularity with the army should begin to pass away.

For Agricola was still the governor of Britain. Accordingly the Emperor ordered that the usual triumphal decorations, the honour of a laurelled statue, and all that is commonly given in place of the triumphal procession, with the addition of many laudatory expressions, should be decreed in the senate, together with a hint to the effect that Agricola was to have the province of Syria, then vacant by the death of Atilius Rufus, a man of consular rank, and generally reserved for men of distinction. It was believed by many persons that one of the freedmen employed on confidential services was sent to Agricola, bearing a despatch in which Syria was offered him, and with instructions to deliver it should he be in Britain; that this freedman in crossing the straits met Agricola, and without even saluting him made his way back to Domitian; though I cannot say whether the story is true, or is only a fiction invented to suit the Emperor's character.

Meanwhile Agricola had handed over his province in peace and safety to his successor. And not to make his entrance into Rome conspicuous by the concourse of welcoming throngs, he avoided the attentions of his friends by entering the city at night, and at night too, according to orders, proceeded to the palace, where, having been received with a hurried embrace and without a word being spoken, he mingled in the crowd of courtiers. Anxious henceforth to temper the military renown, which annoys men of peace, with other merits, he studiously cultivated retirement and leisure, simple in dress, courteous in conversation, and never accompanied but by one or two friends, so that the many who commonly judge of great men by their external grandeur, after having seen and attentively surveyed him, asked the secret of a greatness which but few could explain.

During this time he was frequently accused before Domitian in his absence, and in his absence acquitted. The cause of his danger lay not in any crime, nor in any complaint of injury, but in a ruler who was the foe of virtue, in his own renown, and in that worst class of enemies—the men who praise. And then followed such days for the commonwealth as would not suffer Agricola to be forgotten; days when so many of our armies were lost in Moesia, Dacia, Germany, and Pannonia, through the rashness or cowardice of our generals, when so many of our officers were besieged and captured with so many of our auxiliaries, when it was no longer the boundaries of empire and the banks of rivers which were imperilled, but the winter-quarters of our legions and the possession of our territories. And so when disaster followed upon disaster, and the entire year was marked by destruction and slaughter, the voice of the people called Agricola to the command; for they all contrasted his vigour, firmness, and experience in war, with the inertness and timidity of other generals. This talk, it is quite certain, assailed the ears of the Emperor himself, while affection and loyalty in the best of his freedmen, malice and envy in the worst, kindled the anger of a prince ever inclined to evil. And so at once, by his own excellences and by the faults of others, Agricola was hurried headlong to a perilous elevation.

The year had now arrived in which the pro-consulate of Asia or Africa was to fall to him by lot, and, as Civica had been lately murdered, Agricola did not want a warning, or Domitian a precedent. Persons well acquainted with the Emperor's feelings came to ask Agricola, as if on their own account, whether he would go. First they hinted their purpose by praises of tranquillity and leisure; then offered their services in procuring acceptance for his excuses; and at last, throwing off all disguise, brought him by entreaties and threats to Domitian. The Emperor, armed beforehand with hypocrisy, and assuming a haughty demeanour, listened to his prayer that he might be excused, and having granted his request allowed himself to be formally thanked, nor blushed to grant so sinister a favour. But the salary usually granted to a pro-consul, and which he had himself given to some governors, he did not bestow on Agricola, either because he was offended at its not having been asked, or was warned by his conscience that he might be thought to have purchased the refusal which he had commanded. It is, indeed, human nature to hate the man whom you have injured; yet the Emperor, notwithstanding his irascible temper and an implacability proportioned to his reserve, was softened by the moderation and prudence of Agricola, who neither by a perverse obstinacy nor an idle parade of freedom challenged fame or provoked his fate. Let it be known to those whose habit it is to admire the disregard of authority, that there may be great men even under bad emperors, and that obedience and submission, when joined to activity and vigour, may attain a glory which most men reach only by a perilous career, utterly useless to the state, and closed by an ostentatious death.

The end of his life, a deplorable calamity to us and a grief to his friends, was regarded with concern even by strangers and those who knew him not. The common people and this busy population continually inquired at his house, and talked of him in public places and in private gatherings. No man when he heard of Agricola's death could either be glad or at once forget it. Men's sympathy was increased by a prevalent rumour that he was destroyed by poison. For myself, I have nothing which I should venture to state for fact. Certainly during the whole of his illness the Emperor's chief freedmen and confidential physicians came more frequently than is usual with a court which pays its visits by means of messengers. This was, perhaps, solicitude, perhaps espionage. Certain it is, that on the last day the very agonies of his dying moments were reported by a succession of couriers, and no one believed that there would be such haste about tidings which would be heard with regret. Yet in his manner and countenance the Emperor displayed some signs of sorrow, for he could now forget his enmity, and it was easier to conceal his joy than his fear. It was well known that on reading the will, in which he was named co-heir with Agricola's excellent wife and most dutiful daughter, he expressed delight, as if it had been a complimentary choice. So blinded and perverted was his mind by incessant flattery, that he did not know that it was only a bad Emperor whom a good father would make his heir.

Agricola was born on the 13th of June, in the third consulate of Caius Caesar; he died on the 23rd of August, during the consulate of Collega and Priscus, being in the fifty-sixth year of his age. Should posterity wish to know something of his appearance, it was graceful rather than commanding. There was nothing formidable in his appearance; a gracious look predominated. One would easily believe him a good man, and willingly believe him to be great. As for himself, though taken from us in the prime of a vigorous manhood, yet, as far as glory is concerned, his life was of the longest. Those true blessings, indeed, which consist in virtue, he had fully attained; and on one who had reached the honours of a consulate and a triumph, what more had fortune to bestow? Immense wealth had no attractions for him, and wealth he had, even to splendour. As his daughter and his wife survived him, it may be thought that he was even fortunate—fortunate, in that while his honours had suffered no eclipse, while his fame was at its height, while his kindred and his friends still prospered, he escaped from the evil to come. For, though to survive until the dawn of this most happy age and to see a Trajan on the throne was what he would speculate upon in previsions and wishes confided to my ears, yet he had this mighty compensation for his premature death, that he was spared those later years during which Domitian, leaving now no interval or breathing space of time, but, as it were, with one continuous blow, drained the life-blood of the Commonwealth.

Agricola did not see the senate-house besieged, or the senate hemmed in by armed men, or so many of our consulars falling at one single massacre, or so many of Rome's noblest ladies exiles and fugitives. Carus Metius had as yet the distinction of but one victory, and the noisy counsels of Messalinus were not heard beyond the walls of Alba, and Massa Baebius was then answering for his life. It was not long before our hands dragged Helvidius to prison, before we gazed on the dying looks of Manricus and Rusticus, before we were steeped in Senecio's innocent blood. Even Nero turned his eyes away, and did not gaze upon the atrocities which he ordered; with Domitian it was the chief part of our miseries to see and to be seen, to know that our sighs were being recorded, to have, ever ready to note the pallid looks of so many faces, that savage countenance reddened with the hue with which he defied shame.

Thou wast indeed fortunate, Agricola, not only in the splendour of thy life, but in the opportune moment of thy death. Thou submittedst to thy fate, so they tell us who were present to hear thy last words, with courage and cheerfulness, seeming to be doing all thou couldst to give thine Emperor full acquittal. As for me and thy daughter, besides all the bitterness of a father's loss, it increases our sorrow that it was not permitted us to watch over thy failing health, to comfort thy weakness, to satisfy ourselves with those looks, those embraces. Assuredly we should have received some precepts, some utterances to fix in our inmost hearts. This is the bitterness of our sorrow, this the smart of our wound, that from the circumstance of so long an absence thou wast lost to us four years before. Doubtless, best of fathers, with that most loving wife at thy side, all the dues of affection were abundantly paid thee, yet with too few tears thou wast laid to thy rest, and in the light of thy last day there was something for which thine eyes longed in vain.

If there is any dwelling-place for the spirits of the just; if, as the wise believe, noble souls do not perish with the body, rest thou in peace; and call us, thy family, from weak regrets and womanish laments to the contemplation of thy virtues, for which we must not weep nor beat the breast. Let us honour thee not so much with transitory praises as with our reverence, and, if our powers permit us, with our emulation. That will be true respect, that the true affection of thy nearest kin. This, too, is what I would enjoin on daughter and wife, to honour the memory of that father, that husband, by pondering in their hearts all his words and acts, by cherishing the features and lineaments of his character rather than those of his person. It is not that I would forbid the likenesses which are wrought in marble or in bronze; but as the faces of men, so all similitudes of the face are weak and perishable things, while the fashion of the soul is everlasting, such as may be expressed not in some foreign substance, or by the help of art, but in our own lives. Whatever we loved, whatever we admired in Agricola, survives, and will survive in the hearts of men, in the succession of the ages, in the fame that waits on noble deeds. Over many indeed, of those who have gone before, as over the inglorious and ignoble, the waves of oblivion will roll; Agricola, made known to posterity by history and tradition, will live for ever.

from the ANNALS
(translated by Michael Grant)

It will seem fantastic, I know, that in a city where nothing escapes notice or comment, any human beings could have felt themselves so secure. Much more so that, on an appointed day and before invited signatories, a consul designate and the emperor's wife should have been joined together in formal marriage—"for the purpose of rearing children"; that she should have listened to the diviners' words, assumed the wedding-veil, sacrificed to the gods; that the pair should have taken their places at a banquet, embraced, and finally spent the night as man and wife. But I am not inventing marvels. What I have told, and shall tell, is the truth. Older men heard and recorded it.

The imperial household shuddered—especially those in power, with everything to fear from a new emperor. There were secret conferences. Then indignation was unconcealed. "While a ballet-dancing actor violated the emperor's bedroom," they said, "it was humiliating enough. Yet it did not threaten Claudius' life. Here, on the other hand, is a young, handsome, intelligent nobleman, consul-to-be—but with a loftier destiny in mind. For where such a marriage will lead is clear enough." When they thought of Claudius' sluggish uxoriousness, and the many assassinations ordered by Messalina, they were terrified. Yet the emperor's very pliability gave them hope. If they could convince him of the enormity of the outrage, Messalina might be condemned and eliminated without trial. But everything, they felt, turned on this —would Claudius give her a hearing? Could they actually shut his ears against her confession? . . .

Narcissus watched for an opening. Then, as Claudius prolonged his stay at Ostia, he induced the emperor's two favourite mistresses to act as informers. They were persuaded by gifts, promises, and assurances of the increased influence that Messalina's downfall would bring them.

One of the women, Calpurnia (I), secured a private interview with Claudius. Throwing herself at his feet, she cried that Messalina had married Silius—in the same breath asking the other girl, Cleopatra (who was standing by ready), for corroboration: which she provided. Then Calpurnia urged that Narcissus should be summoned. "I must excuse my earlier silences," said Narcissus, "about Vettius Valens, Plautius Lateranus, and the like—and now, too, I do not propose to complain of her adulteries, much less impel you to demand back from Silius your mansion, slaves, and other imperial perquisites. *But do you know you are divorced?* Nation, senate, and army have witnessed her wedding to Silius. Act promptly, or her new husband controls Rome!" . . .

Meanwhile, Messalina was indulging in unprecedented extravagances. It was full autumn; and she was performing in her grounds a mimic grape-harvest. Presses were working, vats overflowing, surrounded by women capering in skins like sacrificing or frenzied Maenads. She herself, hair streaming, brandished a Bacchic wand. Beside her stood Silius in ivy-wreath and buskins, rolling his head, while the disreputable chorus yelled round him. Vettius Valens, the story goes, gaily climbed a great tree. Asked what he saw, his answer was: "A fearful storm over Ostia!" There may have been a storm. Or it may have been a casual phrase. But later it seemed prophetic.

Rumours and messengers now came pouring in. They revealed that Claudius knew all, and was on his way, determined for revenge. So the couple separated . . . But she instantly decided on the course that had often saved her—to meet her husband and let him see her.

She also sent word that Britannicus and Octavia should go and seek their father's embraces. She herself begged the senior priestess of Vesta, Vibidia, to obtain the ear of the emperor as Chief Priest and urge pardon. . . .

Claudius remained strangely silent. Lucius Vitellius looked unaware of the proceedings. The ex-slave, Narcissus, took charge. . . . There, after a preliminary statement by the ex-slave, Claudius addressed the assembled Guard—briefly, for he could hardly express his indignation (just though it was) for shame.

The Guardsmen shouted repeatedly for the offenders to be named and punished. Silius was brought on to the platform. Without attempting defence or postponement, he asked for a quick death. Certain distinguished gentlemen outside the senate showed equal courage. They too desired a speedy end. The execution of accomplices was ordered.

PLINY'S LETTERS

Pliny the Younger corresponded with emperor, citizen, and slave; his letters are a very important source of information about life in the empire. He almost certainly wrote with the idea that his letters would later be published, and so we see a generous man, a successful lawyer, and later, a representative of Trajan, who was also a loving husband and friend. Although his self-portrait may be painted in over-bright colors, in all likelihood Pliny really was a conscientious, solid citizen. And so were some, even many, of the people he characterizes. His letters, often intimate, advisory, or highly descriptive, stand in sharp contrast to the bitter critiques of a decadent society by other writers.

As Trajan's representative in Bithynia, Pliny makes a suggestion to the emperor:

X:54
(translated by Betty Radice)

Thanks to your foresight, Sir, the sums owed to public funds have been paid in under my administration, or are in process of being so; but I am afraid the money may remain uninvested. There is no opportunity, or practically none, of purchasing landed property, and people cannot be found who will borrow from public funds, especially at the rate of twelve per cent, the same rate as for private loans.

Would you consider, Sir, whether you think that the rate of interest should be lowered to attract suitable borrowers, and, if they are still not forthcoming, whether the money might be loaned out amongst the town councillors upon their giving proper security? They may be unwilling to accept it, but it will be less of a burden to them if the rate of interest is reduced.

Pliny writes to his absent wife Calpurnia:

VII:5
(translation by William Melmoth, revised by W. M. L. Hutchinson)

It is incredible how I miss you; such is the tenderness of my affection for you, and so unaccustomed are we to a separation! I lie awake the greatest part of the night in conjuring up your image, and by day (to use a very common, but very true expression) my feet carry me of their own accord to your apartment, at those hours I used to visit you; but not finding you there, I return with as much sorrow and disappointment as an excluded lover. The only intermission my torment knows, is when I am engaged at the bar, and in the causes of my friends. Judge how wretched must *his* life be, who finds no repose but in toil, no consolation but in dealing with distress and anxieties. Farewell.

Pliny complies with Tacitus' request for a report of Pliny the Elder's death at Pompeii:

VI:14
(translation by William Melmoth, revised by W. M. L. Hutchinson)

Your request that I would send you an account of my uncle's end, so that you may transmit a more exact relation of it to posterity, deserves my acknowledgements; for if his death shall be celebrated by your pen, the glory of it, I am aware, will be rendered for ever deathless. . . .

He was at that time with the fleet under his command at Misenum. On the twenty-fourth of August, about one in the afternoon, my mother desired him to observe a cloud of very unusual size and appearance. He had sunned himself, then taken a cold bath, and after a leisurely luncheon was engaged in study. He immediately called for his shoes and went up an eminence from whence he might best view this very uncommon appearance. It was not at that distance discernible from what mountain this cloud issued, but it was found afterwards to be Vesuvius. . . .

My uncle . . . deemed the phenomenon important and worth a nearer view. He ordered a light vessel to be got ready. . . Hastening to the place from whence others were flying, he steered his direct course to the point of danger, and with such freedom from fear, as to be able to make and dictate his observations upon the successive motions and figures of that terrific object.

And now cinders, which grew thicker and hotter the nearer he approached, fell into the ships, then pumice-stones too, with stones blackened, scorched, and cracked by fire, then the sea ebbed suddenly from under them, while the shore was blocked up by landslips from the mountains. . . .

In the meanwhile Mount Vesuvius was blazing in several places with spreading and towering flames, whose refulgent brightness the darkness of the night set in high relief. But my uncle, in order to soothe apprehensions, kept saying that some fires had been left alight by the terrified country people, and what they saw were only deserted villas on fire in the abandoned district. After this he retired to rest, and it is most certain that his rest was a most genuine slumber; for his breathing, which, as he was pretty fat, was somewhat heavy and sonorous, was heard by those who attended at his chamber-door. But the court which led to his apartment now lay so deep under a mixture of pumice-stones and ashes, that if he had continued longer in his bedroom, egress would have been impossible. On being aroused, he came out, and returned to Pomponianus and the others, who had sat up all night. . . .

It was now day everywhere else, but there a deeper darkness prevailed than in the most obscure night; relieved, however, by many torches and divers illuminations. They thought proper to go down upon the shore . . . There . . . some unusually gross vapour . . . obstructed his breathing and blocked his windpipe, which was not only naturally weak and constricted, but chronically inflamed. When day dawned again (the third from that he last beheld) his body was found entire and uninjured, and still fully clothed as in life; its posture was that of a sleeping, rather than a dead man.

SENECA, DRAMATIST

*It is thought that Seneca was insane; certainly his life was
enough to unbalance a man. He somehow lived through a very
sickly childhood. As a young man he barely escaped death at the
hand of Caligula. He was sent into exile by Claudius whence he
was recalled by Nero, who not only made Seneca his tutor but
also his unwilling accessory in crime, and finally, his victim.
In his lifetime Seneca was as famous a philosopher as he was a
dramatist; today he is known mainly for the plays which seem to
reflect his milieu. They have little stylistic merit; horror-filled,
blood-thirsty, overblown, laden with purple poesy, they are in-
teresting to us chiefly for their influence on Elizabethan drama.
Here Atreus kills the sons of his brother Thyestes, his rival for
a kingdom, and serves their roasted flesh to the unwitting diner.*

from THYESTES

MESSENGER: . . .   (*translated by Ella Isobel Harris*)

Here raging Atreus entered, dragging in
His brother's sons; the altars were adorned—
Ah, who can tell the tale? The noble youths
Have their hands bound behind them and their brows
Bound with the purple fillet; incense
Is there, and wine to Bacchus consecrate,
And sacrificial knife, and salted meal;
All things are done in order, lest such crime
Should be accomplished without fitting rites. . . .
                                     He is himself
The priest. He sang himself with boisterous lips
The sacrificial song, those given to death
He placed, he took the sword and wielded it;
Nothing was lacking to the sacrifice.
Earth trembled, all the grove bent down its head,
The palace nodded, doubtful where to fling
Its mighty weight, and from the left there shot
A star from heaven, drawing a black train.
The wine poured forth upon the fire was changed
And flowed red blood; the royal diadem
Fell twice, yea thrice . . .
So cruel Atreus gazes on the heads,
Devoted sacrifices to his rage;
He hesitates which one shall first be slain,
And which be immolated afterward;
It matters not and yet he hesitates,
And in the order of his cruel crime
Takes pleasure. . . .
He stood unmoved, no useless prayers were heard.
That cruel one hid in the wound the sword,
Pressing it deep within the victim's neck,
Then drew it forth. The corpse was upright still;
It hesitated long which way to fall,
Then fell against the uncle. Atreus then,
Dragging before the altar Plisthenes,
Hurried him to his brother. With one blow

He cut away the head; the lifeless trunk
Fell prone and with a whispered sound the head
Rolled downward. . . .
The sword with double murder wet, forgets
Whom he attacks; with direful hand he drives
Right through the body and the sword, received
Within the breast, passes straight through the back.
He falls and with his blood puts out the fires;
By double wound he dies. . . .
Would he had kept, would that no grave might hide
The dead, no fire burn them, would the birds
And savage beasts might feast on such sad food!
That which were torment else is wished for here.
Would father's eyes unburied sons might see!
O crime incredible to every age!
O crime which future ages shall deny!
The entrails taken from the living breast
Tremble, the lungs still breathe, the timid heart
Throbs, but he tears its fibre, ponders well
What it foretells and notes its still warm veins.
When he at last has satisfied himself
About the victims, of his brother's feast
He makes secure. The mangled forms he cuts,
And from the trunk he separates the arms
As far as the broad shoulders, savagely
Lays bare the joints and cleaves apart the bones;
The heads he spares and the right hands they gave
In such good faith. He puts the severed limbs
Upon the spits and roasts them by slow fire;
The other parts into the glowing pot
He throws to boil them. From the food the fire
Leaps back, is twice, yea thrice, replaced and forced
At last reluctantly to do its work.
The liver on the spit emits shrill cries,
I cannot tell whether the flesh or flame
Most deeply groaned. The troubled fire smoked,
The smoke itself, a dark and heavy cloud,
Rose not in air nor scattered readily;
The ugly cloud obscured the household gods.
O patient Phoebus, thou hast backward fled
And, breaking off the light of day at noon,
Submerged the day, but thou didst set too late.
The father mangles his own sons, and eats
Flesh of his flesh, with sin-polluted lips;
His locks are wet and shine with glowing oil;
Heavy is he with wine; the morsels stick
Between his lips. Thyestes, this one good
Amid thy evil fortunes still remains:
Thou knowest it not. But this good too shall die.
Let Titan, turning backward on his path,
Lead back his chariot and with darkness hide
This foul new crime, let blackest night arise
At midday, yet the deed must come to light.
All will be manifest.

THE NOVEL CREATOR PETRONIUS

Petronius, who was Nero's arbiter of taste before the emperor demanded his life, "spent his days sleeping, his nights working and enjoying himself," according to Tacitus. The rest of Tacitus' biographical sketch of him depicts a man who was witty and urbane—as befits the author of the Satyricon. *A marvel of satire and ribaldry, this book is valuable to us not only as a prototype of the novel and as a compendium of the manners and speech of the different classes in Rome, but also for the sheer entertainment it offers.*

Petronius' three quixotic heroes attend a banquet given by Trimalchio, one of the nouveaux riches:

from the SATYRICON
(translated by William Arrowsmith)

At last we took our places. Immediately slaves from Alexandria came in and poured ice water over our hands. These were followed by other slaves who knelt at our feet and with extraordinary skill pedicured our toenails. Not for an instant, moreover, during the whole of this odious job, did one of them stop singing. This made me wonder whether the whole menage was given to bursts of song, so I put it to the test by calling for a drink. It was served immediately by a boy who trilled away as shrilly as the rest of them. In fact, anything you asked for was invariably served with a snatch of song, so that you would have thought you were eating in a concert-hall rather than a private dining room.

Now that the guests were all in their places, the *hors d'oeuvres* were served, and very sumptuous they were. Trimalchio alone was still absent, and the place of honor—reserved for the host in the modern fashion—stood empty. But I was speaking of the *hors d'oeuvres*. On a large tray stood a donkey made of rare Corinthian bronze; on the donkey's back were two panniers, one holding green olives, the other, black. Flanking the donkey were two side dishes, both engraved with Trimalchio's name and the weight of the silver, while in dishes shaped to resemble little bridges there were dormice, all dipped in honey and rolled in poppyseed. Nearby, on a silver grill, piping hot, lay small sausages, while beneath the grill black damsons and red pomegranates had been sliced up and arranged so as to give the effect of flames playing over charcoal.

We were nibbling at these splendid appetizers when suddenly the trumpets blared a fanfare and Trimalchio was carried in, propped up on piles of miniature pillows in such a comic way that some of us couldn't resist impolitely smiling. His head, cropped close in a recognizable slave cut, protruded from a cloak of blazing scarlet; his neck, heavily swathed already in bundles of clothing, was wrapped in a large napkin bounded by an incongruous senatorial purple stripe with little tassels dangling down here and there. On the little finger of his left hand he sported an immense gilt ring; the ring on the last joint of his fourth finger looked to be solid gold of the kind the lesser nobility wear, but was actually, I think, an imitation, pricked out with small steel stars. Nor does this exhaust the inventory of his trinkets. At least he rather ostentatiously bared his arm to show us a large gold bracelet and an ivory circlet with a shiny metal plate.

He was picking his teeth with a silver toothpick when he first addressed us. "My friends," he said, "I wasn't anxious to eat just yet, but I've ignored my own wishes so as not to keep you waiting. Still, perhaps you won't mind if I finish my game." At these words a slave jumped forward with a board of juniper wood and a pair of crystal dice. I noticed one other elegant novelty as well: in place of the usual black and white counters, Trimalchio had substituted gold and silver coins. His playing, I might add, was punctuated throughout with all sorts of vulgar exclamations. . . .

Suddenly the orchestra gave another flourish and four slaves came dancing in and whisked off the top of the tray. Underneath, in still another tray, lay fat capons and sowbellies and a hare tricked out with wings to look like a little Pegasus. At the corners of the tray stood four little gravy boats, all shaped like the satyr Marsyas, with phalluses for spouts and a spicy hot gravy dripping down over several large fish swimming about in the lagoon of the tray. The slaves burst out clapping, we clapped too and turned with gusto to these new delights. Trimalchio, enormously pleased with the success of his little *tour de force*, roared for a slave to come and carve. The carver appeared instantly and went to work, thrusting with his knife like a gladiator practicing to the accompaniment of a water-organ. But all the time Trimalchio kept mumbling in a low voice, "Carver, carver, carver carver . . ." I suspected that this chant was somehow connected with a trick, so I asked my neighbor, an old hand at these party surprises. "Look," he said, "you see that slave who's carving? Well, he's called Carver, so every time Trimalchio says 'Carver,' he's also saying 'Carve 'er!' and giving him orders to carve."

This atrocious pun finished me: I couldn't touch a thing. So I turned back to my neighbor to pick up what gossip I could and soon had him blabbing away, especially when I asked him about the woman who was bustling around the room. "Her?" he said, "why, that's Fortunata, Trimalchio's wife. And the name couldn't suit her better. She counts her cash by the cartload. And you know what she used to be? Well, begging your Honor's pardon, but you wouldn't have taken bread from her hand. Now, gods knows how or why, she's sitting pretty: has Trimalchio eating out of her hand. If she told him at noon it was night, he'd crawl into bed. As for him, he's so loaded he doesn't know how much he has. But that bitch has her finger in everything—where you'd least expect it too. A regular tightwad, never drinks, and sharp as they come. But she's got a nasty tongue; get her gossiping on a couch and she'll chatter like a parrot. If she likes you, you're lucky; if she doesn't, god help you.

"As for old Trimalchio, that man's got more farms than a kite could flap over. And there's more silver plate stuffed in his porter's lodge than another man's got in his safe. As for slaves, whoosh! So help me, I'll bet not one in ten has ever seen his master. Your ordinary rich man is just peanuts compared to him; he could knock them all under a cabbage and you'd never know they were gone. . . ."

At this point Trimalchio heaved himself up from his couch and waddled off to the toilet. Once rid of our table tyrant, the talk began to flow more freely. Damas called for larger glasses and led off himself. "What's one day? Bah, nothing at all. You turn round and it's dark. Nothing for it, I say, but jump right from bed to table. Brrrr. Nasty spell of cold weather we've been having. A bath hardly warmed me up. But a hot drink's the best overcoat of all; that's what I always say. Whoosh, I must have guzzled gallons. I'm tight and no mistake. Wine's gone right to my head . . ."

"As for me," Seleucus broke in, "I don't take a bath every day. Your bath's a fuller; the water's got teeth like a comb. Saps your vital juices. But once I've had a slug of mead, then bugger the cold. Couldn't have had a bath today anyway. Had to go to poor old Chrysanthus' funeral. Yup, he's gone for good, folded his tent forever. And a grand little guy he was; they don't make 'em any better these days. I might almost be talking to him now. Just goes to show you. What are men anyway but balloons on legs, a lot of blown-up bladders? Flies, that's what we are. No, not even flies. Flies have something inside. But a man's a bubble, all air, nothing else. And, you know, Chrysanthus might still be with us if he hadn't tried that starvation diet. Five days and not a crumb of bread, not a drop of water, passed his lips. Tch, tch. And now he's gone, joined the great majority. Doctors killed him. Maybe not doctors, call it fate. What good's a doctor but for peace of mind? But the funeral was fine, they did it up proper: nice bier, fancy drapes, and a good bunch of mourners turned out too. Mostly slaves he'd set free, of course. But his old lady was sure stingy with the tears. Not that he didn't lead her a hard life, mind. But women, they're a race of kites. Don't deserve love. You might as well drop it down a well. . . ."

He was beginning to be tiresome and Phileros shouted him down. "Whoa there," he cut in, "let's talk about the living. He got what was coming to him. He lived well, he died well. . . . I knew him for ages, and he was horny, right to the end. By god, I'll bet he even pestered the dog. Boys were what he really liked, but he wasn't choosy: he'd jump anything with legs. I don't blame him a bit, you understand. He won't have any fun where he's gone now." . . .

At this moment an incident occurred on which our little party almost foundered. Among the incoming slaves there was a remarkably pretty boy. Trimalchio literally launched himself upon him and, to Fortunata's extreme annoyance, began to cover him with rather prolonged kisses. Finally, Fortunata asserted her rights and began to abuse him. "You turd!" she shrieked, "you hunk of filth." At last she used the supreme insult: "Dog!" At this Trimalchio exploded with rage, reached for a wine cup and slammed it into her face. Fortunata let out a piercing scream and covered her face with trembling hands as though she'd just lost an eye. Scintilla, stunned and shocked, tried to comfort her sobbing friend in her arms, while a slave solicitously applied a glass of cold water to her livid cheek. Fortunata herself hunched over the glass heaving and sobbing.

But Trimalchio was still shaking with fury. "Doesn't that slut remember what she used to be? By god, I took her off the sale platform and made her an honest woman. But she blows herself up like a bullfrog. She's forgotten how lucky she is. She won't remember the whore she used to be. People in shacks shouldn't dream of palaces, I say. By god, if I don't tame that strutting Cassandra, my name isn't Trimalchio! And to think, sap that I was, that I could have married an heiress worth half a million. And that's no lie. Old Agatho, who sells perfume to the lady next door, slipped me the word: 'Don't let your line die out, old boy,' he said. But not me. Oh no, I was a good little boy, nothing fickle about me. And now I've gone and slammed the axe into my shins good and proper.—But someday, slut, you'll come scratching at my grave to get me back! And just so you understand what you've done, I'll remove your statue from my tomb. That's an order, Habinnas. No sir, I don't want any more domestic squabbles in my grave. And what's more, just to show her I can dish it out too, I won't have her kissing me on my deathbed." . . .

The whole business had by now become absolutely revolting. Trimalchio was obviously completely drunk, but suddenly he had a hankering for funeral music too and ordered a brass band sent into the dining room. Then he propped himself on piles of cushions and stretched out full length along the couch. "Pretend I'm dead," he said, "say something nice about me." The band blared a dead march, but one of the slaves belonging to Habinnas—who was, incidentally, one of the most respectable people present—blew so loudly that he woke up the entire neighborhood. Immediately the firemen assigned to that quarter of town, thinking that Trimalchio's house was on fire, smashed down the door and rushed in with buckets and axes to do their job. Utter confusion followed, of course, and we took advantage of the heaven-sent opportunity, gave Agamemnon the slip, and rushed out of there as though the place were really in flames.

SUETONIUS, IMPERIAL BIOGRAPHER

One critic says of Suetonius (c. A.D. 69–c. 140) that he was "a recorder, not a moralist." It seems to be true that he preferred to pile up material rather than to select from it. Consequently he preserved valuable records, for as Hadrian's secretary he had access to files that other historians, even Tacitus, had not seen. Although his lack of selectivity makes his writing gossipy and anecdotal, in many respects it also makes for lively historical reading. De vita Caesarum (The Twelve Caesars), which contains biographies of the emperors from Julius Caesar to Domitian, is the most complete work left of Suetonius' prolific output.

from THE TWELVE CAESARS
(translated by Robert Graves)

Nero was born at Antium on 15 December 37 A.D., nine months after Tiberius' death. The sun was rising and his earliest rays touched the newly-born boy almost before he could be laid on the ground, as the custom was, for his father either to acknowledge or disavow. Nero's horiscope at once occasioned many ominous predictions; and a significant comment was made by his father in reply to friendly congratulations: namely, that any child born to himself and Agrippina was bound to have a detestable nature and become a public danger. . . .

He had reached the age of seventeen when Cladius' death occurred, and presented himself to the Palace Guard that day between the sixth and seventh hours—ugly omens having ruled out an earlier appearance. After being acclaimed Emperor on the Palace steps, he was taken in a litter to the Guards' Camp, where he briefly addressed the troops. He then visited the Senate House, where he remained until nightfall, refusing only one of the many high honours voted him, namely the title "Father of the Country," and this because of his youth.

Nero started off with a parade of virtue . . . On the day of his accession the password he gave to the colonel on duty was "The Best of Mothers"; and she and he often rode out together through the streets in her litter. Nero founded a colony at Antium consisting of Guards veterans, augmented by a group of rich retired centurions, whom he forced to move there; and also built them a harbour at great expense. . . .

He gave an immense variety of entertainments—coming-of-age parties, chariot races in the Circus, stage plays, a gladiatorial show—persuading even old men of consular rank, and old ladies, too, to attend the coming-of-age parties. He reserved seats for the knights at the Circus, as he had done in the Theatre; and actually raced four-camel chariots! . . .

During his reign a great many public abuses were suppressed by the imposition of heavy penalties . . . Punishments were also inflicted on the Christians, a sect professing a new and mischievous religious belief; and Nero ended the licence which the charioteers had so long enjoyed that they claimed it as a right: to wander merrily down the streets, swindling and robbing the populace. He likewise expelled from the City all pantomime actors and their hangers on. . . .

Nero probably felt no ambition to extend the Roman Empire, and even considered withdrawing his forces from Britain; yet kept them there because such a decision might have reflected on the glory won by his adopted father Claudius. The sole additions made during his reign to the list of Imperial provinces were the Kingdom of Pontus, ceded to him by Polemon; and that of the Cottian Alps which, on the death of Cottius, reverted to Rome. . . .

I have separated this catalogue of Nero's less atrocious acts—some forgiveable, some even praiseworthy—from the others; but I must begin to list his follies and crimes. . . .

Though his voice was still feeble and husky, he was pleased enough with his progress [singing and playing the lyre] to nurse theatrical ambitions . . . No one was allowed to leave the theatre during his recitals, however pressing the reason, and the gates were kept barred. We read of women in the audience giving birth, and of men being so bored with the music and the applause that they furtively dropped down from the wall at the rear, or shammed dead and were carried away for burial. . . .

Gradually Nero's vices gained the upper hand: he no longer tried to laugh them off, or hide, or deny them, but turned quite brazen. His feasts now lasted from noon till midnight, with an occasional break for diving into a warm bath or, if it were summer, into snow-cooled water. Sometimes he would drain the artificial lake in the Campus Martius, or the other in the Circus, and hold public dinner parties there, including prostitutes and dancing-girls from all over the City among his guests. Whenever he floated down the Tiber to Ostia, or cruised past Baiae, he had a row of temporary brothels erected along the shore, where a number of noblewomen, pretending to be madams, stood waiting to solicit his custom. . . .

Not satisfied with seducing free-born boys and married women, Nero raped the Vestal Virgin Rubria. . . . Having tried to turn the boy Sporus into a girl by castration, he went through a wedding ceremony with him—dowry, bridal veil and all—which the whole Court attended; then brought him home, and treated him as a wife. He dressed Sporus in fine clothes normally worn by an Empress and took him in his own litter not only to every Greek assize and fair, but actually through the Street of Images at Rome, kissing him amorously now and then. A rather amusing joke is still going the rounds: the world would have been a happier place had Nero's father Domitius married that sort of wife.

The passion he felt for his mother, Agrippina, was notorious; but her enemies would not let him consummate it, fearing that, if he did, she would become even more powerful and ruthless than hitherto. So he found a new mistress who was said to be her spit and image . . .

He believed that fortunes were made to be squandered, and whoever could account for every penny he spent seemed to him a stingy miser. "True gentlemen," he said "always throw their money about." . . .

Nero found himself bankrupt—and financial difficulties were such that he could not lay hands on enough money . . . and therefore resorted to robbery and blackmail. . . .

He tried to poison Britannicus, being not merely jealous of his voice, which was far more musical than his own, but afraid that the common people might be less attached to Cladius' adopted son than to his real one. The drug came from an expert poisoner named Locusta, and when its action was not so rapid as he expected—the effect was violently laxative—he called for her, complaining that she had given him medicine instead of poison, and flogged her with his own hands. Locusta explained that she had reduced the dose to make the crime less obvious. "Oho!" he said. "So you think I am afraid of the Julian law against poisoning?" Then he led Locusta into his bedroom and stood over her while she concocted the fastest-working poison in her pharmacopoeia. This he administered to a kid, but when it took five hours to die he made her boil down the brew again and again. At last he tried it on a pig, which died on the spot; and that night at dinner had what remained poured into Britannicus' cup. . . .

The over-watchful, over-critical eye that Agrippina kept on whatever Nero said or did proved more than he could stand. . . . He tried to poison her three times, but she had always taken the antidote in advance; so he rigged up a machine in the ceiling of her bedroom which would dislodge the panels and drop them on her while she slept. However, someone gave the secret away. Then he had a collapsible cabin-boat designed which would either sink or fall in on top of her. . . he protracted the [a] feast until a late hour, and when at last she said: "I really must get back to Baiae," offered her his collapsible boat instead of the damaged galley. Nero was in a very happy mood as he led Agrippina down to the quay, and even kissed her breasts before she stepped aboard. He sat up all night, on tenterhooks of anxiety, waiting for news of her death. At dawn Lucius Agermus, her freedman, entered joyfully to report that although the ship had foundered, his mother had swum to safety, and he need have no fears on her account. . . . After this he arranged for Agrippina to be killed, and made it seem as if she had sent Agermus to assassinate him but committed suicide on hearing that the plot had miscarried. Other more gruesome details are supplied by reliable authorities: it appears that Nero rushed off to examine Agrippina's corpse, handling her legs and arms critically and, between drinks, discussing their good and bad points. . . .

Life with Octavia had soon bored him, and when his friends criticized his treatment of her, he retorted: "Being an emperor's wife ought surely to be enough to make her happy?" He tried to strangle her on several occasions. . . Though he doted on Poppaea . . . he kicked her to death while she was pregnant and feeling very ill, because she dared to complain that he came home late from the races. . . . There was no family relationship which Nero did not criminally abuse. . . .

Nero was no less cruel to strangers than to members of his family. A comet, popularly supposed to herald the death of some person of outstanding importance, appeared several nights running and greatly disturbed him. His astrologer Balbillus observed that monarchs usually avoided portents of this kind by executing their most prominent subjects and thus directing the wrath of heaven elsewhere; so Nero resolved on a wholesale massacre of the nobility. What fortified him in this decision, and seemed to justify it, was that he had discovered two plots against his life. The earlier and more important one of the two was Piso's conspiracy in Rome; the other, detected at Beneventum, had been headed by Vinicius. When brought up for trial the conspirators were loaded with three sets of chains. Some, while admitting their guilt, claimed that by destroying a man so thoroughly steeped in evil as Nero, they would have been doing him the greatest possible service. All children of the condemned men were banished from Rome, and then starved to death or poisoned. . . .

Nero showed no greater mercy to the common folk, or to the very walls of Rome. Once, in the course of a general conversation, someone quoted the line: "When I am dead, may fire consume the earth," but Nero said that the first part of the line should read: "While I yet live," and soon converted this fancy into fact. Pretending to be disgusted by the drab old buildings and narrow, winding streets of Rome, he brazenly set fire to the City; and though a group of ex-consuls caught his attendants, armed with oakum and blazing torches, trespassing on their property, they dared not interfere. He also coveted the sites of several granaries, solidly built in stone, near the Golden House; having knocked down their walls with siege-engines, he set the interiors ablaze. This terror lasted for six days and seven nights, causing many people to take shelter in the tombs. Nero's men destroyed not only a vast number of tenements, but mansions which had belonged to famous generals and were still decorated with their triumphal trophies; temples, too, dating back to the time of the kingship, and others dedicated during the Punic and Gallic wars —in fact, every ancient monument of historical interest that had hitherto survived. Nero watched the conflagration from the Tower of Maecenas, enraptured by what he called "the beauty of the flames"; then put on his tragedian's costume and sang *The Fall of Ilium* from beginning to end. He offered to remove corpses and rubble free of charge, but allowed nobody to search among the ruins even of his own mansion; he wanted to collect as much loot as possible himself. Then he opened a Fire Relief Fund and insisted on contributions, which bled the provincials white and practically beggared all private citizens. . . .

At last after nearly fourteen years of Nero's misrule, the earth rid herself of him.

MARTIAL, VERSIFIER

Unlike his friend Juvenal, whose work does not seem to have been popular in Rome, Martial (c. A.D. 40–c. 104) became a famous poet and remained so even after he retired to his native Spain. Martial perfected the epigram, the short pithy poem whose last line snaps ferociously at its victim. But he had other moods too; in his Epigrams *there are verses ranging from the obsequious to the obscene and from the sweet to the scathing. Altogether his poems give us a unique view of Roman society.*

I:10
(translated by J. A. Pott)

It is very strange, as it seems to me,
That you and your wife should not agree,
Since each is as vile as vile can be.

I:28
(translated by J. Wight Duff)

'Tis said Acerra reeks of last night's wine:
'Tis false: he always drinks till morning-shine.

II:59
(translated by Robert Louis Stevenson)

Look around: you see a little supper room;
But from my window, lo! great Caesar's tomb!
And the great dead themselves, with jovial breath
Bid you be merry and remember death.

V:10
(translated by F. A. Wright)

"Fame comes not to the living. Strange!" you say,
"How few can love the artists of their day!"
The cause is this, that envy's cross-eyed view
Will always set the old above the new.
Thus haunt we Pompey's ancient porch—and thus
Fools praise the crumbled fanes of Catulus.
So Virgil's Rome pored still o'er Ennius' page,
And Homer lived unhonoured of his age;
Few were his peers to laud Menander's plays;
Who save Corinna knew her Ovid's lays?
Yet soft, my books, no haste, nor hurry fate;
If fame must wait on death, then let it wait.

VIII:16
(translated by Rolfe Humphries)

A baker, once, Cyperus, now
You are a counsellor, and how!
That you are prosperous is clear
From your ten thousand bucks a year,
But—here today and gone tomorrow!—
You're constantly compelled to borrow.
Your old profession, as we know,
You don't forsake, still needing dough.

VIII:43
(translated by J. Wight Duff)

Fabius buries all his wives:
Chrestilla ends her husbands' lives.
The torch, which from the marriage-bed
They brandish, soon attends the dead.
O Venus, link this conquering pair!
Their match will meet with issue fair,
Whereby for such a dangerous *two*
A single funeral will do.

VI:12
(translated by Sir John Harington)

The golden hair that Galla wears
    Is hers: who would have thought it?
She swears 'tis hers, and true she swears,
    For I know where she bought it.

X:61
(translated by Leigh Hunt)

Underneath this greedy stone,
Lies little sweet Erotion;
Whom the Fates, with hearts as cold,
Nipp'd away at six years old.
Thou, whoever thou mayst be,
That hast this small field after me,
Let the yearly rites be paid
To her little slender shade;
So shall no disease or jar
Hurt thy house, or chill thy Lar;
But this tomb be here alone
The only melancholy stone.

X:65
(translated by James Cranstoun)

To boast, Charmenion, is your practice
That you're from Corinth—now, the fact is
Disputed not by one or other—
But why, for heaven's sake, call me Brother—
Me, born in Celteberia's land,
A citizen from Tagus' strand?
Say, is't that everybody traces
A wondrous likeness in our faces?
You walk with sleek and flowing hair,
While my rough Spanish crop I wear;
Your polished skin of pumice speaks,
While I have hairy limbs and cheeks;
You lisp—your tongue's so plaguy weak,
My infant child could louder speak:
Are doves like eagles, prithee tell,
Or like strong lion lithe gazelle?
From saying Brother then desist, or,
Charmenion, I may call you Sister.

Flaminian Gate

Salarian Gate

Pincian Gate

Nomentan Gate

PRAETORIAN CAMP

FLAMINIAN WAY

NOMENTAN WAY

SERVIAN WALL

WALL OF AURELIAN

TOMB OF AUGUSTUS

MAUSOLEUM OF HADRIAN

Aelian Bridge

BATHS OF DIOCLETIAN

Tiburtine Gate

Bridge of Nero

CAMPUS MARTIUS

ARA PACIS

COLUMN OF MARCUS AURELIUS

BATHS OF NERO

BATHS OF CONSTANTINE

ARCH OF DIOCLETIAN

PRAENESTINE WAY

STADIUM OF DOMITIAN

TEMPLE OF HADRIAN

PANTHEON

THEATRE OF POMPEY

BATHS OF AGRIPPA

CIRCUS FLAMINIUS

IMPERIAL FORUMS

PORTICO OF LIVIA

BATHS OF TRAJAN

Bridge of Agrippa

TEMPLE OF APOLLO

TEMPLE OF JUPITER

TEMPLE OF VENUS AND ROMA

Praenestine Gate

THEATRE OF MARCELLUS

ROMAN FORUM

COLOSSEUM

Aurelian Bridge

Aemilian Bridge

ARCH OF TITUS

ARCH OF CONSTANTINE

Aurelian Gate

AURELIAN WAY

Bridge of Cestius

FORUM BOARIUM

PORTICO AND TEMPLE OF CLAUDIUS

Asinarian Gate

Bridge of Probus

IMPERIAL PALACE

CIRCUS MAXIMUS

APPIAN WAY

The Tiber

BATHS OF DECIUS

ROME, FOURTH CENTURY A.D.

GRANARIES OF GALBA

BATHS OF CARACALLA

Latin Gate

Ostian Gate

LATIN WAY

Appian Gate

TEMPLE OF TRAJAN

BASILICA ULPIA

COLUMN OF TRAJAN

THE FORUMS OF ROME

FORUM OF TRAJAN

FORUM OF AUGUSTUS

TEMPLE OF MARS

FORUM OF NERVA

FORUM OF JULIUS CAESAR

TEMPLE OF CONCORD

CURIA

FORUM OF PEACE

BASILICA AEMILIA

TEMPLE OF SATURN

ROMAN FORUM

LIBRARY

BASILICA OF CONSTANTINE

BASILICA JULIA

SACRED WAY

TEMPLE OF VESTA

THE IMPERIAL CITY

The citizens who celebrated Rome's thousandth anniversary in A.D. 248 may have believed that the city that "wasn't built in a day" would never be completed. The imperial capital had spread far beyond its ancient Servian Wall and had not yet seen the end of ambitious construction programs initiated by emperors determined to erect ever more opulent forums, monuments, and public buildings. Within another hundred years, however, such grandiose projects were to end. Some Romans may have felt a premonition when Aurelian decided to surround their suddenly vulnerable city with a new defensive wall.

XI

THE LONG TWILIGHT

The year A.D. 248 saw a great festival in Rome, celebrated with pomp, majestic rites, and games. It had been a thousand years from the time, according to tradition, that the city was founded, and the Romans gathered to honor their millennium. In that time they had accomplished unprecedented feats of growth and survival. Despite all the strife and misfortunes of the preceding century, their capital city stood at the peak of imperial grandeur, vastly enriched since the time of Caesar and Augustus with palaces, baths, gardens, monuments, theatres, thoroughfares, and the looming Colosseum. Despite political and social upheavals, many institutions had survived: the Roman Forum was still the center of daily politics, trade, and administration of law; the hereditary Senate still went through its motions of debate; temples were still thronged with adherents of the state religion. The idea of an eternal nation had deeply entered the Roman mind: on the coins of the boy emperor Gordian, minted not long before the anniversary, stood the words AETERNITAS AUGUSTI. Yet everywhere there were signs of change—and no single one was more significant, perhaps, than that the emperor who presided over the celebration was an Arab chieftain's son who had taken a Christian wife.

Rome had Romanized the world, yet it had lost much of its old identity as non-Romans swarmed in to dilute it. The capital had become the greatest melting pot of antiquity, peopled with swarthy Arabs and Syrians, olive-skinned Berbers, fair-haired Gauls, bearded Dacians from beyond the Danube, and long-haired Scythians from remote regions of southern Russia who congregated in the streets, where the emperor—an Arab like Philip or an Illyrian like his successor Decius—passed in state. Greek merchants were everywhere, and the tonsured priests of Isis, in their immaculate white robes, were seen along with Jewish followers of Christ. So many races crowded into Rome that one might have been hard put to find a Roman face in a given assembly.

As Rome became more mixed it also became more divided. Senators holding military commands sometimes sought the throne for themselves, in opposition to generals raised in the provinces. The imperial bureaucracy, increasingly militarized, became, like the armies themselves, increasingly composed of foreign elements. To strengthen their structure of rule, emperors resorted heavily to the device of requiring members of local aristocracies to act, in effect, as agents of the throne in their communities. Such leading citizens, who were known as *curiales*, were obliged to take on unpaid duties of collecting taxes and cultivating state land; and although such responsibilities could be borne by the rich, they became extremely burdensome on those who were not and who had to sell out and sink to a lower class in the event that they could not meet their obligation. The result was more hostility between classes and more uncertainty in relations between the metropolis and the provinces.

Groups of businessmen—such as shipowners and suppliers of vital products—had been brought together into trade associations and assured of government contracts and profits in exchange for required services. But the demands of a financially and politically unstable state made these benefits increasingly questionable. In the second half of the century many men evidently wanted to leave these associations or corporations; this we know because under the soldier-emperors a process began of requiring them and their heirs to remain within and to put up their landed property as surety for their performance. Such a scheme (a prototype, it has been remarked, for the "corporative state" to be set up on the same parent soil by Mussolini) was a major departure from the older Roman encouragement of independent, private ventures.

Always there were the vast armies posted along the frontiers. They were made greater in importance both by the multiplying barbarian incursions and by their own proven ability to raise their generals to the imperial throne. The logistics of defense had demanded that the frontier armies be recruited locally; every army saw itself as a kingmaker, entitled to the *donativa* that traditionally accompanied the march on Rome and the elevation of a new ruler. The center of Rome's power lay at the mercy of the circumference. Between A.D. 235 and 260, in a time of almost constant civil wars, there were twelve emperors; by 284 another four had come to power. In the West, under the emperor Gallienus, a governor of Gaul named Postumus set up a regional empire of his own, with headquarters at Augusta Treverorum, complete with a senate, a bureaucracy, and several mints; and for over a decade Gaul and to some extent Britain and Spain were ruled not from Rome, but by a usurper from the banks of the Moselle. In the East, a noble named Odenathus, of the Syrian frontier city of Palmyra, proclaimed himself an independent king, and several years later his remarkable widow Zenobia managed to seize not only Syria and most of Asia Minor but Egypt as well, where she briefly established an openly rebellious regime.

Meanwhile the rapid spread of individual conversions to Christianity was causing mounting concern in Rome. Except for brief outbursts of persecution, emperors in the second century A.D. had been inclined toward a policy of toleration: the Christians were only one of many sects worshiping their strange gods here and there in the empire and seemed to pose no danger to the state. But

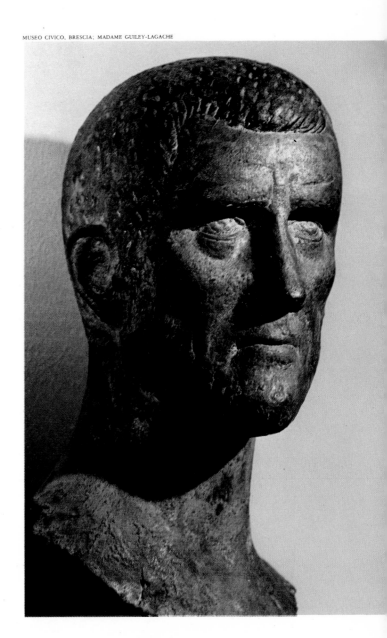

During the turbulent second half of the third century A.D. *many military men were raised to the throne by their legions to live only a few years before being replaced. One of these was Probus (above), who survived almost six years. Diocletian was the first whose reign spanned more than a decade.*

by the middle of the third century the new faith was making serious inroads among the upper classes no less than the lower, bringing with it the specter of wide disaffection. The refusal of Christians to join, even for form's sake, in the loyalty ceremonies of the state religion was thought damaging to public morale. The obloquy that fervid Christian converts poured upon the traditional gods of Rome—often dismissing them not only as false gods but as evil demons—seemed highly impious and a grave offense against propriety. There were many citizens in capital and countryside, shaken by continuing civil wars, mounting barbarian invasions, general disorder, and by a plague, who felt that the old gods were angered at Rome and were intent on bringing disaster down upon it. Put down the offending Christians and the curse might be lifted.

They were put down, only to increase in stature and presence by their courage under persecution. Eventually emperors would see in the Christians a creative rather than just another disruptive force in the state. But before that, strong rulers had to arise to seek to reconstitute the all but sundered empire. An Aurelian or a Diocletian was needed to prepare the way for Constantine. That Rome, with its diluted blood, its disasters, and its declining authority, was still able to provide such men was testimony to its traditions and its stamina.

Marcus Julius Philippus, or Philip the Arab as he was called, ruled from the year A.D. 244 to 249 and was a figure of brief promise in a time of decay. Rising from the post of provincial military commander, like many of his predecessors, he appears to have impressed Romans with his fine-drawn features and his bearing like that of an Arab aristocrat of the desert. (The fact of his marriage to a Christian, coupled with stories of his lack of interest in the pagan rites that marked the millennial exercises of A.D. 248, was to cause Christian commentators to argue that he was, in fact, the first Christian emperor of Rome—a claim not otherwise supported.) We know little about his mind or motives other than that he appears to have been a man who acted with firmness and dispatch amid danger. When Goths came streaming into and across the Balkans he appointed his favorite general Decius, a native of Pannonia, north of the Adriatic, to lead a Danubian army against them. It is said that the two men were friends of long standing and that Decius questioned whether he was the right man to lead the expedition, for he was popular with the army, and the frontier troops might do what they had done before: they might offer him the empire, and then, instead of fighting the Goths, they might march on Rome. Yet Philip took the risk and sent his popular

By A.D. *250 a number of barbarian tribes were attacking borders throughout the empire, and two formidable enemies had risen to threaten the power of Rome. The Goths were making inroads in Asia Minor, Greece, and the Danube area. Although they were subdued temporarily by Claudius Gothicus in 268, they remained a continual harassment to Rome. The other terrible foe was Persia. One of Rome's most humiliating moments is depicted on the Persian relief above: Valerian, the first Roman emperor to be captured, kneels before King Shapur I.*

general against the invaders—and soon afterward Philip himself died in battle at Verona, perhaps betrayed by Decius, who thereupon became emperor.

Coming to the throne a few months before mid-century, Decius was the first of a line of Illyrian rulers of little culture but of soldierly vigor, and under the best of them Rome's house was gradually restored to order. Though connected on his mother's side with an old Italian family, he was himself of provincial peasant background. He had a peasant's heavy, commonplace features, but his mind moved with shrewdness and clarity. In part a stranger to Rome and its traditions, he nevertheless set out to restore the older ways of the empire in the interest of its survival. He recognized the damage done by the unbridled military and felt that the civil authority must be upheld at all costs. Thus he set up a special financial office with broad civic powers, reminiscent of that of censor, and assigned it to a certain Valerian, a senator who had risen to become *senatus princeps*. Moreover, Decius was determined to compel the loyalty of all inhabitants to the state and its religion, and he took the occasion of a general sacrifice and libation to the gods in every village and city of the empire as the means of achieving this. All persons were required by decree to participate in the sacrifices and to procure from special boards of inspection certificates testifying that they had obeyed the order and that they had also made such sacrifices in the past. Those who disobeyed the order were subject to penalties leading up to that of death. Under such proscription and the use of torture the bravest of Christians still refused to forsake their convictions.

Finally, in Decius' design for order, there had to be war to the death against the Goths, those formidable invaders who were breaking down Danubian frontiers and threatening Rome's great military roads to Greece and the Near East. He himself led his legions against them, blunting their power, only to die in battle.

Before the revival that Decius sought was to come, perhaps the lowest point of Roman cohesion and prestige was reached under his successor Valerian, who found the problems confronting him all but insuperable. Barbarians on almost all the frontiers attacked simultaneously, as if by a concerted plan. Goths poured into Dacia, overran the Balkan peninsula, and plundered Roman outposts along the Black Sea's southern shore; the Alamanni appeared in force on the Po plain; in A.D. 253, the first year of Valerian's reign, Franks surged across Gaul and into Spain. So beset, the elderly emperor decided to divide rule of the empire, his son Gallienus taking charge in the West while he himself commanded the threatened East. Apart from its admission of weakness at the center, this move was an indication—more were shortly to come— of the degree to which emperors saw Rome's center of gravity moving eastward. The Persian threat was constantly growing; Palmyra was breaking away. Meanwhile the prevalence of plague in Italy was decimating the Roman population.

While making his division, though, Valerian continued to follow a policy of general attack on the Christians throughout the empire. Many had bowed to Decius' decree and paid their respects to the old Roman gods. This was not enough: they were now to be made to abjure their faith under penalty of having their goods confiscated, their places of worship shut, and their priests deported if they did not recant. The new persecutions lasted only a short time, however, for in A.D. 260, when leading an expedition against the Persian ruler Shapur I, Valerian fell into a military trap and was captured. For the first time a Roman emperor was forced to kneel in abject surrender to a foreign king. The Persians relished and exploited this humiliation, and their artists depicted him in the attitude of a man pleading for his life (see illustration on pages 340–41). "Through all his remaining years," says the historian Orosius, "Valerian was compelled to perform the menial service of helping the king to mount his horse, not in the usual way, by giving his hand, but by bending to the ground and offering his back." After so many Roman triumphs, this was exquisite retribution.

Under the rule of Valerian's son Gallienus, the fate of both the Christians and the empire itself changed for the better. In place of persecution, Christians were accorded an edict of toleration. A conservative man of intellect, who wrote poetry and liked to have philosophers around him, Gallienus felt that the best way of meeting the Christian incursion was not by making martyrs but by reinvigorating the cultural pursuits and values of pagan Rome. He befriended the thinker Plotinus, possibly an Egyptian by birth and distinctly Greek in schooling, who had come to Rome to teach a philosophy derived distantly from Plato's. Plotinus had gathered many followers about him as he set forth his doctrine that the search for truth or reality behind appearance would lead, step by step, toward a recognition of a spiritual "One" beyond all physical things, and to communion with that supreme force. Such a teaching, with its emphasis on quest and mystical union, exerted great challenge in a jaded and sundered society; it embodied perhaps something of the same impulse that had made many Romans and provincials turn to Christ.

At one time Gallienus lent support to a scheme of Plotinus' to found a Platonic community on the site of a ruined Pythagorean settlement in the Campania. Perhaps as an instance of his desire to fuse the best of Roman and Greek traditions, he had himself elected an archon of Athens—a once-powerful office that survived only as a local ceremonial one, but the very name of which conjured up memories of Athenian greatness. His interest appears to have been centered on peace at home and abroad: Gibbon writes that Gallienus married a daughter of one of the Germanic tribal chiefs as a means of achieving it, and other chroniclers record that he married a Christian woman and that he had coins struck bearing the inscription UBIQUE PAX.

There was, however, little peace in his reign, which ended in A.D. 268. Would-be usurpers arose on every hand to threaten his power; he managed to put down no less than eighteen. All the peoples along the frontiers were in revolt. Under Germanic pressure he had to evacuate part of Gaul, but by wise concentration of forces he saved Italy from being overrun. In A.D. 267 he won a major victory over the Goths in his ancestral Illyria, but was killed shortly thereafter by his own staff, possibly at the instigation of one of his generals, the Illyrian Claudius, who succeeded him.

If Gallienus had an intellectual temperament, Claudius was the pure soldier whose only aim was to reach out at the enemy's throat. He fought the Alamanni at Garda Lake and then marched into the Balkans to rout a horde of Gothic and related invaders, some three hundred twenty thousand of whom, with their women and children, had poured over the frontier, not only to conquer but to settle. He crushed them in Serbia after writing to the Senate a letter in which he described the odds against him: "If I conquer, your gratitude will be the reward of my services. If I fail, remember that I am the successor of Gallienus. The whole state is exhausted and worn to the bone. We lack javelins, spears, and shields. We shall perform greatly." Claudius, who took the title of Gothicus after his victory, spoke in accents reminiscent of the consuls of the ancient republic. Hardheaded and single-minded, he not only routed the Goths but eliminated them as a serious threat to the empire for more than a hundred years.

His successor, Aurelian, was to call himself *restitutor orbis*, meaning that he had restored the empire. But the claim could be made more properly of Claudius, who in his brief three years of rule before his tragic death by the plague in 270 had perhaps saved Rome from extinction.

Still, despite the defeat of the Goths, Rome remained vulnerable. Aurelian saw that only a determined and continuing policy of containment could stem the flood. He had to withdraw his far-flung forces to the near, or the south, side of the Danube, but on

One of Aurelian's enemies was Zenobia (above), queen of Palmyra. He accepted her take-over of Egypt, Syria, and much of Asia Minor, but when she named her son to the position of augustus, he destroyed Palmyra as a power and made her a prisoner of his triumph, to be held in Rome for life.
LEONARD VON MATT

343

the other hand he stood off an incursion by Alamanni and others in the Po plains and recovered the lost areas of Gaul. In the East Queen Zenobia had carved out for herself an empire that extended from her capital, in Palmyra, into Egypt; Aurelian had conquered her armies and led her through the streets of Rome. Chroniclers report that there had never been such a dazzling triumphal procession in Roman memory: the queen walked in golden chains before the triumphator's chariot, and there was also a chariot led by the royal stags captured from the king of the Goths. Such spectacles were rare in those days when the fear of invasion had led the Romans to build new walls around their city.

Save for Gallienus, almost all the generals who succeeded one another on the throne were men of remarkably similar stamp. As we see them on their coins, they might be thought of as being brothers. There is little nobility in those heavy, determined, rather sullen faces; they were men of the camp, with hard features and set jaws, lean and often hungry. Few of them possessed personal magnetism; they were harsh disciplinarians who treated their soldiers like cattle, and were in turn brutally disposed of.

Aurelian was murdered; so was Probus, his best and most loyal general, who came to the throne after the brief reign of an elderly senator, Tacitus, who claimed to be descended from the historian of that name. Probus was another Illyrian, hardy and well built, with a talent for strategy and a quality of ruthless determination. Yet his coins and a portrait bust (see illustration on page 339) show him to be another rare exception, a man of sensitivity. He went so far as to speak of a time when there would be no more need for soldiers. "Soon perhaps," he said, "the barbarians will be driven back and there will be no need for an army. There will be no more requisitions in the provinces, no demands for compulsory payments, and the Roman people will possess unfailing revenues. There will be no camps, no sound of trumpets, no fashioning of armaments, and the people will be free to follow the plow and do their own work, learn their own crafts, and sail the seas."

There were few emperors who dreamed of so idyllic a future, but there is little doubt that he was reflecting the common hopes and longings of many of his people. The idea of universal peace, which had haunted the Romans since the days of Numa, was revived during the last years of the third century, becoming all the more appealing the more distant it seemed to be. Probus, however, was fortunate. A brief period of peace descended on Italy during his short reign—the quietest in the later history of the empire.

Everything we know about him suggests he was a man who might have been a great emperor had he lived long enough. He

A third-century A.D. *tomb relief depicts a banker with two of Rome's poor. During that period the empire's economic system decayed badly. Terroristic tax collections that reduced patricians and rich equites to poverty failed to fill the treasury; they only enriched the greediest soldiers and financial agents.*

PALAZZO MASSIMI, ROME; GERMAN ARCHAEOLOGICAL INSTITUTE

treated the senators with respect, permitting them to retain the rights granted them by Augustus. He treated the soldiers without severity and preferred to see them performing useful work rather than fighting. He was on his way to Persia at the head of his army when he decided to stop at his native city of Sirmium, in the Balkans, and he set his soldiers to draining the marshes and building a canal. There, while overseeing their work, he was assaulted by some soldiers opposed to doing it, and was killed. Afterward the army built an enormous tumulus to him and carved on it an inscription testifying to its respect: "Here lies the emperor Probus, a man of probity, conqueror of all the barbarian nations, and victor over tyrants." Such a man illuminated a dark age. Of few emperors would so much be said in so few words.

Two years later, in A.D. 284, there came to the throne a man who seemed to many to be a reincarnation of the great Caesars. The origins of Diocletian are obscure; all that is known is that he was a Dalmatian, and it was said that his father was a freedman bearing the Greek name Diokles. His rise, like that of his predecessors, was due to his military skills, and when he was acclaimed emperor by his troops at Nicomedia, near the Bosporus, there were perhaps few people in Rome who expected him to survive for more than a short time before a new mutiny or palace revolution overtook him in the familiar fashion. However, he accomplished the extraordinary feat of staying safely on the throne for twenty-one years and then retiring at his own volition to relax in the splendid palace he had built for himself in his Dalmatian homeland.

In this, as in all the other elements of his rule, Diocletian was a highly original person. He was the most absolute of monarchs. He surrounded himself with the aura of the representative on earth of Jupiter Optimus Maximus and required (according to the historian Aurelius Victor) that persons appearing in his presence afford him the obeisance, or *adoratio*, due to a god. On the other hand, aware of the difficulties of one-man rule of the empire, he appointed a favorite soldier-in-arms, Maximian, as co-emperor to rule in the West, while he himself ruled in the East, moving his headquarters to Nicomedia and only rarely visiting Rome.

Although virtually dividing the empire, he was no less great an administrator than an innovator. In A.D. 301 he published his edict concerning maximum prices and wages that was intended to put an end to the spiraling increase in the cost of living. At the same time he reformed the coinage and introduced a fixed relationship between the worth of the coin and its metal content. He established a new system of taxation, uniform for all the provinces and based on the value of the land, and saw to it that the tax gatherers

In order to mitigate the instability of the economy and administration, in A.D. 293 Diocletian divided the rule of the empire. Constantius Chlorus, father of Constantine the Great, was chosen as caesar in the West and set off immediately to recapture Britain. His success is commemorated on the medal above.
STUDIO DRANCOURT, ARRAS, FRANCE

345

produced correct accounts. By reorganizing the financial basis of the empire he put an end to the financial anarchy that had been sapping the energies of the people.

He did much else: he reorganized the army and the bureaucracy, abolished the secret police, dealt with revolts in Britain and Egypt, and defeated the Persians and brought the upper Tigris valley under Roman rule. Even so, there was no escaping the necessity of the empire's division. Constitutionally, when he gave his co-ruler Maximian the title of augustus in A.D. 286, he endowed him with powers equal to his own—though in practice he retained a right of veto as senior augustus. Soon he decided that not even two rulers were sufficient to deal with the complex problems of the empire, and arranged the appointment of two further men who were to serve in effect as deputy co-emperors with the title of caesar—Constantius Chlorus in the West and Galerius in the East. Both these men, vested with dignity and authority, were to conduct major military operations; and as lieutenants of their respective chiefs, they were designated eventually to succeed them—an ingenious way of solving the perennial Roman problem of succession. Together, the four men constituted what became known as the tetrarchy, an order of governance unknown before or since.

Amid these innovations Diocletian returned to another problem, namely that of the Christian presence, which he attacked in the spirit of Valerian rather than of Gallienus and with utter ruthlessness. What is known as the Great Persecution now began. Lactantius, a teacher of Latin at Nicomedia, who had become a convert to Christianity, was to recount in a tract called *De mortibus persecutorum (On the Deaths of the Persecutors)* his own version of the cause of the new assault upon believers. According to him, Diocletian was performing a sacrifice before the state gods when he observed that some of the attendants were making the sign of the cross, thereby counteracting the influence of the pagan deities and in effect canceling out the supplications and prayers offered by the emperor. In the eyes of Diocletian an act of desecration had been committed by people whom he regarded as atheists. In a state of high excitement he discussed the wanton behavior of the Christians with his deputy Galerius, and it probably was Galerius who goaded him into suppressing them.

It is more likely that Diocletian's action, far from being a fit of imperial temper, represented cold-blooded policy. Conversions had been increasing; Christian basilicas were flourishing in many cities; the imperial court itself was peopled with votaries of the new faith. A rapid series of edicts, beginning in February, A.D. 303, therefore undertook to root out the infection totally. The first or-

Diocletian was proclaimed emperor by the army, as many of his predecessors had been. But his abilities enabled him to revive some of the strength of the empire; he brought about extensive tax reform, stabilization of currency, and reorganization of the bureaucracy, the provinces, and the army. When he became ill in A.D. 305 he retired to his palace at Salonae (above), in Dalmatia, thinking that the system of succession that he had instituted would ensure a continuity of rule the empire badly needed.
HOLLE VERLAG, *Rome and Her Empire*

dered all copies of the Scriptures surrendered and burned and the churches destroyed; all meetings of Christians were forbidden. Next the Christians were deprived of all civil rights, including that of holding any public office. Regardless of their social rank, they could be submitted to torture after trial; Christian slaves were not to be liberated. In further edicts, setting up a progressive scale of punishments, Christian priests and then Christian laymen were to be executed unless they recanted and worshiped state gods.

In A.D. 305, a year after promulgating his last and sternest edict, and at the height of his power at the age of sixty, Diocletian abruptly abdicated and spent the rest of his days gardening the grounds of his vast palace in Dalmatia, leaving his lieutenant Galerius in full command of the empire in the East. At the same time his old and faithful friend Maximian also retired in the West, leaving his deputy Constantius Chlorus in command. Galerius, a skillful soldier, though lacking Diocletian's spacious quality of command, followed his predecessor's footsteps and also persecuted Christians with unabated vigor. Constantius, on the other hand, now the junior emperor after Maximian's retirement in the West, left them alone. He was a highly efficient ruler, who had been admired as a military leader ever since he had put down a rebellion in Britain in A.D. 296, rescuing Londinium (London) with such dispatch that a gold medallion was struck hailing him as the REDDITOR LUCIS AETERNAE—restorer of the eternal light of Rome. His extraordinary pallor won him the cognomen of Chlorus, or the "pale one." His later fame was to rest on the fact that he sired, either with his wife or with his concubine, the man who was to become known as Constantine the Great.

Diocletian had been a man with a prodigious passion for building. The baths he constructed in Rome cover over thirty acres. The fortress palace he ordered for himself and hundreds of his retainers on the Dalmatian coast remains to this day a major, though ruined, monument to an emperor's leisure. Venetian conquerors embellished it, streets were to be built through it, and where the Roman emperor worshiped his gods, Christians erected their own churches out of the stone he had imported. When he retired he seems to have believed that he had built so firm an architecture of government that there would be no more civil wars, that the caesars or deputies would automatically acquire power on the deaths of the emperors, and that an ample bureaucracy would resolve all the problems confronting the peace and security of the empire. He could not have been more mistaken. When Constantius Chlorus died in the British city of Eboracum in A.D. 306, the succession in the West was thrown into disorder. The younger Constantine, dis-

Diocletian's plan for sound rule and orderly succession was based on dividing the realm into eastern and western portions, each ruled by an emperor or augustus, with a deputy or caesar under him who was to become his heir. The four men together formed a tetrarchy: above are shown the augusti Diocletian and Maximian, with their respective caesars, who were their sons-in-law, Constantius of the West and Galerius of the East.

ALINARI-GIRAUDON

tinguished like his father for his soldierly and human qualities, was promptly proclaimed emperor by the troops in Britain. Meanwhile a son of Maximian named Maxentius, who had been passed over in the naming of heirs, was living as a private citizen in Rome. There a mass of Praetorians, riding a wave of popular unrest over the capital's diminishing prestige in the imperial system and the imposition of heavy taxes, proclaimed Maxentius caesar, with rights to the throne. Both these proclamations were in effect acts of usurpation since under Diocletian's system the eastern emperor Galerius as senior augustus held the right of appointment in the West as well as in the East. Galerius had gone so far in accommodation as to recognize young Constantine as a caesar in the West, but not as augustus; to that higher rank he elevated one of his own lieutenants, Severus. But he could not brook the rival upstart Maxentius—a threat to the whole order especially since Maxentius' father, the elderly Maximian, had come out of retirement to support his son's cause. Severus was ordered to march against Maxentius, only to be captured at Ravenna. Maximian, playing a crafty game, journeyed to Gaul to make an alliance with Constantine by giving him his daughter in marriage and independently bestowing upon him the title of augustus in exchange for which the new son-in-law was to recognize Maxentius as augustus also.

In this gathering storm, with the fate of the empire at stake, Galerius called a conference of Rome's senior statesmen at Carnuntum, on the Danube, in A.D. 308. Diocletian came out of retirement to attend it, but refused the suggestion that he himself return to the helm. Maximian, on the other hand, was asked to relinquish his new bid for power, which he refused to do. With no less than six augusti now holding claims in the East and the West, Galerius tried to resolve the disorder by asking that another of his lieutenants, Licinius, a Dacian peasant who had risen to high military rank, be accepted as lawful emperor in the West. Young Constantine was urged to abandon the acclamation given him by his troops and to place himself as a caesar under the authority of Licinius. Constantine, who had kept his troops in training against Franks and Germans, bided his time.

His chance came soon. In 310 the aging Maximian seized Massilia, but Constantine's opposition is thought to have led Maximian to suicide. In the next year Galerius died. Licinius hurried to consolidate control of the western areas while another lieutenant of the late emperor Galerius, Maximinus Daza, set out to organize the East. Between them stood Maxentius, augustus at Rome. Constantine saw his opportunity.

In his twenties Constantine had served under Diocletian in Egypt and under Galerius against the Persians. In A.D. 306 he had been posted to Britain to assist his father against the Scots. Vigorous, handsome, square-jawed, with eyes remarkable for their leonine brightness, he was a commanding presence at thirty-two when his father died. He also had unusual patience and a sense of the proper moment to strike. His mind was fired with high ambitions—not only to win the West but ultimately the East as well, where Rome's greatest resources lay. Amid all the contests of empire, he soon identified Maxentius as his chief rival for mastery, and when in sure command of Gaul, prepared carefully for a march on Rome. His campaign of A.D. 312 was a masterpiece of speed and dispatch; it has been likened to Napoleon's first Italian campaign. Maxentius' numerically superior forces were destroyed little by little at Turin, at Verona, and then at the Mulvian Bridge, outside Rome, leaving the young conqueror master of the West.

Among the matters discussed at the Carnuntum conference of A.D. 308 may have been that of the religion that should now govern the state. The cult of Mithra had become a favorite of the soldiers, and there is evidence that a temple was restored by the emperors assembled on the Danube in honor of Mithra, protector of the empire (*fautori imperii sui*). Worship of an eastern god had long been established in polytheistic Rome, and worship of a savior was not to be arrested. When Constantine took up arms against his foe Maxentius he appears to have felt the need of the protection of the strongest god of all—and for reasons that can only be surmised, he found this in the Christian god as against a pagan one. He was—at least this is how he recounted it to the historian Eusebius—overtaken by a vision in the form of a cross in the sky, and a command that he go into battle under that sign. Whatever the source of his guidance, his troops put down Maxentius with the sign of Christ's cross on their shields.

The event was to have vast consequences. Victory was now coupled with Christianity in the eyes of the western empire—a recognition highly welcomed in the far more Christianized eastern half. A merging of spiritual influences emanating from the East with the tribal vigor of the West seemed in prospect. And so it was to be. For the better part of a decade Constantine was to rule the West in an uneasy relationship with Licinius, who had become Galerius' successor in the East. When Licinius wrongheadedly resumed persecution of Christians, Constantine overthrew him in A.D. 324, and thus fulfilled his ambition: he had resolved centuries of conflict between East and West, old faiths and new, and reunited the empire under one hand.

As soon as Diocletian and Maximian retired, it became clear that the carefully-thought-out system of succession was going to fail. Within a few years there were six claimants to the title of augustus. Two decades of civil war began; in A.D. 312 Constantine (son of the man who had been the legitimate caesar in the West before he died) won a battle near Rome that made him ruler of the West. He destroyed the eastern augustus in 324 and became sole ruler of the empire. He is shown above in a contemporary bust.

A DISTINCTION
IN PAINTING

When the techniques of painting borrowed from the Greeks and the Etruscans were exposed to the forces of the Roman imagination, the art found a distinct, new idiom. The interests of the Roman painter were far wider than his forerunners'; he, too, painted mythical and historical subjects but was also drawn to scenes of architecture and landscape. Genre or anecdotal painting and the still life appear to have been Roman innovations.

The talent of these men is known to us almost exclusively through wall paintings, which, with their limitations as decorations, had to be subordinated to the scheme of a house. Freestanding paintings, such as the very few portraits on plaques that have survived, no doubt offered greater freedom of composition and tone to Roman masters.

Styles of painting, of course, changed over the centuries. Augustan artists employed the carefully outlined, polished Hellenistic style as in the detail opposite from the Villa of the Mysteries, near Pompeii. After the mid-first century, painters created a purely Roman form of expression, representing their subjects in a warmer, freer way. Concentrating on the effects of light, the most talented could convey a feeling of mood and scene with a few broad brush strokes. As the empire began to fail so did the ability to handle paint; Roman painting became rather crude, and influenced by the East, somewhat stylized.

Most of the surviving Roman paintings are from the towns of Stabiae, Pompeii, and Herculaneum, which were destroyed by the eruption of Vesuvius in A.D. *79; excavations in those places have revealed innumerable painting styles. At top,* Houses at Noon *from Pompeii demonstrates the impressionistic manner, developed after* A.D. *50. Opposite,* Hercules and Telephus *from Herculaneum shows its creator's interest in statuesque representation of the human body. The* Sleeping Maenad *(detail at bottom) is a storytelling painting showing a Bacchic reveler after an orgy.*

The two paintings on these pages, charming and extremely skillfully executed, nevertheless illustrate one problem that Roman artists were never able to solve—perspective. The picture above is in a common Pompeiian style that always depicted architecture; it indicates depth and solidity, but a close look reveals that the spatial relationship of the structures is obscure. Opposite is a detail from a mural excavated at Pompeii; although the plants and animals are convincing, there is almost no depth behind them.

HIRMER VERLAG, MUNICH

There is a great gap in our knowledge
of Roman painting between A.D. 79
and the third century when the Christians began to paint on catacomb walls.
And though the subject of those works
is religious, there is reason to believe
that contemporary pagan Roman painting was of about the same quality.
Apparently during the second century,
painters had worked hard to convey
dimension, but by the time of these two
late-third-century catacomb paintings,
the work was frontal and less rounded,
due in part to oriental influences.

Nowhere in the empire were there finer portrait painters than in the Faiyûm area of Egypt (see page 294), although they had many close rivals. And the Faiyûm painters, remote as they were from Italy, were not exempt when the general change in style and character of painting came about in the third century. At right, a painting of about A.D. *60 from Pompeii represents a young couple; their features are delicately molded with light and shade, and no realistic detail has been avoided. The Faiyûm Portrait above (about* A.D. *280 in origin) is sketchy and flat, and the figure and clothes are stylized.*

XII

ROME BECOMES CHRISTIAN

Against the advice of the augurs, in spite of his military counsellors, unsupported by the troops of Licinius, with incredible audacity Constantine had risked everything on a single hazard—and won. How shall that success be explained? Constantine himself knew well the reason for his victory: it had been won instinctu divinitatis, *by a* virtus *which was no mere human valor, but was a mysterious force which had its origin in God . . . Victory had been promised him by the God of the Christians; he had challenged the Christian God to an Ordeal by Battle and that God had kept his pledge.*

Lactantius, On the Deaths of the Persecutors

The character of Constantine, who was to leave so vast an imprint on the history of the West, remains an enigma. The brute facts of his reign, his journeys and battles and laws, are extensively recorded, and his physical appearance has been brilliantly rendered in statues and on coins; but we do not know the workings of his mind. He was to make great decisions that would change the course of history, but we can only guess why he made them. With a mysterious logic of his own he brings down the curtain on hallowed Roman traditions of antiquity, and when at last the curtain rises again, a new Rome has appeared nearly a thousand miles to the east, and an entirely new cycle of history has begun.

The two greatest achievements of Constantine were so vast in their scope that they give the impression of being carefully planned and pondered over for many years. But as Constantine himself made clear, both of them came about as the result of dreams or visions. He compelled his army to adopt the sign of Christianity after he had seen a vision of a flaming cross, and he chose Byzantium as the new capital of his empire. Yet he was not by nature a visionary; he was a man of intense practicality.

The battle at the Mulvian Bridge, at which Constantine won his empire, was not one of those battles that at the time seemed to have decisive importance. Both Maxentius and Constantine were usurpers, possessing no legal or justifiable claim to the throne, and it might be expected that in the course of time both of them would have vanished before the superior forces of the imperial armies. But Constantine managed to hold on to his power. He was to claim that he won the battle and reached the throne because the Christian God had protected him; his enemies, with greater logic, might have claimed that the battle was won by default or through the malice of the god who presided over the Tiber. When Maxentius was retreating across the Mulvian Bridge with part of the army he was forced into the river and drowned, and his army was thrown into a panic. By an accident Rome fell to Constantine.

This victory over Maxentius confirmed his devotion to Christianity. But to speak of the conversion of Constantine is to misunderstand the quality of his mind. He did not immediately try to impose the Christian faith on his subjects. He continued to celebrate pagan festivals, minted coins in honor of Apollo, Hercules, Mars, and Jupiter, and even after his conversion, presented himself on coins wearing the spiked crown of *sol invictus*, the unconquered Sun. He was tolerant of all religions, and as Augustus had, he showed a special predilection for Apollo. He attached great importance to the externals of religious conduct and insisted that all services should be conducted with propriety, for he liked his religions to have clear contours and well-defined lines of command. When necessary he would himself enter as umpire and supreme religious authority, even though he had little understanding of the philosophical subtleties his bishops were arguing about. He believed that it was an emperor's right and duty to lay down all laws, even the laws of religion.

How deeply Constantine believed in the tenets of Christianity is a question that has puzzled historians, as it may very well have puzzled Constantine himself. His complex mind appears to have been capable of believing simultaneously in the Christian God and the entire pagan tradition. He acknowledged a *summus deus*, a supreme god who ordered and commanded the entire universe, but beyond this he apparently was not prepared to go, though he would pay lip service to Christ or to the unconquered Sun whom his father had worshiped. Toward the end of his life he caused to be erected, near the Colosseum, a magnificent triumphal arch in his honor, bearing an inscription testifying that all his victories were the result of the inspiration of the divine—*instinctu divinitatis*. Perhaps he was paying tribute to his own divinity or to all divinities. Certainly the ambiguous phrase does not reveal a special preference for the Christian God.

Constantine was not, after all, so deeply interested in religion; what interested him almost to the exclusion of everything else was the exploration of power, and he realized very early that toleration was itself a form of power. In a remarkable series of edicts he displayed a genuinely humane attitude toward the poor and the oppressed. He did not, of course, abolish slavery, but he made certain that slaves were given every opportunity to prove their right to freedom; a master who dealt brutally with a slave would have to answer for it; the families of slaves on an imperial estate were to be kept together even if the estate was sold. We hear of laws protecting peasants who fell into debt, and others protecting children from brutal or avaricious parents. Prisoners in jail, he decreed, must not be harshly treated, rather they must be given exercise and light; and callous jailers were to be severely punished. Condemned prisoners were not compelled to become gladiators.

The growing influence of Christianity had brought a greater emphasis on mercy and fair dealing. Sometimes the laws betray a Christian origin, as when the emperor issued an edict against the branding of criminals on the face, since the face is created "in the likeness of divine beauty," or when he abolished crucifixion or protested against gladiatorial displays, describing them as "bloody spectacles displeasing in a time of peace and quiet." Again, when he ordered that parents who exposed their children

The direct cause and effect relationship between Christianity's rise and Rome's fall cannot be determined, but it is true that the fortunes of Christians rose as the empire sank into chaos. A late fourth-century drawing on glass depicts saints Peter and Paul, who did most to establish the new faith.

should be forever disbarred from claiming any rights over them, he was following the lead of the Church Fathers, who viewed the abandonment of children as a crime against God. Christian influence is evident, too, in Constantine's proclamation of a special day in the week when factories, shops, and law courts would be closed, even though the day of rest was to be called the venerable day of the Sun. The laws of Constantine consistently demonstrate a high degree of social consciousness and decency. He was one of the few Roman emperors who seems genuinely to have desired peace and to have hated bloodshed.

Constantine's efforts to establish peace and a stable government brought changes in the administration as well as in the law. He tightened imperial control over the lives of his subjects through taxation and through the enforcement of the edicts that bound people to their work. It was almost impossible for any peasant to leave the farm on which he was born, or for any worker to obtain a job different from that of his father's. These rules were harsh, but they were designed to maintain stability in every sector of society. He invited vigorous German tribesmen to settle uncultivated lands within the empire's boundaries, welcomed them into the army and the civil service, and encouraged their advancement into positions of responsibility. He confiscated the treasures of pagan temples and summoned an ecumenical council of the Christian Church—the first to take place.

To increase his control over his subjects, Constantine surrounded himself with an aura of divinity. Of course, he could not, as a Christian, claim to be a god. Nevertheless his new religion gave the emperor the opportunity to announce that he was "ordained by God to oversee whatever is external to the Church"—a statement that was to have awesome consequences in the Middle Ages when emperors and popes struggled for supremacy.

Yet Constantine also established a foundation for the papacy's claims to temporal power when he gave the rights and duties of magistrates to all the bishops in his empire. Many of the bishops carefully searched their consciences before they agreed to accept the post, for Christian tradition, centuries old, looked on the state and all of its work as being corrupt. But finally, with gratitude, they assented to the change and regarded it as a sign of the new era that was dawning.

With astonishing clarity Constantine saw that the fulcrum of imperial power lay in the East and that the time had come to reinvigorate the empire by building an entirely new capital there. Already Diocletian had realized that, on strategic grounds, the empire required a capital nearer to the border where Europe met Asia.

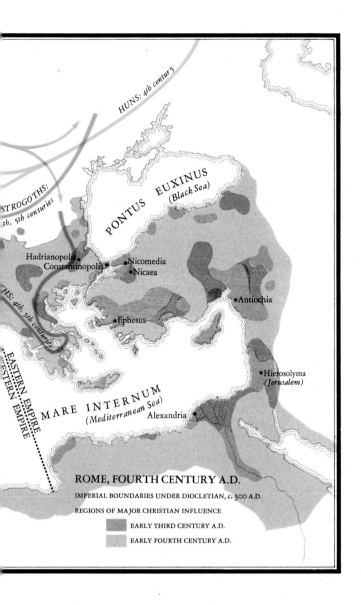

ROME, FOURTH CENTURY A.D.

IMPERIAL BOUNDARIES UNDER DIOCLETIAN, c. 300 A.D.

REGIONS OF MAJOR CHRISTIAN INFLUENCE

EARLY THIRD CENTURY A.D.

EARLY FOURTH CENTURY A.D.

THE TRIUMPH OF HEATHENS AND CHRISTIANS *In concluding his famous study of Rome's decline and fall, the historian Edward Gibbon remarked that he had "described the triumph of barbarism and religion." There is little doubt that the barbarians, whose migrations are traced above, wasted Rome's resources and helped to shatter its unity. Christianity bolstered the late empire only temporarily, if at all. As shown on the map, the Church, despite proscriptions and persecutions, greatly extended its sway during the third century. Constantine, recognizing it as the principal source of authority and cohesion in many localities, enlisted it in government by appointing bishops as magistrates, but at a time when the Church itself was about to suffer grave schisms.*

Diocletian chose Nicomedia. Constantine, however, decided against Nicomedia, and after toying with the idea of rebuilding ancient Troy, he finally chose the old Greek fishing port of Byzantium, the junction of all the roads between Asia and the West. There on May 11, 330, in the presence of high ecclesiastical officials, the city of New Rome was formally inaugurated with great pomp. Christian commentators, who carefully noted the presence of the Churchmen, appear to have glossed over the fact that the ceremony was also pagan and modeled on the legendary inauguration of Rome by Romulus.

With the founding of the new capital, old Rome lost its aura of power; it was drained of its nobility, its craftsmen, and its soldiers, who found a more prosperous outlet for their energies in Constantine's city, which was at first named New Rome, but which came to be called Constantinople after the ceremonies in 330. In its beginning New Rome was largely populated by Romans, and Latin was the language heard at court as well as in the market place. The laws were written in Latin, and so they continued to be for more than two centuries. New Rome fed on the old until it had taken all it could; and then it drank at the inexhaustible wells of Greek culture, and also became Greek.

At its founding the city had been dedicated to the Trinity and to the Virgin Mary, for Constantine's encouragement of Christianity went hand in hand with his establishment of a new capital. Both were designed to strengthen and unify the empire. Both, however, proved in the end to be divisive forces. The new capital took some of the glory away from Rome, but not all; and in the century after its foundation, the vast and unwieldy empire tended to divide more and more into eastern and western halves.

Christianity, too, failed to unify Constantine's domain. Even before he brought the new religion to dominance, the Church had been plagued with dissension, and its divisions often fell along social as well as doctrinal lines. In North Africa, one religious squabble aligned the old Berber and Punic elements in a bitter struggle against the Roman colonists. About the year 318 a more serious controversy erupted in Egypt, splitting the entire Church into factions that opposed each other in the political as well as the religious sphere.

The argument—over the nature of Christ—aroused the passions not only of theologians but of the workers and artisans of Alexandria as well, men who followed the philosophical controversy with as much enthusiasm as some men devote to athletic contests. To resolve the differences between the two parties—the Arians, who claimed that Christ must have originated after God and was not equal to Him, and their opponents, who believed that Christ was coeternal with God—the First Ecumenical Council was called at Nicaea in 325 to settle all disputes. There the doctrine of the Trinity was formulated. Although greater unity was thus achieved, a few Arians refused to accept the concept, and the Church and empire remained divided over the question until the year 381 when the emperor Theodosius the Great made heresy a crime.

In that same year Theodosius made paganism a crime too. It had enjoyed a brief revival under the sponsorship of the emperor Julian—called the Apostate—who had acceded to the throne in the year 361. Julian had studied at the ancient university of Athens, where he developed a profound reverence for the ideals that had inspired classical society. Some of his teachers, pagan philosophers, were attempting to combat the inroads of Christianity by developing ethical rationalizations for the old pagan ceremonies. Many of them were Neoplatonists, followers of the philosopher Plotinus, who encouraged men to see all the gods as aspects of one great God and to seek union with Him.

When Julian came to the throne he tried to establish a pagan church throughout the empire, with bishops, priests, and most important, ethics like those of Christianity; but paganism was unable to compete with the vigorous new faith. A few years after Julian's death paganism itself was moribund. The ancient temples were abandoned or transformed into market halls, and their estates and revenues were requisitioned by their priests or by local magnates for their own benefit. Everywhere citizens converted to Christianity and left behind the cults of their ancestors. Athens and the Peloponnesus and Rome itself, where the ancient senatorial families proudly guarded their heritage, remained bastions of paganism; but as time went on they became more and more isolated. Most significant of all, during the reign of Gratian (375–383) the statue of Victoria, before which sacrifices had been offered since the days of Augustus, was removed from its prominent position in the Senate house in Rome.

Ironically, that happened at a time when Rome desperately needed the favor of the goddess Victoria, for the age of major barbarian invasions had begun. For centuries German tribes had been pressing relentlessly along the northern frontiers of the empire. From time to time they were massacred or driven back; when they became too strong they were appeased with generous grants of land; when they became stronger still they were permitted to enter the Roman army. In a strict sense they were not really barbarians. They had their own cultures, their own traditions in the arts, in commerce, and in warfare, and many of them were even

The triumphal arch of Constantine seems to symbolize his desire to restore the Roman empire, for he had fragments from the monuments of many great Romans built into it. One way in which he tried to achieve his goal was to adopt Christianity. He believed that its votaries would be united, moral, and obedient subjects under a Christian emperor.

Christians. Once they became Roman mercenaries they were in a position to defy the emperor, for they guarded the frontiers, and when rival elements were struggling for the throne these tribal mercenaries often held the balance of power.

Although the West finally succumbed to them, the East suffered the first successful incursion. Toward the end of the fourth century the most powerful of the barbarian tribes were the Goths, who had probably originated in southern Sweden and in the second century had moved into the Baltic region. They then traveled across Europe and western Asia until they came to settle peacefully in what is now Rumania, Hungary, and southern Russia. One of the Gothic tribes known as the Visigoths had settled in Transylvania. They spoke a pure and primitive Teutonic, and the majority of them embraced Arian Christianity with the passion of converts. They wore their flaxen hair long, and they dressed in skins, but their towns and cities were halfway civilized. They might have remained there indefinitely, trading with Constantinople and acting as frontier mercenaries if it had not been for the sudden, massive attack by marauding Huns from central Asia. These wild Mongolian people were to remain the scourge of Europe for centuries to come. Merciless, devoid of any sense of law, they destroyed for the sake of destruction, and they proved to be masters of the art of raiding.

About 370 a Hunnish invasion of the Gothic kingdoms forced the Visigoths to appeal to Constantinople for shelter, and they were permitted to settle south of the Danube in the region of Lower Moesia. Some eighty thousand of them crossed the Danube, only to find that the Roman officials treated them unjustly and with contempt. Goaded into action, in 378 they marched against the imperial army. In a narrow valley near Adrianople the mailed cavalry of the Goths hacked the army of the eastern emperor Valens to pieces. The emperor was pierced by an arrow and died. It was a second Cannae.

Seventeen years later, in 395, under their newly chosen warleader Alaric, whose name means "all powerful," they began to sack the empire as the Huns had ravaged their own land. Alaric struck at Thessaly, marched down the eastern coast of Greece, battered at the walls of Athens, crossed into the Peloponnesus; Corinth, Argos, and Sparta all fell before him. Nothing could stop him, and Arcadius, the eastern Roman emperor, fearing that the whole empire might fall to the Goths, tried to buy him off, rewarding him with high honors and surrendering large areas of Illyria for him to rule as an imperial viceroy. Alaric, standing between East and West, was now in a position to attack one or the

The statue above probably represents Julian the Apostate, who gained the throne in 361. Although brought up a Christian, he renounced the religion and became the last emperor to try to destroy it. He did not persecute Christians physically, but he took away their rights and organized a pagan priesthood.

LOUVRE; GIRAUDON

other at his leisure. In 400 he decided to attack Italy and to carve out for the Visigoths a settlement on Italian soil.

Like many of his successors, he regarded Rome as the most desirable of conquests, its capture being the crown of his military career. The church historian Socrates Scholasticus tells the story of a monk who came to Alaric's royal tent and begged him to stop plundering the towns and villages of Italy. "There is something within me which every day urges me irresistibly forward," said Alaric. "It says to me, 'Go to Rome and make that city desolate.' " At last in 408, after two abortive sieges in 401 and 402, Alaric had Rome at his mercy, the city ringed by his troops and the people starving. When ambassadors came to plead for clemency he answered grimly that he would not raise the siege until they offered him all their gold, silver, movable property, and slaves. "And what will you leave us?" the ambassadors asked. "Your lives," Alaric answered, and he was as good as his word.

But in 410, one of the imperial legions broke the truce agreed to after the ransom, and Alaric moved to lay waste the city. The Visigoths sacked Rome with a quiet fury that was all the more terrible because it was so calm and methodical. There was looting, and Saint Augustine also tells of slaughter and rape and arson, but apparently the Visigoths committed far fewer atrocities than other ancient conquerors had before them. A terrified people watched the wealth of the city heaped up in the carts of the barbarians. They were only three or four days in the city, but they swept it clean. Not since the destruction of Rome by the Gauls, eight hundred years earlier, had the city known a conqueror.

Tertullian, in the second century, had believed that Rome would last as long as the world, enduring until the Day of Judgment. A special sanctity was attached to the inviolate city. But Alaric had proved that it was a city like any other, only too vulnerable. In far-off Bethlehem, Saint Jerome lamented: "The entire human race is implicated in the catastrophe. My voice is choked, and my words are broken with sobs while I write: The city now is taken that once held the world." *Capitur urbs quae totum cepit orbem* —those last words read like a funeral inscription for an empire. Saint Augustine viewed the capture of Rome with horror, but also with Christian detachment. He found some consolation in the thought that Rome—an essentially pagan city—had richly deserved its fate. "The City of God endureth for ever," he wrote, "though the greatest city on earth is fallen. . . ."

Meanwhile, other German tribes were striking at the vulnerable western provinces. For centuries, for as long as the Romans themselves had been in Gaul, Germans had been making forays into the land. But now their invasions were no longer turned back. In the year 406, marauding bands of Vandals, Alans, and Sueves marched through Gaul and devastated it. Three years later the Vandals pushed into Spain and wrested the peninsula from the Romans. Nominally Spain was still a part of the empire, but the barbarians controlled it completely, for in 411 they negotiated a treaty with the Roman emperor Honorius that put them in charge of defending the peninsula. Later in the century Britain was lost to invading Saxons, and Visigoths established a kingdom in Gaul, centered about the town of Tolosa. The Vandals moved on into North Africa, and they were succeeded in Spain by the Sueves, whose earlier domain in Gaul was in turn taken over by the Franks. Province after province was claimed and reclaimed by the barbarians, and the imperial city itself had fallen; the greatness of Rome was no more.

Attila the Hun, the most ruthless of barbarian invaders, who destroyed for the joy of destruction, was persuaded partly by his own fears not to harm Rome. In 452 he destroyed the great city of Aquileia, in northern Italy; its citizens fled to the lagoons to found a new and safer town—Venice. He intended to attack Rome, but his army was racked with disease, and Alaric's death, shortly after the sack of the city by the Goths in 410, had filled the barbarians with superstitious horror. When Pope Leo I came to him to ask his leniency, therefore, Attila was ready to grant it. Attila turned back and Rome was saved. Three years later, in 455, Leo confronted Gaiseric, the Vandal, whose armies were camped outside the walls. Once again the pope was able to save Rome from destruction. Gaiseric wanted plunder, and this was given to him on condition that there would be no rape, no murder, no firing of houses, churches, and ancient palaces. For fourteen days he was permitted to strip the city of its valuables, even the precious vessels in the churches, although it was stipulated that the three most sacred basilicas were to be left unharmed. Gaiseric kept his bargain and sailed to Africa with the greatest treasure ever accumulated in Europe up to that time. For Leo it was pure victory; he had exchanged the gold tiles of the temple of Jupiter on the Capitoline and all the baubles of pagan Rome for a Christian peace.

Again and again the barbarians struck at the city in search of the loot that had escaped their predecessors. In 472 Ricimer, a Suevian, besieged and sacked Rome. He was followed four years later by Odoacer, a son of one of Attila's generals. He proclaimed himself king of Italy, independent of Romulus Augustulus, the puppet emperor of the West who had been appointed by the Roman emperor in Constantinople, and then abandoned the city for

By the beginning of the fifth century the threat of the barbaric tribes was greater than the sum of all the rest of the empire's problems—and was, in part, a cause of them too. A seal represents Alaric, king of the Visigoths. Although forced from their own land by the Huns, the Visigoths were able to sack Rome.

Ravenna, which could be more easily defended than Rome. The chroniclers of the time paid very little attention to Odoacer; he was merely one more of the usurpers who rose to power and vanished after stamping his features and his name on coins. Romulus was a fourteen-year-old boy. He was charming, and when Odoacer deposed him and was on the point of killing him, the usurper decided that nothing was to be gained by murdering a defenseless child. The last of the western emperors, therefore, was granted a pension by a barbarian king and ordered to spend the rest of his life with his relatives in a luxurious villa near Naples. Nothing more was ever heard of the boy, whose name combined the names of the first Roman king and the first Roman emperor.

"The western Roman empire, which started with Augustus, finished with Augustulus," wrote the chronicler Marcellinus. But in essence the western Roman empire had perished long before, dying when Constantine transferred the capital to Byzantium. After Odoacer, invading chieftains fought for power and looted and burned the city; Italy began to split into its many principalities, which were not to be reunited until the nineteenth century. But the civilizing mission of Rome did continue through the agency of the Church—especially through the monasteries, which grew in usefulness and importance during the years of the barbaric invasions when men turned in relief from war to contemplation. These monasteries preserved the manuscripts of ancient Rome and Greece, many of which have come down to us only because the monks copied them. Meanwhile, the Church grew in power and authority, for no other voice spoke so clearly in the dark ages. A few years after Romulus Augustulus vanished into obscurity, Pope Gelasius formulated the "doctrine of the two powers," which maintained that the Church should be independent of the imperial power. But when Pope Gelasius spoke, temporal power was all but gone from Rome: the empire that once had radiated from antiquity's greatest city had vanished.

What caused this breakdown of Roman power—a power that had held the world in thrall for centuries? It is tempting to search for an answer, but of course no one really knows. The great eighteenth-century historian Edward Gibbon claimed that one of the reasons was that Christianity had sapped the vigor of the Roman people. Other scholars attribute the decline and fall of the empire to the plagues, which frequently ravaged the Mediterranean world in the fourth century. Still others assert that the economy of the empire became so disorganized that its collapse was inevitable. Today's scholars are less inclined than those of the past were to explain away such a complex historical process as the empire's fall

Theodosius the Great is shown in his box at the games in Constantinople. He was virtually the last Roman emperor to have control of both halves of the empire. He was also the last ruler to hold off the barbarians; he did so in some cases by battle but in others by appointing tribes as imperial allies or granting them rights to the land. When he died in 395 his two inept sons divided his realm. Fifteen years later, hordes of barbarians had taken over much of the empire and had entered the gates of Rome.

with a glib generalization. They admit quite frankly that they do not know the reasons and that they can only guess at them; and they go on to study the age's history in terms of continuity as well as in terms of change.

For although the Celtic and Roman population that inhabited Gaul, Britain, and Spain was severely tried by the atrocities of the barbarian invasions, in many ways society was not vastly different from the way it had been when imperial power was still unchallenged. True, the towns were decaying, the peasants were little more than serfs, brigandage was rife, corruption was widespread, taxes were burdensome, and the service that the taxes brought was minimal, but this had been so for a century before the sack of Rome by the Visigoths. Long after the emperor had lost all effective power in the West, most of the inhabitants—Roman and barbarian—of these lands, still considered him their overlord. The idea of Roman domination had not died and would not die until more than a thousand years later.

For the barbarians who hammered at its gates, the city of Rome itself presented problems that almost defied solution. It could be conquered easily; it could be destroyed as the Gauls had destroyed it long ago. But what were the advantages of conquering it or putting it to flames? Powerless, it was still powerful—with the power of legends and of traditions and of the knowledge of government. The ruined city was still teaching law to the world, and with law went civilization, order, the quiet pursuit of trade, the flourishing of arts. Eventually the barbarians were to one degree or another to come under the spell of Rome.

The Roman empire had had many virtues and many vices; it deployed its enormous strength for good and evil alike. Never before had such vast regimented power been visited on the earth; never before—and never again until modern times—had so many lands been conquered and subjected to the commands of a single government. Power was used wantonly and peace came rarely. But in those intervals of peace the human spirit flowered, magnificent buildings arose, great poems were written, and the slow march of civilization was continued. Even those who had reason to hate that empire built up over the centuries by the Romans also were forced to find virtue in it. When Saint Augustine wrote *De civitate dei* (*The City of God*) he catalogued the evils committed by Rome, and yet he offered the city a supreme tribute: "Between the city in which it has been promised that we shall reign and the earthly city there is a great gulf as wide as the distance between heaven and earth. Yet . . . there is a faint shadowy resemblance between the Roman empire and the heavenly city."

369

A NEW PRESENCE

While the hills and forums of Rome remained peopled with statues of gods and emperors, the sanctuaries and catacombs beneath the city became the seats of a new faith that ultimately was to overtake the empire and rule its remains. At left, a third-century painting from one of the Roman catacombs shows Christ in an attitude of benediction. The course of Christian art, from the first-century subterranean scratchings to the beautiful shrines of the fourth century, attests to the rise of the religion from its tenuous period of persecution to its time of triumph.

The burning zeal of the Christian believers brought that triumph about. They exhorted the world to accept the gospel, and their ardent promises of salvation and afterlife converted an ever-widening circle of citizens, subjects, and slaves. The apostles of the first and second centuries not only spread the word of Christ but they organized His rapidly growing groups of followers in each community and made them responsible to the larger structure of the Church that was then beginning to come into being.

Constantine, aware of Christianity's growing popularity, tried to shore up the crumbling empire by declaring himself Christian and moving his capital to the East, to Constantinople. He did not know that rancor and schisms between the intellectual eastern Church and the western Church were already growing, and that his adopted religion would serve as an additional lever to pry the empire apart.

CATACOMB OF DOMITILLA, ROME; HIRMER VERLAG, MUNICH

371

A CATHOLIC FAITH

The Christian religion that triumphed in the fourth century
was no longer based only on the simple teachings of Jesus; it
was a composite of the theologies and philosophies and personal credos of most of the peoples of the eastern and western
parts of the empire. From Judaism came the concept of one
omnipotent, omniscient God, a strong moral code, and a belief in an imminent apocalypse, which made many early Christians foreswear earthly pleasures. Theologians influenced by
Greek philosophies transformed Christianity into a highly
sophisticated religion in which abstract concepts joined with
messages of love and hope. Christianity shared many rites and
holidays with the mystery religions, which proliferated in the
East, and from the Romans came the tight hierarchical organization that was to unify the Church. But Jesus' words gave
the religion a humanitarianism that was not to be encountered
in most faiths, and the transcendent Christ—the man-god who
suffered and died to save all men—made the religion unique.

In early representations, Jesus was commonly depicted as the Good Shepherd (left); the motif was taken directly from Greek sculptures of the god Apollo. The Jewish tomb relief (center) is by a pagan sculptor; during most of the first century Christians considered themselves to be Jews. The apostles Peter and Paul are shown above. They, perhaps more than any other individuals, were responsible for spreading the religion, and Paul, an educated Roman citizen from Tarsus, was first to give it its Greek-based theology.

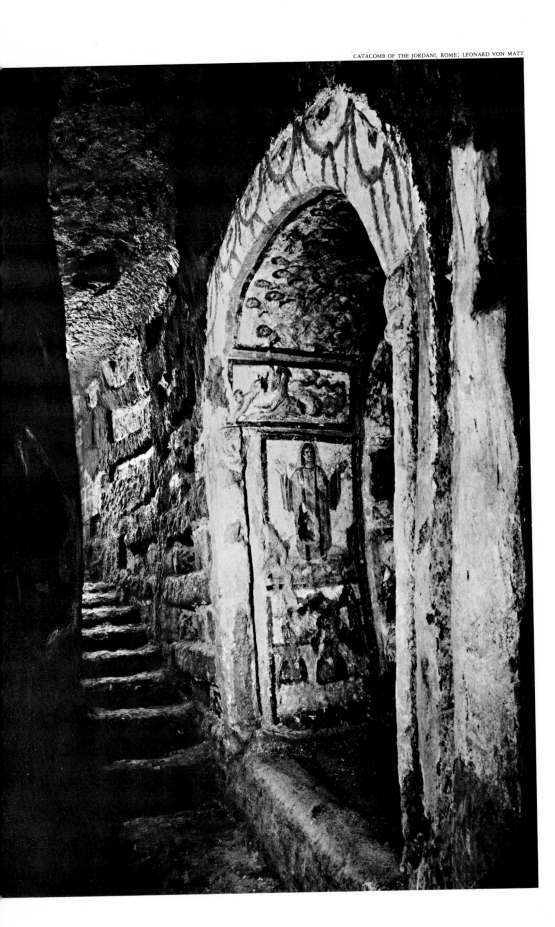

CENTURIES OF DARKNESS

In the first few centuries of their existence, Christians were despised by most other people in the Roman world. Their beliefs seemed fantastic to outsiders. As the writer Lucian put it: "These lunatics believe that they are immortal . . ." The pagans more or less believed in their gods and disliked Christian condemnation of their worship. The aloofness and self-containment of the new sect did not enhance its popularity either, and in the early days its appeal to the degenerates and thieves, whom the sectarians succored, gave the whole community an unsavory flavor. The Christians' refusal to worship the emperor made them truly revolutionaries. And so, being politically and socially in the wrong, they became the ideal group to blame for calamities, and to torture and burn to allay the Romans' insatiable bloodthirst.

The early Christians tunneled under Rome, forming miles of catacombs in which to bury their dead; during persecutions they hid in them as well. It was in those sepulchers that their first art appeared, as in the catacomb of the Jordani at left. The symbolic graffito at right shows the fish, whose letters in Greek form an acronym for "Jesus Christ, Son of God, Saviour," and the anchor, which in Christian iconology represents hope and steadfastness. A Christian sculpture (far right) shows a martyr being devoured by a lion.

Constantine's adoption of Christianity caused its transformation from a highly moralistic, flesh-denying sect to one whose members were, for the most part, as worldly as other Roman citizens. No longer shunning or shunned by the rest of society and secure from persecution, they began to build beautiful places to worship, to shelter their relics, and to honor their martyrs, and they had elaborate tombs made for themselves. An example of the vigorous Christian building program in the fourth century is the church of Santa Constanza (above), in Rome, erected about 340. At right is the lavishly carved sarcophagus of a Roman prefect, Junius Bassius, who died in 359 shortly after he converted.

THE CHURCH TRIUMPHANT

By the fourth century Christianity was finding wide acceptance, despite the fact that intermittent persecutions continued to take place. In fact the bravery with which the martyrs met their deaths in itself brought the sect respect. The chaotic state of the empire had driven people by the thousands to find security and comfort in religion, and many wealthy and educated people chose Christianity. Its new, enlarged flock changed the character of the Church; it became enormously wealthy and gradually dropped its puritanical attitudes, accepting the money and worldly ways of many of its worshipers.

OVERLEAF: *A sixth-century Ravenna mosaic depicts Justinian and his court; in Byzantium Christianity burst into flower.*

MAXIMIANVS

XIII

A SPACIOUS LEGACY

The Roman empire perished and went on living. Long after the capital had become a small town outside the frontiers of the Byzantine empire and long after the last Roman legionary marched down the Flaminian Way, its civilization held sway in the West. The legacy of this most worldly of empires was to lie largely in the realm of ideas—in law, language, literature, government, attitudes, and styles. In innumerable ways, as century followed century, men's minds were to respond to a presence that was shorn of all the panoply of power while gradually becoming transfigured into a dominion of the spirit and of thought.

The legacy was a mixed one, inextricably compounded of Greek influence on Rome and Rome's original contributions. What we call Roman civilization was very largely a Greco-Roman civilization; but it was Rome that gave it the endurance that enabled it to survive down through the centuries. The Romans were great borrowers, great adapters, and great transmitters. In later ages men learned the Greek legends and studied Greek philosophy through the writings of Roman authors, and they saw Greek sculpture through the eyes of copyists working to the Roman taste. Even in decline and defeat, Rome had the remarkable power of assimilating other peoples. Its barbarian invaders at first thought to stay aloof from the fallen conquerors, but they soon fell under the spell of a culture so much richer than their own. When the Lombards swept through Italy and intermarried with local citizens they were soon adopting the Latin tongue in their inscriptions and incorporating some principles of Roman law in their tribal code.

The Roman scheme of universality was shattered by the breakup of the empire; yet the concept was to survive in a new form—that of a Christian commonwealth in which state and Church were united. When Constantine founded his new capital in the ancient seaport of Byzantium he took with him the power of the Roman name and the faith in the divine mission; and Constantinople was "the second Rome." To the very end the Byzantine emperors regarded themselves as Romans: not merely as the inheritors or imitators, but as Romans in fact, and by descent, and by renown. They employed the word *Rome* as though there had been no sea change. Rome was eternal, but it was also portable. These emperors, moreover, were also heads of the Church. But since their temporal reach was limited by the barbarian incursions and disorders in the West, there arose in Rome—the old Rome—a line of Christian bishops who exercised virtually independent spiritual leadership there, although they recognized the authority of the distant emperor. Eventually what could be called a working partnership came into being between the presiding bishop or pope of Rome and his suzerain, the head of state beside the Bosporus.

The Roman empire seen from the new capital at Constantinople differed in many ways from the empire of the Caesars. It was not only that Rome was uprooted and transplanted to the borders of Asia, subject to all the winds that blow across the Black Sea, from Asia Minor and Persia and the coasts of Palestine, but the orientalizing influence was now firmly established, and it was precisely this influence that Rome had combatted through all the centuries of its growth and power. The new Rome was an oriental city.

To Augustus Caesar it would have seemed the strangest of all fates that there should come into existence a city that called itself Rome, inhabited by Greeks, ruled by an emperor and by governing officials who spoke in Latin and pronounced their edicts in Latin, dedicated to a divinity born during his lifetime in Judaea, borrowing openhandedly the luxuries and sometimes the ceremonies of the Persians, once the hereditary enemies of Rome. It would have surprised him that these people and their emperors would have regarded themselves as genuine Romans, and he would have been still more surprised to discover that the new Roman empire, founded on so many fictions, would produce a tolerable and workable civilization.

As the years passed the eastern and western empires gradually drifted apart; Constantinople surrendered to the luxuries and dialectics of the East. The Byzantine emperors cultivated splendor as it had perhaps never been cultivated before. They appeared in public in jeweled garments, their gestures were minutely studied, and they almost vanished beneath the weight of their panoply. They were gods walking the earth, remote and inaccessible, moving in that breath-taking splendor that was the mark of their divinity. Their palaces were plated in gold, they sat beneath gold crowns suspended from the ceiling, and sometimes they concealed themselves behind jeweled curtains. By the time of Justinian the Byzantine court had surrendered to almost unimaginable luxury. The great palaces on the Bosporus shimmered like the Christian churches with brilliant mosaics, and the Roman emperor moved like a ghost appareled in majesty. He was no longer merely the emperor. He was the king of kings, the vicar of Christ, the giver of all blessings, the divinely appointed one. The distance between the ruler and his subjects, always great, now became so great that they seemed to live in different worlds.

To this eastern realm Rome left a legacy of imperial organization if not order, and in the sixth century the glittering emperor Justinian emerged in Constantinople as a man imbued with the

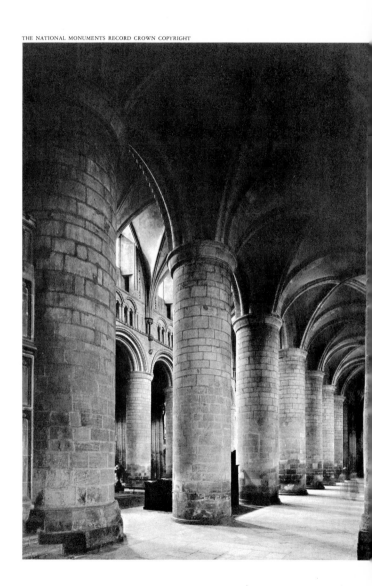

To later civilizations Rome bequeathed its language, literature, law, governmental ideas, and the awesome example of its architecture. The arches and massive piers of the twelfth-century cathedral nave in Gloucester, England, illustrate the impulse of Romanesque builders to emulate Roman grandeur.

381

old Roman sense of grandeur and an impulse to revive Rome's lost greatness. A major lawgiver, codifier of laws, and builder of churches and palaces, he succeeded in reconquering North Africa and parts of Italy, bringing them back into allegiance to Constantinople. But his triumphs, accompanied by the squandering of vast sums on his palaces and fawning bureaucracy, proved to be short-lived. Later Byzantine emperors imitated his conquests, driving across Asia Minor, Syria, and Egypt, showing the panoply of their power in the deserts of the Negeb and on the borders of Persia, but about all their conquests there was an air of impermanence. The Arab invasions of the seventh century made them withdraw gradually toward the center, and thereafter the imperial pretensions grew wider as their power weakened. Finally, in 1453, after eleven centuries of grandeur, Constantinople fell to the Turks.

To the West, Rome left a legacy of quite another order; it was passed in the first instance through the Church, which inherited much of Rome's talent, character, and learning. The early Church had been the foe of the pagan Roman state; gradually it was to become the preserver and adapter of much of what had been best in it. Justinian's triumphs against the Goths in Italy only left the state in complete disorder: after 541 there were no more consuls in Rome, the Senate withered away, and only the prefect of the city, *praefectus urbis*, remained to testify to the ancient traditions of the capital.

Out of the storm of the Gothic wars there emerged one strong western power—the papacy. In the hands of Pope Gregory I, himself a former *praefectus urbis*, the office began to exert strong influence. A monkish priest who never learned Greek, though he spent many years on an embassy to Constantinople, he seemed to symbolize the ancient Roman virtues, and by the singular force of his personality he was able to bring some order to a ruined land. He believed in old wives' tales, relished mysteries, wrote a vivid and interminable commentary on the Book of Job, and pronounced himself to be the arbiter of Roman destinies.

At first he held very little power, for the papal states reached scarcely farther than Naples. But in time Italy was to become dappled with territories owing allegiance to the papacy; and the kings of Europe would find compelling reasons to accept the doctrine that all spiritual power was vested in the pope and that earthly power should receive the sanction of the spiritual. When Charlemagne permitted himself to be crowned by Pope Leo III on Christmas Day, 800, he was under no illusions that any rights had been conferred on him. Nevertheless the coronation laid the foundations for the Holy Roman Empire. For many centuries kings would struggle for possession of that crown and the title, which gave them the inheritance to an empire that had long perished. German and Norman kings would try to wrest that crown by force, seeing themselves as the divinely appointed successors of Augustus. Not until the time of Napoleon was the dream of the divine Roman empire ultimately abandoned.

What happened was that the Church had gradually acquired many qualities of the old imperial order. The Roman genius for organization, along with the Roman sense of hierarchy, had given shape to Church institutions. The Roman political imagination, which had once brought so many peoples into one orbit, had lent strength to the idea of a Church universal. Roman jurisprudence had become the basis of canon law. The Church, which had begun by being an enemy of Rome, became the chief stronghold and preserver of the ancient Roman traditions.

The Latin language—that stern, hard, and metallic language that was finally hammered into shape during the last years of the republic—continued to be spoken in western Europe, carrying with it the ideas and concepts that were to become an integral part of the culture of Italy and France, and to a lesser extent of England and Spain. There was no break. The Romance languages which grew out of ancient Latin, developed slowly and almost imperceptibly, with the result that it is quite impossible to determine when Italian, Spanish, French, Portuguese, and Rumanian came into existence. They arose not from the elegant phrases of Cicero but from the language of the camp, which tended to be happily insulting and convivial, with no pretensions to dignity. So the French word *tête*, "head" derives from the Latin *testa*, "pot," and *jambe*, "leg," derives from *gamba*, "fetlock"; *cheval* and *caballo* come not from the regular Latin *equus*, "horse," but from the horseman's *caballus*, "nag." In adapting Latin to their own use, the French showed a genius for softening a language that was essentially hard and masculine. The Latin *lux*, "light," becomes *luz* in Spanish and *luce* in Italian, and was wholly transformed by the French into the tender and feminine *lumière*. A new resilience had entered common speech; the hard outlines became blurred; the words lost the monumental, graven quality, which was the delight of Roman orators, who spoke as though they were reading inscriptions carved in stone.

The Latin of the Church was a subtle and intricate rendering of classical Latin. In that amazing fourth century when Saint Jerome and Saint Augustine were inventing new words to describe Christian ideas, ecclesiastical Latin took shape. Saint Jerome's translation of the Bible, completed at last in 405, became the ac-

Roman themes were a treasure-trove for medieval and Renaissance poets and artists, and a source of much play of imagination. Here a fifteenth-century illustrator depicts in terms of his own times the arrival of Cleopatra in Asia Minor on her voyage to Rome. Though the setting is incongruous, the artist may have been familiar with Plutarch's description of the queen, attended by maids "dressed like sea nymphs and graces," being borne in a lustrous ship whose "silver oars beat time." Certainly Shakespeare was when he wrote: "The barge she sat in, like a burnished throne,/ Burned on the water; the poop was beaten gold . . ."

cepted version of the scriptures in the West; and in Saint Augustine's prose we find Latin quivering with an excitement it never possessed before. The hymns of Ambrose, written with a quiet perfection, reflect the classical temper. And sometimes Saint Gregory the Great would find himself rebuking his priests for reading so deeply in classical authors.

Greek philosophy survived in Latin, even though knowledge of Greek had nearly disappeared in the West. Boethius, a scholar at the court of the Ostrogothic king Theodoric at Ravenna, translated Aristotle into Latin and wrote commentaries on Greek philosophy, music, and mathematics. Shortly before he was executed on a charge of treason he wrote *De Consolatione Philosophiae (On the Consolation of Philosophy)*—a work in which he sought to recall Platonic, Stoic, and Vergilian ideas to Christian society. King Alfred translated the work into Anglo-Saxon.

In the Middle Ages men almost seemed to breathe in Latin. If it was not the language of trade, it was the language of nearly everything else. Roman themes continued to influence the western imagination. One of the most popular medieval romances, the *Roman de Troie*, by Benoît de Sainte-Maure, recounts the conflict of Greeks and Trojans, evidently derived from a Latin original. Troubadours and courtiers of love drew widely on ancient Roman episodes of passion: Héloïse and Abelard, the most philosophical of medieval lovers, quoted Ovid to each other in their letters in Latin. The spirit of Vergil hovered over the *Divine Comedy*, written in colloquial Italian. (Even after Dante had completed the work, there were intelligent men like Dante's friend Giovanni del Virgilio who regarded it as a waste of time to write poetry in the vernacular and asked him to write an epic on the contemporary great conquerors in Latin, "the language common to us all." Dante replied in a Latin poem, regretting his inability to write a Latin epic, and offered his friend ten cantos of the *Paradiso* as proof that there was some merit in the vernacular.)

Petrarch drew on Livy; Chaucer on Ovid at his most boisterous. The English playwrights Kyd, Marlowe, Jonson, and Shakespeare drew on the brutalities of Seneca; Shakespeare read deeply in Plutarch. The example of Plautus helped re-establish social comedy and farce; Lucan's rodomontade passed into Spanish epic; the oratory of Cicero was transformed into English political prose. Rough comedy, satire, lyric poetry, essay, oratory, drama, epic—all those forms admired by Romans passed in adaptations to the West. The wit of Cervantes and the rhetoric of Milton both derived from Rome. The cult of antiquity never died out. Charlemagne in the ninth century ordered his scribes to copy ancient

An illustration from an early edition of the Inferno *shows Dante (at left, in black) and his guide, Vergil, encountering giants who, having waged war against heaven, are condemned to stand in a great well. At right, the two poets are carried to another part of hell by the giant Antaeus. Dante regarded Vergil as the most inspired of Rome's poets.*

manuscripts to preserve them for posterity; the copyists succeeded so well that we can trace most of the surviving Latin manuscripts to the scribes employed in his monasteries. Carolingian palaces were adorned with sculptures, marbles, silks, textiles, and mosaics removed from Rome and Ravenna, and his court poets modeled their verses on the classics. Architects in the eighth, ninth, and tenth centuries constructed great cathedrals in the style known as Romanesque, because it was once thought to be a grotesque deformation of Roman architecture. In fact it derived straight from Rome.

Although the heritage of Rome had survived, it had done so really only at the whim of emperors and popes—by the sheerest chance. Monasteries were sacked, treasuries were emptied, old buildings were torn down to provide stones. And although the Carolingians were the first to make a conscious effort to imitate the ancient Roman forms, the scholars at the end of the fifteenth century made an even more determined effort to recover the treasures of the past. Petrarch himself discovered many lost letters of Cicero. The Florentine bibliophile Poggio Bracciolini scoured monastery libraries in search of ancient and forgotten manuscripts.

The unearthing of the Laocoön group of sculptures near the baths of Trajan in 1506 revived the classical presence. So, too, did the discovery of the *Apollo Belvedere* a few years later. Both statues were promptly acquired by Pope Julius II. A passion for excavating, restoring, and imitating old sculpture arose; the young humanist, painter, and architect Raphael pleaded with Pope Leo X to halt the continuing despoliation of Roman edifices. The pope appointed the young man general superintendent or conservator of Roman antiquities, and there exists an unsigned letter, which appears to have been written by Raphael and Baldassare Castiglione, urging the pope to preserve the relics of ancient Rome:

> *Many people, Holy Father, when observing the great relics of Rome with its wonderful art, its wealth, and its ornaments, and the grandeur of the buildings, lamely judge them to be more fabulous than real. But with me it seemed, and still seems, otherwise, for when I consider the many relics which are still to be seen in the ruins of Rome, and the divine gifts which dwelt in the men of ancient times, I think it not impossible that many things which seemed impossible to us seemed very easy to them. . . .*

So he wrote with fervor in a long letter that remains a classic account of a Renaissance man's devotion to antiquity. Raphael himself died too young to prevent the erosion of the city, but his influence spread throughout Italy, and soon we find the architects

Eighteenth-century political idealists looked on the assassination of Caesar as part of a great, symbolic confrontation between autocracy and representative government. Above is an illustration from a 1709 edition of Shakespeare's Julius Caesar, *a play that did much to establish the image of Brutus as the classic martyr who gave his life to save a republic.*

becoming increasingly immersed in studying Roman architecture. Palladio, Borromini, and Bramante became earnest students of the past. Bramante, the first architect of the new basilica of St. Peter's, planned to surmount it with a low dome, following the model of the Pantheon; his successor Michelangelo, more daring, undertook to raise the dome on a high support or drum—a brilliant adaptation of Roman example. When Wren was invited to rebuild St. Paul's Cathedral, in London, he wished to design it "after a good Roman manner," refusing to follow "the Gothic Rudeness of the old Design." The "good Roman manner" swept across Europe, with the result that the rather heavy, four-square forms of Roman temples were soon adapted to the needs of France and England. Although Renaissance builders adhered to a concise use of Roman motifs, the baroque designers, who followed them, rang exuberant changes on these, luxuriating in twisted columns, split pediments, and swirling volutes. The rococo fashion of the eighteenth century then carried these variations to such unbounded excess that the result was another upheaval of taste and a return to Rome in the form of the neoclassical style. Newer excavations, such as those at Pompeii, helped to influence and shape this movement, once again reviving, copying, and widely adapting the forms that had been popular during the time of the Caesars.

In the realm of civil engineering, Roman precepts and achievements survived the centuries because they were so practical and so durable. No pope or emperor thought of dismantling a Roman bridge or uprooting a Roman road; such structures outlasted the ages. Not until the introduction of the steel suspension cable and cantilever was a method found of bridging a river that improved on the old Roman masonry span. Not until the introduction of macadam as a road-surfacing material was there an appreciable improvement on the old Roman use of paving blocks. In France and Spain there are small Roman bridges still in use today; they support heavy buses and trucks, though once, two millennia ago, they supported only carts. Roman roads, with their heavy ballast, culverts, and embankments, underlie many a highway in the tourist's Italy today.

From the time of Machiavelli political historians have searched through Roman chronicles in their quest for the principles of political science. Since Roman history involved nearly every conceivable permutation and combination of forces that act on governments, students have sought to codify Roman history and to extract from it not only those principles that they desired to defend but also those that they desired to attack. Revolutionary republics would invoke the example of the Roman republic, tyran-

The republicanism of Cicero and of those Romans who thought as he did was influential in shaping the ideas of the men who founded the American nation. Like the Senate of Rome, the United States Senate was created as a select, deliberative body. The splendid orations of Cato, Scipio, and Cicero became models for public men such as Daniel Webster, seen here in a painting recording his greatest triumph—his "Liberty and Union now and forever" peroration in 1830.
FANEUIL HALL, BOSTON

nies would invoke the name of Caesar. To the American and French revolutionaries all Roman history seemed to converge on the brooding and remorseless figure of Brutus, the champion of society that had overthrown dictatorship. They saw him as an incarnation of fury aroused to stamp out the vestiges of authoritarian rule—the first free man. The legend of Brutus haunted the Middle Ages; local rulers dreaded his name, for he represented the libertarian strivings of the spokesmen of common people.

Machiavelli believed that Rome attained its lasting place among the nations not because it was favored by the gods or by divine fortune, but because it practiced virtue. In his eyes and in the eyes of many who followed him, the republic was the embodiment of a golden age of frugality, honesty, simplicity, and courage. Like Cincinnatus, the husbandman worked his fields with his sword near at hand, prepared to defend the republic to the death, quietly content with his few worldly possessions, with no desire for the blandishments of wealth. This golden age was legendary, but the idea satisfied a human belief that there must have been a time when tyrants were powerless before the armed might of the people. The Renaissance philosopher Giordano Bruno commended the "magnanimity, justice, and mercy" shown by the Romans under the republic, though the pages of Livy testify to a remarkable absence of these virtues.

The American revolutionaries were steeped in Roman history and saw themselves as inheritors of the republican tradition. The delegations from the free American states that met in Philadelphia in 1787 to achieve "a more perfect union" included men of varying degrees of education; but nearly all of them, being persons of standing and distinction in their communities, knew the classics by heart and were intimately familiar with the works of Caesar and Plutarch. The Federal Convention debated bitterly and brilliantly the question of the allocation of powers in the future United States, but there was never any doubt in its mind that there should be a select upper legislative house, patterned distantly on the Roman Senate, as well as a lower popular legislative house armed with the powers of the Roman assemblies.

The ultimate and most pervasive Roman legacy resides, of course, in Roman law—that vast accumulation of precepts and practices concerning the ordered relationships of man to fellow man, husband to wife, parent to child, injured to innocent, citizen to state, accused to magistrate, and finally, of state to state—on which so much of the western scheme of equality, justice, and fair dealing depends. The Romans possessed a particular gift of law—a sense of a world brought together by unbreakable bonds of

Several ages meet in an engraving executed by Piranesi in the 1750's. In the foreground is Trajan's column, surmounted by the statue of Saint Peter, which Pope Sixtus V erected in 1587 to replace an ancient likeness of Trajan and which still tops the monument. Behind it, at right, is the eighteenth-century church of Nome di Maria—a late baroque structure deriving in part from ancient models.

rights and obligations. They thought of themselves as trustees of a legal contract, which they entered at birth and which was to be continued long after their death. Discipline, order, piety, instant obedience to commands—all these were merely different aspects of the law that guided and governed them.

The law had deep roots among the Romans, who were taught from childhood to respect it, obey it fully, and defend it with their lives. At a very early age children were taught the Twelve Tables, which were believed to have been compiled about 450 B.C. and which had been handed down little changed through the ages. Cicero in his boyhood had to learn them by heart. These laws were inscribed on wooden tablets, and the originals, or perhaps direct copies, survived well into the second century A.D. in the place reserved for them in the Forum.

The Twelve Tables were regarded with reverence, but they were not thought to possess divine sanction. In this they were fundamentally different from the Ten Commandments of the Jews. And though in earliest times Roman laws had been surrounded by an aura of mystery and had been administered by priests, there gradually emerged about the Twelve Tables a huge body of practical enactments devised and interpreted and then reinterpreted by a professional caste of laymen—the *jurisprudentes* of Rome. Nearly a thousand years after the compilation of the Twelve Tables a supreme effort at codification appeared in the form of the *Corpus Juris Civilis* of the emperor Justinian. This monument of legal and historical study (in the course of which the Twelve Tables were restated) consisted of the *Code* in twelve books, the *Digest* in fifty, the *Institutes* in four, and a supplement of one hundred sixty new laws called the *Novels*. A Christian emperor in Byzantium gave final shape to the laws of Rome.

The three greatest gifts the Romans left to the world—their language, their traditions of republicanism, and their laws—all owed a major debt to Greece, for even the Roman language was influenced by Greek turns of phrase and ways of thought. The Greek genius for liberty and compromise sometimes took on Roman dress, and Greek philosophy entered into the mainstream of Roman thought. In law especially Greek ideas were prevalent, and when Cicero made his famous pronouncement on the nature of true law in the course of his essay *De republica*, he was following the Greek philosophers who asserted the existence of law arising from man's own soul and nature, and reigning supreme:

> *True law is right reason consonant with nature, pervading all things, constant, eternal. Its commands and prohibitions apply effectively to good men, and those influenced by them are evil.*

It is not lawful to alter this law, to derogate from it, or to repeal it. Nor can we possibly be absolved from this law, either by the Senate or by the Assembly. This law does not differ for Rome or for Athens, for the present and the future, for one unchanging and eternal law shall be valid for all nations and for all times; and so it becomes, as it were, the general master and governor, the one God of all men, being itself its own author, promulgator, and enforcer.

As Cicero described this universal law, he was not of course describing Roman law as it was practiced in the courts. Nothing could have been more alien to the Roman spirit than the idea of an immutable code. He was saying that everyday laws should seek to approach the ideal of universal law and try justly to reflect it. This involved constant search and exploration. For all their veneration of ancient tablets, the Romans with their pragmatic sense realized that law should grow and respond to new situations and needs. "We are servants of the law in order that we may be free," Cicero remarked. This was another way of saying that self-subordination to basic principles, far from confining the human spirit, would enlarge it; and that the very respect for tradition and authority would heighten the stature of man and bring worth and responsibility to his own exercise of judgment.

Often the Romans failed to live up to this concept. Their official cult of unloved state gods often belied their critical intelligence. They produced no philosophers equal to those of Greece. Their ideals of *pietas, gravitas,* and *humanitas* were repeatedly despoiled, and in the later stages of the empire, fewer and fewer men stood up for them. Yet the idea of moral governance of men's actions never lost hold, even if Rome itself grossly violated it. The states of western Europe, all formed between A.D. 500 and 1200 under the tutelage of the Roman presence, picked and chose from it, but all remained indebted to the Roman idea of law as supreme over men and as penetrating into the remotest corners of their lives. When the framers of the United States Constitution erected what they termed "a government of laws, not men," they were in effect reasserting Rome's better self.

More lasting than Rome's victories, the vast edifice of Roman jurisprudence survives in the codes of many western nations, and the precedents and procedures established by men beside the Tiber more than two millennia ago are echoed today in the courthouses of western Europe and two Americas. The Roman genius for logic and order is with us yet. The architect poring over his drawing board, the bridgebuilder studying stresses, the attorney invoking high principles, all hark back to Roman ways; in countless ways we still live under the sign of the spacious mind of Rome.

Early in the nineteenth century the Italian neoclassic sculptor Antonio Canova was commissioned by the North Carolina legislature to carve a life-sized figure of George Washington. What he delivered in 1812 was the image of a soldier-consul in toga and tunic, holding a tablet, reminiscent of Michelangelo's figure of Moses pointing to his laws. The design was artificial, yet it reflected a deep-rooted impulse among Americans to identify themselves with classical tradition.

SURVIVAL
OF A
STYLE

Rome's influences, transmitted throughout the West in innumerable ways, have undergone mutations in each new age. Though only a small portion of Rome's architecture, art, and literature has survived, this has been enough to provide a source of inspiration for each succeeding epoch. The so-called dark ages and the medieval era that followed were keenly aware of Roman style and content in building and sculpture as well as in thought and writing, and many efforts were made to adapt Roman models. The Renaissance, with its return to classical ideals, brought with it the antiquarian, the excavator, the imitator as well as masters such as Palladio or Michelangelo, ringing their mighty changes on Roman themes. The baroque period exulted in further variants, with its grand façades, swirling columns, split pediments, fanciful fountains, and dramatic vistas. After the excesses of the rococo, the neoclassical movement in Europe and America returned to stricter Roman forms, often in turn to romanticize them. More recent times have seen a leaning away from Roman models—it is no longer fashionable to erect Roman cupolas over court houses or to design railroad stations in the style of the baths of Diocletian—but much of today's sculpture, for instance, remains in debt to Rome, and the haunting image of a classical presence informs such a work as the nostalgic, imaginary landscape (opposite) painted by the contemporary Italian surrealist Georgio de Chirico.

ROME REVISITED

Citizens of the nations that eventually sprang out of the lands of the Romans were never far removed from the tangible evidence of ancient glory, represented by some surviving monument, in repair or in ruins. The awe with which medieval man regarded Rome and its works gave way in the Renaissance to the flattery of imitation as Europeans sought to build a new civilization among the imposing remnants of the old. Gifted architects adapted and recombined classical forms, producing structures that were, in effect, largely original. Their patrons and masters were often less imaginative, contenting themselves with collections or copies of Roman works in their efforts to glean some part of Rome's ancient luster.

The isolotto, *a small islet set in a quiet pool, at the Boboli Gardens, in Florence, is illustrated in an eighteenth-century print above; it was inspired by the so-called marine theatre of Hadrian's magnificent villa at Tivoli. Opposite (at top) is a drawing of the church of Il Redentore, in Venice, designed by Andrea Palladio and demonstrating the new uses to which architects of the sixteenth century were putting such Roman specialties as the arch and the dome. At right is a representation of the arch erected in the* Place du Carrousel, *in Paris, by Napoleon Bonaparte, heir of the Roman empire builders.*

Nineteenth-century notions of Rome often dwelt on its carnivals and excesses. In The Romans of the

Decadence, *the neoclassicist Thomas Couture presented a scene that drew on an ample imagination.*

MAN'S LIKENESS

The view that western art sprang primarily from Greek roots is especially difficult to maintain with respect to portrait sculpture. Master sculptors from the Renaissance to modern times, as they turned toward increasingly personal interpretations of their models, seem to have owed much less to the Greeks' achievement of ideal beauty than to the Romans' uncompromising attempts to record every revealing truth to be discovered in a given subject's face (see portfolio, The Roman Face, page 201).

Portrait sculptures from the early Renaissance to the present era, all reflecting some Roman influences, appear at left in chronological order. At top, from left to right, are busts attributed to the fifteenth-century artists Donatello, Verrocchio, and Antonio Rossellino; in the second row are portraits by Michelangelo, Bernini, and Houdon; in the third row, by Frank Dobson, Rodin, and Medaro Rosso; and at bottom, by Matisse, Marini, and Giacometti. The last three works, products of the twentieth century, complement the powerful figure by Jacob Epstein (opposite), infused with a realism reminiscent of Roman portraiture at its best.

ECHOES IN A
NEW WORLD

Americans in the age of George Washington and Thomas Jefferson acquired a taste for Roman architecture that matched their interest in Rome's history and literature. Jefferson himself, after studying Roman works, designed Monticello and the Virginia State Capitol—fairly modest structures suitable for a nation that could not yet build on an imperial Roman scale. In the 1860's, however, citizens of a war-torn but burgeoning United States saw their national Capitol crowned with a dome that was worthy of their country's aspirations, a great structure patterned after the most ambitious efforts of European builders who had exploited ancient Rome's rich architectural tradition.

The statue at left, in which the goddess of victory leads General William Tecumseh Sherman's mount, shows that the Roman style has survived even in New York's Central Park. At top is Monticello, the stately hilltop home that Jefferson modeled, in large part, after Roman villas. The light-filled interior of Thomas Walter's lofty Capitol dome (right), in Washington, recalls the harmonies of supreme architectural achievement, the Pantheon.

Romulus, Remus, and the she-wolf, who figure in Rome's most persistent myth, are shown on an ancient coin.

A SELECTION OF BOOKS ON ROME

Any exhaustive Roman bibliography would extend to epic length. The purpose of what follows is neither to list the works of ancient Roman authors nor to give a balanced summary of the literature about Rome subsequently produced by innumerable distinguished historians, commentators, anthologizers, and interpreters. All that is presented here is a group of studies, most of them recent, which the editors have found particularly valuable in their own pursuit of the subject.

GENERAL STUDIES

Abbott, Frank Frost

A History and Description of Roman Political Institutions. New York, Biblo and Tannen, 1963.

Adcock, F. E.

Roman Political Ideas and Practice. Ann Arbor Paperbacks, 1964.

Atlas of the Classical World

A. A. M. Van der Heyden, and H. H. Scullard, eds. London, Nelson, 1963.

Barrow, R. H.

The Romans. London, Pelican, 1949.

Bloch, Raymond

The Origins of Rome. New York, Praeger, 1960.

Butterfield, Roger

Ancient Rome. New York, Odyssey Press, 1964.

The Cambridge Ancient History, Vols. VII, VIII, IX, X, XI, and XII.

S. A. Cook, and others, eds. Cambridge University Press, 1954.

The Cambridge Medieval History, Vol. I.

H. M. Gwatkin, and J. P. Whitney, eds. Cambridge University Press, 1924.

Cary, M., and Haarhoff, T. J.

Life and Thought in the Greek and Roman World. London, Methuen, 1940.

A Companion to Latin Studies

John Edwin Sandys, ed. New York, Hafner, 1935.

Dudley, Donald R.

The Civilization of Rome. New York, Mentor, 1962.

Durant, Will

The Story of Civilization: Caesar and Christ. New York, Simon and Schuster, 1935.

Grant, Michael

The World of Rome. Cleveland, World, 1960.

Grimal, Pierre

The Civilization of Rome, trans. by W. S. Maguinness. New York, Simon and Schuster, 1963.

Hadas, Moses

A History of Rome, New York, Anchor, 1956.

Jerome, Thomas Spencer

Aspects of the Study of Roman History. New York, Capricorn Books, 1962.

Mommsen, Theodor

The History of Rome, Rev. ed. New York, Meridian, 1958.

Oxford Annotated Bible

Herbert G. May, and Bruce M. Metzger, eds. New York, Oxford University Press, 1962.

Oxford Classical Dictionary

M. Cary, and others, eds. London, Oxford University Press, 1953.

Perowne, Stewart

Hadrian. New York, Norton, 1960.

Robinson, Charles Alexander

Ancient History. New York, Macmillan, 1951.

Rostovtzeff, M.

Rome, trans. by J. D. Duff. New York, Oxford University Press, 1960.

Scullard, Howard H.

A History of the Roman World. London, Methuen, 1961.

Shepherd, William R.

Historical Atlas. New York, Barnes and Noble, 1956.

Starr, Chester G.

A History of the Ancient World. New York, Oxford University Press, 1965.

Westermann, Georg

Atlas zur Weltgeschichte. Berlin, 1963.

HISTORIES OF ERAS

Africa, Thomas W.

Rome of the Caesars. New York, Wiley & Sons, 1965.

Bainton, Roland H.

Early Christianity. New York, Van Nostrand, 1960.

The Horizon History of Christianity, Chaps. II and III. New York, American Heritage Publishing Co., 1964.

Burckhardt, Jacob

The Age of Constantine the Great, trans. by Moses Hadas. New York, Doubleday, 1956.

Bury, J. B.

History of the Later Roman Empire, Vol. I. New York, Dover. 1958.

Charlesworth, M. P.

The Roman Empire. London, Oxford University Press, 1951.

Cowell, F. R.

Cicero and the Roman Republic. Baltimore, Pelican, 1964.

Dill, Samuel

Roman Society from Nero to Marcus Aurelius. Cleveland, Meridian, 1956.
Roman Society in the Last Century of the Western Empire. Cleveland, Meridian, 1958.

Gibbon, Edward

The Decline and Fall of the Roman Empire. D. M. Low, ed. Harcourt, Brace and Company, 1960.

Gough, Michael

The Early Christians. New York, Praeger, 1961.

Haywood, Richard Mansfield

The Myth of Rome's Fall. New York, Crowell, 1962.

Jones, A. H. M.

The Later Roman Empire, Vols. I and II. Norman, University of Oklahoma Press, 1964.

Nilsson, Martin P.

Imperial Rome. New York, Schocken Books, 1962.

Perowne, Stewart

Caesars and Saints. New York, Norton, 1963.

Rowell, Henry Thompson

Rome in the Augustan Age. Norman, University of Oklahoma Press, 1962.

Rostovtzeff, M.

The Social and Economic History of the Roman Empire, Vols. I and II. Oxford, Clarendon Press, 1957.

Scullard, Howard H.

From the Gracchi to Nero. London, Methuen, 1963.

Starr, Chester G.

Civilization and the Caesars. New York, Oxford University Press, 1965.

IMAGINATIVE BIOGRAPHY

Graves, Robert

I, Claudius. New York, Modern Library, 1961.

Vidal, Gore

Julian. Boston, Little, 1964.

Wilder, Thornton

Ides of March. New York, Harper, 1948.

Yourcenar, Margaret

Memoirs of Hadrian. New York, Noonday, 1963.

DAILY LIFE

Assa, Janine

The Great Roman Ladies, trans. by Anne Hollander. New York, Evergreen, 1960.

Balsdon, J. P. V. D.

Roman Women. New York, John Day, 1962.

Carcopino, Jérôme

Daily Life in Ancient Rome, trans. by E. O. Lorimer. Henry T. Rowell, ed. New Haven, Yale University Press, 1940.

Cowell, F. R.

Everyday Life in Ancient Rome. London, Batsford, 1961.

Seltman, Charles

Women in Antiquity. New York, St. Martin's Press.

THE ETRUSCANS

Bloch, Raymond

The Etruscans. New York, Praeger, 1958.

Cottrell, Leonard

The Horizon Book of Lost Worlds, Chap. XIII. New York, American Heritage Publishing Co., 1962.

Heurgon, Jacques

Daily Life of the Etruscans, trans. by James Kirkup. New York, Macmillan, 1964.

Pallottino, Massimo

The Etruscans, trans. by J. A. Cremona. London, Pelican, 1955.

Von Vacano, Otto-Wilhelm

The Etruscans in the Ancient World, trans. by Sheila Ann Ogilvie. New York, St. Martin's Press, 1960.

LITERARY HISTORY

Duff, J. Wight

A Literary History of Rome in the Silver Age. A. M. Duff, ed. New York, Barnes and Noble, 1964.

A Literary History of Rome from the Origins to the Close of the Golden Age. A. M. Duff, ed. New York, Barnes and Noble, 1960.

Hadas, Moses

A History of Latin Literature. New York, Columbia University Press, 1952.

Highet, Gilbert

The Anatomy of Satire. New Jersey, Princeton University Press, 1962.
Poets in a Landscape. New York, Alfred A. Knopf, 1957.

MILITARY

Adcock, F. E.

The Roman Art of War Under the Republic, Rev. ed. New York, Barnes and Noble, 1960.

Fuller, J. F. C.

A Military History of the Western World, Vol. I. New York, Funk and Wagnalls, 1954.

RELIGION

Fowler, W. Warde

The Religious Experience of the Roman People. London, Macmillan, 1914.

Grant, Michael

Myths of the Greeks and Romans. Cleveland, World, 1962.

Hus, Alain

Greek and Roman Religion. New York, Hawthorn, 1962.

Rose, H. J.

Ancient Roman Religion. London, Hutchinson's University Library.

Larousse Encyclopedia of Mythology

Intro. by Robert Graves. New York, Prometheus Press, 1960.

ART, ARCHITECTURE, AND TECHNOLOGY

Brion, Marcel

Pompeii and Herculaneum. New York, Crown, 1960.

Brown, Frank E.

Roman Architecture. New York, George Braziller, 1961.

Caputo, Giacomo

Tunisia, Ancient Mosaics. Paris, New York Graphic Society, 1962.

Eydoux, Henri-Paul

La France Antique. Paris, Librairie Plon, 1962.

Goldscheider, Ludwig

Etruscan Sculpture. New York, Phaidon Edition, Oxford University Press, 1941.

Hanfmann, George M. A.

Roman Art. Greenwich, New York Graphic Society, 1964.

A History of Technology, Vol. II.

Charles Singer, and others, eds., Oxford, Clarendon Press, 1955.

Kahler, Heinz

The Art of Rome and Her Empire. New York, Crown Publishers, 1963.

MacDonald, William L.

Early Christian and Byzantine Architecture. New York, George Braziller, 1962.

Maiuri, Amedeo

Roman Painting. Geneva, Skira, 1953.

Maiuri, Bianca

The National Museum. Novara, Italy, Instituto Geografico de Agostini, 1959.

Nash, Ernest

Pictorial Dictionary of Ancient Rome, Vols. I and II. New York, Praeger, 1961.

Pallottino, Massimo

Art of the Etruscans. New York, Vanguard, 1955.
Etruscan Painting. Geneva, Skira, 1952.

Pobé, Marcel, and Jean Roubier

The Art of Roman Gaul. Toronto, University of Toronto Press, 1961.

Robertson, D. S.

A Handbook of Greek and Roman Architecture. Cambridge University Press, 1964.

The Splendors of Italy. Réalités, trans. by Geoffrey Braitwaite. New York, G. P. Putnam's Sons, 1964.

Toynbee, J. M. C.

Art in Roman Britain. London, Phaidon Press, 1962.

Von Matt, Leonard

Ancient Sicily. New York, Universe Books, 1960.
Architektur im Antiken Rom. Würzburg, Echter Verlag, 1958.
Early Christian Art in Rome. New York, Universe Books, 1961.
Romische Bildwerke. Zurich, NZN Buchverlag, 1958.

Von Matt, Leonard, and Hans Kühner

Les Césars. Paris, Librairie Hachette, 1965.

Zachietzschmann, W.

Hellas and Rome. New York, Universe Books, 1960.

ROME'S LEGACY

Bolgar, R. R.

The Classical Heritage and its Beneficiaries. Cambridge University Press, 1958.

The Legacy of Rome. Cyril Bailey, ed.

Oxford, Clarendon Press, 1923.

Highet, Gilbert

The Classical Tradition. New York, Oxford University Press, 1949.

ACKNOWLEDGMENTS

The editors wish to acknowledge the following individuals and institutions for their generous assistance and for their co-operation in making available pictorial material in their collections. We are especially grateful to Dr. Gilbert Highet, Chairman of the Department of Greek and Latin of Columbia University, New York, for his valuable advice.

Mrs. Sylvia Abrams
American Academy, Rome
   Dr. Ernest Nash
Archivo MAS, Barcelona
Mrs. Jane Horton de Cabanyes
Gabinetto Fotografico Nazionale, Rome
Gabinetto Fotografico dello Stato, Rome
Gallerie Musei Vaticani, Rome
   Dr. Herminia Speyer
German Archaeological Institute, Rome
   Dr. Ulrich Rudigher
Glyptothek und Museum Antiker Kleinkunst, Munich
Instituto Espanol de Arqueologica, Consejo Superior de Investigaciones Cientificas
   D. Antonio Garcia y Bellido
Mrs. Mary Jenkins
Kunsthistorisches Museum, Vienna
   Dr. E. M. Auer
Louvre, Department of Roman and Greek Antiquities
Mr. M. A. McKenzie
Musei Capitolini, Rome
   Dr. Carlo Pietrangeli
Museo Archeologico, Florence
Museo Arqueologico Nacional, Madrid
Museo Nazionale, Naples
   Dr. Giuseppe Maggi
Museo Nazionale, Rome
   Dr. Eleonora Bracco
Museo Nazionale di Villa Giulia, Rome
   Dr. Mario Moretti
Scala
Anton Schroll & Co., Vienna
Soprintendenza alle Antichità della Campania, Naples
Soprintendenza alle Antichità dell'Etruria Meridionale, Florence
Soprintendenza del Palatino e Foro Romano;
   Dr. Itala Dondero
Miss Bianca Spantigati
Mrs. Maria Todorow

PHOTOGRAPHY: Italy, Leonard Von Matt; London, R. B. Fleming and Co., Ltd., Roger Wood.

Maps and drawings by Cal Sacks.

Samnite house at Herculaneum on page 180 is reproduced from *Pompeii and Herculaneum,* by Marchel Brion, by permission of Elek Books Ltd., London. Edwin Smith, photographer. Pantheon façade on page 255 is reproduced from *Rome and Her Empire,* by Holle Verlag. Art of the World.

Grateful acknowledgment is made for permission to quote from the following works (the page on which the quotation appears is indicated in boldface type):

THE VOICES OF REPUBLICAN ROME: **128–44** **130–31** from Plautus' "Amphitryon," in *Six Plays of Plautus,* ed. and trans. by Lionel Casson. Copyright © 1960, 1963 by Lionel Casson. Reprinted by permission of Doubleday & Company, Inc. **132–34** from Lucretius' *On the Nature of Things,* trans. by Cyril Bailey. Reprinted by permission of The Clarendon Press, Oxford. **135** Poem LXXXV from *The Poems of Catullus,* trans. by Horace Gregory. Copyright © 1956 by Horace Gregory. Reprinted by permission of Grove Press, Inc.; Catullus' Poem XI from *Poets in a Landscape,* by Gilbert Highet. Copyright © 1957 by Gilbert Highet. Reprinted by permission of Alfred A. Knopf, Inc. and Curtis Brown, Ltd. **135, 138–39** Catullus' Poem LXXII, trans. by Eric A. Havelock; from Cicero's *The Second Philippic,* trans. by Norman J. DeWitt; from Cicero's *On Duty,* trans. by Paul MacKendrick: All in *Classics In Translation,* ed. by MacKendrick & Howe. Copyright © 1952 by The University of Wisconsin Press. Reprinted by permission of The University of Wisconsin Press. **135** Catullus' Poem CI, trans. by Robert Fitzgerald, from *The Hudson Review,* Vol. V, #1, Spring 1952. Copyright © 1952 by The Hudson Review, Inc. Reprinted by permission of The Hudson Review, Inc. **136, 137** Catullus' Poems VIII and V, trans. by Horace Gregory, from *The Poems of Catullus,* trans. and intro. by Horace Gregory. Copyright © 1956 by Horace Gregory. Reprinted by permission of Grove Press, Inc. **137** Poem XLVI, from *The Poems of Catullus,* trans. by William A. Aiken. Copyright © 1950 by William A. Aiken. Reprinted by permission of E. P. Dutton & Co., Inc. **140** Cicero's letter to Atticus, July, 65 B.C., from *Letters of a Roman Gentleman,* by Arthur Patch McKinley. Reprinted by permission of

Houghton Mifflin Company. 140–41 Cicero's letters to Atticus, February 24, 49 B.C. and March 12, 49 B.C., from *Cicero's Letters to Atticus,* Vol. II, trans. by E. O. Winstedt. Reprinted by permission of The Harvard University Press. 141–43 Letters: Cicero to Caesar, March 19, 49 B.C.; Caesar to Cicero, April 16, 49 B.C.; Cicero to Atticus, December 19, 45 B.C.: All from *Cicero's Selected Works,* trans. by Michael Grant. Reprinted by permission of Penguin Books, Ltd., Harmondsworth, England. 142–44 from Caesar's *The Gallic War,* Book IV, trans. by H. J. Edwards. Reprinted by permission of The Harvard University Press.

MASTERS OF THE GOLDEN AGE: 208–24
210–15 from Vergil's *Aeneid,* trans. by Rolfe Humphries. Reprinted by permission of Charles Scribner's Sons. 214–15 from the *Elegies,* by Propertius, trans. by Gilbert Highet, in *Poets in a Landscape,* by Gilbert Highet. Copyright © 1957 by Gilbert Highet. Reprinted by permission of Alfred A. Knopf, Inc. and Curtis Brown, Ltd. 217 Horace's Ode I:23, from *Including Horace,* by Louis Untermeyer. Copyright © 1919 by Harcourt, Brace & World, Inc., renewed 1947 by Louis Untermeyer. Reprinted by permission of Harcourt, Brace & World, Inc.; I:25, trans. by Robert Fitzgerald, from *The Hudson Review,* Vol. V, #1, Spring 1952. Copyright © 1952 by The Hudson Review, Inc. Reprinted by permission of The Hudson Review, Inc. 217–18 I:38, trans. by Eugene Field; III:30, trans. by William Ewart Gladstone: Both from *A History of Latin Literature,* by Moses Hadas. Reprinted by permission of The Columbia University Press. 218–19 from Horace's *Satires,* trans. by Franklin P. Adams, in *The Classical Age,* ed. and intro. by Lionel Casson. Published by Dell Publishing Co., Inc. Reprinted by permission of the Executrix of the Estate of Franklin P. Adams. 219 from Horace's *Letters,* in *Poets in a Landscape,* by Gilbert Highet. © Copyright by Gilbert Highet. Reprinted by permission of Alfred A. Knopf, Inc. 221–22 from Ovid's *Metamorphoses,* trans. by F. A. Wright, in *The Latin Poets,* ed. by R. B. Godolphin. Reprinted by permission of Routledge & Kegan Paul, Ltd.

222 from Ovid's *Art of Love,* trans. by Rolfe Humphries. Reprinted by permission of The Indiana University Press. 223–24 from Livy's *History of Rome,* trans. and intro. by Moses Hadas and Joe P. Poe. Copyright © 1962 by Moses Hadas. Reprinted by permission of Random House, Inc.

THE FREE MINDS OF THE EMPIRE: 320–36
325 from Juvenal's Satire I, in *Latin Poetry in Verse Translation,* trans. by L. R. Lind. Reprinted by permission of Houghton Mifflin Company; from Juvenal's Satire VI, trans. by John Paul Heironimus, in *Classics in Translation,* Vol. II, ed. by MacKendrick and Howe. Reprinted by permission of the copyright owners, The University of Wisconsin Press; from Juvenal's Satire VIII, in *Juvenal the Satirist,* trans. by Gilbert Highet. Reprinted by permission of The Clarendon Press, Oxford. 326, 327–29 from *The Complete Works of Tacitus,* trans. by Alfred John Church and William Jackson Brodribb. Published by the Modern Library, Inc. Reprinted by permission of Random House, Inc. 326 from *Tacitus on Britain and Germany,* trans. by H. Mattingly; 329 from Tacitus' *Annals of Imperial Rome,* trans. by Michael Grant; 330 X:54, from *The Letters of the Younger Pliny,* ed. and trans. by Betty Radice: All reprinted by permission of Penguin Books, Ltd., Harmondsworth, England. 330 VII:5 and VI:14, from *Pliny the Younger,* trans. by William Melmoth and revised by W. M. L. Hutchinson. Reprinted by permission of The Harvard University Press. 331 from Seneca's "Thyestes," trans. by Ella Isobel Harris, in *The Complete Roman Drama,* ed. by George E. Duckworth. Copyright 1942 by Random House, Inc. Reprinted by permission of Random House, Inc. 332–33 from Petronius' *Satyricon,* trans. by William Arrowsmith. Reprinted by permission of The University of Michigan Press. 334–35 from Suetonius' *Twelve Caesars,* trans. by Robert Graves. Copyright © 1957 by International Authors N. Y., Penguin Books, Ltd. Reprinted by permission of Willis Kingsley Wing. 336 Martial's Epigram I:10, from *The Twelve Books of Epigrams,* trans. by J. A. Pott and F. A. Wright. Reprinted by permis-

sion of Routledge & Kegan Paul, Ltd.; I:28 and VIII:43, from *A Literary History of Rome in the Silver Age,* by J. Wight Duff, ed. by A. M. Duff. Reprinted by permission of Barnes and Noble, Inc.; V:10, trans. by F. A. Wright, from *The Latin Poets,* ed. and intro. by Francis R. B. Godolphin. Reprinted by permission of Routledge & Kegan Paul, Ltd.; VIII:16, from *Selected Epigrams,* trans. by Rolfe Humphries with intro. and notes by Palmer Bovie. Copyright © 1963 by The Indiana University Press. Reprinted by permission.

PAGE 12 from Lucretius' *On the Nature of Things,* trans. by Cyril Bailey. Reprinted by permission of The Clarendon Press, Oxford.

PAGE 116 from *The Histories of Polybius,* Vol. I, trans. from the text of F. Hultsch by Evelyn S. Shuckburgh. Reprinted by permission of The Indiana University Press.

PAGE 158 from *Selected Speeches of Cicero,* trans. by H. E. D. Blakiston. Reprinted by permission of Methuen & Co., Ltd., London.

PAGE 236 from Suetonius' *Twelve Caesars,* trans. by Robert Graves. Copyright © 1957 by International Authors, N. Y., Penguin Books, Ltd. Reprinted by permission of Willis Kingsley Wing. 227, 240 from *The Complete Works of Tacitus,* trans. by Alfred John Church and William Jackson Brodribb. Published by the Modern Library, Inc. Reprinted by permission of Random House, Inc.

PAGE 262 from Edward Gibbon's *Decline and Fall of the Roman Empire.* ed. by D. M. Low. Reprinted by permission of Chatto and Windus, Ltd., London and Harcourt, Brace & World.

PAGE 338 from Lactantius' *Divine Institutions,* in *The Later Roman Empire,* Vol. II, by A. H. M. Jones. Reprinted by permission of The University of Oklahoma Press.

A